Clinical Handbook of Child Abuse and Neglect

Lane J. Veltkamp, M.S.W.
Thomas W. Miller, Ph.D., ABPP

with contributions by

Gary Kearl, M.D.
Katherine L. Bright, M.D.

INTERNATIONAL UNIVERSITIES PRESS, INC.
MADISON, CONNECTICUT

Second printing, 1994

Library of Congress Cataloging in Publication Data

Veltkamp, Lane J., 1940–
 Clinical handbook of child abuse and neglect / Lane J. Veltkamp,
Thomas W. Miller with contributions by Gary Kearl and Katherine L.
Bright.
  p. cm.
 Includes bibliographical references and indexes.
 ISBN 0-8236-0950-2
 1. Child abuse. 2. Abused children. I. Miller, Thomas W., 1943–.
  II. Title.
 [DNLM: 1. Child Abuse. WA 320 V445c 1992]
 RC569.5C55V45 1994
 616.85'822—dc20
 DNLM/DLC
 for Library of Congress   93-15721
                                                               CIP

Manufactured in the United States of America

This book is dedicated to our children, Daniel, Stacey, Stephanie, David, and Jeanine, whom we love.

Table of Contents

Foreword

The Honorable William F. Stewart

The publication of the *Clinical Handbook of Child Abuse and Neglect* comes at a time when professionals dealing with abused and neglected children and their families are required to strive for understanding of a broad range of complex issues involved in the victimization of children. This handbook collects in one resource much of the pertinent information available on a range of problems from recognized experts in their fields.

Each of us, though, must look beyond our own personal or professional limits and move toward the goal of being broadly knowledgeable on these varied subjects. This handbook provides us with such an opportunity. Veltkamp and Miller have given us a source, within which much of the available information is accessible for use and application, thus allowing not only consolidation of the expanding nature of the information, but stimulation of new thought and direction.

The increased awareness of the issue of child sexual abuse has not only impacted the field of law enforcement, mental health, child protective service, and medicine, but also the court system, including juvenile, circuit, and criminal courts. In addition, child sexual abuse is highly inflammatory when brought out in custody cases, and is making its debut in civil litigation by victims vs. abusers. This increased activity in the court system requires a much higher level of information and understanding by a wide variety of professionals and practitioners. I have learned from presiding over cases from juvenile court to family court and criminal court that it is readily apparent that a great many of the participants will welcome the publication of this handbook.

So often, many of the sources quoted in court are unavailable and much information is given out of context. This volume will become an indispensable and key component in any library which provides information on these difficult issues.

Preface

This manual is intended for professionals in the fields of health, mental health, child protective services, and law enforcement who are beginning to work with abused or neglected children and their families. We trust that this volume will provide conceptual clarity and scholarly direction in our growing understanding of this most complex and devastating of traumas. It is our intention to build upon the important contributions of several scholars and clinicians who have already contributed to the field of study, including, but not limited to, Roland Summit, David Finkelhor, Anne Burgess, Nicholas Groth, Suzanne Sgroi, and B. Gomez-Schwartz, in an attempt to synthesize the relevant clinical information and research into an organized set of applied clinical information. The manual is also designed to stimulate new hypotheses and generate new clinical intervention skills and research in this most important area of clinical practice and study.

We have attempted to organize a compendium of empirically based observations that will assist the practitioner in reaching a clear understanding of the victim of child abuse and making a diagnosis, and also of family members. In an effort to explicate the nature and consequences of the trauma involved in child sexual abuse, the following are the specific objectives we have in mind:

1. We want to clearly define child abuse and provide a framework for understanding its impact on the lives of victims throughout the life span.
2. We want to educate professionals regarding the scope of child abuse, along with its characteristics and effects; in order words, provide the information that is essential to an understanding of the subject.
3. It is our aim to develop a framework by which one can easily understand and recognize the behavioral, psychological, and medical indicators of abuse.
4. We have attempted to identify clearly the principles helpful in aiding courts in addressing this complex issue.

In communities throughout the country, professionals struggle daily with a wide range of issues pertaining to child abuse, a problem that has reached epidemic proportions. We trust that readers will find this manual helpful in their work.

Thomas W. Miller, Ph.D.
Lane J. Veltkamp, M.S.W.

Acknowledgments

Appreciation is extended to Deborah Kessler, Tag Heister, and Katrina Scott, Library Service; and Eleanor Royalty, Virginia Lynn Gift, and Debbie Howard, Department of Psychiatry, University of Kentucky, and Lisa Michele Webster, Eastern Kentucky University, for their assistance in the preparation of this manuscript. The authors are indebted to Betty Lawson, secretary and typist; Toni Byrne for typing assistance; Pat Garr, Virginia Lynn Gift, Debbie Howard and Wendy Stolldorf for word processing; and Tag Heister for library assistance.

1

Purpose and Objectives

In every community throughout the country professionals struggle with a wide range of issues pertaining to child abuse prevention, including early identification, evaluation and treatment, child placement, and courtroom testimony. We hope this manual will acquaint mental health, child protective service, and health and law enforcement professionals with the principles and strategies helpful in these areas. We want in particular to help professionals (1) understand the scope of the problem of child abuse and neglect; (2) understand the effects of abuse and neglect on victims and their siblings; (3) gain an understanding of the characteristics of those families where there is a risk for abuse or neglect; (4) recognize the behavioral, psychological, and medical indicators of abuse; (5) move toward more effective cooperation and communication between agencies; (6) gain an understanding of the placement issues in order to serve the best psychological interests of the child; (7) learn principles helpful in aiding the court through written reports and courtroom testimony.

2

Introduction and Historical Perspectives

HISTORY

Child abuse and neglect have been present in society throughout recorded history. Infanticide, ritual killings, maiming, and severe physical punishments are well recorded over the centuries. Charles Dickens, for example, wrote of the problems of children growing up in an industrialized society.

The 1874 Mary Ellen case in New York was the first reported instance of child abuse in the United States (Lazoritz, 1990). Mary Ellen had been beaten by her foster parents, and in an attempt to get help for her, a social worker finally took the child to the Society for the Prevention of Cruelty to Animals. Out of this experience, the Society for the Prevention of Cruelty to Children was formed in New York in 1885. Thus, laws for the protection of animals were in existence in this country long before corresponding legislation was used to help children.

Dr. C. Henry Kempe's article, ''The Battered Child Syndrome,'' published in the *Journal of the American Medical Association* (Kempe,

3

Silverman, Steele, Droegemuller, and Silver, 1962), brought the impact of child abuse to the attention of the medical community and general public. Yet it must be understood that this particular syndrome is only one small, although severe, portion of the whole area of maltreatment of children.

Physical abuse is generally defined as nonaccidental acts which cause injury to the body of the child. Emotional abuse is more difficult to define, but refers to any behavior which endangers the child's health, morals, or emotional well-being.

Neglect pertains to negligent treatment or maltreatment of a child by an adult, which harms the child's health, welfare, and safety, and may often be an act of omission which disregards the child's needs in these areas. Failure to provide food, care, clothing, shelter, or medical and dental care fits within this category.

THE LAW

Every state has now enacted laws to obtain reports of child abuse. In the majority of states, physicians, therapists, psychologists, teachers, and clergy are required to report suspected cases and are guilty of a misdemeanor if they fail to do so. All fifty states provide immunity from civil and criminal prosecution for those required to report.

IMPACT

Mental health and health care professionals have recognized the concept of child abuse and its impact on the lives of both the parenting figures and the child or children involved. Maltreated and abused children have been the focus of public concern (Gomez-Schwartz, Horowitz, and Sauzier, 1986), clinical assessment (Koppitz, 1968; Klepsh and Logie, 1982), and treatment (Conte, Berliner, and Schuerman, 1987). National epidemiological surveys (National Center for Child Abuse and Neglect, 1981, 1982) have provided convincing evidence that child abuse and neglect may well be occurring at an alarmingly high rate. The impact on children is realized in physical, emotional, and intellectual impairment in later life. Gold (1986) has studied the long-term effects of victimization in childhood, finding that victimized individuals differ significantly from those who have not been victimized. Of considerable significance is the impaired coping ability and inability to make use of social support systems that arc common features of victims of child abuse when they reach adulthood. Where a social support system, including a parent, failed to respond to the victimized child, the likelihood of adjustment in adulthood was seriously compromised.

Cicchetti and Olsen (1987), in the Harvard Maltreatment Project, realized that adults abused as children, like most other posttraumatic stress victims, were either under- or overcontrolled in their management of feelings, impulses, and arousal. The findings suggested that when maltreated children reach adulthood, they are at significant risk for developing psychopathology. A Factor Analytic Guide (Giaretto, 1981) suggests that the following characteristics were significant contributors to adult nonsurvival; that is, the child victim's failure to adjust in adulthood: (1) a history of family violence, abuse, or neglect; (2) family chaos and disorganization; (3) the family's lack of acceptance and lack of interest in the juvenile; (4) low quality of family members' communication with others; and (5) self-destructive behavior.

3

Physical Abuse of Children

DEFINITION

The following definition is derived from the Model Child Protective Services Act:

1. An "abused or neglected child" is one whose physical or mental health or welfare is harmed or threatened with harm by acts of omission or commission on the part of his or her parent or other persons responsible for the child's welfare.
2. "Harm" occurs when a parent or other person responsible for the child's welfare:

   a. Inflicts, or allows to be inflicted, upon the child, physical or mental injury, including injuries sustained as a result of excessive corporal punishment; or
   b. Commits, or allows to be committed, against the child, a sexual offense, as defined by law; or
   c. Fails to supply the child with adequate food, clothing, shelter, education (as defined by law); or

7

    d. Abandons the child; or

    e. Fails to provide the child with adequate care, supervision, or guardianship by specific acts of omission.

3. "Threatened harm" means substantial risk of harm.

4. "A person responsible for the child's welfare" includes the child's parent, guardian, foster parent, an employee of a public or private residential home, institution, or agency, baby-sitters, or teachers.

5. "Physical injury" means death, disfigurement, or the impairment of any bodily organ.

6. "Mental injury" means an injury to the intellectual or psychological capacity of a child as evidenced by an observable and substantial impairment in his ability to function within a normal range of performance and behavior.

SCOPE OF THE PROBLEM

1. Children of both sexes, of all ages, of all races, with parents of all educational and income levels, and from urban, suburban, and rural settings are subjected to child abuse and neglect.

2. Four in 1000 children are physically assaulted in the United States annually (National Center for Child Abuse and Neglect, 1986).

3. An estimated "bare minimum" of 652,000 (10.5 per 1000 children) children are confirmed to have been abused and neglected each year. This number is viewed as the tip of the iceberg. Eighty-four percent were moderately or severely injured or impaired (National Center for Child Abuse and Neglect, 1986).

4. It is likely that the actual number of children abused and neglected annually in the United States is at least 1 million (National Center for Child Abuse and Neglect, 1986).

5. It is estimated that only one-fifth of children recognized as maltreated by professionals in community institutions are reported (National Center for Child Abuse and Neglect, 1982).

THE IMPACT OF CHILD ABUSE AND NEGLECT

1. Physical abuse may have an impact on the child's feelings about himself, his perception of others, and his behavior toward others.

2. Physical effects of child abuse and neglect may include damage to the brain, vital organs, eyes, ears, arms, or legs. These injuries may result in mental retardation, blindness, deafness, or loss of limb. Abuse or neglect may cause arrested development.

3. Abused or neglected children may be impaired in self-concept, reality testing, and overall thought processes. Frequently they have a higher level of aggression, anxiety, low impulse control, self-destructiveness, and antisocial behavior.

4. Abuse and neglect may restrict cognitive development. Language, perceptual, and motor skills may be underdeveloped, further hindering the child's chances to succeed.

5. Physical abuse may affect the child during the time he is being abused, during adolescence when he begins to develop closer emotional and physical relationships with peers, or may affect him when, as an adult, he marries and parents his own children. The impact on the child during the time he or she is being abused is clearly identified under "Behavioral Indicators of Physical Abuse" (p. 000). As an adolescent he may become physically abusive during his dating years. As an adult he may abuse his own children or his spouse.

CAUSES OF CHILD ABUSE AND NEGLECT

1. Severe emotional pressure, psychopathology, or family stress.
2. Multigenerational patterns; family heritage of violence.
3. Burdens resulting from poverty, other external stresses such as marital discord, unemployment, presence of extended family members, poor housing conditions, lack of financial security, and lack of social contact.
4. Parental attitudes and values toward children, changing family roles, and the use of corporal punishment in disciplining the child.

FAMILY PROFILE

The family profile is made up of those characteristics often seen in abusive families. These characteristics may occur with any type of family dysfunction and may show up in families where abuse is not a problem. However, generally speaking the more characteristics one observes in a given family, the greater the risk to the child. The clinician can get this information regarding family characteristics by using open-ended questions, specifically related to the child's symptoms and family history. In addition, the use of reframing as an interviewing skill may help avoid the need for the parent to initially assume the role of the abuser and for the child to be viewed as a helpless victim. When talking to parents, it may be important to focus on the child initially because the parents may become too threatened or defensive if they feel the clinician is focusing on them. The following questions and statements are examples of the technique of reframing:

1. "Is he a pretty tough kid to handle?"
2. "It must be difficult to find affordable baby-sitters."
3. "Sometimes kids just refuse to mind."
4. "Sometimes when a parent is being affectionate with a child. . . ."

Intrafamily Abuse of Children

The following are characteristics often seen in families where children are abused. The greater the number of characteristics present in a particular family, the greater the risk to the child.

1. The parents experience a crisis of unmet needs. Parents are not getting their needs met in the marital relationship or in their relationships with their children; therefore, frustration and anger leads to an emotional crisis, and possible abuse of the children.
2. There is role reversal between child and parent—one or both parents look to the children for support and nurturance rather than to each other; generational boundaries are unclear; and parents look to children to fill an emotional need.
3. Parents and children are isolated from others—may lack a support system, particularly at a time of crisis.
4. Parents have difficulty coping with stress constructively.
5. Parents may have inadequate coping skills when handling routine child problems.
6. An abusing family may "hospital shop"—go from hospital to hospital to avoid detection.

7. The abusive family moves or relocates frequently.
8. Parents may attempt to conceal the child's injury or protect the perpetrator.
9. There is a lack of a sense of order or responsibility within the family.
10. The family demonstrates a lack of productivity or "getting things done," in such areas as schoolwork, employment, or chores.
11. Conflict is not resolved constructively within the family; it may lie dormant only to recur.
12. Family members constantly manipulate one another; negotiation between family members is infrequent.
13. Parents and children may show a variety of symptoms related to their feelings or behavior. Examples of symptoms seen in parents include depression, alcohol or drug abuse, spouse abuse, etc. Symptoms seen in children are identified on pages 13–15.
14. Parents have difficulty handling feelings constructively, have difficulty verbalizing their feelings, and tend to act out their feelings.
15. There is a high level of suspiciousness between family members.
16. Parents often give semiplausible reasons when explaining the cause of the abuse or neglect.
17. The history may reveal the mysterious death or injury of a sibling of the victim.
18. There are unusually high stress levels within the family. This stress may be caused by a combination of external events, internal stress within each parent, and difficulty in coping with stress constructively.

The Parent(s)

Once again, not all of these characteristics may occur in a single family. However, the more of these characteristics that are present the more the child is at risk.

1. One parent is often overly involved with activities outside the home to such a degree as to exclude meaningful involvement with the family.
2. The other parent, in order to get his or her emotional needs met, is overly involved with the children, often looking to them for support and nurturance not found in the marital relationship.

3. There is a lack of intimacy between the parents in the marital relationship.
4. The abusing parent and the nonabusing parent both have low self-esteem, but each handles it differently; one is more dependent, the other more aggressive.
5. There is a history of marital discord.
6. Parents may have relinquished custody of a child or children.
7. One or both parents may have been abused as children.
8. Pregnancy may have occurred at an early age or was unwanted.
9. The parents assumed too much responsibility at an early age; they require the child to take too much responsibility.
10. The parents misuse alcohol or drugs; for example, use alcohol during times of stress.
11. Parents have unrealistic expectations of the child.
12. The history often reveals spouse abuse in the parents' childhood.
13. The parents may show immaturity in handling conflicts, handling their own feelings, and dealing with crises.
14. The parents appear unconcerned about the child's needs for dental or medical care, for nurturance or support, or for affection.
15. Parents lack knowledge regarding child rearing.
16. The parents routinely employ harsh, unreasonable discipline which is inappropriate to the child's age, or the transgression.
17. The history shows that the parents were unable to depend on their own parents for love and nurturance.

The Child

1. The child may be "different"; for example, hyperactive, mentally retarded, racially different, physically handicapped. These children are at greater risk for being abused.
2. The child is often viewed as "bad," "evil," a "monster," or "witch."
3. The child was born prematurely.
4. The child is often required by the parent to take too much responsibility. For example, taking care of the parent, being the parent's companion, taking care of younger siblings.
5. The child is often overly involved with one parent.
6. The child cannot depend on the parents for love and nurturance.

7. The child is often expected to fill an emotional void for the parents.
8. The parents look to the child for emotional support and nurturance not found in the marital relationship.

The Multigenerational Pattern

1. The past: Abusive parents were often subjected to abuse as children; there is a pattern of abusive behavior in the family of origin. Being abused as a child increases the risk for abusing one's own children later in life.
3. The present: The current pattern is abusive.
4. The future: An abused child will be at risk of abusing his or her own children. In addition, they may abuse their parents later in life.

BEHAVIORAL INDICATORS OF PHYSICAL ABUSE

Child abuse and neglect can often be identified by recognizing behavioral indicators. The presence of a single indicator does not necessarily prove that child abuse or neglect is occurring. The repeated occurrence of an indicator or the presence of several indicators in combination should alert the clinician to the possibility of child abuse or neglect.

The following behaviors are the child's way of saying something is wrong. The child's behavior is purposeful and goal-oriented and is his way of "getting it out" or communicating how he feels about himself or his relationships with others. In evaluating these behaviors and in order to have a longitudinal view of the child, it is often helpful to obtain information from individuals (i.e., schoolteachers) who have observed the child over time.

The following behavioral indicators are seen in preschool, latency, and adolescence:

1. There may be regression from age-appropriate behaviors or activities. For example, a toilet-trained child may become enuretic or encopretic, or use baby talk.
2. The child may behave aggressively toward other children or adults or toward things (e.g., breaking toys).

3. The child withdraws from age-appropriate activities in his or her peer group.
4. The child is overcompliant or shows overly adaptive behavior in response to unresolved parental needs.
5. Physical symptoms increase; the child is sick more frequently.
6. There are lags in the child's physical, emotional, and/or intellectual development.
7. The child is agitated.
8. The child is hyperactive.
9. The child has temper tantrums.
10. The child's attention span is shorter than it should be, given the developmental stage.
11. The child is overdependent on the parents or parental figures.
12. The child seeks constant affection.
13. The child shows role reversal.
14. Emotional constriction or blunted affect is apparent.
15. The child is wary of adult contact.
16. The child is apprehensive, fearful, and self-blaming.
17. There are sleep disturbances.
18. The child has habit disorders such as tics, biting, rocking.

In addition, symptoms seen primarily in the latency-age child include:

1. The child shows poor peer relationships—child is undersocialized, withdrawn from others, or engages in fighting behavior.
2. The child shows an unwillingness or inability to participate in school-related activities where bruises or other injuries may be revealed.
3. Child may be truant from home or school.
4. Child may be depressed.
5. Child may show phobias, obsessions, or compulsive behaviors.

In addition, the adolescent may:

1. engage in drug or alcohol abuse;
2. engage in sexually promiscuous behavior;
3. make suicidal gestures or attempts.

PSYCHOLOGICAL INDICATORS

In addition to the behavioral indicators listed above, the following are psychological indicators seen in severely abused children. Once again, these symptoms are goal-oriented and are the child's way of saying something is wrong. The greater the abuse, the less the child will trust other people or reach out to them and the more time he or she will need to respond to love and care.

The following are grouped according to the child's developmental stage:

Preschool Child

1. The child does what the abusive parent wants without regard to his or her own needs; expects nothing in the way of love and support.
2. There are inhibited verbal or crying responses (depression).
3. There is inordinate shyness (withdrawal).
4. There is immobility due to depression or fatigue.
5. Extreme dependence on others is exhibited.
6. The child lacks curiosity, or there is a fear of appearing curious.
7. The child is wary of physical contact due to fear of offending someone.
8. There is excessive concern for the parents' needs; this derives from a need to keep the parents happy.
9. The child is excessively self-controlled so as not to bother others.
10. The child may be frightened of one or both parents.
11. The child states he or she is afraid and may cry when it is time to go home.
12. The child becomes apprehensive when other children cry.

Latency-Age Child or Adolescent

1. The child or adolescent does what the abusive parent wants without regard to his or her own needs; does not expect love and support.
2. There is extreme dependence on others.
3. There is excessive concern for the parents' needs in order to keep parents happy.

4. The child or adolescent is excessively self-controlled so as not to bother others.
5. He or she seems frightened of the parents.
6. The child or adolescent states that he or she is afraid to go home or cries when it is time to leave.
7. The child reports injury by a parent.

MEDICAL INDICATORS OF PHYSICAL ABUSE

1. There are different-aged bruises or lacerations.
2. There are bruises or lacerations on different planes of the body. For example, it is unlikely that accidental injury would cause bruises on both the back and the chest.
3. There are bruises inflicted by specific objects (belt, cord, etc.).
4. There are burns in clearly defined areas indicating that the child was forcibly held or that cigarettes or other objects were held to the child.
5. There are dislocations and/or fractures.
6. There are multiple, unexplained injuries, fractures, lacerations, or abrasions.
7. Family members give contradictory versions of the history of the injuries.
8. There is delay in seeking medical attention.
9. There is a history of repeated hospitalizations.
10. The child is given inappropriate food, drink, or drugs.
11. The parents may refuse to allow the child to receive diagnostic tests or treatment. For example, when a child has an injury from shaking or twisting an arm, the parent may refuse evaluation or treatment for the child in an emergency room.

4

Physical Neglect of Children

DEFINITION

Physical neglect of children involves inattention to the basic needs of the child for food, clothing, shelter, medical care, and supervision. While physical abuse tends to be episodic, neglect tends to be chronic. When considering the possibility of neglect, it is important to note the consistency of indicators. Do they occur rarely, or frequently? Are they chronic (present most of the time), periodic (noticeable after weekends or absences), or episodic (seen during a time of family stress)?

In identifying neglect be sensitive to:

1. Issues of poverty versus neglect. Parents who are unable to afford a well-balanced diet on a daily basis may not be neglectful.
2. Differing cultural expectations and values versus neglect. Some parents, due to heavy work commitments, may have others take care of their children. Some parents may expect children to do much more for themselves, while others may view this as neglectful.

17

SCOPE OF THE PROBLEM

1. There are 5.3 per 1000 substantiated cases of physical neglect of children each year (National Center for Child Abuse and Neglect, 1986, p. 18).
2. There are 2.9 per 1000 substantiated cases of educational neglect of children each year (National Center for Child Abuse and Neglect, 1986, p. 18).

PHYSICAL INDICATORS OF NEGLECT

The greater the cluster of symptoms or behaviors, the greater the chance that neglect is occurring (Miller and Veltkamp, 1989c).

1. Abandonment: Leaving the child unsupervised, uncared for, alone.
2. Lack of supervision: Failing to provide the child with sufficient direction or management.
3. The child lacks clothing or wears inappropriate clothing.
4. There is a lack of medical or dental care; unattended physical problems such as:
   a. Vision problems
   b. Anemia
   c. Hearing deficit
   d. Poor dental health
5. The child is constantly hungry; malnutrition is evident.
6. Adequate shelter is lacking.
7. Skin hygiene is poor.
8. Failure to thrive; infant not gaining or losing weight.
9. Immunizations are inadequate.
10. Adequate education is lacking. The child is not getting to school.
11. There is constant fatigue or listlessness.

BEHAVIORAL INDICATORS OF NEGLECT

1. Truancy.
2. The child is begging or stealing food.

3. There is fatigue or listlessness.
4. The child comes to school very early and leaves very late.
5. Delinquency (vandalism, theft, etc.).
6. The child states there is no one to look after him or her.

CHARACTERISTICS OF NEGLECTFUL PARENTS

1. Home life may be chaotic.
2. Living conditions may be unsafe (no food; garbage and excrement in living areas; exposed wiring; drugs and poisons kept within the reach of children).
3. The parents may abuse drugs or alcohol.
4. The parents may be mentally retarded.
5. The parents may be impulsive individuals who seek immediate gratification without regard to long-term consequences.
6. The parents may be employed, but unable or unwilling to find child care.
7. The parents generally may not have experienced success in relationships.
8. The parents' emotional needs were not met by their parents.
9. The parents have low self-esteem.
10. The parents have little motivation or skill to effect changes in their lives.
11. The parents tend to be passive in relationships or in dealing with people outside the family.

5

Emotional Maltreatment of Children

DEFINITION

Emotional maltreatment is defined as blaming, belittling, or rejecting a child; treating siblings unequally on a continuing basis; or deliberate and enforced isolation or continuous withholding of security and affection by the child's caretaker. Emotional maltreatment is not necessarily manifested in physical signs. Speech disorders, lags in physical development, and failure-to-thrive syndrome in infancy (a progressive wasting away associated with lack of parenting) are a few examples of physical indications of emotional maltreatment.

In addition, a child witnessing the abuse of a sibling or a parent, or a child experiencing being snatched or kidnapped (e.g., when a noncustodial parent kidnaps a child from a custodial parent or a natural parent kidnaps a child from foster parents) are examples of emotional maltreatment. Emotional maltreatment may also include exposing a child to criminal or immoral influences.

21

SCOPE OF THE PROBLEM (NATIONAL CENTER FOR CHILD ABUSE AND NEGLECT, 1986)

The following are substantiated cases:
1. 1 child per 1000 children is emotionally neglected each year.
2. 2.2 per 1000 children are emotionally abused per year.
3. 5.3 per 1000 children are emotionally, educationally, and physically neglected each year.

PHYSICAL INDICATORS

1. Speech disorders are often seen in preschool and latency-age children.
2. Lags in physical development are seen in preschool children.
3. Failure to thrive in infancy.

BEHAVIORAL INDICATORS

Once again, in viewing the following behavioral indicators, it is important to realize that the greater the cluster of behaviors or the more intense the behavior, the more the child is at risk, and the greater the family dysfunction:

1. Behavioral extremes such as withdrawal, explosiveness, impulsivity;
2. Overly adaptive, compliant behavior;
3. Attempted suicide, suicide gesture or attempts;
4. Habit disorders (nail-biting, hair-pulling);
5. Conduct disorders (acting out behaviors, disrespect for authority);
6. Sleep disturbances (nightmares, insomnia, wakefulness);
7. Inhibitions (fear of others, fear of expressing self);
8. Obsessions, a preoccupation with pleasing others, attempting to be perfect;
9. Lack of purpose or direction, lack of goals;
10. Depression, a sense of sadness, hopelessness, or helplessness;

11. Night terrors, panic state, usually seen at night, when child cannot be calmed down;
12. Excessive fears of dark, people, and anger;
13. Impulsivity, poor behavior control;
14. Self-destructive behaviors, hurting self;
15. Hyperactivity.

6

The Sexual Abuse of Children

INTRODUCTION

Maltreated and sexually abused children have become the focus of public concern (Gomez-Schwartz, Horowitz, and Sauzier, 1986), clinical assessment (Sgroi, 1978; Veltkamp and Miller, 1988), and treatment (Giaretto, 1981; Goodwin, McCarty, and DiVasto, 1982). National epidemiological surveys (National Center for Child Abuse and Neglect, 1982; Goodwin, Willett, and Jackson, 1982) have provided convincing evidence that child sexual abuse and neglect may well be occurring at an alarmingly high rate. The impact on children is realized in physical, emotional, and intellectual impairment (Kreiger, Rosenfeld, and Gordon, 1980).

The purpose of this chapter is to provide a clinical perspective on the problem of sexual abuse. It further addresses critically important components that medical and health care professionals must address in accurately diagnosing and treating child sexual abuse.

The American Humane Association reports that the true extent of the problem of sexual abuse of children may not actually be known. Most data come from large urban centers and much less is known

25

about rural communities. The most recent data from the American Humane Association (1988) indicate that the total number of children reported for child abuse and neglect nationally is 2.2 million per year. Forty percent of these cases have been substantiated from the twenty-five states in which data have been collected. Of the approximately 2 million cases reported, 27.6 percent involve physical abuse, 54.9 percent involve neglect, 15.7 percent involve sexual abuse, 8.3 percent involve emotional abuse, and 7.9 percent involve other categories including abandonment. The most recent figures suggest that 132,000 children have been sexually abused in the most recent report year, with 77.2 percent of these being female while 22.8 percent are male. The average age of the abused child is 9.19 years of age.

DEFINITION

Sexual abuse includes any contact or interactions between a child and an adult in which the child is sexually stimulated or is being used for the sexual stimulation of the perpetrator or another person. Sexual abuse includes fondling, exhibitionism, forcible rape, sexual exploitation and/or prostitution. When these acts are committed by an adolescent who is either older than the victim or in a position of power or control over the victim, it is also considered sexual abuse. Father–daughter incest appears to be the most common, but father–son and brother–sister incest are also prevalent. Mother–son sexual contact seems less common, but may be more prevalent than we realize.

SCOPE OF THE PROBLEM

1. The National Center on Child Abuse and Neglect (1981) reports that the true extent of the problem of sexual abuse of children is unknown.
2. It is estimated that between 10 and 25 percent of all preadolescent females had some sexual contacts with adults. Some authors have said that the risk is the same for young males.
3. Finkelhor (1979) reports that 19 percent of females and 9 percent of males were sexually abused prior to age 12 by a person at least five years older.

4. One-third of 500 college students studied indicated they had been sexually abused as children (Finkelhor, 1979).
5. Russell (1983) found 38 percent of females before age 18 had sexual abuse experiences involving physical contact.
6. Sexual abuse, like other forms of abuse, is a grossly underreported problem; most victims never report their abuse.

TYPES OF SEXUAL ABUSE

Incestuous relationships often involve a series of escalating contacts over many years beginning with fondling and possibly moving toward penetration of the child. Such relationships include:

1. Sexualized or erotized fondling and caressing.
2. Using the child to sexually stimulate the parent.
3. Sexual stimulation of the child.
4. Sexual exploitation of the child; there are at least 264 pornographic publications involving children.
5. Intercourse or oral–genital contact.
6. Rape.

WHEN THE CHILD IS AFFECTED

The sexually abused child may show symptoms when the abuse occurs, or the impact of the trauma may not be experienced until later in life; for example, during adolescence and/or adulthood.

1. When the abuse occurs, the child will often show symptoms associated with feelings, behavior, and/or attitude. The child may also exhibit a wide range of physical symptoms. These symptoms are listed on page 34.
2. Symptoms may appear during adolescence, particularly as relationships become more emotionally and physically intimate.
3. Adults who were sexually abused as children may withdraw from sexual activity, or may experience sexual dysfunctions.
4. In relationships with children, adults may be overly protective or sexually abusive of children.

CRITERIA USEFUL IN DETERMINING THE DEGREE OF PSYCHOLOGICAL HARM

Psychological harm to the child is dependent on the following variables. These should be viewed as a cluster: the more of these that occur the more psychologically traumatic they are for the child. In addition, the greater the trauma the greater the need for treatment.

1. *The age of the child.* The younger child may not actually realize what is going on, but may experience physical pain which makes the initial sexual experience an emotionally and physically painful one, and contributes to an overall negative attitude regarding sex. More confusion is seen in the older child, who is bewildered, angry, depressed, and guilt ridden.
2. *Duration.* The longer the abuse continues, the more traumatic it becomes.
3. *Aggression.* The greater the level of aggression, the more physically and psychologically traumatic its effects become.
4. *Threat.* The abusing parent often threatens the child. The greater the threat, the more traumatic the event is to the child. Examples include threat of removal of the child from the family, of physical abuse to the child, or the parent being imprisoned.
5. *The kind of adult.* If the perpetrator is known to the child, the child is more confused and guilt ridden than if the perpetrator is a stranger. In addition, when the perpetrator is known it has a profound impact on the child's ability to trust.
6. *Degree of activity.* The more frequent the activity, the more psychologically traumatic it is to the child.
7. *If adults do not believe or protect the child,* the experience of abuse becomes more traumatic. If the parent overreacts the child may feel guilty and responsible for the abuse.

In addition to the factors above, it is helpful in determining the need for treatment of the victim, to assess the following factors as they apply to the situation.

1. *The child's symptomatology.* The greater the degree of symptomatology, the greater the need for treatment.

2. *The siblings' reaction.* Siblings may blame the victim for the family breakdown, father's incarceration, and so on.
3. *The parent's reaction.* They may blame the child or someone outside the family for the abuse.
4. *The community reaction.* The community may be outraged; overreaction is common, and may cause guilt on the part of the child.
5. *The victim's placement of blame.* The victim may place the blame on self, on the abusive parent, on the nonabusive parent, or others.
6. *The victim's selection of which side to take.* The victim must either betray the abusing parent or be loyal to him; in the latter case, the abuse will continue.

MAPPING THE TRAUMA OF ABUSE

The trauma of child abuse and in particular sexual abuse has been discussed in the psychiatric literature for some time (Finch, 1962; Russell, 1983; Landis, 1985). Clinicians have come to understand some of the real or anticipated trauma experienced by children who are the objects of sexual abuse. Sexual trauma can occur when a child is seduced or pressured by an individual in a power position, by reason of authority or age, into a sexual activity that is not age-appropriate or desirable and may be life-threatening. The activities will continue as long as the child is intimidated or coerced into remaining silent.

Roland Summit of Harbor-UCLA Medical Center (1983) discusses the "Child Sexual Abuse Accommodation Syndrome." The author suggests that the sexually abused child is often fearful and confused about the outcome of disclosure. Adults, including parents, health care professionals, and the courts, often offer little support, and in fact tend to disbelieve the child. A typical response is that the child's story is merely fantasy, confusion, or displacement of the child's own wish for seductive conquest. The sexually abused child responds in a contradictory and unexpected manner, unexpected, that is, from the adult perspective. The following are the five categories of the syndrome suggested by Summit: (1) secrecy; (2) helplessness; (3) accommodation; (4) delayed, conflicted, and unconvincing testimony; (5) retraction: the child is likely to reverse his or her story because of ambivalence, obligation to preserve the family, and fear.

Children have great difficulty in discussing any aspect of sexuality and in particular sexual activities where they are victimized (Goodwin, Sahd, and Rada, 1982). If the child has been unable to disclose the content of sexual activities, alternative methods include the use of (1) anatomical dolls; (2) human figure drawings; and (3) fables (Miller and Veltkamp, 1986, 1989a). These methods can be used to assist in relieving the usually well-defended systems that prevent children from sharing these experiences with adults or professionals. The content and quality of such projective measures as fables can reflect evidence of concealment, avoidance, and vagueness. It can also permit the child to disclose in a less threatening way activities which might otherwise be too difficult for direct discussion.

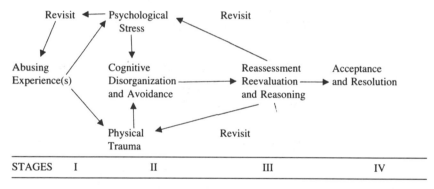

Figure 6.1. Four Stages of Experiencing Sexual Abuse and Emotional Trauma in Children

The child confronted with such sexual victimization often passes through a series of stages in dealing with this trauma (Miller and Feibelman, 1987) (**Figure 6.1**) The initial stage of the victimization, which is recognized as the stressor, usually brings about acute physical and/or psychological trauma. The child's response is usually one of feeling overwhelmed, intimidated, and powerless. It is not uncommon for the child to think recurringly of the stressful experience and to focus on the intimidating act as well as physical pain associated with the act. This acute stage of trauma is followed by a stage involving more cognitive disorganization and confusion. This stage is marked by a vagueness in understanding both the concept of sexual abuse and the expectancies associated with the demands of the adult in the relationship.

The second stage involves a denial or avoidance which can take two directions and may vary in its choice at various within-phase considerations. The first is a phase of conscious inhibition during which the child tries actively to inhibit thoughts and feelings related to the sexual trauma. This can involve a recurrence of the cognitive disorganization phase and the earlier memories and flashbacks to the acute physical and psychological trauma. The second phase is one of avoidance, involving unconscious denial. The child is unaware that he or she is avoiding the psychological trauma associated with the sexual abuse and therefore unconsciously denying the issues and reconsideration of the sexually abusing experience and the confusion which followed. This unconscious denial less frequently allows a revisitation to the cognitive disorganization stage and the confusion phase.

The cognitive disorganization or confused thinking phase is followed by a stage of therapeutic reassessment during which a parent or significant other usually supports the child's reevaluation of the psychological and physical trauma associated with the sexual abuse. At this phase, the child victim may begin to disclose the abuse through drawings, fables, or specific content relevant to the experiencing of the sexual abuse. The phase of therapeutic reevaluation and reasoning is significant because it indicates that conscious adult support has been realized by the child in passing from the avoidant phase to the actual issues, activities, and the trauma of the sexual abuse.

The final stage is one of acceptance and resolution wherein the child has been able, through the support of parents, professionals, or significant others, to deal with the issues. The child will arrive at a better understanding of the abuse and its significance. He or she will develop coping strategies that will allow self-acceptance without shame, doubt, or guilt, and progress to a stage of resolution. At this stage the child is (1) more open and talks about the incident; (2) is able to express thoughts and feelings more readily; and (3) is able through assessment and play therapy to discharge some of the aggressive feelings toward the perpetrator which are a healthy part of the child's response. It is at this phase that the child develops an alliance with significant others and/or professionals in (1) exploring the original traumatic life experience; (2) dealing with both the physical and psychological stressors involved; (3) attending to the repressed material and the process of either conscious inhibition or unconscious denial utilized during the avoidant phase; (4) focusing on self-understanding and emotional support from others in understanding the reasons for the abuse; (5) exploring appropriate psychological and social patterns of living to determine the extent to which further professional help may be needed (Miller and Veltkamp, 1986).

FAMILY PROFILE

The family profile contains two parts: there is the family constellation or nuclear family and the multigenerational pattern which takes into account the abusing parents' own families of origin and also looks into the future of the child who is currently being sexually abused and their likely patterns of behavior. The family profile identifies a cluster of characteristics often seen in sexually abusive families. The greater the number of characteristics, the greater the risk is to the child.

We believe that children should remain with their families if at all possible. Removal from parents, siblings, peer group, and school where the child feels comfortable is psychologically detrimental because continuity of relationship and place is broken and the psychological bonds a child has developed with parents and siblings may be destroyed. When removal occurs it is necessary to maintain the child's psychological attachments and to preserve as much continuity as possible. The issue of removal will be discussed in more detail later.

Family Constellation

1. One parent (e.g., the mother, in father–daughter incest) may be passive, dependent, and reluctant to be assertive for fear of destroying the family unit.
2. Mother–daughter relationships (in father–daughter incest) are often characterized by detachment, hostility, and competition.
3. The marital relationship is poor, with little constructive communication, and a poor sexual relationship.
4. Father or mother turns to the child to get emotional and physical needs met.
5. The child feels emotionally deprived, and turns to the parent for support and emotional nurturance.

6. Generational boundaries between parents and child are unclear.
7. There is a lack of social contacts outside family.
8. The parents have inadequate coping skills, particularly under stress.

The Multigenerational Pattern

1. One or both parents experienced patterns of sexual exploitation and abusive behavior in the family of origin.
2. Later on the sexually abused child may select a marital partner who will sexually abuse her own children, or she may abuse her own children or children in her care.

CHARACTERISTICS OF SEXUALLY ABUSIVE PARENTS

1. They have low self-esteem.
2. Their emotional needs were not met by their own parents.
3. They have inadequate coping skills.
4. They may have experienced the loss of a spouse through death or divorce.
5. The family may be experiencing overcrowding in their home.
6. The parents may have marital problems; one spouse may be seeking physical affection from a child rather than from the other spouse (a "solution" the "denying" husband or wife might find acceptable).
7. The parents may abuse alcohol or drugs.
8. There is often a lack of social and emotional contacts outside the family.
9. The family may feel isolated.
10. The perpetrator often has a blurring of the boundaries between the expression of affection and sexual expression. This blurring developed in childhood, often due to the offender having been subjected to sexual victimization.
11. The abusing parent may feel uncomfortable in sexual encounters with agemates, and therefore turns to children.

THE ADULT SEXUALLY ABUSING MALE

1. There is a need on the part of the abuser to be in control of the family, and he is often a rigid disciplinarian.
2. The abuser is passive outside the home.
3. The abuser does not usually have a police record nor is he known to have been involved in any public disturbance.
4. The abuser may not engage in social activities outside the home; he is often isolated socially.
5. The abuser is jealous and protective of the child he victimizes.
6. The abuser pays special attention to the child victim which usually results in sibling jealousy.
7. The abuser has a distorted perception of the child's role in the family.
8. The abuser often initiates sexual contact with the child by hugging and kissing which tends to develop over time into more intimate caressing, genital–genital and oral–genital contacts.
9. Sometimes the sexually abusing male will gravitate toward jobs involving close contact with children; for example, he will seek work in institutions for children or youth groups.

WHEN THE ADULT FEMALE ALLOWS SEXUAL ABUSE OF A CHILD TO OCCUR OR CONTINUE

1. She may be cognizant of the sexual abuse but consciously or subconsciously she denies it.
2. She may hesitate reporting the abuse for fear of destroying the marriage and being left on her own.
3. She may see sexual activity within the family as preferable to extramarital sexual activity.
4. She may feel that the sexual activity between the husband and daughter is a relief from her wifely sexual responsibilities and will make certain that time is available for the two to be alone.
5. She may feel a mixture of guilt, anger, and jealousy toward her daughter.

BEHAVIORAL INDICATORS OF SEXUAL ABUSE

The following behaviors are frequently seen in children who are, or have been, sexually abused. Any one of these behaviors may be the child's way of revealing that something is wrong, that he or she is being sexually misused or abused. A mistake frequently made by professionals is to view these behaviors as the problem rather than as symptoms of a far greater family problem. Explicit sexual behaviors are the most reliable indicators of abuse.

The following behavioral indicators are seen often in sexually abused children. Many of the symptoms seen in physically abused children may also occur in those who have been sexually abused.

Preschool, Latency Age, or Adolescent

1. The child displays bizarre, sophisticated, or unusual sexual knowledge or behavior.
2. The child states he or she has been sexually assaulted.
3. Such a child may "come on" sexually with children, adolescents, or adults.
4. The child is unwilling to participate in physical activities (i.e., gym class).

PHYSICAL INDICATORS OF SEXUAL ABUSE

1. There are complaints of pain, itching, or irritation in the genital area.
2. There is evidence of trauma (e.g., bruises or bleeding) of the mouth, anus, external genitalia, or vaginal area.
3. There is torn, stained, or bloody underclothing.
4. Semen is present.
5. Pregnancy, especially in early adolescence, is a possible indicator.
6. The child suffers from a sexually transmitted disease (STD).
7. The child has difficulty in walking or sitting.
8. In addition, the sexually abused child may present to a physician a variety of physical complaints over many years.

MOTHER–SON INCEST

While the literature gives attention to father–daughter incest, mother–son incest may be more prevalent than most professionals realize. What is commonly referred to as overprotectiveness or overindulgence may often involve overt or covert sexual themes. For example, provocative nudity, mother sleeping with a son, or mother and son bathing together, may produce sexual stimulation as well as anxiety and guilt on the part of the child.

THE ISSUE OF BELIEVABILITY

At times parents, agencies, or the courts question the believability of a child's report of sexual abuse. In general, the child should be believed and the following criteria can be used as guidelines to demonstrate that the child is believable:

1. The child's vivid description of the event: The more vivid the description, the more believable.
2. The child's detailed description of the event: The more detailed the description, the more believable.
3. Does the child's story hold up over time? If so, the child is more believable. A caution here is that there is often family pressure on the sexually abused child to change his or her story. If a child retracts the story, it does not indicate that the abuse did not occur (see section on the "Child Sexual Abuse Accommodation Syndrome") (Summit, 1983).
4. Is the child's story corroborated by others, by the child's drawings, play, fables, and by the physical exam?
5. Is there congruity between the child's affect and his or her description of the event? The more congruity, the more believable the child. However, in some children, flat affect may be due to depression.

THE CHILD SEXUAL ABUSE ACCOMMODATION SYNDROME

It is well known that the sexually abused child is often fearful and confused about the continuation of the abuse. In addition, the child is fearful of the outcome of disclosure. Adults, including parents, health care professionals, and the courts offer little support; in fact, they often do not believe the child. Summit (1983) explains that many abused children delay their disclosure and may later retract their accusation because they have been pressured or threatened to keep it a secret, and they feel helpless to prevent the abuse. Often when the disclosure is finally made, the reaction of the adults is disbelief, which further convinces the child to withhold information and to retract the claim of abuse. As noted above, Dr. Summit refers to this as the "Sexual Abuse Accommodation Syndrome." The following reactions are normal in a child who has been abused:

1. *Secrecy*: The majority of victims never tell anyone.
2. *Helplessness*: The child feels betrayed, abandoned, untrusting. The child has no choice but to submit and to keep the abuse a secret.
3. *Entrapment and accommodation*: The only option available to the child is to learn to accept the situation.
4. *Delayed, conflicted, and unconvincing disclosure*: The victim usually remains silent about the abuse until she has established a separate life for herself and can challenge the authority of her parents.
5. *Retraction*: Because of ambivalent feelings, a child is likely to reverse his or her disclosure about being sexually abused. While there is intense fear of the abuse continuing, there is simultaneous fear of the family breaking up, and strong feelings of obligation to preserve the family.

DISCUSSION AND CONCLUSIONS

It is essential that the entire family of the child victim be considered when diagnosing and treating a child who has been sexually abused or assaulted. The victimization is a traumatic, stressful event, externally imposed; the psychopathology resides in the offender, triggering him or her to behave in a sexually deviant manner. Clinically relevant research indicates that the child experiences an acute disorganizational phase, which may well be exemplified in human figure drawings or other measures, such as fables, even when the child is unable to describe the experience or any feelings associated with it. Drawings relating to child abuse are much more clearly defined than the child's other drawings and not of a random or diffuse nature. The psychodynamics of child sexual trauma suggest that children are often able to draw what they are unable to communicate verbally, and that the verbal reluctance is often a reaction to straightforward questioning from an adult and a reluctance on the child's part to disclose the victimization.

Within the framework of child sexual abuse (Miller and Veltkamp, 1989c), multigenerational patterns of sexual abuse may be of greater frequency than national statistics reveal. It is not unlikely that both parents of the sexually abused child have experienced patterns of sexual exploitation and abusive behavior. In the family of origin, both the mother and the father may well have been abused sexually as children by parents, grandparents, or extended family members. The sexually abused child may select a marital partner who will sexually abuse her own children and may even select a partner who will be accepting of her own abuse of her children. Generally speaking, sexually abusing parents tend to be avoidant, isolated individuals of low self-confidence and self-esteem. Within the family, there is often a blurring of the boundaries between the expression of affection and overt sexual abuse. This blurring develops during infancy and becomes an ever-greater factor in the prepubertal years. It is not unlikely that the emotional needs of these sexually abusing adults were not met by their parents when they were children and have resulted in poorly developed marital relationships. These marital relationships find the sexually abusing parent or parents seeking either sexual gratification or physical affection from a child rather than from a spouse, a solution that the other spouse might well find more acceptable than separation or divorce.

Characteristics of these families include a likelihood of this pattern of incestuous relationships and lack of social and emotional contacts outside the family continuing into the next generation. While the sexually abusing male often desires rigid control within the family, he may be seen as more passive and dependent outside the home. There is usually no indication of a police record. This individual, while generally isolated from the community, is not recognized as a violator of public laws or community norms. The adult sexually abusing male may also be a person who uses his spouse to intimidate and threaten the child who is the object of sexual abuse. The adult female may be cognizant of the sexual abuse, but consciously or subconsciously denies it or chooses to participate in it in a more passive manner. The female spouse may often be hesitant to report the child sexual abuse, both for fear of physical response as well as the destruction of the marital relationship. The myths and rituals maintained in families relate to cultural aspects of sexual activity and may lead the female spouse to believe that sexual activity with the child is a ritual which must be fostered in order for the child to reach adulthood. DeJong (1985) suggests the following objectives be addressed in the treatment of child sexual abuse: (1) Identify the sexually abused child. Some children will complain directly about the assault, while others exhibit various physical and emotional symptoms. (2) Manage the acute medical problems of the child, including physical injury, sexually transmitted disease, and pregnancy. (3) Obtain and record an accurate history of the assault, including the answers to the questions of who, when, what, where, and how. (4) Manage the acute emotional problems of the child and family resulting from the assault itself, the act of disclosure, police involvement, and the medical exam. These problems are often exacerbated for the child by mixed feelings of anger, guilt, and frustration. (5) Safeguard the child against further sexual abuse by determining whether the child and other children at home are under unusual risk for sexual abuse and need to be placed in temporary custody. (6) Formulate treatment follow-up plans for the child's medical and emotional well-being. (7) Comply with legal requirements for collection of evidence, documentation, and, depending upon the laws of a particular state, reporting of the assault as a crime or as child abuse. The objectives presented are best achieved through a multidisciplinary effort involving health and mental health care providers, the legal justice system, child protective service agencies, and social support agencies (Sgroi, Porter, and Blick, 1982).

THE CLINICAL ASSESSMENT OF ABUSE VICTIMS

INTRODUCTION

Clinical interest in the assessment of child sexual abuse has been addressed in several recent clinical research studies (Green, Lindy, and Wilson, 1985; Janoff-Bulman, 1985; McCann, Pearlman, Sakheim, and Abrahamson, 1988). The inclusion of posttraumatic stress disorder in DSM-III-R (American Psychiatric Association, 1987) led to increased interest in understanding the commonalities in response patterns across a variety of seriously stressful life events, including child sexual abuse. Researchers are searching for better ways to understand the unique responses of victims by seeking to understand the interaction among pretrauma characteristics, characteristics of the event, and posttrauma variables (Green et al., 1985).

The impact of stressful life events plays an integral role in the process of psychological development (Hultsch and Plemons, 1979). Antecedent life event stressors, whether positive or negative, involve an interactive process between the individual and the life stress situation. Holmes and Rahe (1967) and Dohrenwend, Krasnoff, Askenasy, and Dohrenwend (1978) have researched the effects of stress on behavioral change and found that separation and divorce require considerable social readjustment and coping skills for those who are impacted by the divorce process.

Considerable attention has been addressed toward the competency and capability of preschool and primary grade level children in providing testimony on stressful life events, specifically relating to sexual trauma (Burgess, Holmstrom, and McCausland, 1979). Clinicians and researchers alike have attempted to understand the inner experiences of children, recognizing that their comprehension and language skills are still at the formative stages and, therefore, may not accurately reflect the comprehension, substance, and detail that mature individuals may offer.

Clinicians have placed considerable emphasis on children's drawings in assessing their ability to testify regarding abuse. Such drawings have not only allowed clinicians to assess intellectual and cognitive capabilities (Goodenough, 1926), but have also allowed for psychometric analysis of ego functioning, the clarification and understanding of psychological dynamics inherent in the child and his or her relationship with others (Koppitz, 1968), and the child's ability to serve as a witness in a criminal prosecution (Burgess and Laszlo, 1976). The research literature by far suggests that efforts to assess the impact of acute stress have most often involved human figure drawings. Sturner and Rothbaum (1980) studied sixty-eight children, ages 4 to 12, who were facing the acute stress involved in hospitalization for elective surgery. Each child in the study was asked to draw human figures, one shortly after admission and again ninety minutes later. During the ninety-minute period, they received either a stress-provoking situation (venipuncture) or no stress-provoking experience (no blood test until after the second drawing), and were either prepared (information and nursing supportive care) or not prepared (allowed free play) during the stressful situation. The results of this study indicated that the children who were unprepared for the blood test and subjected to the venipuncture showed statistically significant increases in levels of acute stress.

In a similar setting, Thomas (1980) requested human figure drawings from sexually abused children and found that each of the children in the study focused on sexually relevant genital body parts. There has, however, been some concern among both clinicians and legal experts that human figure drawings alone may not be able to yield adequate information appropriate to the thorough diagnosis and psychological assessment of the child's capability for accurately understanding and cognitively processing the impact of sexual abuse.

Several techniques are utilized to assist in assessing the psychological needs and maturity of the child who may have been sexually abused. These include family drawings, the use of family dolls, and imaginative stories (fables).

FAMILY DRAWINGS

Considerable clinical data can be gathered by the traditional use of family drawings and they can be used to help assess the quality of the child's relationship to parents and siblings. The role of the evaluator in interpreting the child's drawings is of critical importance, and only those who have been clinically trained should attempt to evaluate and interpret these drawings.

FAMILY DOLLS

The use of doll play in evaluating the interactive patterns of parents and children has long been a valuable technique in the evaluation process. Such efforts encourage young children to express their feelings, attitudes, and thoughts about how parents perceive them and how they perceive their parental figures.

IMAGINATIVE STORIES

Utility and relevance of imaginative stories developed by children who are experiencing stressful life events, including sexual abuse, physical abuse, and neglect, can assist the young child in expressing feelings. Unstructured and open-ended stories can reveal what the child is thinking about and most preoccupied with. Underlying or subconscious issues related to dependency, security, and esteem may well be revealed through the child's stories.

There are several methods of assessment that range from the clinical psychometric measures to the clinical interview (Miller and Veltkamp, 1989a), each of which has its own place in the assessment process. Each method can provide important and needed data, and the use of psychometric assessment, for example, can help to clarify issues important to child sexual abuse cases. Projective measures may allow features of the personality to manifest themselves in a way that is less likely to occur in a structured interview. More structured than the clinical interview, the psychological and projective tests present the subject with a series of stimuli to which the subject is asked to respond. Such measures are based on the psychodynamic assumption that the individual's true conflicts and motives must be drawn out indirectly because they are largely unconscious. This process involves presenting the individuals with ambiguous stimuli, such as fables, and allows them to project their private selves into these responses.

Accordingly, the projective measures expose the subjects to vague stimuli into which they must read some meaning or significance. While there is no right or wrong answer, whatever meaning the subject gives to the stimuli tends to be a reflection of what the individual is thinking about, and may contain some clues to the subject's unconscious thought process and require interpretation by a professional psychometrician. Murstein (1961) suggests that projective measures like fables assume (1) that no response is accidental on the part of the individual, so every response is interpretable; (2) that the subject is unaware of what he or she is revealing; and (3) that verbal responses to the test parallel the subject's behavior in the social environment. Human figure drawings, use of family dolls, three wishes, and imaginative stories have all been recognized for their diagnostic value and as a projective measure of personality.

FABLE ASSESSMENT OF CHILD TRAUMA

The use of fables allows the child to identify with a particular situation and to generate, through metaphor, his or her comprehension and cognitive processing of the issues and implications involved in stressful life events and in particular, sexual trauma. Despert (1943) developed ten fables dealing with various aspects of life and with important issues related to the psychological understanding and development of the individual. These fables deal with questions that relate to the child's relationship to parents or whether the child is independent. They help clinicians ascertain whether the child may have witnessed the primal scene or whether there may be jealousy toward the parents' union. The fables deal also with sibling rivalry issues or address certain anticipatory fears or consequential stressors that the child might well envision but find too difficult to express to either a familiar or unfamiliar adult.

We outline a series of fables used as a means of understanding the complexities and readiness of the child to yield clinically relevant information in cases where life stress and/or personal or sexual trauma are indicated. The fables have been modified, making them more relevant for use with children of abusing parents or for cases involving trauma to the child, including sexual abuse. The fables (Veltkamp and Miller, 1984) include, but are not limited to, the following, and are read to the child for his or her interpretation and projective response.

1. *The Anger Fable*: To determine how family members—specifically the parents—handle their anger.

   A Daddy frog, Mommy frog, and their baby frog live together in a small pond. One day, the Daddy frog comes home very angry and upset. What does he do? What does the Mommy frog do? What does it feel like to you?

2. *The Worry Fable*: To determine what children worry about or what's on their minds.

   A dog family—a Daddy, Mommy, sister, and brother—live together on a farm. The sister (or brother) worries a lot at bedtime, as well as during other times of the day. What could she or he be so worried about?

3. *The Incest Fable*: To determine if there is an incestuous relationship in the family.

   A family of cats—a Daddy, Mommy, sister, and brother—live together in a barn. The Daddy (or Mommy) cat is very affectionate; there is a lot of hugging and kissing. Sometimes the Daddy (or Mommy) touches parts of the body that makes the sister (or brother) feel funny. What could be happening? What is he or she touching?

4. *The Discipline Fable*: To determine if the parents physically abuse their children.

   A Daddy bear, Mommy bear, and child bear live in the woods. Sometimes the Daddy or Mommy must discipline or correct the little bear. What does he or she do?

5. *The Spaceship Fable*: To determine the child's strongest psychological attachment.

   Let's pretend you are going to drive a spaceship to the moon. If you could take one person with you, who would that be? If two? If three?

6. *The Drug/Alcohol Fable*: To determine if the parents are using drugs or alcohol.

   A child's parent is drinking something or taking something that makes him or her feel different. Sometimes the drink (or the other stuff he or she is taking) makes the father (mother) act in a different way. What could the parent be taking? How often does the parent do this?

7. *The Abandonment/Left-Alone Fable*: To determine if a child is neglected.

   A family of fish—a Daddy, Mommy, and two babies—live together in a large pond. The babies need someone to watch them every minute, but sometimes Daddy and Mommy want to go off together. What happens then?

8. *The Fear Fable*: To determine if a child is anxious or fearful.

   A young child is sitting in school (or lying in bed at night). He says to himself, "I am really afraid." What could he be afraid of?

9. *The Dream Fable*: To determine a child's fears, concerns, and/ or worries.

   A child wakes up in the morning and says to himself, "What a bad dream I had last night." What could he have dreamed about?

10. *The Separation/Divorce Fable*: To determine if there is marital discord or a separation.

    A child comes home from school and finds that his mother is not at home but his father is. His father says, "I have something important to tell you." What could it be?

11. *The Parental Violence Fable*: To determine if there is parental violence.

    A young boy (girl) is watching television. He hears his mother and father arguing. He gets scared and wonders what will happen. What do you think will happen? How does the child feel?

Administration and Scoring

The Fable Assessment of Child Trauma (FACT) may be administered in two forms. Form A utilizes each of the eleven fables. Each fable is read to the subject, followed by the questions. The administrator may summarize the full responses of the child to each of the questions in the appropriate space provided on the administration and scoring sheet.

A short form of the Fable Assessment of Child Trauma may be administered by using one or more of the fables in similar fashion (Veltkamp and Miller, 1989). Tape-recorded instructions and items may be used for either form of administration. The administrator can mark the answers on specifically designed answer sheets. The tape-recorded format is useful with respondents who cannot read or those who may have short attention spans. It may be beneficial to have more than one testing session if the administrator wishes to give more than

one form of the scale; this may decrease fatigue and clearly differentiate between the various themes addressed by each of the fables.

Test–retest reliability may be utilized by administering one or
more of the same fables a second time, with perhaps a one-week
interval, to assess the reliability of themes which emerge from the
fables.

The Efficacy of Fables in Clinical Assessment

Preliminary data from the use of fables as a part of the assessment
process in cases involving child sexual abuse have revealed that the
content of the responses given to the fables has been extremely helpful
in drawing attention to the recurrence of certain themes. If certain
themes keep reappearing in the subject's interpretation, then, depending on the nature of the theme, the clinician may well be able to
recognize clues to the presence of underlying psychopathology. As
with the efforts of Despert (1943), the fables have assisted in the
examination process and have yielded clinically relevant data that have
been beneficial in defining issues of psychological attachment, neglect,
marital discord, and physical, sexual, and psychological abuse of the
child.

THE USE OF ANATOMICAL DOLLS

Anatomical dolls are useful for children of all ages, including adolescents. They are particularly useful with the preschool child; the latency-age child with delays in speech; children who are experiencing
external or internal conflict and therefore have difficulty talking about
what happened to them; and with handicapped children.

How Are Dolls Useful?

Dolls help a child describe what has happened to him without personal-
izing the experience. If the child personalizes the experience, he or
she is more likely to be defensive, withdrawn, or nonverbal. Dolls
help keep the experience at a distance, making it easier for the child
to discuss the event. The dolls are extremely useful during evaluation

and treatment of incest or child molestation cases. They can be used in courtroom testimony, and used therapeutically to help children talk about their experiences and feelings. Such dolls can be useful also in reducing the anxiety a child or young adolescent may experience by explaining what will take place during a vaginal exam.

Steps in Using the Dolls

1. Show the dolls to the parent or guardian when the child is not present. Explain to the parents just what you will do with the dolls and how they help you in the course of the evaluation. This will help reduce the parent's anxiety or fears.
2. Explain to the child that these dolls and toys belong to you and that the child may look at them and play with them.
3. Mention to the child that he or she will probably notice that these dolls are different from other dolls that they have seen.
4. Let the child hold the dolls and name different parts of the body. It is important that clinicians not name the parts of the body themselves.
5. Ask the child to identify who the dolls are. If, for example, the child says, "That's my daddy," ask her about her father.
6. In cases of incest or molestation ask child to show what happened by using the dolls to re-create the scene and the situation.
7. If a child is uneasy, that is, visibly anxious or nonverbal, set the dolls aside but have them clearly visible. The child may return to the dolls at a later point when he or she feels more comfortable.
8. After the session take detailed notes using the child's words as much as possible. In court cases, many clinicians prefer to take some notes during the session or to tape the session in order to have a clear record of the sequence of events and the words specifically used by the child (Boat and Everson, 1986).

USE OF DRAWINGS

Environmental Conditions in Evaluation

Of all cases evaluated and treated in outpatient clinics, that of the sexually abused child is among the most difficult. Many victims, particularly preschoolers and early latency-age children, often do not have the knowledge or vocabulary to tell clinicians what has happened to them. Not only is it difficult for the child to put feelings into words, but when the perpetrator is a family member, the child is often too conflicted to talk openly about what has happened. Clinical strategies employed to assess accuracy and the child's ability to provide testimony have placed considerable emphasis on children's drawings. Human figure drawings have not only allowed expert clinicians to assess intellectual and cognitive capabilities but have also allowed for psychometric analysis of personality (Goodenough, 1926). Clarification and understanding of psychological dynamics inherent in the child and the child's relationship with others (Drucker and Shapiro, 1979) have been beneficial in identifying clinically relevant information. Sturner and Rothbaum (1980) and others studied children facing acute stressful situations. Results of human figure drawings of sexually abused children revealed that each of the children studied focused on sexually relevant genital body parts.

It is our purpose to examine the use of drawings in the treatment and evaluation of child victims of sexual abuse. Drawings have long been used as a source of nonverbal communication. Klepsh and Logie (1982) studied human figure drawings to learn what they reveal about children's personalities, perceptions, values, and attitudes. Human figure drawings have also been used by teachers and psychologists to measure a child's developmental or intellectual maturity. Hjorth and Harway (1981) found that drawings by physically abused children differed from those by nonabused children. Factors examined were detail, symmetry, position on the page, size, and erasures. The studies show that drawings by abused children were less symmetrical, had less detail, and few erasures. According to the authors, these findings indicate that the abused children had more feelings of insecurity than nonabused children, and a poor body image. While this article discussed many of the characteristics of abused children, it failed to discuss the implications of these findings for practice.

Adams-Tucker (1984) addresses the use of drawings with victims of incest from preschool age through adolescence. These children are often the ones most fearful of sharing the secret of incest and often have been threatened with reprisals should they tell anyone. Stemper (1980) found art to be a useful and nonthreatening vehicle for pulling these children's feelings together. Sexually abused children need appropriate ways to ventilate their anger, fear, hostility, and other feelings that may be inhibited or repressed. Drawings can be a way of bringing the incident out into the open and can help clear the way for healing and growth to occur. These and other authors have written about the use of drawings as a form of ventilation, but little has been written about the use of drawings in evaluating sexually abused children.

Drawings in Clinical Evaluation

It is widely understood that in the evaluation of children, the more conflicting the material is to the child, the more difficult it is for the child to express feelings. Not only is it difficult to put feelings into words, but in those sexual abuse cases where the perpetrator is a family member, the child is often too conflicted to talk openly about what has happened.

A variety of techniques are used to ascertain how a child feels about himself, and what the child has experienced. The use of wishes, fables, anatomical dolls, puppets, drawings, and a variety of play therapy techniques are used by most clinicians in working with victims of sexual abuse. Drawings are particularly useful in the evaluation and treatment process.

In the course of an evaluation, the child often will refer to something that has happened, a dream, a daydream, a specific fear, but be unable or refuse to talk about it or not know how to express his feelings about it in words. At this point in the evaluation the clinician may say, "We don't have to put it into words. Sometimes it's easier to draw a picture of what we feel about what has happened." It has been our experience that often a child will accept the drawing as an alternative to talking. Several of the following suggestions may stimulate projective materials.

1. Draw a feeling, such as sadness, anger, guilt, fear, confusion.
2. Draw what happened, for example, the abusive incident.
3. Draw a solution to a problem, what would solve the problem.
4. Draw a way to feel safe; that is, what would help the child feel safe.
5. Draw a family.
6. When the child talks about the victimization, have him or her draw the offender.

7. Draw a bad dream.
8. If the child states he is afraid, suggest he or she draw the fear.
9. If the child refers to a dream/daydream, suggest he or she draw it.
10. Draw a home (inside or outside).
11. If the child has discussed worries, ask the child to draw the worry.
12. Draw what parents do; for example, when they feel angry.
13. Draw a wish.

Environmental Considerations in Evaluation

In the clinical evaluation of the child, it is necessary to create a non-threatening environment with familiar toys and objects. If the evaluation takes place in a medical setting, white coats and medical equipment should be avoided. A playroom or a room that looks like a family room is ideal. The therapist's vocabulary should be easily understood by the child. The word *abuse* should not be used by the therapist since often the child does not equate what has happened to him or her with abuse. The object is to create an atmosphere that will encourage the child to tell his story.

During the evaluation, the child may talk freely about the incident or may refuse to talk. In either case, the use of fables and drawings can be useful tools for the clinician. The child who cannot talk freely about the incident may prefer to draw a picture of what has happened. For this child, the drawing may help the clinician understand the details, including who was present, where the abuse occurred, what happened and where, and what clothing the child was wearing. The therapist should involve the child in play using dolls or puppets or some other toy. During the course of this evaluation the child may bring up dreams, feelings, or a secret and be able to draw these feelings or dreams. There are statements a therapist can make to help facilitate the process. For example, in a case involving incest, the therapist may say, "Adults sometimes touch children in ways that are scary or feel funny, the kids we see sometimes prefer to draw pictures rather than talk about this." The therapist can ask the child to draw a feeling, a family, a daydream, a worry, or a wish. Many times the child will quickly accept the drawing as an alternative to talking.

Case Illustrations

Case 1

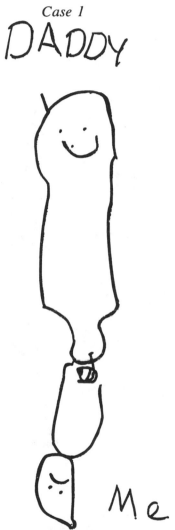

This 5-year-old girl was unable to talk about her sexual abuse. This drawing, during the evaluation, clearly reveals three primary themes: (1) the type of sexual abuse; (2) who the perpetrator is; and (3) the victim's feelings. Once she drew the picture, she was able to talk about the sexual abuse involving penetration, that the perpetrator was her father, and her feelings of sadness and anger.

Case 2

This 8-year-old boy was referred to the clinic because "my butt started hurting." His drawing reveals the perpetrator and where the abuse took place. Notice the detail around the genital area. In addition, the detail across the room, television, dresser, and lamp, on, is typical; the victim of sexual assault frequently focuses on something away from himself and the trauma.

Case 3

This 7-year-old sibling of a 5-year-old girl victim is looking through a door and observes his father having oral sex with his sister. The clinician can observe father's head between the victim's legs. This drawing was used in court and played a part in convicting the father.

The Use and Interpretation of Drawings

The drawing is a child's way of communicating, a way of letting the therapist know how he feels or what has happened to him, in short a way of telling his story. In interpreting the drawings, the clinician should observe such primary themes as feelings, the child's perspective, specific events, and what happened. Drawings by sexually abused children tend to be more sexualized, often with emphasis on genital areas or breasts. They may show sexual contact between people. These drawings indicate sexual knowledge beyond a child's years.

Several features can be used in interpreting the drawings. Some suggested interpretations include the following:

1. If the sizes of the figures are small, it may represent helplessness or feelings of inadequacy.
2. The way the child positions figures on the paper may indicate what happened during the incident, the child's self-image, and how he feels about others.
3. Feeling abandoned or helpless may be indicated by the omission of specific persons or features.
4. The facial expressions on the characters may indicate feelings, such as anger or fear.
5. The drawings may show people in dangerous situations or using dangerous objects. This can be an indication of an abusive or dangerous environment.
6. Drawings may show sexual themes. This may be the child's way of communicating that she has been sexually abused or observed sexual behavior between others.
7. Sometimes drawings show compartmentalization, a child's way of protecting himself from danger.

The interpretation of the drawings is not only based on what the child has drawn, but on the specific themes observed and also what the child has stated about the drawings. It has often been our experience that once a child has drawn a picture, he or she goes on to elaborate verbally on the details.

Utilization of Drawings

Human figure drawings can be used in the evaluation process, the treatment process, and in courtroom testimony. In the evaluation process, drawings help identify the child's feelings about himself and others. They help identify the traumatic events that have taken place, and may bring out specific themes such as anger, fear, or helplessness. In addition, they may bring out specifics regarding incidents involving sexual or physical abuse, such as who the perpetrator was or where the victimization occurred. Drawings may identify where treatment is indicated; for example, a child may feel responsible for the abuse, demonstrate low self-esteem, or have fears of the future.

The use of drawings during treatment helps a child focus on self-help issues. The child may draw solutions to the problem or ways to make himself feel safe. This can help reduce the child's anxiety or feelings of helplessness. Drawings can also be a useful and effective tool in courtroom testimony. Some specific uses we have found for these strategies involve court cases relating to family violence, contested custody cases, contested visitation cases, and cases involving termination of parental rights. The drawings represent the child's story.

Implications for Clinical Practice

Drawings have been found to be particularly useful in the evaluation and treatment process for a number of reasons. Drawings are a permanent record which can later be used in courtroom testimony if necessary, or later drawings can be compared to earlier drawings during the course of treatment. Also, drawings and fables can be discussed in detail on more than one occasion. One can often determine progress or lack of progress, by evaluating the degree of change, if any, in drawings or fables at different stages. In addition, drawings and fables are an aid in helping understand how a child feels about himself, significant others, as well as his home environment. Furthermore, since children enjoy drawing and storytelling, this is a relatively easy way to gather information.

Utilization of fables and drawings as a part of the assessment process helps the clinician spot recurring themes which may provide clues to understanding psychopathology (Nunnally, 1978).

Use of drawings has assisted in the examination process and yielded valuable clinical data that have been beneficial in defining issues of psychological attachment, neglect, and physical, sexual, and psychological abuse of children. Several issues emerge from a psychometric perspective in using these measures. Tests such as these allow the interviewer sustained freedom in interpreting the subject's responses, and this becomes a critical issue with respect to projective assessment. Those opposed to projective measures suggest that the chain of inference leading from the subject's response to the interviewer's report may well be too complex and subjective (Stemper, 1980b). Proponents of projective testing claim that tests such as these are the only assessment methods that can explore and expose the patient's unconscious processes. Such information, even if the validity may be scientifically questionable, may still be beneficial to the clinical assessment process (Miller and Veltkamp, 1989a).

In cases involving sexual abuse, unconscious motivation becomes crucial in the evaluation process and plays an important role in the use of projective measures as a part of the psychometric assessment. Unconscious motivation suggests that there are aspects of the personality that the patient may be unaware of, and if so, the person cannot be expected to report adequately in these areas through the use of a simple, straightforward clinical interview.

Issues in the Use of Projective Assessment

Numerous issues emerge from a psychometric perspective because of all the varieties of psychological testing. Projective measures consistently allow the individual the greatest freedom in self-expression. They also allow the interviewer the greatest freedom in interpreting the subject's responses, and herein lies the critical issue and major problem with projective testing. The use of fables falls well within the category of this particular issue. Opponents of projective measures claim that the chain of inference leading from the subject's response to the interviewer's report may well be too complex and subjective. This argument has been supported in numerous studies (Mischel, 1968). Supporters of projective testing, on the other hand, claim that tests such as these are the only assessment methods that can be open and flexible enough in providing information about the subject's unconscious processes, and that such information, even if the validity may be scientifically questionable, can still be useful to the clinician.

Another issue deals with whether it is better to use a projective measure such as fables or clinically relevant data collected as part of the clinical interview. While statistically relevant questions regarding reliability and validity are raised with respect to projective measures, the self-report interview may not always represent an accurate estimate of the patient's level of functioning. Self-report relies heavily on an honest response from the subject. The interviewer utilizing the self-report measures suggests to the subject what the best response might be and, therefore, estimates of this type can be faked. Even if the patient is being honest and clearly understands the questions involved in a clinical interview or structured self-report measure, it is unlikely that the person is aware of all aspects of his or her personality that are important and relevant to the measure.

Summary

The use and function of fables and other projective measures in the evaluation of child sexual abuse is viewed as beneficial. It is essential that mental health professionals who are competent to make such evaluations make them based on historical as well as contemporary psychological data and evidence. It would seem that the greatest benefit of having such data available lies in its potential for assisting the court in understanding the processing of the trauma by the child and rendering a decision that is in the best interests of the child who has been sexually abused.

ASSESSMENT OF THE SEXUALLY ABUSING ADULT

Groth (1979) has identified two primary etiologies or causes of sexual abuse—a fixation at an early stage of sexual development or a regression from an adult sexual relationship. While the typical child molester is usually fixated the typical incestuous parent is usually regressed, although there are exceptions to each. The following is designed to help the clinician differentiate between the two.

Fixation at an Early Stage of Psychosexual Development

1. The history reveals primary sexual orientation is to children.

2. The sexual interest in children began in adolescence.
3. There is generally no precipitating stress; no subjective distress.
4. The offender shows a persistent interest in children and often demonstrates compulsive behavior.
5. The offense is usually premeditated.
6. Equalization: The offender identifies closely with the victim and he behaves at the child's level; the offender becomes a pseudopeer of the victim.
7. Same-sexed victims are primary targets.
8. The offender has little or no sexual contact with agemates; is usually single, but may marry as a cover for the sexual interest in children.
9. There is usually no history of alcohol or drug abuse.
10. Characterological immaturity; the offender has poor sociosexual peer relationships.

Regressed Offender

1. The history reveals the offender's primary sexual orientation is to agemates.
2. The sexual interest in children emerges in adulthood.
3. Precipitating stress is usually evident.
4. The sexual involvement with children may be episodic.
5. The initial offense may be impulsive, not premeditated.
6. Substitution: The offender replaces a conflictual adult relationship with involvement with the child; the victim is a pseudadult.
7. Victims of the opposite sex are primary targets.
8. The sexual contact with the child coexists with sexual contact with agemates; the offender is usually married or in a common law relationship.
9. In many cases the offense may be alcohol related.
10. The offender has a more traditional life-style but underdeveloped peer relationships.

The fixated pedophile cannot be treated effectively on an outpatient basis because this only increases the risk to other children in the community. The regressed offender can be treated effectively on an outpatient basis if the offender recognizes the problem, takes responsibility for his behavior, and is motivated for therapy. Clearly, the evaluation process is very important in determining the type of offender being assessed, as well as the prognosis.

8

The Medical Evaluation of Child Sexual Abuse

Gary W. Kearl, M.D., M.S.P.H.
Katherine L. Bright, M.D.

INTRODUCTION

Responsibilities of Health Care Providers

Health care providers have a responsibility to assist suspected victims of child sexual abuse or assault. All 50 states require physicians to report suspected cases of child abuse to appropriate civil agencies (e.g., child protective services or police). Unfortunately, physicians are often loathe to become involved in what they perceive to be a highly specialized, emotionally stressful form of medical care. Furthermore, the implicit threat of future involvement in legal proceedings (as a material or expert witness) seems to discourage many physicians from acting upon personal suspicions of child abuse raised during routine medical care. Nevertheless, abused children and their families should be provided with the following:

- Emotional support

- Medical assessment and treatment of injuries

- Documentation of the alleged assault by collection of evidence for police

- Referral for appropriate counseling services

- Expert medical testimony in subsequent litigation

PROBLEMS IN EVALUATING SEXUALLY ABUSED CHILDREN

The physician's task of evaluating suspected victims of child sexual abuse may be complicated by:

1. *Strain on the family system.* When children are sexually abused by a relative or close acquaintance, the family system may become so strained by the revelation of abuse that the perpetrator may actually be protected by persons normally responsible for protecting the victim. In such instances, the victim may either be blamed for the incident or his or her story may be vigorously denied.

2. *Delay in seeking care.* Children are often brought in for evaluation of alleged sexual abuse days, months, and even years after the event. Consequently, little or no physical evidence may be found to corroborate the child's story. A lack of physical evidence may further reinforce denial on the part of the family. As a result: *It is critically important for physicians to thoroughly evaluate any child who provides a detailed story of sexual abuse.*

RESPONSIBILITIES OF OFFICE PERSONNEL

Patient Appointments

Victims of sexual abuse should always be seen expeditiously. However, as already noted, many cases are identified weeks to months after the most recent sexual contact. As a result, the medical evaluation can usually be postponed until the child has been interviewed by child protective service personnel and fully prepared for the medical examination. When the most recent sexual contact has occurred within the past 48 hours, or if the child presents with acute signs of anogenital injury, then he or she should be seen immediately, either in the office or a hospital emergency room. The initial examination should follow the general guidelines set forth for the evaluation of rape victims and carefully document the extent of any visible injuries.

Patient Registration

The office receptionist is responsible for expediting the registration process for victims of child sexual abuse. Patient confidentiality is of special concern in these cases. One way to maximize patient confidentiality is to prepare a child sexual abuse case folder that is filed in a separate location from the regular medical record. This folder is used to hold sensitive case notes and is cross-referenced to the regular chart. In this way, any information pertaining to the child's evaluation for suspected sexual abuse can be easily retrieved, yet routine scrutiny of the child's regular medical chart will not automatically reveal sensitive examination data. When access to this information is requested from insurance carriers or other agencies, specific permission should be obtained from the child's parents or guardians.

Nursing Responsibilities

The nurse in attendance assists the examiner in performing the physical examination. The nurse should:

1. Prepare the room for the examination and place following supplies in the exam room prior to the examination:

   Appropriately labeled bacteriology slips

   Iced chlamydia culture transport tubes: 3

   Warmed gonorrhea culture (Transgrow) media: 3

   Microscope slides

Sterile cotton-tipped applicators: 1

Sterile "minitip" culturette swabs: 3

KOH/Normal saline solutions

Papanicolaou fixative

3 or 5 percent acetic acid solution

Sterile specimen collection cup filled with (nonbacteriostatic) sterile saline solution

Bright light source (e.g., goose-neck lamp)

Magnification device (hand-held lens, magnifying loop, colposcope if available)

Tape recorder and audiotapes (if the examiner wishes to record the interview)

Tape measure (marked in millimeters)

Various sized (**Huffman** and **Pederson**) vaginal specula

2. Measure and record in the chart the patient's height, weight, and temperature.
3. Take a Polaroid photograph of the patient (this is an optional entry in the child's medical record).
4. Completely label all laboratory specimens and verify with the examiner that each specimen container is properly marked *before leaving the exam room*.
5. Ensure that the laboratory specimens are expeditiously forwarded to an appropriate lab facility.

Interviewer/Examiner Responsibilities

The interviewer and the examiner are usually the same person. Prior to starting the evaluation, the interviewer should provide a general explanation of the interview process and obtain informed consent from the child and the parents or guardian to begin the evaluation process. The interviewer is responsible for obtaining a history of the abuse. The examiner is responsible for performing a complete physical examination, and providing appropriate medical treatment to victims of child abuse. In addition, the examiner should discuss the need for counseling services and make referrals to other specialists when appropriate. Although the examiner may be the health care provider for the entire family, the victim's safety and well-being must take precedence over the family's needs, particularly when the perpetrator is a family member.

EVALUATION OF CHILD SEXUAL ABUSE

Medical History

Documentation of sexual abuse is primarily dependent upon the history in the majority of cases (Solomons, 1980, p. 503). As a result, the interview should be conducted in a tactful yet thorough manner. The child should always be interviewed **privately**, if possible. In some instances children may request that a parent or caretaker remain with them during the interview. In such cases, the examiner should arrange for the child to sit in such a way as to be unable to receive nonverbal cues from the parent or caretaker. The parents or caretakers should also be interviewed separately and apart from the child.

In addition to the usual parts of the medical history, the interviewer should try to obtain a clear description of the nature of the abuse including: what happened; where it happened; when it happened; who did it; and whether any threats or acts of violence were employed. It is important for the interviewer to attempt to identify the perpetrator of the abuse for two reasons:

1. The first goal of medical treatment is to protect the victim from further abuse. It is very difficult to protect the victim if the identity of the perpetrator of the abuse is unknown.
2. Victims of child sexual abuse may contract sexually transmitted diseases. Public health policy dictates that when a sexually transmitted infection is diagnosed, each sexual contact of the index case be identified if possible, contacted, tested for sexually transmitted diseases, and treated so that such infections may be eradicated from the community.

The interviewer should remember the following points while interviewing the child (Tipton, 1989, pp. 10–11):

1. *Setting*. Arrange for a neutral interview setting.
2. *Credibility*. Reassure the child that you are experienced in evaluating children who have been sexually abused.
3. *Anxiety*. Maintain a relaxed atmosphere during the interview.
4. *Terminology*. Use simple terminology and clarify meanings of the child's informal terms for anatomical structures.
5. *Time*. Assess the child's sense of time and use the child's scale of time measurement to clarify the chronology of important events.
6. *Continuum of exposure*. Try to document both the duration and progression of the abuse over time.
7. *Multiple interviews*. Arrange for follow-up interviews (if necessary) in order to obtain a more complete history.

Victims of child sexual abuse should be encouraged to use their own words to describe what happened. (This portion of the interview may be audiotaped to preserve the child's own terminology.) The interviewer should ask the child to point to *all* parts of his or her body which received sexual contact (e.g., mouth, breasts, genitals, anus, etc.). Information as to whether penetration occurred and whether ejaculation took place should be sought and recorded. Finally, it is important to understand the child's concept of sexual intercourse, particularly when children report what sounds like vaginal or anal penetration.

    Sexually abused children are often emotionally manipulated by their assailants. Some victims may be offered special favors or privileges while others may be threatened with physical harm in order to prevent them from disclosing details of the abuse. As a result, it is frequently difficult for victims of child sexual abuse to make a straightforward disclosure about the nature of the abuse. In circumstances like this it may be helpful for the interviewer to ask the child if she or he has any "special secrets to share" or is "feeling scared about anything." In some cases, a child may be more inclined to provide details about the nature of the abuse if the interviewer asks the following: ***"I am wondering if somebody has done something to your body that has frightened you. Would you tell me about it?"*** Another way of reassuring a child, who is feeling conflicted about disclosing details of abusive contacts, would be to say: ***"Sometimes I see children here because someone has touched them in a way that*** *feels wrong or uncomfortable. Has anything like that happened to you?''*

Regardless of whether the victim provides a detailed history of the abuse, the interviewer should conduct a review of systems which should include inquiry as to recent or past episodes of gastrointestinal (GI), genitourinary (GU), and behavioral signs and symptoms (**Table 8.1**).

Table 8.1
Significant Signs and Symptoms from the Review of Systems

GU Symptoms	GU Signs	GI Symptoms
Enuresis	Genital Irritation	Encopresis
Dysuria	Genital Sores	Constipation
Polyuria	Vaginal Discharge	Bloody Stool
Recurrent UTI	Amenorrhea	Anal Discomfort

Behavioral Symptoms	Behavioral Signs
Headaches	New Contraceptive Use
Abdominal Pains	New Sexual Activity
Insomnia/Hypersomnia	Public Masturbation
Changes in Appetite	"Sexualized" Play
Depressive Symptoms	School Problems/Phobia
Suicidal Ideation	Drug/Alcohol Use/Abuse

The review of systems is particularly important when the abuse history is nonspecific.

Legal Aspects of the Medical History

The manner in which the child's history is obtained has an important effect on the value of the history in establishing the facts in the case (Tipton, 1989, p. 11; Indest, 1989, p. 150). Once child abuse is considered as a diagnosis, the interviewer should document precisely:

1. The source of the information by name and relationship to the victim.
2. In addition, whenever possible, the interviewer should also try to obtain details as to the following:
   a. The duration of time which has elapsed between the most recent episode of abuse and the child's statements;

   b. Whether the child's statement was made in response to questioning by an adult or was spontaneous;
   c. Whether the statement was elicited by open-ended, direct, or leading questions;
   d. Whether the child was excited or distressed at the time of the questions (record all nonverbal cues);
   e. Whether the child was calm or placid prior to making the statement;
   f. The child's physical condition at the time of the statement;
   g. Who was present when the statement was made;
   h. The characteristics of the event and the exact words used;
   i. Whether the statement was made at the first opportunity when the child felt safe to talk;
   j. Whether the child had any apparent incentive to fabricate or distort the truth.

THE PHYSICAL EXAMINATION: PRELIMINARY CONSIDERATIONS

Prior to beginning the physical exam, the examiner should obtain informed consent for the examination procedure by providing an explanation of the examination process to the child and parents or guardians using terms which both can understand. Most children are able to cooperate with the examination, if care has been taken to establish a satisfactory level of rapport during the preceding interview. Nevertheless, in some instances, multiple appointments may be required in order to achieve enough rapport to guarantee sufficient cooperation and relaxation for a complete examination.

Use of Physical Restraints During the Examination

With the exception of infants, children should never be restrained during an examination because this usually produces increased fear and physical resistance on the part of the child, and it is impossible to perform an adequate genital examination on a resisting, frightened, squirming child. Moreover, placement of restraints may be interpreted by the child as a prelude to another sexual assault. Under these circumstances, the medical examination may end up actually hurting rather than helping the child by reenacting the original abusive episode.

Special Problems with the Examination of Sexually Abused Children

Victims of sexual abuse frequently express a wide range of emotions during the evaluation process. Such feelings should always be acknowledged and any underlying fears identified and addressed by the examination personnel. Two emotional responses to the examination pose special problems for physicians evaluating suspected victims of child sexual abuse:

1. *The frightened young child.* Many children become frightened at the prospect of the examination either because they don't fully understand the purpose of the examination or because they fear the exam will be traumatic. The examiner can usually reassure the child by carefully reexplaining the rationale for and nature of the examination. A frightened child may be further persuaded to cooperate with the physical examination if a supportive adult remains in the room during the examination and if the examiner proceeds slowly through the examination, explaining each step, and allowing the child to have as much control over the progress of the examination as possible. *We have found that sedatives such as chloral hydrate are generally ineffective at facilitating the examination of an uncooperative, frightened child.*
2. *The older unwilling child.* An older child may sometimes refuse to be examined because of a difference of opinion between the child and his or her parents about the nature of the incident (e.g., real or imagined, consensual or abusive, etc.). In this instance, the examiner should attempt to ask the parents to leave and to arrange for another, more supportive, adult to come into the exam room and reassure the child about the nature of the examination.

Examination under Anesthesia

Although there are a few instances in which a child victim of sexual abuse should be examined regardless of his or her wishes, the desire to document medical evidence of abuse must *never* override sound medical judgment or compassionate caregiving. Thus, we believe that *no child should be forcibly examined against his or her will*. If the facts of the case require a prompt examination for medical reasons and the child is uncooperative, the examiner should consider arranging for an examination under anesthesia (EUA). The indications for an EUA are virtually always medical (e.g., presence of an injury which requires immediate assessment or repair in an uncooperative child).

GENITAL EXAMINATION TECHNIQUES

Prior to the examination, the examiner should be comfortably seated and arrange for a bright source of lighting to be available in the exam room.

1. **Positioning**. Younger children are usually best examined while lying supine either on the exam table or in their mother's lap. Such patients are usually placed in "frog-leg" position as illustrated below (**Figure 8.1**):

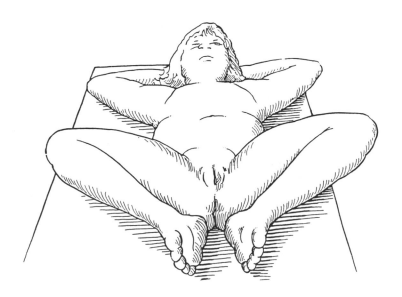

Figure 8.1. The "Frog-Leg" Exam Position

Older children (particularly adolescents) may prefer to be examined in the conventional lithotomy position with their feet in stirrups. Both examination positions afford the examiner an excellent view of the external genitalia.

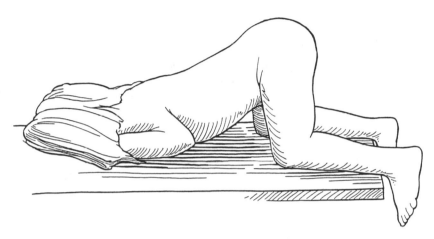

Figure 8.2. Prone Knee–chest Exam Position

The **prone knee-chest** position can help clarify the anatomy of the hymen and vagina in prepubertal females. This examination position affords the examiner a clearer view into the vaginal canal. Foreign bodies in the vagina, missed in the supine (frog-leg) position, are more easily found when the child is placed in the prone knee–chest position. The examiner should allow the child to relax in the prone knee–chest position for a few seconds and then apply gentle upward and lateral tension on the buttocks in order to adequately expose the hymen and vagina (**Figure 8.2**). It is important to remember that some children have been abused while in the knee–chest position. Accordingly, *if a child becomes unusually distraught at being placed in this position, he or she should not be forced to continue with this part of the examination.*

2. **Draping**. In general, preadolescent girls usually do not like to be draped; however, older girls may feel more comfortable when draped. In either case, it is important to respect the child's modesty at all times.

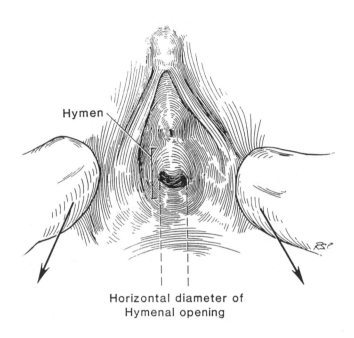

Figure 8.3. Vaginal Examination—Labial Separation

3. **Exposure of the female genitalia for the exam**. Two standard examination techniques, **labial separation** and **traction,** are commonly used to expose the female genitalia during the physical examination. Labial separation is obtained by placing thumbs on the labia majora and applying gentle pressure laterally and downward. Labial traction is produced by grasping the labia majora and gently pulling them simultaneously downward and toward the examiner. *It is important to avoid creating iatrogenic physical abnormalities from the use of "heavy-handed" examination techniques during this phase of the physical examination.*

4. **Examination of the external female genitalia**. The examiner should document the Tanner stage of sexual development (Johnson, Moore, and Jeffries, 1978) and then carefully inspect each portion of the external genitalia including the labia majora, labia minora,

clitoris, fossa navicularis, posterior fourchette, and periurethral and perihymenal mucosal surfaces; for signs of fresh or healed injury.

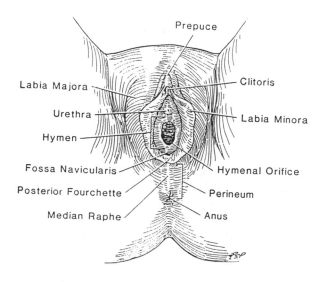

Figure 8.4. Female Genitalia

Although the external genitalia of prepubertal children are normally quite pale and delicate in appearance, the periurethral and perihymenal tissues are frequently very erythematous. The presence of any genital discharge, hyperpigmentation, bruising, laceration, or scarring is abnormal and should be fully described in the medical record (see **Figure 8.4**).

5. **Examination of the hymen**. The hymen should be inspected closely and measurements of the vertical and horizontal dimensions of the hymenal opening can be recorded in millimeters (see **Figure 8.3**). A recent study (McCann, Wells, Simon, and Voris, 1990) of a population of nonabused girls suggests that there is considerable variation in the *normal* configuration and dimensions of the hymenal opening. Moreover, these characteristics appear to vary substantially depending on the examination position used and the degree of relaxation achieved during the examination. Accordingly, the examiner should record the exam position and estimate the level of pelvic relaxation achieved during the examination of the hymen.

Although the external genitalia can be examined quite well without the use of a magnification device, magnified views of the surface anatomy of the genitalia may occasionally reveal signs of physical injury missed during the unaided examination (Murram and Elias, 1989, p. 333). An **otosope** lens or a **magnifying loop** (**Figure 8.5**) can be used to provide an inexpensive source of magnification for this purpose.

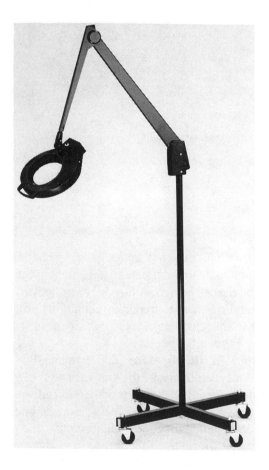

Figure 8.5. Magnifying Loop

The **colposcope** (**Figure 8.6**) is also being used with increasing frequency during child sexual abuse evaluations (McCann,

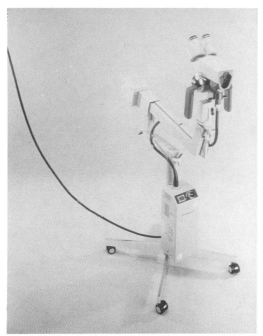

Figure 8.6. The Colposcope

1990). The colposcope is particularly helpful because it provides excellent lighting, magnification, and may be used to take high-quality photographs during the examination. During this portion of the examination, the examiner should describe, both in writing and with a sketch, any hymenal abnormalities such as: rounding/thickening of the hymenal edges, tears, transections, scars, adhesions, abrasions, bruises, or abnormal vascular patterns.

6. **Vaginal speculum examination**. Pubertal females who report a history of sexual abuse should receive a speculum examination (including a Papanicolaou smear) to look for vaginal and cervical pathology.

7. **Examination of the male genitalia**. Both the penis and the scrotum are potential targets of sexual abuse. A complete description of the appearance of the penis including the location of any erythema, bruising, suction marks, excoriations, burns, or skin lacerations should be noted. Tenderness of the testicles or epididymis and urethral discharge are additional physical signs which may reflect evidence of traumatic injury and/or the presence of a sexually transmitted infection (**Figure 8.7**).

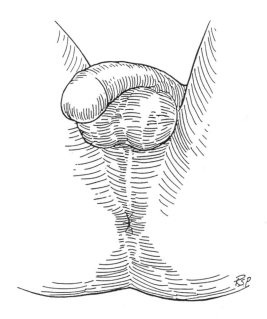

Figure 8.7. Male Genitalia

8. **The anal examination**. Anal penetration may occur without leaving any sign of physical injury. As a result, it is not unusual for
the anus to have a "normal" appearance despite a history of anal
abuse (Reinhart, 1987, p. 235). The anal examination should be
conducted with the child in the prone, knee–chest, position (**Figure
8.2**). Older children may be placed in the lateral decubitus or the
supine position (with the knees curled up toward the chest). The
examiner should first inspect the buttocks and the perianal skin for
bruising, hematomas, deep fissures (off the midline), abrasions,
lacerations, inflammation, thickening, and pigmentation changes.
The anal sphincter of patients who have been sodomized may dilate
abnormally during the course of the anal examination. Anal sphincter dilatation may be quantified by measuring the diameter of the
anal opening after the child has been in the prone knee–chest position for 2 minutes or longer. Dilation greater than 20 millimeters
in the midline anteroposterior diameter with gentle buttock traction
(while the patient is in the prone knee–chest position) and without
the presence of stool in the rectum, is considered abnormal

(McCann, Voris, Simon, and Wells, 1989, pp. 187, 189, 190). The tone of the anal sphincter may be assessed by eliciting the "anal wink" reflex. If there is any sign of significant anal sphincter injury, referral to an appropriate specialist may be required.

SEXUALLY TRANSMITTED DISEASES

Although relatively few victims of child sexual abuse acquire sexually transmitted diseases (**STDs**), the presence of an STD in a child is strongly suggestive of sexual abuse (Neinstein, Goldenring, and Carpenter, 1984, p. 67). Many sexually transmitted pathogens can also be transmitted nonsexually from mother to infant at birth (**Table 8.2**). Nevertheless, transmission via sexual abuse should be considered whenever a child is found to have an STD.

Table 8.2
Modes of Nonsexual Transmission of Sexually Transmitted Pathogens
(adapted from Neinstein, Goldenring, and Carpenter, 1984, p. 74).

Pathogen	Maternal Transmission Intra-uterine/Perinatal	Nonsexual Human Transmission[a]	Transmission by Fomites[b]
Neisseria gonorrhea	Well documented	Not documented	Not documented
Chlamydia trachomatis	Well documented	Not documented	Not documented
Herpes Simplex Virus (HSV)	Well documented	HSV I only	Not documented
Trichomonas vaginalis	Well documented	Not documented	Not documented
Human Papilloma Virus (HPV)	Well documented	Possible	Not documented
Trepomena palladium	Well documented	Well documented	Not documented
Chancroid	Not documented	Not documented	Not documented
Granuloma inguinale	Documented	Well documented	Not documented

[a] Includes skin to skin or skin to mucous membrane and auto inoculation.
[b] Includes such inanimate objects as pens, pencils, toys, etc., which can become coated with a disease-producing organism (excludes laboratory accidents).

Although gonorrhea is considered to be a strong indicator of sexual abuse, chlamydia is also thought to be a marker of sexual abuse (American Academy of Pediatrics Committee on Child Abuse and Neglect, 1991). The prevalence of gonorrhea in our area is much lower than that of chlamydia. We routinely screened *all* suspected victims of child sexual abuse for both gonorrhea and chlamydia during a two-year period and found that *none* of the children tested positive for gonorrhea and 6 percent tested positive for chlamydia. We also found that neither the history nor the results of the physical examination were reliable predictors of chlamydia infections. As a result, although we continue to collect routine chlamydia cultures from children we evaluate, we now obtain gonorrhea cultures only when the child presents with symptoms or a history which places them at higher risk for contracting gonorrhea (e.g., the suspected perpetrator is known to have gonorrhea or another victim is found to have gonorrhea). Routine culture samples for chlamydia should be obtained from the oropharynx, rectum, and vagina of prepubertal females or the cervix of pubertal females. Males should be cultured from the oropharynx, rectum, and urethra. We recommend using a sterile, saline-soaked "minitip" culturette swab (Becton Dickinson Microbiology Systems) to obtain gonorrhea and chlamydia cultures because the tip of this swab is much smaller than a regular cotton swab and seems to cause less discomfort to the child.

Culture Techniques for Sexually Transmitted Diseases

1. *Neisseria gonorrhea*. Cultures for gonorrhea should be plated directly onto a **warmed** transgrow medium and sent to the bacteriology lab within 30 minutes or placed in storage in a warmer set at 35 to 36°C. Rectal swabs for gonorrhea should be free of obvious fecal contamination since rectal flora will overgrow gonococcal organisms and possibly result in a false negative culture result. All positive gonorrhea cultures should be confirmed by a second independent biochemical test to avoid the possibility of a false positive culture result (Alexander, 1988, p. 1).
2. *Chlamydia trachomatis*. Chlamydia is an obligate intracellular bacterial pathogen. Although chlamydia prefers to grow within the columnar epithelium of the mature female genital tract, it is able to infect the vaginal mucosa of prepubertal females. Rapid antigen detection methods are *not* reliable for use in child abuse evaluations (Hammershlag, Rettig, and Shields, 1988, p. 11). Accordingly, chlamydia cultures are the preferred method of screening for anogenital chlamydia infections. Chlamydia is cultured by scraping

epithelial cells directly from the suspected infection site with a sterile swab and quickly dropping the swab into a *cooled*, buffered transport solution. The transport solution should then be transported on ice to the lab.

3. *Human Papilloma Virus (HPV)*. The human papilloma virus is the causative agent of cutaneous and genital warts (*Condyloma acuminata*). Studies of the HPV genome have identified more than 60 distinct subtypes of DNA. These studies have also confirmed that HPV lesions tend to be site specific and that anogenital warts are most frequently caused by HPV DNA subtypes 6, 11, 16, 18, 31, 33, and 35 (Hanson, Glasson, McCrossin, and Rogers, 1989, p. 230). Suspicious genital lesions can be soaked with a 3 or 5 percent solution of acetic acid and observed for "aceto-whitening" of the epithelial surface (Pfenninger, 1989, p. 287). (Some children may experience a burning or stinging sensation upon application of the acetic acid solution.) Unfortunately, aceto-whitening is a nonspecific epithelial response. As a result, genital lesions which turn white in response to application of acetic acid should be tested for the presence of intracellular HPV DNA using one of several commercially available tests (**Table 8.3**) to confirm whether they actually represent HPV lesions of a type which are known to be sexually transmitted (Nuovo and Nuovo, 1992, p. 189).

A combination of vaginal/cervical cytology and HPV testing may eventually prove to be the best method for confirming a clinical diagnosis of genital HPV infections.

Table 8.3
Human Papilloma Virus Detection Kits

Product	Method	Number of Tests/Kit	Cost/Test
Digene	In situ	20	$15
Enzo	In situ	40	10
ONCOR	Southern blot	60	7
Virapap	Slot blot	50	7
Viratype	In situ	20	15

Although it is well accepted that anogenital HPV infections are generally transmitted through sexual contact (**Table 8.2**), it is uncertain whether this is the *only* mode of transmission of this virus (American Academy of Dermatology Task Force on Pediatric Dermatology, 1984, p. 529). Furthermore, the long latency period (1 to 20 months) between initial infection and development of visible HPV lesions makes a definitive determination of the source of genital warts in young children problematic. Currently, the best recommendation is to consider a *sexual* mode of transmission whenever anogenital HPV lesions are identified in a young child (except when the child is under the age of 2, the mother has a history of having genital warts, *and* there are no other historical factors or physical findings suggestive of abuse). DNA typing studies of cutaneous/genital HPV lesions may become particularly helpful in clarifying the mode of transmission in ambiguous cases.

4. **Other Sexually Transmitted Diseases**. The decision to screen for other STDs should be based upon the local prevalence of each STD (Koop, 1988). For example, we do not routinely test for HIV antibodies because of the low prevalence of AIDS in our area (Frost, 1989). Moreover, we do not test for *Treponema palladium* unless the victim has either been assaulted by a stranger or has been previously documented to have another STD. Finally, we don't routinely test for other STDs (except as noted above) unless the physical findings suggest a specific diagnosis.

5. **Other Laboratory Tests**. Additional laboratory testing should be ordered as indicated by the history or physical exam and the results recorded in the medical record.

MEDICAL TREATMENT OF SEXUALLY ABUSED CHILDREN

Contraception

The risk of pregnancy (Abramowicz, 1989, p. 93) following unprotected intercourse is 20 percent at three days prior to ovulation; 25 percent one day prior to ovulation; and 15 percent on the day of ovulation. The risk of becoming pregnant as a result of unprotected intercourse approaches zero two days following ovulation. High-dose estrogens have been shown to significantly lower the risk of pregnancy following unprotected intercourse. However, such "postcoital contraception" is reserved for cases where the nature of the abuse could result in pregnancy (e.g., pubertal female victim of vaginal intercourse who presents for evaluation within 48 hours of the assault). In such cases, the victim should be tested for pregnancy and receive an explanation of the risks and benefits of this form of contraception prior to receiving any postcoital contraceptive drugs. The risks include the following:

1. An inability to guarantee that such treatment will prevent a pregnancy resulting from a sexual assault. The pooled failure rate is reported to be 1.8 percent (Abramowicz, 1989, p. 93).
2. These contraceptive agents produce unpleasant side effects (nausea, vomiting, breast tenderness, dizziness, and menstrual irregularities).
3. In the event that the pregnancy persists, there is a theoretical risk that the treatment will produce fetal malformations.

A common postcoital contraceptive regimen consists of two tablets of Ovral (50 μg of ethinyl estradiol and 0.5 mg of norgestrel per tablet) given initially (within 72 hours of unprotected intercourse) followed 12 hours later by another two Ovral tablets (Yupze and Lancee, 1977, p. 238). Compazine 5 to 10 mg (prochlorperazine) can be given two hours prior to the second dose to prevent nausea. Other methods of postcoital contraception currently under development include progestational agents and luteinizing hormone releasing hormone analogues. Mefepristone (RU 486) is a competitive, progesterone antagonist which is now undergoing clinical testing as a postcoital contraceptive in Europe.

Treatment of Sexually Transmitted Diseases

Prophylactic treatment of STDs among victims of child sexual abuse is generally *not* recommended. The decision to prescribe antimicrobial therapy should be guided by the results of the physical exam and screening tests for STDs. Optimal antimicrobial treatment regimens for sexually transmitted diseases are published annually by the Centers for Disease Control in the *Morbidity and Mortality Weekly Report.*

CHART DOCUMENTATION OF THE MEDICAL EVALUATION OF CHILD SEXUAL ABUSE

The final record of the evaluation of suspected victims of child sexual abuse is an important legal document (Indest, 1989, p. 144). Even if

Table 8.4
Classification of Anogenital Findings

Category	Findings
1	Normal—does not rule out the possibility of sexual abuse.
2	Nonspecific—findings which could also be caused by accidental or nonsexual trauma.
3	Specific—findings which are most likely to have been caused by sexual contact.
4	Definitive—findings which could only have been caused by sexual contact (e.g., presence of sperm/semen on the victim).

the interview is routinely audiotaped and transcribed, a legible chart note detailing the results of the history, physical exam, and the lab studies should be entered into the child's medical chart immediately following the examination. We have found it helpful to use a standardized examination form developed by the Office of the Attorney General of Kentucky (**Appendix 8.1**) to document our historical, physical, and laboratory findings. We currently use Murram and Elias' classification system (1989) to rate the specificity of the physical findings for abuse (**Table 8.4**).

In addition, we always include a written description of our findings within each child's Sexual Abuse Case Folder. Appropriate ICD-9/CPT codes for child sexual abuse examinations are listed in **Appendix 8.2**.

REFERENCES

Abramowicz, M., ed. (1989), Ovral as a "morning-after" contraceptive. *The Medical Letter*, 31/803:93–94.

Alexander, E. (1988), Misidentification of sexually transmitted organisms in children: Medicolegal implications. *Pediatr. Infect. Dis. J.*, 7:1–2.

American Academy of Dermatology Task Force on Pediatric Dermatology (1984), Genital warts and sexual abuse in children. *J. Amer. Acad. Dermatol.*, 11:529–530.

American Academy of Pediatrics Committee on Child Abuse and Neglect (1991),
    1991 Guidelines for the evaluation of sexual abuse in children. *Pediatrics*,
    87:254–260.
Frost, N. (1989), Ethical considerations in testing victims of sexual abuse for HIV
    infections. *Child Abuse & Negl.*, 14:5–7.
Hammerschlag, M., Rettig, P., & Shields, M. (1988), False positive results with the
    use of chlamydial antigen detection tests in the evaluation of suspected sexual
    abuse in children. *J. Pediatr. Infect. Dis.*, 7:11–14.
Hanson, R., Glasson, M., McCrossin, I., & Rogers, M. (1989), Anogenital warts in
    childhood. *Child Abuse and Negl.*, 13:225–253.
Indest, G. (1989), Medico-legal issues in detecting and proving the sexual abuse of
    children. *J. Sex & Mar. Ther.*, 15:141–160.
Johnson, R. T., Moore, W. M., & Jeffries, J. E. (1978), *Children Are Different:
    Developmental Physiology*, 2nd. ed. Columbus, OH: Ross Laboratories, pp.
    26–29.
Koop, C. E. (1988), The Surgeon General's Letter on Child Sexual Abuse. Washing-
    ton, DC: U.S. Department of Health & Human Services, Public Health Service,
    Bureau of Maternal and Child Health and Resources Development, Office of
    Maternal and Child Health.
McCann, J. (1990), Use of the colposcope in childhood sexual abuse examinations.
    Pediatr. Clin. N. Amer., 37:863–880.
———— Voris, J., Simon, M., & Wells, R. (1989), Perianal findings in prepubertal
    children selected for non-abuse: A descriptive study. *Child Abuse & Negl.*,
    13:179–193.
———— Wells, R., Simon, M., & Voris, J. (1990), Genital findings in prepubertal
    girls selected for nonabuse: A descriptive study. *Pediatrics*, 3:428–439.
Murram, D. (1989), Anal and perianal abnormalities in prepubertal victims of sexual
    abuse. *Amer. J. Obstet. & Gynecol.*, 161:278–281.
———— Elias, S. (1989), Child sexual abuse—Genital tract findings in prepubertal
    girls II. Comparison of colposcopic and unaided examinations. *Amer. J. Obstet.
    & Gynecol.*, 160:333–335.
Neinstein, L., Goldenring, J., & Carpenter, S. (1984), Nonsexual transmission of
    sexually transmitted diseases: An infrequent occurrence. *Pediatrics*, 74:67–76.
Nuovo, G., & Nuovo, J. (1992), Should family physicians test for human papilloma-
    virus infection? An opposing view. *J. Fam. Pract.*, 32:188–192.
Pfenninger, J. (1989), Androscopy: A technique for examining men for condyloma.
    J. Fam. Pract., 29:286–288.
Reinhart, M. A. (1987), Sexually abused boys. *Child Abuse & Negl.*, 11:229–235.
Solomons, G. (1980), Trauma and child abuse: The importance of the medical record.
    Amer. J. Dis. Child, 134:503.
Tipton, A. C. (1989), Child sexual abuse: Physical examination techniques and inter-
    pretation of findings. *Adol. Pediatr. Gyn.*, 2:10–25.
Yupze, A. A., & Lancee, W. J. (1977), Ethinyl estradiol and *dl*-norgestrel as a
    postcoital contraceptive. *Fertil. Steril.*, 28:932.

SELECTED BIBLIOGRAPHY OF CHILD SEXUAL ABUSE

These articles are recommended to the reader who would like to review
additional literature on this subject.

Demographics of Child Sexual Abuse

Berkowitz, C. (1987), Sexual abuse of children and adolescents. *Adv. Pediatr.*, 34:275–312.

Kendall-Tackett, K., & Simon, A. (1987), Perpetrators and their acts: Data from 365 adults molested as children. *Child Abuse & Negl.*, 11:237–245.

Levitt, C. (1986), Sexual abuse in children. *Postgrad. Med.*, 80:201–215.

Summit, R. (1983), Child sexual abuse accommodation syndrome. *Child Abuse & Negl.*, 7:177–193.

Woodling, B., & Kossoris, P. (1981), Sexual misuse: Rape, molestation and incest. *Pediatr. Clin. N. Amer.*, 28:481–499.

Diagnosis of Child Sexual Abuse

Abrams, M. E., Shah, R. Z., & Keenan-Allyn, S. (1988), Sexual abuse in children and adolescents: A detection and management guide. *Female Patient.*, 13:17–33.

Adams, J., Ahmad, M., & Phillips, P. (1988), Anogenital findings and hymenal diameter in children referred for sexual abuse examination. *Adolesc. & Pediatr. Gyn.*, 1:123–127.

Chadwick, D. L., Berkowitz, C., Kerns, D., McCann, J., Reinhart, M., & Strickland, S. (1989), *Color Atlas of Child Sexual Abuse*. Chicago, IL: Yearbook Medical Publishers.

Durfee, M., Heger, A., & Woodling, B. (1986), Medical evaluation. In: *Sexual Abuse of Young Children*, ed. K. McFarlane & J. Waterman. New York: Guilford Press, pp. 52–66.

Emans, J., Woods, E., Flagg, N., & Freeman, A. (1987), Genital findings in sexually abused symptomatic and asymptomatic girls. *Pediatrics*, 79:778.

Goff, C. W., Burke, K. R., Rickenback, C., & Buebendorf, D. (1989), Vaginal opening measurement in prepubertal girls. *Amer. J. Dis. Child.*, 143:1366–1368.

Jenny, C., Kuhns, M. L., & Arakawa, F. (1987), Hymens in newborn female infants. *Pediatrics*, 80:399.

Heger, A. (1985), *Response: Child Sexual Abuse, a Medical View*. New York: Guilford Publications.

Hobbs, C. J., & Wynne, J. M. (1989), Sexual abuse of English boys and girls: The importance of anal exam. *Child Abuse & Negl.*, 13:195.

Krugman, R. (1986), Recognition of sexual abuse in children. *Pediatr. in Rev.*, 8:25–30.

Ladson, S., Johnson, C., & Doty, R. (1987), Do physicians recognize sexual abuse? *Amer. J. Dis. Child.*, 141:411–415.

McCann, J., Voris, J., & Simon, M. (1988), Labial adhesions and posterior fourchette injuries in childhood sexual abuse. *Amer. J. Dis. Child.*, 142:659–663.

————— Voris, J., Simon, M., & Wells, R. (1990), Comparison of genital examination techniques in prepubertal girls. *Pediatrics*, 85:182–187.

Mor, N. (1988), Congenital absence of the hymen only a rumor? [letter] *Pediatrics*, 82:679–680.

Paradise, J. (1990), The medical evaluation of the sexually abused child. *Pediatr. Clin. N. Amer.*, 37:839–862.

Sexually Transmitted Diseases Among Victims of Child Sexual Abuse

Emans, S. (1986), Vulvovaginitis in the child and adolescent. *Pediatr. in Rev.*, 8:12.

Fuster, C., & Neinstein, L. (1987), Vaginal chlamydia trachomatis prevalence in sexually abused prepubertal girls. *Pediatrics*, 79:235–238.

Pokorny, S. (1989), Child abuse and infections. *Obstet. & Gynecol. Clin. N. Amer.*, 16/2:401–415.

Legal Issues Related to Child Sexual Abuse

Baum, E., Grodin, M., Alpert, J., & Glantz, L. (1987), Child sexual abuse, criminal justice and the pediatrician. *Pediatrics*, 70:437–439.

Chadwick, D. (1990), Preparation for court testimony in child abuse cases. *Pediatr. Clin. N. Amer.*, 37:955–970.

De Jong, A., & Rose, M. (1989), Frequency and significance of physical evidence in legally proven cases of child sexual abuse. *Pediatrics*, 84:1022–1026.

Herbert, C. (1987), Expert medical assessment in determining probability of alleged child sexual abuse. *Child Abuse & Negl.*, 11:213–221.

Peters, J. (1989), Criminal prosecution of child abuse: Recent trends. *Pediatr. Ann.*, 18:505–509.

Ricci, L. (1988), Medical forensic photography of the sexually abused child. *Child Abuse & Negl.*, 12:305–310.

APPENDIX 8.1. CHILD SEXUAL ABUSE EXAMINATION FORM

Child Sexual Abuse Exam Form

FAMILY MEDICAL CENTER
Child Sexual Abuse
Evaluation Form

Chief Complaint(s) in Child's Own Words *(Use additional sheets if necessary)*

Chief Complaint(s) of Person Providing History if other than child *(Use additional sheets if necessary)*

Name of Person Providing History   Relationship to Child

Full Address and Phone

Date(s) or Timeframe and Location(s) of Incidents
  ACUTE = Occurred w/i 48 hours; use forensic sexual assault evidence kit
  CHRONIC = Occurred beyond 48 hours; use of forensic kit not mandatory

1. Acute/Chronic Incident   2. Single/Multiple Incident(s)   3. Single/Multiple Perpetrator(s)

D. Acts Described by Patient/Other

	Patient	Other
Vaginal Contact		
Penis	___	___
Finger	___	___
Foreign object(s)	___	___
Describe object(s)	___	___
Anal Contact		
Penis	___	___
Finger	___	___
Foreign object(s)	___	___
Describe object(s)		
Oral Copulation of Genitals		
of victim by assailant	___	___
of assailant by victim	___	___
Oral Copulation of Anus		
of victim by assailant	___	___
of assailant by victim	___	___
Masturbation		
of victim by assailant	___	___
of assailant by victim	___	___
Did ejaculation occur outside body orifice?	___	___
If yes, describe location:		

	Patient	Other
Foam, jelly, condom used (Circle)	___	___
Lubricant used (Specify)	___	___
Fondling, licking or kissling (Circle)	___	___
If yes, describe location:		

Symptoms Described by Patient/Other

	Patient	Other
Physical Symptoms		
Abdom/pelvic pain	___	___
Vulvar pain	___	___
Dysuria	___	___
UTI	___	___
Enuresis (day/night)	___	___
Vaginal itching	___	___
Vaginal discharge	___	___
describe color, odor, amount below		
Vaginal bleeding	___	___
Rectal pain	___	___
Rectal bleeding	___	___
Rectal discharge	___	___
Constipation	___	___
Incontinent of stool	___	___
Lapse of consciousness	___	___
Vomiting	___	___
Physical injuries:	___	___
pain or tenderness, describe below		
Behavioral/Emotional Symptoms		
Sleep disturbances	___	___
Eating disorders	___	___
School	___	___
Sexual acting out	___	___
Fear	___	___
Anger	___	___
Depression	___	___
Other Symptoms	___	___

Child Sexual Abuse Exam Form (continued)

Other acts _____

Additional Information: _____

_____

_____

_____

_____

_____

_____

Was force or threat of harm used upon patient? _____

If yes, describe _____

_____

Was patient threatened regarding disclosure? _____

If yes, describe _____

_____

_____

_____

_____

E. PERTINENT PAST MEDICAL HISTORY

1. Pre-existing physical injuries (fractures, concussions) _____ Yes _____ No

If yes, describe _____

2. Pre-existing medical conditions _____ Yes _____ No If yes, describe _____

3. Previous surgery (particularly ano-rectal-genital) _____ Yes _____ No

If yes, describe _____

4. Previous history of known or suspected neglect/physical/sexual abuse _____ Yes _____ No

If yes, describe _____

5. For female patient, complete the following:

Menarchal _____ Yes _____ No   Date LMP _____   Age of menarch _____

Use of tampons _____ Yes _____ No   History of vaginitis _____ Yes _____ No   Etiology of vaginitis _____

F. GENERAL PHYSICAL EXAMINATION

Date/Time of Exam _____

NOTE: If the patient is examined within 48 hours of the reported incident, forensic evidence must be obtained by use of Sexual Assault Evidence Collection Kit during the physical examination. See specific instructions in Kit and page 6.

1. BP _____ P _____ R _____ T _____ WT _____ HT _____

2. General Physical Condition (excluding genitalia, anus, rectum)—Comment on general features, eg. state of nutrition, cleanliness, dental hygiene as well as more specific anatomic abnormalities next to appropriate heading.

Child Sexual Abuse Exam Form (continued)

3. Physical examination—Record on accompanying body diagrams location, shape and size of any injuries including abrasions, bites, bruises, burns, contusions, erythema, fractures, lacerations, etc. Also record any abnormalities.

HEENT	( ) Within normal limits	( ) Abnormal	Pulses	( ) Within normal limits	( ) Abnormal
Dental/oral	( ) Within normal limits	( ) Abnormal	Abdom	( ) Within normal limits	( ) Abnormal
Neck	( ) Within normal limits	( ) Abnormal	Extrem	( ) Within normal limits	( ) Abnormal
Chest	( ) Within normal limits	( ) Abnormal	Neuro	( ) Within normal limits	( ) Abnormal
Heart	( ) Within normal limits	( ) Abnormal			

Oropharyngeal cultures for GC and chlamydia should be obtained at the end of the examination.

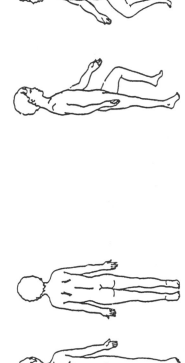

Description of Findings:

G. ANAL-GENITAL EXAMINATION

Female/Male General	WNL	ABN
Tanner Stage		
Breast 1 2 3 4 5	( )	( )
Genitals 1 2 3 4 5	( )	( )
Inguinal adenopathy	( )	( )
Medial aspect/thighs	( )	( )
Perineum	( )	( )
Vulvovaginal discharge ( )Yes ( )No		
Urethral discharge ( )Yes ( )No		
Condyloma acuminata ( )Yes ( )No		

Female/Male Anus	WNL	ABN
Buttocks	( )	( )
Perianal skin	( )	( )
Anal verge/folds/rugae	( )	( )
Tone	( )	( )
Anal spasms ( ) Yes ( ) No		
Anal laxity ( ) Yes ( ) No		
Note presence of stool in rectal ampulla ( ) Yes ( ) No		
Anoscopic exam ( ) Yes ( ) No ( ) N/A		
Proctoscopic exam ( ) Yes ( ) No ( ) N/A		
Exam Position ( ) Supine ( ) Prone ( ) Lateral recumbent		

Female	WNL	ABN
Labia majora	( )	( )
Clitoris	( )	( )
Labia minora	( )	( )
Periurethral tissue/urethral meatus	( )	( )
Perihymenal tissue/(vestibule)	( )	( )
Hymen	( )	( )
Record diameter		
( ) Horizontal	( )	( )
( ) Vertical	( )	( )
Posterior fourchette	( )	( )
Fossa Navicularis	( )	( )
Vagina	( )	( )

Male	WNL	ABN
Penis	( )	( )
Circumcised ( ) Yes ( ) No		
Urethral meatus	( )	( )
Scrotum	( )	( )
Testes	( )	( )

Additional Comments:

Child Sexual Abuse Exam Form (continued)

Exam Position ( ) Supine   ( ) Knee Chest

8

9   *Child Sexual Abuse Exam Form (continued)*

H. CLINICAL SPECIMENS TO HOSPITAL LABORATORY

STD Cultures	GC	Chlamyda	Other (Specify)
Vaginal			
Rectal			
Urethral			
Oral			

Other Tests Performed	Yes	No	Comment
Pregnancy			
Syphilis serology			
Hepatitis B. serology			
Other (specify)			

Photographs Taken   ( ) NO   ( ) YES   ( ) Photo # _____

Area of body _____

Photographer _____

I. PERSONNEL INVOLVED—PRINT

	Print	Phone
History taken by:		
Specimens labeled/sealed by		
Assisting nurse		

Additional narrative by physician ( ) Reported attached ( ) N/A

Child Sexual Abuse Exam Form (continued)

SUMMARY OF PHYSICAL FINDINGS: (   ) Unable to Examine (   ) Normal Exam

Genital Findings   Anal Findings

_____   _____

_____   _____

_____   _____

(   ) The foregoing abnormal findings are non-specific but do not rule out the possibility of child sexual abuse.

(   ) The foregoing abnormal findings are indicative of ano-genital trauma which is consistent with child sexual abuse.

(   ) The foregoing abnormal findings **definitive** for child sexual abuse.

Name of Examining Physician _____

Physician's Signature _____ Date _____

APPENDIX 8.2. ICD-9 CODES FOR CHILD SEXUAL ABUSE EVALUATIONS

Child Abuse Services:

V61.21	—	As reason for family seeking advice
V62.5	—	Legal exam for investigation/prosecution
V68.2	—	Request for expert legal evidence
V70.4	—	Medical–legal examination
V71.5	—	Examination of victim/culprit of alleged rape or seduction
V71.6	—	Examination of child victim of battering/assault

Child Abuse Codes:

959.9	—	Rape
995.5	—	Child maltreatment syndrome

Genital Codes:

054.10	—	Genital herpes
054.11	—	Vulvo-vaginal herpes
078.1	—	Condyloma acuminata
091.0	—	1° genital syphilis
091.3	—	2° genital syphilis (condyloma lata)
098.0	—	Acute gonococcal vaginitis
098.15	—	Acute gonococcal cervicitis
098.2	—	Chronic (> 2 mos) gonococcal vaginitis
098.35	—	Chronic (> 2 mos) gonococcal cervicitis
099.8	—	Venereal vaginitis (NEC)
112.2	—	Urogenital candidal infection
131.0	—	Urogenital trichomoniasis
131.01	—	Trichomonas vulvovaginitis
752.49	—	Hymenal septum/labial adhesions
867.6	—	Genital organ injury
878.4	—	Vulvar wound
878.6	—	Vaginal/hymenal wound
911	—	Vaginal/perineal/pubic abrasions
939.0	—	Foreign body in genitourinary tract
939.2	—	Foreign body in vulva and vagina
959.1	—	Vaginal injury

Pharynx Codes:
078	—	Chlamydia (nonconjunctival)
098.6	—	Gonococcal pharyngitis
091.2	—	1° oral syphilis
112.0	—	Oral candidiasis (thrush)

Urinary Tract Codes:
054.13	—	Penile herpes
078	—	Chlamydia (nonconjunctival)
078.1	—	Condyloma acuminata
098.0	—	Acute gonococcal urethritis/epididymitis
098.12	—	Acute gonococcal prostatitis
098.2	—	Chronic (> 2 mos) gonococcal epididymitis
098.32	—	Chronic (> 2 mos) gonococcal prostatitis
099.4	—	Nongonococcal urethritis
112.2	—	Candidal balanitis
131.02	—	Trichomonas urethritis
131.03	—	Trichomonas prostatitis
878.0	—	Penis wound
911	—	Penis/scrotal/perineal abrasions
939.3	—	Foreign body in penis

Anorectal Codes:
007.3	—	Intestinal trichomoniasis
078	—	Chlamydia (nonconjunctival)
078.1	—	Condyloma acuminata
091.1	—	1° anal syphilis
098.7	—	Gonococcal proctitis
565.0	—	Anal fissure
863.45	—	Rectal injury
863.89	—	Anal sphincter tear
879.6	—	Anal wound
937	—	Foreign body in anus

CPT CODES FOR CHILD SEXUAL ABUSE EVALUATIONS

Physician's Current Procedural Terminology (CPT) is a uniform system of terms used by physicians to report medical services and procedures to other physicians, patients, and third parties. In 1992, the physician evaluation and management (E/M) codes were revised extensively to reflect the changes in reimbursement for cognitive services. These descriptors now recognize seven components of physician service: history, examination, decision making, counseling, coordination of care, nature of the presenting problem, and time. The first three components are considered the key components in selecting the appropriate E/M code, whereas the others are considered to be contributory components. The reader should consult the most recent edition of the AMA's CPT manual for complete details.

99204 — Office evaluation of a *new patient* with a presenting problem of high severity in which the examining physician obtains a comprehensive history, performs a comprehensive examination, employs medical decision making of high complexity, and spends 60 minutes or more face to face with the patient/family.

99215 — Office evaluation of an *established patient* with a presenting problem of high severity in which the examining physician obtains a comprehensive history, performs a comprehensive examination, employs medical decision making of high complexity, and spends 40 minutes or more face to face with the patient/family.

99245 — Complex initial consultation (requires documentation of the request for the consult in the medical record).

99275 — Complex confirmatory consultation

99284 — Emergency room evaluation of a *new or established patient* with a presenting problem of high severity which requires urgent evaluation but which does *not* pose a significant threat to life or physiologic function and in which the examining physician obtains a detailed history, performs a detailed examination, and employs medical decision making of high complexity.

99285 — Emergency room evaluation of a *new or established patient* with a presenting problem of high severity which requires urgent evaluation and which poses a significant threat to life or physiologic function. The examining physician obtains a comprehensive history, performs a comprehensive examination, and employs medical decision making of high complexity.

99362 — Interdisciplinary team conference to coordinate activities of patient care 60 minutes.

99075 — Medical testimony
99090 — Special Reports
99071 — Patient educational materials provided by the physician

Procedure Codes:

55899 — Androscopy (males)
57452 — Colposcopy (females)
57410 — Pelvic examination under anesthesia
81000 — Urinalysis with microscopy
82270 — Stool hemoccult screening
87081 — Bacterial culture
87086 — Bacticult, urine culture, and sensitivity with colony count
87110 — Chlamydia culture
87205 — KOH exam
87207 — Herpes smear
87252 — Herpes (tissue) culture
87210 — Wet prep
86592 — VDRL, RPR

9

Treatment Strategies and Considerations

THE TREATMENT TEAM

Treatment of the abused child and the abusive family is a complex process which usually involves several professionals from different agencies. These professionals vary from case to case, but often include a physician specifically trained in the evaluation and treatment of child abuse, a mental health specialist in child abuse, a child protective services worker, the police, and the prosecuting attorney. Collaboration, cooperation, and mutual respect and understanding of each other's roles are essential to the success of the treatment process. The reporting law recognizes the need for open communication in the area of child abuse and recognizes no privileged relationships beyond that of attorney and client. While respecting the client's confidentiality, it is important for the treatment team, often composed of professionals from different agencies, to be able to communicate openly. Many areas have found it helpful to develop advocacy centers, where professionals from different disciplines and agencies can meet regularly to evaluate and treat the victim and family.

THE CHILD

When a case of sexual abuse becomes known to mental health or child protective agencies, frequently the child is forgotten. Often there is strong emphasis placed on prosecuting the abuser, which means the child and his feelings, as well as reactions of other family members such as the nonabusing parent and siblings, may go unattended.

The following are important considerations in all cases of abuse and neglect:

Medical Considerations

A physical exam is important when there is evidence of physical or sexual abuse or neglect. The physical exam may yield the necessary information and cause court action to be initiated if necessary. Court action may coerce the offender and his family into an evaluation or treatment program.

Psychological Considerations

It is psychologically traumatic when a child is removed from parents, siblings, peer group, and school. Therefore the child should be kept at home if at all possible to preserve the psychological attachment and continuity of relationships and place. It may be possible to influence the abusing parent to leave until a full evaluation has been completed and treatment indicates he or she may return. It may be possible for all family members to remain in the home with adequate supervision being given to the child by the nonabusing parent by not allowing the child to be alone with the abusing parent. These two options are less psychologically detrimental than removing the child.

In addition, it is crucial to evaluate the psychological impact on the child. This can be accomplished by determining the degree of harm and assessing the impact on the child.

AREAS TO EXPLORE WHEN EVALUATING THE CHILD

The following are general areas to explore to determine how the child is symptomatic:

1. Assess the child's peer relationships.
2. Evaluate school behavior and academic performance.
3. Assess the parent–child relationship.
4. Evaluate the use of drugs and alcohol in the family.
5. Identify fears and inhibitions.
6. Evaluate aggressive–passive behavior.
7. Determine intellectual ability.
8. Assess social skills.
9. Evaluate the possibility of role reversal—the child being asked to meet the parents' emotional or physical needs.
10. Determine if the victim has elevated status in his sibling group; that is, a special relationship with the abusing or nonabusing parent.
11. Assess the possibility of a sleep disturbance—sleep walking, nightmares, restlessness, insomnia.
12. Identify any appetite disturbance.
13. The child may be perceived as "different" (i.e., handicapped, biracial, premature, etc.).
14. Assess whether bed-wetting or soiling is present.
15. Determine if there are behavioral regressions.
16. Identify separation problems (e.g., refusal to go to school).

Burgess, Holmstrom, and McCausland (1978) and Mrazek (1981) suggest that the therapy which follows such a stressful life experience as abuse should include several key concepts: it should (1) help the child put feelings and needs into words; (2) strengthen impulse control by channeling aggression into play activities; (3) improve interpersonal relationships with family and peer group; and (4) provide play therapy for children who show low self-esteem, depression, aggressiveness, and severe management or behavior problems to help them more appropriately deal with the traumatic sexual abuse.

Specific techniques useful in evaluating preschool and latency-age children include:

- Fables. The child is asked to respond to stories with specific themes.

- Three wishes. The therapist suggests playing a game; the child can wish for anything he wants, or any change he wants.

- Drawings.

- <u>Free play.</u>

- <u>Structured play.</u>

- <u>Mutual story-telling.</u> The therapist suggests to the child that they tell a story. The therapist can begin by identifying the persons in an animal family and begin a specific theme. Then ask the child to continue and alternate between the child's story-telling and bringing out specific themes or issues that are relevant to the child's situation.

- <u>Anatomical dolls</u> are used to elicit information about the abuse.

These techniques are discussed in detail throughout this manual.

SIBLINGS

In physical and sexual abuse cases, the community may focus on apprehension of the alleged offender and trial, and the child may be forgotten in this process. This is also true of the siblings because it is often unrecognized that the siblings have been exposed to similar family themes as the abused child and in many cases the siblings may also have been abused. In addition, they may feel guilty that they have not attempted to intervene and stop the abusive pattern.

1. It is important to preserve the psychological attachment, the psychological bond, that the siblings have with their parents and with each other.
2. Continuity of relationships and place.
3. Risk for siblings should be reduced by providing supervision (i.e., by monitoring the relationship with the abusing parent).
4. Determine if the siblings are showing symptoms of abuse or other kinds of stress.
5. If siblings cannot be protected in their home, they should be removed.

THE ABUSING PARENT

The community's reaction against the abuser may take the form of arrest and prosecution. Initially a family evaluation must occur to determine if the family is treatable. In cases of extreme physical or sexual abuse it is often helpful to have the perpetrator hospitalized or leave the home for three or four weeks in order to complete the evaluation. The following are techniques helpful in the evaluation and treatment process:

1. The therapist should allow a dependent relationship to develop with the abusing parent.
2. Emotional and practical support should be offered to the family.
3. The therapist must tune in to the abuser's feelings (loneliness, anger, fearfulness, etc.).
4. The parent must be made aware of his feelings by the therapist and also of the need to communicate them verbally.
5. The therapist must help the parent deal with feelings constructively.
6. The therapist needs to teach the parent to communicate his needs and desires verbally.
7. The abusing parent must be helped to improve impulse control.
8. Appropriate child-rearing practices must be taught.
9. The abuser must be taught to have appropriate pleasurable experiences with children.
10. The therapist must teach appropriate expectations of children.
11. Developmental milestones for children must be described.
12. The parent needs help in integrating effective parenting techniques.
13. The therapist can help the parent get his needs met within age-appropriate relationships.
14. The parent can be helpd to differentiate between affectionate behavior and coming on sexually. Often this is blurred because of the sexually abusing parent's early life experiences, which may have included sexual abuse.
15. Win the parent's cooperation by viewing abusive behavior as a solution to a problem (i.e., being affectionate with the child,

the need for sexual release, etc.). Initially accommodate to his perception of the problem.

16. Initially relabel inappropriate behavior; for example, with a sexually abusing parent the therapist may state, "This was your way of being affectionate with your child," or "This was a way of getting your sexual needs met." This is not to condone the behavior, but a way of beginning to talk about the sexually abusive behavior.

SPECIFIC TECHNIQUES USEFUL IN TREATING THE PHYSICALLY ABUSIVE PARENT

Physically abusive parents often have difficulty differentiating between the expression of anger and abusive behavior. It is important for parents to understand that anger is a feeling, an emotion, whereas abuse is behavior. Angry feelings are normal; everyone has them many times in the course of their lives. Abuse of a child is an expression of anger and frustration, but there are many other more appropriate ways to express these feelings. However, if anger is to be handled more constructively, the parent must first learn to recognize his or her feelings. Parents who do not recognize their feelings may find that their anger comes out very quickly and they explode. The reason for this is that as children, many were taught that anger is bad; as a result, they may have learned to pay little attention to these feelings, and if they are aware of them, they keep them inside.

There are many ways in which parents deal with anger: some push it inside, others allow it to escalate, and some direct it in a constructive way. When feelings of anger are pushed inside, they build up, and a parent may explode. The term *escalating feelings* means a parent first criticizes, then verbally attacks, and, finally, may abuse the child.

Some methods of handling anger more constructively include the following:

1. The parent must learn to be aware of feelings of anger and frustration.

2. Take time-out. Time-out is a method used with children to help them control their feelings, to handle them more constructively. It can also be used by adults. When a parent feels anger building, he or she can take a time out by leaving the house for a period of time or leaving the room. Doing something physical helps, like jogging, walking, or pushups.

3. Rational self-talk. Dr. Maxie Maultsby (1984), in his book, describes positive self-talk. This technique will help the parent keep his angry feelings from escalating. When a parent blames, criticizes, or verbally attacks, he or she directs the anger toward the child. If the self-talk is changed to a positive form, the parent begins to say to himself that he is angry with his child and needs to take a time-out; that he must do some physical exercise so he won't lose control.

4. Stress reduction. Parents who abuse their children usually have high levels of stress, both within family relationships and in general. Stress is a physical and emotional response within us to something we view as a threat. Stress can be caused by a change, a loss, an event we feel helpless about, conflict, or frustration. Relaxation exercises can be helpful in keeping stress at a manageable level (Sorkin and Durphy, 1982).

5. Communication. When parents are aware of their feelings, it is very helpful to put these feelings into words. This can be directly done toward the child (e.g., "I feel furious," or "I really feel angry") or toward a spouse. Putting feelings into words can help get it out so it won't build up (Dinkmeyer and McKay, 1982).

6. If a parent does not say "no," he may end up angry and frustrated. It is important to say "no" and to stick to it. This will prevent anger and stressful feelings from developing.

7. Stop the use of alcohol. A high percentage of abusive episodes are drug related, that is, alcohol or some other drug was used prior to the abusive act. Alcohol makes a person less inhibited and less in control of his behavior.

Families where child abuse is a problem must curtail the use of alcohol and the user must get specific intervention for the problem. Examples include an inpatient alcohol treatment unit to "dry out," Alcoholics Anonymous, and psychotherapy.

THE NONABUSING PARENT

1. The nonabusing parent needs to be helped to offer support to the abuser.
2. Marital intervention should be started, focusing on communication patterns, sexual relationships, and the couple's ability to "tune in" to each other and meet each other's needs.
3. The nonabuser needs help in becoming more assertive in protecting herself and her children. Assertiveness training groups are often effective.
4 The nonabusing parent needs help to build closer relationships with the children, particularly the victim.

BUILDING RELATIONSHIPS OUTSIDE THE FAMILY, DEVELOPING A SUPPORT SYSTEM

Abusive families are dysfunctional. Usually they do not look outside their family for support, nurturance, or help at a time of crisis or extreme stress. An extremely important aspect of the total treatment plan is to help the adults in the family form friendships and other constructive relationships with adults outside the family. It is equally important for the children to form satisfactory relationships with their peers. There are a number of ways in which families can be encouraged to reach out and establish a network of relationships:

1. Activity groups for preschool or latency-age children are very helpful.
2. Therapy groups are especially helpful for adolescents.
3. Church groups for children, adolescents, and adults can be a major source of support.
4. The use of Parents Anonymous as a support group for adults can help both the abusing and nonabusing parent realize that there are others with similar problems and that nonjudgmental support is available.

THE ISSUE OF PARENTAL DENIAL

The use of denial by abusing parents is frequent, and frustrating to mental health and child protective service professionals. Frequently in these cases there is no clear evidence of physical or sexual abuse or neglect, meaning that there are no physical indicators that abuse or neglect has occurred and the behavioral indicators are not conclusive. The following strategies can prove useful:

1. With the parents, be careful not to confront or intimidate them initially, but rather accommodate to their perception of the problem and support them in their role as parents and marital partners.
2. If parental denial continues, treatment cannot be effective. More simply stated, if a perpetrator does not accept responsibility for the abusive behavior, then he or she cannot be effectively treated.
3. Let children know what they can do if anyone physically hurts them or touches them in a physical or sexual way, who they can call, and what they can do to feel safe within their family. Assure them that they can say "no" to an adult.
4. In cases of severe abuse, and when parents continue to deny responsibility, it is usually necessary to remove the children.

ISSUES SPECIFIC TO THE TREATMENT OF NEGLECTED CHILDREN AND NEGLECTING PARENTS

Goals in Treating the Neglected Child

1. The child should be helped to establish trust in others, and his or her developmental needs must be met. Allow the child to experience being a child.
2. Encourage individuation and the development of the child's capacity to tolerate separation.
3. Help the child to develop a positive self-image or self-concept through improved peer relationships and participation in age-appropriate activities.
4. Help the child to improve interpersonal relationships and socialization.

5. The child should be helped to experience positive interaction with adults and peers.
6. The child will need help in learning how to communicate feelings and needs verbally.
7. The child can be helped to strengthen impulse control by channeling aggression into play, music, art, and sports.
8. The child will need help in developing more functional coping skills.

Goals in Treating the Neglecting Parent

1. The neglecting parent needs help in developing trust in others, overcoming their fear of relationships, and reducing isolation.
2. The parent needs help in developing a positive self-image and learning to self-nurture.
3. Help is essential in developing support systems. The parent needs to learn how to make contact with others and how to use community resources.
4. The parent needs to learn how to communicate his or her needs and feelings appropriately.
5. Help is needed for the parent to improve impulse control and learn appropriate ways of channeling aggression.
6. The parent needs help in developing the ability to have pleasurable experiences.
7. The parent needs to learn how to care for a child appropriately and how to nurture a child.
8. Appropriate and consistent child-rearing practices must be learned. Not only do parents need to learn appropriate child-rearing practices and child-rearing techniques but they need to learn how to integrate these techniques into their daily interaction with the child. This is a difficult process and usually requires individual or family counseling more than parent education. In general, the greater the family dysfunction the less an educational approach will be effective in and of itself.

ISSUES SPECIFIC TO TREATMENT OF THE VICTIM OF SEXUAL ABUSE

Techniques for an Investigative Interview of a Sexually Abused Child

1. The interviewer should see the child without a parent present.
2. Someone whom the child knows and trusts should be present if possible. For example, you may ask the child if she would like her teacher present.
3. The interview should take place in a private setting.
4. The interviewer should be close enough to reach out to the child if needed. Do not be behind a desk or at a table.
5. After a brief warm-up conversation tell the child why you're there. Examples: "We've received a call that there are problems in your home," or "I understand that you've told your counselor."
6. If the child is reluctant to talk, tell him or her that most kids the interviewer talks with feel uncomfortable at first. Tell her the purpose of the interview is to make things better.
7. Focus on behaviors. For example, ask, "And then what happened?" instead of "How did that make you feel?"
8. Ask the child if she has any questions to ask you before she tells you about what has happened.
9. Once the child begins to talk, do not ask him for a lot of details regarding time and place. You can get that later if necessary.
10. Ask the child to clarify words and terms if you're not certain what they refer to.
11. Never display any shock, surprise, or disapproval of parents, child, or situation.
12. If the child indicates feelings of guilt say, "Most children feel that somehow they are partly to blame, but that's not true. These are complicated family problems."
13. Assume the child is telling you the truth. Use encouragers such as "uh, huh" and "Then what happened?"
14. Ask, "Who else have you told?" If child names an individual, ask casually, "What did she say when you told her?"
15. Let the child know you believe her, will stick by her, and will try your best to help her and her family through this problem.

16. Tell the child to the best of your knowledge what will probably happen next.

CRITICAL TREATMENT FACTORS SPECIFIC TO INTRAFAMILY SEXUAL ABUSE

1. Always believe the child; protection of the child is our highest priority.

2. If the child is not safe at home, suggest that the perpetrator leave the home.

3. In evaluating the perpetrator, determine if he is fixated or regressed. If the perpetrator is fixated the safest alternative is institutionalization. If the perpetrator is regressed often outpatient treatment of the family can be effective.

4. For treatment to be effective, the offender must admit guilt and accept responsibility for his behavior.

5. The child should never be left in the home unless the mother is supportive.

6. Any family member removed is encouraged to move in with a relative or friend.

7. If a family member is removed, frequent visitation, supervised if necessary, is strongly recommended.

FACTORS THAT HELP ADJUSTMENT OF THE SEXUALLY ABUSED CHILD IN FATHER–DAUGHTER INCEST CASES

1. Mother's support of the child is an essential aid to adjustment.

2. Father's ability to admit guilt is of great importance.

3. The abusive parent's statement that the child is not at fault goes a long way toward helping the adjustment process.

4. The abusive parent's willingness to accept treatment is important.

Susan Sgroi (1982) has identified the following treatment issues regarding the victim of sexual abuse. These come from her book, *Handbook of Clinical Intervention in Child Sexual Abuse*.

1. The *Damaged Goods Syndrome*. Frequently, the child is fearful of physical injury, and a physical exam is extremely helpful in order to rule this out. It can be reassuring to the child for the physician or other health professional to inform him or her that there is no physical damage. In addition, society's response contributes to the child's perception that he or she is damaged. Because the child is often removed from the home and family members may not believe the child, he or she feels more guilty and responsible.

2. *Guilt*. The child feels responsible for the abuse, responsible for the disclosure, and responsible for the disruption in the family. Treatment should be designed to help the child understand his or her own feelings and to sort them out. It is important for the therapist to tell the child over and over again that she is not responsible and to inform the child that disclosure was good and that he or she has the right to be protected.

3. *Fear*. The child is often afraid of future disability as a result of reprisals from the perpetrator. These fears often take the form of nightmares or sleep disturbance. It is helpful in the course of treatment to identify the fears, have the child express them, and move in the direction of making the child's environment safe.

4. *Depression*. Depression is a common reaction in most victims. Clinically, it is necessary to look for signs of depression, to anticipate suicidal thoughts, and to support and believe the victim.

5. *Low Self-Esteem and Poor Social Skills*. These are additional symptoms that are frequently seen in victims. Treatment can help the child identify and ventilate their feelings and offer support to the child. In addition, group therapy is helpful in teaching the child new social skills.

6. *Repressed Anger and Hostility*. Victims are frequently angry at the perpetrator, at family members who have failed to protect them, and at others in the community who didn't respond to their disclosures about the abuse. Treatment is helpful in helping victims get in touch with their repressed rage in a healthy and constructive manner and to learn not to be afraid of their own anger.

7. *Inability to Trust*. If the child has been abused by a trusted person, problems regarding trust can be expected. Frequently, this is

linked to low self-esteem, a feeling of being betrayed, and problems in forming close, intimate relationships in the future. Trust can only begin to develop when a child gradually experiences more satisfying relationships with others.

8. *Blurred Role Boundaries and Role Confusion.* If the offender is a parent or person trusted by the child, blurred role boundaries and role confusion are magnified. In treatment it is crucial that family members assist the therapist by establishing appropriate role boundaries, by believing the child, and by treating the child as a child by being supportive and affectionate.

9. *Pseudomaturity and Failure to Complete Developmental Tasks.* The sexual stimulation and preoccupation with sex interferes with the developmental tasks of childhood and adolescence. In incest cases, the child takes on an adult position in the family, leading to role confusion. Treatment of the child, as well as the family, can help the victim relinquish adult responsibilities and assume a child role.

10. *Self-Mastery and Control.* The sexual abuse has violated the child's right to self-mastery and control. The offender gave the message, "You have no rights"; now the therapist, over and over, must give the message to the child, "You *have* rights." Family treatment is important here and the family must support the child's control of herself. Peer group support and positive peer pressure are also helpful for the child.

Other important treatment considerations include the child being able to ventilate her feelings about the sexual trauma in relation to: (1) guilt and shame, by helping the child gain a new perspective; (2) positive and negative feelings toward the offender; (3) positive and negative feelings toward the nonabusing parent; (4) feelings regarding reactions of siblings; (5) feelings about reactions of peers; (6) impact of the criminal justice system on the victim's life; (7) the parent–child relationship and family roles; (8) communication patterns within the family; (9) relationship with peers both of the same and opposite sex; and (10) sex education and birth control.

CHILD PLACEMENT AND CUSTODY ISSUES

This is a particularly crucial issue because abuse or neglect often prompts placement of the child outside his home or provokes a custody dispute. The questions are: "What impact does this have on children?"; "What is in the child's best psychological interest?"; "What are the implications for professionals in evaluation and treatment of these complex cases?"

It is invariably traumatic to the child when he is pulled between divorced parents, shuffled between foster parents, natural parents, and institutions, or left with grossly inadequate parents.

Solnit, Freud, and Goldstein (1973) state, "Each time the cycle of grossly inadequate parent/child relationship is broken, society stands to gain a person capable of becoming an adequate parent for children of the future" (p. 7). At the same time, each time adequate parent–child relationships are maintained and each time inadequate parents are rehabilitated, society gains someone who continues to have the ability to trust, to know how to develop meaningful relationships, and ultimately to be an adequate parent.

The following are criteria that are useful in determining when a child should be removed, or if the child has been removed, when the child should be returned to the family. Clearly if these criteria are not met and the child is removed and the criteria continue not to be met, the child cannot be returned to the family. After a period of time has elapsed, approximately six months to a year, if the family has shown no motivation to change, termination of parental rights should be considered.

CRITERIA USED IN CONSIDERING REMOVAL OF THE CHILD FROM THE FAMILY

1. The degree of abuse or neglect. The more severe, the more quickly the child should be removed
2. The greater the level of emotional upset, the more urgently removal should be considered.
3. The younger the child, the more vulnerable he or she is to neglect or abuse.
4. If parents are psychotic, have severe character disorders, or have handicaps that prevent them from caring adequately for the child, removal should be considered.
5. Has there been a recent crisis in the family? What are the stress levels in the family? Are they likely to increase in the immediate future?

6. The nonabusing parent's willingness and ability to protect the child is a major factor in considering removal.
7. The child's level of fear. If the child is fearful of returning home, removal may be necessary.
8. If the offender is unwilling to move out, the child may need to be removed.
9. Alcohol or drug abuse on the part of the parents.
10. A past history of abuse, with parents not accepting responsibility or services.
11. Evaluate the parents' willingness and ability to cooperate. For example, note their response to "Please take your child to the hospital this afternoon."
12. Evaluate the parents' plan to protect the child from future harm. If parents are unable to come up with an acceptable plan to ensure the child's safety, or they form a plan but show little willingness or ability to implement it, move toward removal.

CRITERIA USEFUL IN DETERMINING WHEN A CHILD SHOULD BE RETURNED TO THE HOME

These criteria should be observed over time:

1. The return should be gradual, that is, with increased and prolonged visitation over time. It is important that the interaction between parents and children be monitored so one can closely assess the behaviors and feelings of both parents and children.
2. Cooperation of parents with the treatment plan is vitally important; for example, as expressed by keeping appointments, cooperating with a visitation plan, showing a general interest and concern, and a willingness to discuss their problems.
3. Evidence shows that stress in the family has been significantly reduced and/or new coping techniques have been learned. Behaviors demonstrate that the situation has changed, that is, the parents have more than just good intentions, and there are behavioral indications that things are different.
4. The parents have developed trusting relationships with persons outside the family who they are willing and able to turn to for help, not

only for concrete services, but more importantly, for nontangible services such as parent–child problems, marital problems, and problems with feelings.
5. That parents have shown the ability to sustain good parenting over a period of time.
6. Parents take responsibility for their feelings (anger, for example) and their behavior (the abuse or neglect).

CRITERIA FOR INDICATING A NEED TO PETITION FOR TERMINATION OF PARENTAL RIGHTS

If the parent has been unwilling or unable to follow through with these criteria over a period of 6 to 12 months, termination of parental rights should be considered when:

1. Parents fail to cooperate sufficiently with a realistic, inclusive treatment plan.
2. Parents are beyond rehabilitation due to serious mental or physical conditions.
3. One parent is beyond rehabilitation and the other fails to show sufficient interest.
4. Children have developed a strong psychological attachment with foster parents who want the child permanently, while the child has become totally detached from parents who failed to follow a visitation agreement and/or comply with the total treatment plan.
5. When the child, because of special physical or emotional needs, is needy beyond the scope of the parents' abilities to provide adequate physical and emotional care and supervision for the child.
6. Parents have failed to make any contact for a period of six months to one year.
7. In the presence of one or more of the above conditions, termination may be necessary to ensure permanent placement.
8. In the case of an *adolescent*, it is often unnecessary to terminate parental rights if the child is in a permanent foster placement.
9. Particularly with older children, it is usually important to take the child's feelings and desires into consideration.

10. The level of stress in the family has not been reduced.
11. The parents have not developed trusting relationships outside the family.

Some parents are able to show adequate parenting only for sporadic periods. A child deserves good parenting over time. A parent's inability to sustain adequate parenting, in spite of the fact that they may show adequate parenting for brief periods, indicates that termination should be considered. Changes in placement are always traumatic and characterized by guilt, anger, and sadness. The child frequently feels he may have provoked the change. Separation from psychological parents has different effects depending on the child's age. The following are symptoms often seen at different developmental stages:

1. *Infant (0–18 months)*: Food refusals, digestive upsets, sleeping difficulty, irritability, and delays in development.
2. *Preschool child (1¹/₂–5 years)*: Affects those achievements which come from the intimate relationship with the stable parent figure. Regression is frequently seen, particularly in the area of verbal skills and bathroom habits.
3. *Latency-age child (6–12 years)*: Anger, depression, school problems (both academic and/or behavioral), lack of trust, withdrawal, aggressive outbursts.
4. *Adolescence*: Many will show aggression, outbursts against society, truancy, drug or alcohol use to deal with their feelings, or school problems (Gomez-Schwartz, Horowitz, and Sauzier, 1986).

GUIDELINES FOR CHILD PLACEMENT

The following criteria (Solnit et al., 1973) are useful in determining placement in contested child custody cases. In child abuse cases, a child abuse report may trigger a contested case involving custody or visitation. The following guidelines are useful in these evaluations:

1. Psychological parenthood: Differentiate between the biological, or natural parent, and psychological parenthood. Psychological parents carry on the day-to-day maintenance, support, and nurturance of the child. Clearly, this cannot be achieved by an absent or noncaring parent. In extreme cases, because of abuse or neglect, it is necessary to remove the child from unstable or unfit parents, but this remains emotionally painful for children. Clearly, it is crucial for the emotional well-being of the child to have these psychological bonds maintained.

2. Continuity of relationships and surroundings is essential for the child's emotional development. Since the need for continuity is not as important in later life, the importance is often underrated by adults. Maintaining continuity of relationships and place is extremely important for the child.

3. The child's sense of time refers to the amount of time it takes to break an old and develop a new attachment. Placement and custody arrangements, as well as a visitation plan, should reflect a child's rather than adult's sense of time. In addition, when a child is removed from an abusive home, it is necessary to maintain frequent enough visitation so that the psychological bond between parents and child is not broken down. The following indicate the amount of time a child can tolerate being away from the psychological parent:

   a. 0–2: The child can tolerate a separation of a few days to a few weeks and will then latch onto someone else.

   b. 3–5: The child can tolerate a separation of from two weeks to two months.

   c. 6–10: The child can tolerate a separation from two months to six months.

   d. 11–14: The child can tolerate a separation up to one year.

   e. 15 and up: Adolescents of this age have an adult time sense.

4. The adequacy of the parents:

   a. There are two primary considerations: the quality of time and the quantity of time. The quality of time refers to the quality of the interaction between the child and the parent, the parent's ability to get on the child's level, the parent's ability to tune in to the child's feelings. It is important for the parents not to displace their feelings on children, project their feelings on their children, or use their children as pawns in the custody struggle. The quantity of time is a bit more vague and more difficult to pin down. The younger the child the more available the parents should be to the child. It is important for parents to make a special effort to be available to the child.

   b. Clearly, abusive parents are inadequate in the sense of dealing with their feelings and behavior in a constructive fashion.

5. The way the parents have handled stress: Some parents are unable to deal with stress constructively. The parents may turn to alcohol or act out impulsively.

6. The child's desire: The older the child the more weight should be given to the child's desire. It is important to evaluate the child's purpose behind the stated desire.

7. The child's developmental stage: Children have different needs depending on their stage of development. Some parents can better meet the needs of a preschool child, others can deal best with adolescents.

8. The least detrimental alternative. There are four primary considerations here: (a) Any change in psychological parenthood or continuity is detrimental. (b) Each case should be considered only after the seven previous variables are considered. (c) The placement must maximize the child's chance for continuity and allow the child to live and grow in an atmosphere that would best meet his psychological needs. (d) It is critical to maintain the psychological bond between parent and child. In abusive families when children are removed, this bond can be maintained through regular supervised visitation. Guidelines for visitation are based on the child's sense of time. Only after parental rights are terminated should visitation cease.

IMPLICATIONS FOR PROFESSIONALS

1. Do not break the psychological tie between parents and child and between siblings unless absolutely necessary. Remember, psychological ties can exist even if parents are "unfit."

2. When it is necessary to remove the child from psychological parents for even a temporary period, such as in the case of abuse or neglect, it is crucial that the child see his parents on a regular basis. Also, the younger the child the more frequent the visits must be. Those visits should be supervised if necessary.

3. All placements, except those for brief temporary care, should be permanent if possible.
4. In the case of divorce or separation, usually one parent should have custody. Split custody is generally detrimental to children because it literally splits them up and destroys the psychological attachment between them. Joint custody is workable when parents live close to each other and have demonstrated solid communication patterns and the ability to plan constructively for the children.
5. Once a new psychological tie has developed, for example, with foster parents, it should be maintained, if at all possible.
6. The child's needs must be kept primary.

ASSESSMENT AND TREATMENT OF THE JUVENILE SEX OFFENDER

Nicholas Groth (1982) and others have identified a number of criteria which are useful in the assessment and treatment of the juvenile sex offender (under age 18):

1. The age relationship between the persons involved. If the age difference is over five years, the sexual contact is more serious, and there is a possibility that the offender is fixated at an early stage of psychosexual development.
2. The social relationship between the persons involved. Is the victim a sibling or close acquaintance of the offender or a stranger to the offender? If the victim is a stranger, there will be a greater need for inpatient treatment or incarceration.
3. What type of sexual activity is being exhibited? This should be viewed as a continuum; if the activity involves fondling, caressing, sexual touching, it is less serious than specific sexual acts such as intercourse, anal penetration, oral sex, or ritualistic sexual activity.
4. How does the sex act take place? Is it in the context of an ongoing relationship, in the context of affection, or is the child coerced, physically hurt, or abducted?
5. How persistent is the sexual activity? The more often the activity occurs, the more serious the situation, and the more need there is to at least begin treatment on an inpatient unit, or for incarceration with treatment being a part of the long-range plan.

6. Is there evidence of progression in regard to the nature or frequency of sexual activity? Is the offender progressing from fondling and caressing to specific sexual acts? If this occurs, it is more serious.
7. What is the nature of the juvenile's sexual fantasies? If these fantasies involve sex with agemates, it is not considered problematic. If they involve rape, sexual rituals, torture, or specific sexual acts with young children, the fantasies may be indicative of future behavior.
8. Are there distinguishing characteristics about the targets? Does the offender seek out a certain type of child, with certain physical characteristics? If so, it is more pathological.

TREATMENT AND REHABILITATION OF THE ADULT SEX OFFENDER

Overview

The sociological and psychological literature has yielded numerous documents and studies addressing the issue of the adult sexual offender. The literature indicates that a significant number of adult sexual offenders experienced the trauma of sexual abuse in their own childhood, resulting in anger, hostility, and frustration which were often repressed, suppressed, or redirected through pedophiliac and other incestuous types of relationships.

Clinical literature clearly argues the case that repressed anger, guilt, and anxiety result in the eventual overt expression of psychosomatic illness, impotent rage, passive–aggressive manifestations, displacement and projection onto others of what is one's own hostility and internalized aggression. Nicholas Groth (1982) has provided us with considerable information about child sexual abusers, their assessment, their treatment, and their rehabilitation.

In considering the assessment of sexual offenders, it then becomes increasingly clear that the ideology and onset of sexual abuse is most often rooted in the childhood experiences of the adult offender. It is also clear that sexual abusers exhibit few consistent personality characteristics that provide a unique profile. They do, however, tend to be manipulative and expeditious, thus diminishing the possibility that honest and accurate self-appraisal and self-disclosure can be expected. While no formal testing devices exist to measure the credibility and deviant acting-out behaviors of accused or admitted offenders, there are some psychological tests that help to infer some possibilities and uncertainties about the total picture of the suspected or admitted pedophile.

There is a growing body of evidence to suggest that males may be abused much more frequently than originally suspected. Earlier research studies in the 1980s suggested that the large majority of abused children were girls. However, studies completed by Groth (1979) and O'Brien (1980) suggest that boys may be sexually abused as commonly as girls and that this may be the most prominent in the preschool child. It should also be noted that pedophiles who abuse children outside the family more often choose males as their victims than females.

What remains clear is that the true incidence of child sexual abuse and of the factors that lead to the onset and victimization are still blurred because of unreported cases. The socioeconomic status of those involved in child sexual abuse is confounded by the fact that some agencies, in an effort to avoid controversy, do not collect specific systematic information regarding class or ethnicity of families. Upper socioeconomic level families have been able to camouflage abuse, and thus affect data reporting. What is clear, however, is that child sexual abuse occurs in every stratum of our society.

The increased reported incidence of preschool sexual abuse has helped to sensitize community agencies and national organizations to respond with both educational as well as clinical treatment interventions. What does seem clear are the following:

1. There is general agreement that children who are sexually abused are often abused by people who are close to them.
2. In incestuous relationships, brother–sister incest is considered to be among the most common. It is significantly underreported.
3. Father–daughter incest is the most documented form of incest. However, incestuous relationships involving fathers and sons as well as other male adult relatives may be more common than earlier suspected.
4. The clear majority of sexual perpetrators are males, but there is a growing amount of evidence of female perpetrators as well, especially involving very young children.

5. The forms of sexual abuse that emerge include noncontact activities such as exhibitionism; nonviolent activities such as touching; and violent activities involving contact, such as rape.

GENERAL TREATMENT STRATEGIES IN CHILD ABUSE

The literature on treatment of child abuse clearly advocates a model involving a family systems approach combined with individual psychotherapy as needed, depending on a variety of important considerations in the evaluation of the child. The methodologies that have been outlined suggest a series and process of psychotherapy involving individual therapy with the child, the perpetrator, and family members, followed by conjoint sessions and eventually group psychotherapy which may be directed or of a self-help nature. Sgroi's work involves a multimodal, multitherapist approach. Her initial efforts include the assignment of each family member to a separate individual psychotherapist. Dyadic therapy may follow and may occur simultaneously with group therapy. The rationale Sgroi (1978) offers is that group therapy is the preferred treatment of choice for most victims of child abuse. Group therapeutic activities have been strongly advocated for adolescent victims of sexual abuse and many programs refer adolescent and preadolescent individuals who have experienced abuse to peer level self-help groups. While group therapeutic interventions for younger sexually abused children have been used, this modality has been utilized less frequently. The length of treatment appears to be directly related to the age, impact, and accommodation of the experience by the victim. Long-term treatment programs are often necessary where the physical and emotional impact has been significant and where social support is not readily available to the child. Multiple incidents of sexual abuse and multiple perpetrators often confound the adjustment picture and lead to the need for more long-term intervention strategies. It is not uncommon to see individuals who have experienced multiple abuse by multiple perpetrators.

There are numerous issues which emerge in the provision of psychotherapy for individuals who have been sexually abused as children. Among the most significant issues include the emotional response of the therapist both to the abuse as well as to the sexualized behavior of the child in psychotherapy. The treatment of sexually abused children and adolescents requires well-grounded individuals with an ability to understand and develop a ready awareness of transference and countertransference issues in psychotherapy. There is a growing need for the development of clinical models and research to study the effectiveness of providing therapeutic intervention for victims of child sexual abuse. Well-controlled studies that compare the effects of numerous types of treatment models (including individual, family, and group therapeutic modalities) need to be explored, as do the benefits and impact of short-term versus long-term effects of these therapeutic models.

Models that will help family members and significant others in understanding and processing the impact of stressful experiences such as child sexual abuse and accommodating their nonjudgmental perception of the victim is especially important. Parental support groups to help cope with extrafamilial molestation are especially important.

Of significance as well is the development of educational and training programs for physicians, teachers, clinicians, and other health care professionals who have ready access to children, and who, if they are sensitized, may be able to recognize the medical, physical, psychological, and behavioral signs and symptoms of child sexual abuse. Community education in this regard becomes critically important and must be advocated as a core ingredient in understanding and resolving the complex dilemmas faced by the victim of child sexual abuse.

SEXUAL DEVIANCE AND THE OFFENDER

Efforts to understand the offender's thought process have gained considerable interest among clinicians (Groth, 1982), the court system, and clinical researchers. There appears to be a growing recognition that pedophiles tend to provide profiles that suggest cognitive, behavioral, emotional, and social characteristics unique to this population. Such traits include but are not limited to (1) low self-esteem; (2) limited social skills with noted withdrawal and isolation; (3) limited communication skills that often impair conflict resolution; (4) a history of antisocial behavior; (5) limited ability to experience remorse or guilt in the conduct of antisocial behavior; (6) clear problems in identity, the appropriateness of psychosocial and psychosexual roles in society; (7) poor impulse control and low frustration tolerance; (8) poor interpersonal relationships and inability to develop close and intimate relationships; (9) strong self-centered narcissistic and dependency needs; (10) poor core facilitative conditions including empathy, genuineness, and positive regard; (11) consistent use of projection, regression, repression, and rationalization; (12) obsessive–compulsive features including addictive levels in work, and chemical dependence; (13) limited ability to benefit from cognitive strategies aimed at changing attitudes.

It is not uncommon to find that the sexual offender has conflict with people in an authority role, nor is it unusual to note a lack of commitment in his life. Prominent personality and behavioral patterns include manipulation of individuals, self-protective avoidance patterns, and a cunning pattern of being able to lie and mislead individuals in an effort to achieve personal gain and satisfaction. It is for all of these reasons that the usual methodologies of psychotherapy may not be appropriate in the rehabilitation process of the sexual offender. Specific risk factors that suggest an individual may be a poor candidate for therapy include but are not limited to the following (Briere, 1984): (1) limited ability to learn from insight; (2) limited ability to develop consciousness of the impact of one's behavior on another person; (3) limited conscience development; (4) a history of maladaptive behavior in all spheres of life; (5) persistent use of regressive activities including alcohol and substance abuse, bizarre ritualistic behavior, and polymorphous perversion; (6) psychological diagnosis as a personality disorder, organic impairment, or a history of psychosis.

Therapeutic modalities for a sexual offender involve gradience of behavior; reward and reinforcement are deemed crucial and must be closely tied to the judicial system. For the sexual offender to benefit from a program of rehabilitation, several key ingredients must emerge as a part of the therapeutic process. These include but are not limited to the following: (1) acceptance of responsibility for one's thoughts and behaviors; (2) a developing awareness of the motivations and dynamics of pedophilia; (3) empathic understanding of the victimization process and its impact on the abused individual; (4) awareness of one's own sexuality and appropriate parameters of thinking and behavior; (5) development of skill in managing sexual and social behavior;

(6) the development of a system of social support; (7) continued commitment even in the face of relapse to the rehabilitation program.

There is considerable evidence to support the group therapeutic process as a core ingredient in the rehabilitation of sexual offenders. Group therapeutic intervention strategies tend to diffuse the potential for the offender to deny or rationalize the cognitions and behaviors. Being part of a peer group of sexual offenders presses the individual to develop a sense of honesty and openness, for it is extremely difficult to manipulate individuals who are also perpetrators. Group confrontation often serves the useful purpose of both challenging and encouraging the sexual offender to develop an awareness of self, an empathy for victims, and a plan or strategy for sound impulse control. Goals of group therapy should include: (1) recognition of the problem; (2) taking full responsibility for the problem; (3) developing self-awareness; (4) understanding the impact on the victim; (5) a motivation to change; and (6) a monitoring of the offender's behavior by law enforcement and child protective services. Treatment strategies must be directed toward affective experiential work and appropriately channeling sexual desires, needs, anger, hostility, and frustration. Assertiveness training should be offered to the offender in the development of appropriate self-assertiveness skills aimed at impulse control and appropriate behavioral patterns. Cognitive behavioral therapies should address dysfunctional patterns of thought and coping styles to develop role-specific and sexually appropriate guidelines for self-behavioral management. Finally, reality oriented directive techniques should be offered to the sexual offender to help him rechannel motives, drives, and energy into constructive, socially acceptable thoughts and behavior.

While little is known about sexual deviance, there is a growing body of information that has aided in the identification of sexually deviant individuals and their victims. Furthermore, there is a growing consciousness in our society toward encouraging greater responsibility for social, psychological, and behavioral matters on the part of individuals, and toward cognitive and behavioral life-styles acceptable to societal norms. All of this requires a coordinated effort on the part of the health care and judicial systems to help improve the quality of life not only of the offender but the victim as well.

THE ADULT NONSURVIVOR OF CHILD SEXUAL ABUSE

Introduction

Clinical research has found that as many as 44 percent of females who have received help in a clinical setting were sexually victimized as children (Finkelhor, 1979). Gold (1986) has studied the long-term effects of victimization in childhood, finding that victimized individuals differ significantly from those who have not been victimized. Of considerable significance is the coping effectiveness and social support systems available to victims of child abuse. More specifically, where a social support system, including a parent, failed to respond to the victimized child the likelihood of adjustment in adulthood was seriously compromised (Briere, 1984).

The adult nonsurvivor is therefore defined as a person who, as a result of child abuse or neglect, molestation, or sexual abuse, experiences a massive failure during adulthood in the ability to cope with life stresses and, as a result, enters into conflict with the legal system resulting in institutionalization.

The Harvard Maltreatment Project (Cichetti and Olsen, 1987) studied victims over time and concluded that adult nonsurvivors, like most other posttraumatic stress victims, were either under- or overcontrolled in their management of feelings, impulses, and arousal as adults. The findings suggested that maltreated children are at significant risk as adults for developing psychopathology. A factor analytic study (Conte, Berliner, and Schuerman, 1987) suggests that the following characteristics were significant contributors to adult nonsurvival: (1) a history of family violence, abuse, or neglect; (2) family chaos and disorganization; (3) the family's lack of acceptance and lack of interest in the juvenile; (4) low quality of family members' communication with others; and (5) self-destructive behavior.

Based on the literature review, there are clear indications of a high potential for abused children becoming adult nonsurvivors. Presented below are two case studies, each presenting an individual who was abused as a child, had difficulty in adjustment during adolescence, and emerged as an adult nonsurvivor.

CASE PRESENTATIONS

Case 1

A 22-year-old single female was convicted of the murders of five elderly people and sentenced to death. The history revealed that her early childhood years were chaotic and unpredictable. Her parents' relationship was characterized by considerable marital discord and father's violent abuse of mother, much of which was observed by the patient. They separated when the patient was about 3 years of age. During these early years, she lived in at least five foster homes, as well as living with mother and maternal grandmother. During the first seven years of her life, she was subjected to sexual abuse by a great-uncle, physical abuse, and the psychological trauma that occurs when a child witnesses abuse of a parent.

The impact of these early life experiences took a substantial toll in her ability to trust, the development of a negative self-image, and a reservoir of anger and rage, which at times was expressed outwardly and, at other times, toward herself. A sense of learned helplessness during these early years resulted in an inability to: (1) take care of herself; (2) ask for help; and (3) develop relationships. For example, at age 5, while sitting in a shed while her father was abusing her mother, she found herself killing baby chickens whom she loved. Even at this age, the intense anger was clearly evident, as well as the loss of control and violent lashing out. Her interpretation of this is interesting; she perceived the chickens wiggling off her lap and out of her hands as rejecting her. This indicates, already, at the young age of 5 years, a distorted perception of relationships, caring, and attachment, as well as loss of impulse control.

During the latency years, prior to adolescence, the patient's life continued to be chaotic and unpredictable. Her attempts to get the attention of her parents were often met with rejection or abandonment. At age 9, after searching for father for a number of months, she walked two miles and found him with a number of prostitutes. He was unable in any way to care or provide for her. By age 11, she had made a suicide attempt, in an apparent effort to get her mother's attention; she felt mother was rejecting her in favor of her stepfather. Also, during these years, there were frequent instances of truancy, fights, and substance abuse beginning about age 11 with glue- and paint-sniffing.

During the elementary school years she changed schools on twelve different occasions, averaging two changes per year. At age 7, she saw two therapists who were told about her sexual abuse. There is clear evidence from their records that she was not believed and, therefore, the family could not receive the help they needed.

By early adolescence, she was involved in regular drug and alcohol use, prostitution, and truancy. She had by then made numerous suicide attempts and, during this period, was placed in four group homes. There was little continuity in her life, a great deal of chaos, unpredictable behavior on her part, as well as unpredictable behavior on the part of those within her family. Her alcohol and drug abuse, prostitution, truancy, and suicide attempts in later life were coping mechanisms she learned while growing up in her dysfunctional family. Running away from problems, and the manipulation and exploitation of others was a way to survive and cope. She had learned that she could turn to no one, except herself, and by early adolescence, she did not have trust or faith in anyone. Furthermore, she did not have the ability to form positive, constructive relationships, no longer had trust in the helping system, and was on a self-destructive path.

At age 15, she was placed in another foster home, where she was again exploited and sexually abused. The relationships that she developed during adolescence were disastrous. She was physically abused by all the men with whom she attempted to develop a romantic relationship. Every attempt to search out her father or her mother resulted in feelings of deeper rejection and abandonment. Her level of rage and anger only escalated; she continued on a self-destructive course. By the time she was a late adolescent and into her early twenties, she was out of control. She made numerous suicide attempts, was a chronic drug abuser, engaged in aggressive acting out, and her behavior was unpredictable and self-destructive. However, upon her return home, she again experienced a continuation of the rejection she had experienced throughout her life. Two months later, she married a man she thought genuinely cared for her. However, four months later, after a marital argument, he apparently ripped up the marriage license and threw it in her face. This rejection triggered off a violent episode and the patient shot him, superficially wounding him. From this point on, her life became totally disorganized. She immersed herself in drugs, particularly cocaine. At one point, her habit reached $600 a day. She no longer had the will to live, using drugs only as a measure of surviving for another day. In the spring of 1986, after two months in jail, she returned to the streets and, during a nine-day period, used up to 15 grams a day of cocaine, and suffered sleep deprivation having gone the last four days of the period without sleep. She was at a point where her self-destructive pattern could not continue and could only be stopped by suicide or incarceration.

In April 1986, she participated with another woman in killing five elderly people, four of whom were friends, and three of whom she nurtured and cared for when they were sick. The victims were shot, burned, stabbed, and run over. The motive was confusing. She did not kill them for money or drugs, and the apparent motive came out of her rage toward others, particularly older persons, similar to those who had exploited, abused, and neglected her throughout her life. In addition, she reported to the author that her life was out of control, she was afraid of her own future, her later life. Indeed, the killings may represent a striking out at herself, an attempt to prevent herself from deteriorating and remaining out of control as she grew older.

There are a number of themes that emerge which are important in assessing the psychological components in this case:

1. The seriousness of the patient's psychological problems, going back into her childhood, are extreme. Even prior to adolescence, she was a substance abuser, had attempted suicide, and had killed animals, indicative of the rage, the distortion of perceptions regarding relationships, caring, and love.
2. There is a long history, going back to her infancy, of severe and continued family dysfunction, including inadequate parenting.
3. There is a multigenerational pattern of abuse and neglect which goes back at least four generations and has led to a sense of learned helplessness on the part of all family members, particularly in dealing with conflict, relationships, and feelings of anger and depression.
4. There is a life-long pattern, going back into early childhood, of self-destructive patterns of behavior, which include suicide, beating herself, chronic substance abuse, truancy, and involvement with abusive men.
5. There is a repeated failure on the part of various agencies and professionals to properly evaluate and treat her problems. In addition, there is evidence that she was placed, at least on two occasions, in homes where she was sexually abused.

6. The lack of stability and security throughout her life is obvious. Before age 7, she lived in at least seven homes. From ages 6 through 12, she had changed schools twelve times during the six elementary school years. During adolescence, she was in four group homes.

Case 2

A 30-year-old single male was convicted of rape and murder and sentenced to twenty-five years in prison without parole. The history reveals that his relationship with his father was characterized by distance, hostility, and criticism. There are frequent examples of father degrading him and providing a psychologically abusive environment that would make it difficult for a growing boy to form a positive identification with his father. The result was low self-esteem, a lack of confidence, and sexual identity problems.

The patient's relationship with his mother is somewhat of a paradox. Mother worked the second shift throughout most of his growing years, not being available to him in the sense of offering him supervision, support, or nurturance. This relationship was characterized by a great deal of distance on the one hand, but on the other hand, a sense of overprotectiveness and overinvolvement. There was a mutual dependency, both mother and son being dependent on each other. Throughout his latency and adolescent years, the children were left in the care of the oldest of the four children. Mother was repeatedly subjected to physical abuse by the father and reports that on one occasion she was hit up to a hundred times. By mother's count she was abused on an average of twice a month.

An additional theme which emerges in this family is the exploitation of women. Father was sexually involved with women outside the family, but, in addition, there is evidence of sexual exploitation of the daughters. For example, there apparently was a hole in the wall between the bathroom that the daughters used and a closet. This closet was used frequently by father and the patient's older brother to peek at the girls. The impact of these themes on the patient's life was considerable. There was a great deal of anger toward father as well as anger toward mother. The humiliation, degradation, and criticism from his father and the confusion brought on by the relationship with his mother—which on the one hand was distant, but on the other hand was overly protective and mutually dependent—left the patient with a reservoir of anger and confused sexual identity.

The patient is angry, lonely, and confused about his own sexuality and, in particular, how to respond to women. He has never had a normal sexual relationship and, outside of the rapes, has had sex on only one other occasion and that was with a prostitute. He was unable to form a close emotional attachment to women. During his adolescence he was a loner, particularly uncomfortable around girls, and confused about how to relate to his peers. The feelings and thoughts come out in a form of fantasy material and dreams regarding sexual conquests and being in control, leading to rape, physical abuse, and eventually murder. During his adolescence, according to members of the family, he was obsessed with detective magazines, with frequent depictions of violence, specifically physical and sexual violence toward women. This interest was the result of obsessions and fantasies that came from an effort to deal with his own inadequacy, lack of self-confidence, confusion regarding his own sexuality, and strong feelings of rejection. In a sense, these obsessions were the only way he could get close to a woman, the only way he could feel powerful and in control, and the only way he could have a sexual relationship. His confusion regarding how to relate, his fear of rejection, his reservoir of anger, and confused sexual feelings which were repressed, led to his sexual violence toward women.

During his five years in prison for rape, from ages 25 to 30, the patient was obsessed and preoccupied with violence toward women, specifically rape and murder. These obsessional thoughts, fantasies, and dreams were a frequent and repeated occurrence. The combination of repression and these obsessions made the patient extremely dangerous. Two months after his parole, the murder took place.

DISCUSSION

The adult nonsurvivor, as exemplified in these two case studies, focuses on the long-term impact of child abuse for these individuals. Maltreated and sexually abused children have been the focus of public concern (Gomez-Schwartz, Horowitz, and Sauzier, 1986), clinical assessment (DeJong, 1985), and treatment (Mrazek, 1981). National epidemiological surveys (National Center for Child Abuse and Neglect, 1984, 1986) have provided convincing evidence that child abuse and neglect may well be occurring at an alarmingly high rate. The impact on children is realized in physical, emotional, and intellectual impairment in later life.

Consistent with the pattern of "adult nonsurvival" noted in these two cases, Ressler, Burgess, Hartman, Douglas, and McCormack (1986) report that those sexually abused in childhood are significantly more likely than nonabused offenders to report the following symptoms in childhood: cruelty to animals, isolation, convulsions, cruelty to children, and assaults on adults. In addition, those men sexually abused in childhood are more likely to report experiencing the following symptoms in adolescence: sleep problems, isolation, self-mutilation, and temper tantrums. Likewise, sexually abused adolescents are more likely than nonabused offenders to report the following symptoms in adolescence: running away, fire-setting, and cruelty to animals. In adulthood, differences are noted in the areas of poor body image, sleep problems, isolation, self-mutilation, and temper tantrums. In adulthood, differences for those sexually abused in adolescence include the behavioral indicators of nightmares, daydreams, rebelliousness, and cruelty to children and adults.

MacCulloch, Snowden, Wood, and Mills (1983) observed that perpetrators of sexual abuse had sadistic fantasies from an early age and often experienced difficulties in both interpersonal and sexual relations as adults. The inability to control events in the real world moves the person into a fantasy world. This fantasy state yields thoughts of control and dominance and is bound to be reported because of the relief it provided from a pervasive sense of failure. MacCulloch and colleagues suggest that when sexual arousal is involved in the sadistic fantasy, the further shaping and content of the fantasy may be viewed on a classical conditioning model; the strong tendency to progression of sadistic fantasies may then be understood in terms of habituation.

ADULT ADJUSTMENT TO CHILD ABUSE

Gold (1986) explored the relation between the experience of childhood victimization and adult functioning. One hundred and three adult women who were victimized as children or adolescents served as subjects, and eighty-eight women who were not victimized served as controls. Members of both groups completed a questionnaire about their present social, psychological, and sexual functioning. Sexually victimized women also provided information about their victimization experiences. Victimized women differed significantly from nonvictims on the following measures: (1) childhood family and social experiences; (2) adult attributional style; and (3) level of depression, psychological distress, self-esteem, and sexual problems. Results of this study suggested that the sexually victimized women's adult functioning was related most strongly to their attributional style for negative events. Perception of the victimization experience and quality of social support were also important factors related to adult functioning.

While Briere (1984) and Finkelhor (1979) suggest that as many as one of every four girls in North America may be sexually victimized before she reaches adulthood, recent studies (Veltkamp, Miller, Kearl, Barlow-Elliott, and Bright, 1992) note close to half of all women who have received help in clinical settings were sexually victimized as children. While most studies have found that some victims exhibit no specific pattern of response to childhood sexual abuse, certain symptoms and posttraumatic stress are commonly observed (Miller and Feibelman, 1987). These include depression, low self-esteem, guilt feelings, and interpersonal difficulties characterized by feelings of isolation and difficulty in trusting others (Sgroi, 1982; Landis, 1985; Veltkamp and Miller, 1989). Symptoms such as these were clearly evident in both cases summarized.

In summary, the long-term effects of child sexual abuse in adults suggest the following: (1) There tends to be clear evidence of self-destructive behaviors in victimized as opposed to nonvictimized patients. In the two case studies there is clear evidence of self-destructive behaviors emerging in adolescence and adulthood. These are seen both in suicidal and homicidal activities. (2) Women who have been abused show significant adjustment difficulties in adulthood with problems related to both interpersonal and sexual relationships with males and females. More specifically, it appears that incest victims carry hostile feelings toward significant adults in their adulthood. In the first case the impact of homicidal activity against the five adults is a clear indication of this. (3) Sexually abused female children as adults also seek adult relationships which involve sexual abuse. Herein the cases reveal that two of three male partners in Case 1 were physically abusive to the adult nonsurvivor and in the case of the husband who was not abusive, a violent response was realized when she shot him. (4) The most significant diagnostic profile for adults who are physically and sexually abused as children includes the following symptomatology: depression, self-destructive behavior, anxiety, and traumatic stress; a feeling of isolation; poor self-esteem, a tendency toward revictimization; substance abuse; difficulties in trusting others; and sexual maladjustment in adulthood.

It is clear from the research in the Harvard Maltreatment Project (Cicchetti and Olsen, 1987) that most maltreated children have experienced more than one distinct type of maltreatment, that siblings of maltreated children are highly likely to be maltreated, even though their maltreatment experience may not be legally documented; that different types of maltreatment have differential impact on various domains of development; and that the vast majority of maltreated children have insecure attachment relationships with their caregivers and guardians.

10

The Court Report and Courtroom Testimony

The expert testimony of health care professionals has a profound impact on the lives of both plaintiffs and defendants. In the case of family violence, including child abuse and child sexual abuse, there is a growing body of scientific evidence addressing the issues of diagnostic significance and the predictive accuracy of health care professionals in providing expert testimony. It is the purpose of this chapter to review the literature on and characteristics of this most important component of the broad spectrum of services provided in the course of dealing with family violence.

The value of professional clinical judgment is well recognized, even though the interrater reliability between clinicians can vary. Stoller (Stoller and Geerstma, 1975) found that when the judgments of health care professionals were compared with those of lay personnel, highly experienced clinicians who viewed the same psychiatric interview could not agree on the patient's diagnosis, intrapsychic motivations and conflicts, or conscious and unconscious feelings. There appears to be a slight advantage for the lay person, but most often the groups perform similarly. When lay interviewers are allowed to use standardized questions, the information produced is of equal or greater validity than that produced by psychiatrists conducting interviews in their preferred manner. Carkhuff and Berenson (1968) have found that students and professionals working from a common data base experienced comparable difficulty in predicting violent behavior and weighted data similarly. The similarity in data interpretations suggested that both groups relied on common assumptions about potentially violent individuals and also that they shared cultural stereotypes with respect to those individuals. Similar studies have suggested that specific cues can be used and professionals and lay persons show little difference in being able to recognize such cues in outcome comparative studies. This leads to the suggestion that when judgment is based on conventional beliefs or stereotypes rather than empirical knowledge, health care professionals are unlikely to surpass lay persons in quality of clinical judgments made.

Focused research relating to the performance of health care professionals warrants familiarity with legal standards for expert status. The two critical guidelines appear to include that the expert must be able to state opinions with reasonable certainty. Reasonable certainty encompasses both the issues pertinent to the case and also the quality of the measures and assessments used. A second marker is that the health care professional should be able to assist the court in achieving a valid conclusion that enhances the court's understanding of the issues and pathology involved. All health care professionals are limited by their competence and by the state of their science. Actuarial methods which are based solely on empirically established frequencies consistently equal or outperform both professional clinical judgments and lay judgments. It has been demonstrated over a twenty-five-year period that there is a consistency with respect to the superiority of actuarial over clinical judgment. There is evidence to suggest that when actuarial methods and more specific well-established indices such as the Minnesota Multiphasic Personality Inventory (MMPI) are incorporated into clinical judgment, that such indices improve the accuracy of the analyses made.

Recent research methods that compare subjective impressions to objective measures of data utilization yield several discrepancies. Health care professionals may experience overconfidence because their view of both their ability to make successful judgments and their decision-making processes is that they are based on a complex configural analysis or data integration. Clinicians who commonly propose that their conclusions rest on a careful weighing of many variables, actually demonstrate that only a few variables, perhaps two or three, exert a significant impact on the decisions made. Faust (1985), in a review of several studies, concludes that no health care professional can begin to manage the complexity of cognitive operations required, provide expert testimony, and make accurate judgments in the courtroom setting. However, the role of expert testimony, even with the limitations noted, will continue to be an important and vital aspect of our judicial system. Within that context it becomes imperative that the health care professions generate ethical and competent experts for testimony to meet the current demands of our legal system. The evaluation must be case specific, must involve specific evaluation strategies, and answer specific questions.

After completing an evaluation, the court asks for a report of the evaluation process. After the report is submitted to the court, the clinician may be asked to give a deposition or to appear in court personally to give testimony.

THE COURT EVALUATION

The Evaluation Should Be Case Specific

1. In custody cases, the clinician must see all parties involved and ascertain the psychological bond, continuity, where the child is more comfortable, and the adequacy of the parents; and evaluate all allegations made against each parent.
2. In evaluating a victim of sexual abuse, the use of drawings and anatomical dolls is a necessary part of the assessment.
3. It is necessary to evaluate whether the perpetrator of sexual abuse is fixated or regressed. In addition, if treatment is to be effective, he has to be motivated and willing to accept responsibility for his feelings and his behavior.

The Court Report

Once a thorough evaluation has been conducted, a report detailing findings and conclusions should be written. The evaluation report should be no more than two to three pages in length. It should include who was seen and when, specific questions that are going to be answered, a brief history, a brief review of the current situation, primary themes that emerged during the evaluation and recommendations for the court.

After the clinical evaluation has been completed, three possible scenarios emerge. First, based upon the findings of the evaluation, the alleged abuse may not be substantiated. In this case, a decision must be made regarding whether treatment services continue to be warranted or necessary. A second possible scenario is where the evaluation findings lend support to the abuse allegation, but the prosecuting attorney does not feel there is sufficient evidence to pursue the allegations in a criminal trial. In this case, the evaluator may still believe the child has been victimized. Thus, one proceeds by offering and providing treatment services to the victim and family. In the third scenario, the evaluation findings substantiate the abuse allegations, and the prosecuting attorney believes there is sufficient evidence to proceed legally. In this case, whether or not the perpetrator is found guilty, treatment services need to be offered to the victim and family. A determination has to be made as to whether the family can be united or whether other custody or placement arrangements are better suited for the family and the victim's needs. The following is one example of how to write a court report. The report is divided into five paragraphs:

1. "In response to the court's request for an evaluation in this case." In this initial paragraph, state who was seen, when they were seen, and one or two specific questions that you attempt to answer in the course of the evaluation.
2. "This history reveals." Spell out important dates and other information that is pertinent in the history.
3. "The current situation reveals." Spell out important aspects of the current situation, such as where people live, schools they attend, important relationships, and important dates.
4. "The following themes emerged as important in the course of this evaluation." Spell out specific themes including criteria and other issues that are relevant in helping you come to your conclusions regarding the best custodial parent, best visitation plan, or best placement at this time; whether the child has been abused, what is

the best placement at this time and best treatment plan; an assessment of allegations made against the parents.

5. "Based on this evaluation I make the following recommendations for the court's consideration." Go back to the one or two questions outlined in paragraph 1 and briefly state specific recommendations, making your report free of psychological jargon and easy for the court to understand.

COURTROOM TESTIMONY

The following comes from Brodsky (1980) and Caulfield (1978), as well as our own experiences in the courtroom.

General Considerations

1. The definition of an expert witness is anyone who has had experience or training in a designated field.
2. It is crucial to have confidence in yourself and your evaluation.
3. Do not increase your fees per unit of time for court work as this makes you vulnerable in the court room. Include all planning, preparation, evaluation, discussion with attorneys, depositions, and testimony in your fee.
4. Evaluate the possibility that parents fake well when dealing with custody or abuse cases, or fake badly, for example, in personal injury cases. It is often helpful to see all family members to help get a more objective view, rather than only interviewing the victim.
5. You will be asked questions regarding your qualifications. Include your professional training, any additional training, licensure, workshops you have given, consultations, academic appointments, professional organizations, all publications and research.

PREPARATION FOR COURT

1. Do not look sloppy or flamboyant. Dress in conservative clothes.

2. Instruct the attorney to ask specific questions to trigger your memory.
3. Prepare adequately. Don't memorize the testimony. Be spontaneous; such responses are more believable. Use visual aids where appropriate.
4. Review Jay Ziskin (1981), who addresses how to cross-examine mental health professionals.
5. Prepare for testimony by acquainting yourself with the following:

   a. Be knowledgeable of five or six studies that are current and that address diagnostic issues.
   b. Know with accuracy the social, work, family, and health history of the client.
   c. Make detailed records of all contacts with client and attorneys.
   d. Review clearly all diagnostic data and be clear on your interpretation of all testing materials.

6. Do not bring a case record of the medical history into the courtroom but know what is in the record. Many times there are inconsistencies in your personal record and a good attorney will try to use this against you.
7. Assess whether the child's story is based on fantasy, something he saw in a movie or a magazine, or whether it is something that really happened.

BEHAVIOR IN THE COURTROOM

1. Be likable and humble; these behaviors are more believable.
2. It is important to be clear, specific, precise and articulate. Do not use empty adjectives, direct quotations, words that dramatize. Do not be repetitious.
3. Be sincere and dignified, but warm. Make eye contact with the judge and jury.
4. Never use slang or psychological jargon. When technical terms are used, define each word clearly and simply for the court.
5. Answer questions that are asked; if you don't know, don't guess, say you don't know. Saying you don't know makes you more believable.

6. Allow the attorney to develop your testimony.
7. Be aware of how you handle your anxiety. For example, some individuals slouch down when they are anxious, or speak too loud or too soft. These behaviors make the witness less credible.

Specific Issues in Cross-Examination

Often an attorney will present you with what he or she describes as new information in an effort to get you to contradict yourself and thereby weaken your testimony. Be aware that this is a strategy used by the attorney. How you respond is critical if the court is going to find your testimony believable. The following are examples of specific cross-examination:

1. The hypothetical question: "Would your opinion be different if you knew that . . ." Be relaxed and believe that if your evaluation was valid before, it is valid now. Either respond to surprise information as hypothetical, say you don't know, or go back to your evaluation.
2. Another example: If an attorney asks, "If she read some book on how to show symptoms of acute stress disorder and knew what symptoms to report, etc.," you should respond in a relaxed, matter-of-fact manner, remember you have evaluated whether the patient was faking, stand by what you've done, then state, "It is my opinion that she . . ."
3. Attorneys often try to get you to testify on information outside your evaluation; for example, to testify regarding other people's testimony, other theories, books, articles. Always stick to your own evaluation.
4. Sometimes attorneys attack you personally or attack your entire profession. This is an indication that they are desperate.
5 When you are using specific children's drawings in the courtroom, the attorney may ask, "Are there other possible interpretations of these drawings?" Remember that if you say "no," you look naive, but if you say "yes," the attorney will ask you for other possible interpretations, thereby weakening your previous testimony. The best answer is to say, "This is my interpretation . . ." and explain your interpretation of the drawing to the court.

6. An attorney states, "Do you believe everything a child tells you?"
    If you say "yes," you look naive, but if you say "no," then the
    attorney will ask you to explain for the court those instances when
    you wouldn't believe a child. If you answer this, you are weakening
    your previous testimony. Avoid this problem by saying, "I believe
    this child because . . ."
7. Regarding a child who has possibly been sexually abused, an attor-
    ney may state, "Isn't it possible that she was reporting a fantasy
    or something she saw on TV?" Respond that in the course of your
    evaluation you always take fantasy and other experiences the child
    has had into account, and in your opinion this child is reporting
    what actually happened.
8. Cross-examination is critically important. Ziskin suggests six key
    areas that apply to the credibility of psychology. These include the
    following:
    a. Psychology is an inexact science and lacks a systematic theoret-
        ical framework, resulting in frequent disagreements among
        practitioners.
    b. Diagnoses in the mental health field, including those made by
        psychologists and psychiatrists, are very problematic, subject
        to low reliability validity, and interrater reliability.
    c. Most diagnostic measures can be criticized for *reliability* and
        validity issues.
    d. Clinical interviews are subject to several problems and may be
        influenced by the bias and prejudice of the evaluator.
    e. There are specific errors, omissions, short-cuts, and biases in
        the evaluation and testimony of the expert.
    f. The credentials of the mental health professionals are inade-
        quate or not appropriate to the case in question.

EXPERT WITNESS QUALIFICATION STATEMENT

The following components should be addressed, summarized, and
clearly understood for the health care professional who is an expert
witness. Each of the factors should be known to both the attorney and
to the witness.

1. Name
2. Occupation/profession
3. Present practice of profession
4. Length of time in profession
5. Location of office
6. License to practice
7. Date of license
8. Professional degrees
9. Dates and schools where degrees have been obtained
10. Additional training
11. Dates of training
12. Nature, duration, and place of training
13. Professional associations
14. Articles published
15. Teaching/training experience
16. Number of investigations/evaluations
17. Number of cases (families and children) in practice
18. Previous qualification as expert witness
19. Date and court where you appeared as an expert witness

TESTIMONY IN CHILD ABUSE

There is convincing evidence from numerous sources that the trauma for the child witness is greatest when the child is a victim of physical or sexual abuse. Roland Summit (1983) of Harvard-UCLA has introduced a sexual abuse accommodation syndrome, a series of stages or phases which face the child victim of trauma. Health care professionals have recently introduced a series of changes in courtroom procedures that show a specific sensitivity to the feelings commonly experienced by child witnesses, the most significant of which is the fear of retaliation by the perpetrator. Such court procedures that have been proposed include but are not limited to the following:

1. The use of a skilled interviewer who puts the child at ease and allows rapport to develop between the child and the evaluator.
2. The use of a multidisciplinary team including health care professionals, prosecutors, and law enforcement officials.

3. The use of diagnostic evaluation measures including human figure drawings, anatomically correct dolls, and fables that will allow younger children to recount the events through displacement and more easily facilitate discussion of the traumatic events that have occurred.

4. Allowing the child to testify via closed circuit television has raised considerable objections because of the accused's right under the Sixth Amendment to be confronted with the witnesses against him.

5. The introduction of a videotape of the child's testimony made at an earlier point for presentation in the court proceedings is seen as an effective method. It reduces the number of times the child has to relive the experience while yielding a clear account of the child's testimony. What is most clear is that to ask a child to provide testimony in an adult environment creates several barriers. The legal system must be sensitive to considering the developmental age and physiological needs of the child and his or her intellectual competency to provide testimony in an adult environment. There are numerous studies that have demonstrated that children have more difficulty than adults in narrating their observations and are more likely to make errors or omit important facts. Some researchers have suggested that the difficulty results from the child's lack of relevant prior knowledge that helps them to organize elements in a cohesive whole or relate one set of events to another. Loftus and Davis-Graham (1984) further suggest from their research studies that children have greater difficulty in retrieving information from long-term memory resulting in challenges to their competency to testify.

GUIDELINES FOR TESTIMONY

Both mental health and the legal professions have continued to search for guidelines which can assist in making better judgments about the child's role in testimony and in accurately conveying clinically relevant information in issues relevant to the legal system. A series of guidelines (American Academy of Child and Adolescent Psychiatry, 1988) are defined for use by both clinicians and legal experts in evaluating child sexual abuse. They include, but are not limited to, the following:

1. The competency of the child to testify.
2. The credibility of the child's allegations.
3. Whether the child is emotionally disturbed and in need of treatment.
4. Whether the child will be able to cope with the stress of giving testimony, or whether alternatives be considered, such as videotaped testing or closed circuit television with the victim in the judge's chambers.
5. Whether the child would be further damaged psychologically by giving testimony.
6. Ensuring that the child receives psychological preparation for the court appearance.
7. To further evaluate if it is in the child's best interests to have contact with the alleged perpetrator prior to court proceedings.

Operationally, the following may be extremely beneficial in making decisions relevant to an evaluation of the child:

1. The child's level of intellectual functioning as measured by a standardized intellectual test battery.
2. The child's level of ego functioning and psychosocial dynamics as measured by the use of human figure drawings, anatomically correct dolls, and play therapy.
3. The child's response to the use of clinically relevant fables and projective measures; for example, the ways in which the child identifies with the characters in the fables.

The courts, as well as social agencies, must address the issue of credibility in the reporting of child sexual abuse. In both court testimony and in the reporting of data to social agencies, there are guidelines relating to this issue (Miller and Veltkamp, 1989b). The guidelines regarding credibility should include the following:

1. Consistency in the details defined by the child's description. The more detailed the description, the more credible the event.
2. Where more than one child reports consistency in the pattern of behavior of the abusing parent, the greater the likelihood that the incidents have occurred.

3. The consistency with which the child's revelations are corroborated by other adults or children or supported by means of fables, human figure drawings, or thematic apperception testing materials.
4. The level of continuity between the child's level of affect and the perception of the emotional impact of the event or events. The greater the continuity, the more credible the child.

It is not unlikely that abused children may be both fearful and confused over the experiences that they have had and be intimidated as well by the potential for future sexual and/or physical abuse. The process of disclosure creates a profound impact on the child and it must be realized that the child may feel both entrapped and helpless in the revelation of these experiences. It is not uncommon for the sexually abused child to consider reversing the revelation of materials, mainly because of ambivalence, the dedication and obligation to preserve the family, or pressure from family members.

SOURCES OF STRESS IN COURTROOM TESTIMONY

When sexual abuse cases are prosecuted, for the child and family, the court process can be as much of a crisis as the actual assault. Victims and their families display a multitude of intense reactions in going through the court process.

The sources of stress which may impact the child during the court process include:

- Revealing sexually intimate details;
- The overall courtroom atmosphere;
- Repeated interrogations;
- Cross-examination by the perpetrator's attorney;
- Having to face the perpetrator, who is often a known and trusted adult;
- Guilt and fear of abusing parent going to jail;
- Family conflict, pressures, and humiliation;
- Guilt and fear of the family breaking up.

In addition, the psychological effects which result from the stresses associated with the legal system can be substantial and may include a sense of hopelessness, a sense of insignificance, feelings of guilt, fear, distrust, embarrassment, and humiliation.

Society, through its system of administering justice, requires that a person charged with an offense has a right to trial, to be confronted and to be cross-examined by those who have brought the charges. Unfortunately, police and prosecutors may have little training in non-damaging methods of interviewing children and tend to use the same adversarial approaches appropriate for adults.

If the jurisdiction requires the child's testimony, or the family or victim decides to prosecute, the therapist should prepare them for the court experience. The therapist's goal in the court process is to help maintain a tolerable stress level for the victim and family and to always keep the child's best interests in mind. The therapist's tasks may include:

1. Providing psychological support;
2. Interpreting the routine courtroom protocol;
3. Neutralizing the stressful feelings that may develop between the victim and people encountered in the court process.

Factors that increase stress for young witnesses and their families have been identified as including the following:

1. The public setting of the courtroom and presence of the media.
2. Being unfamiliar with a courtroom and court personnel.
3. Being sequestered and seeing no familiar faces in the court.
4. Confusing questions under cross-examination and/or the use of legal or technical jargon by the attorneys.
5. Seeing the defendant.
6. Long delays and postponements.

Factors which decrease stress include:

1. Family and/or familiar persons present throughout the preparation process.
2. Providing an overview of the court process.
3. Visiting and walking around an empty courtroom.

4. Presence of a parent or supportive familiar person in the courtroom.
5. Attorneys using language that is clear and simple.
6. Refreshing the victim's memory of the evaluation.
7. The child testifying in the judge's chambers via closed-circuit television.

11

Future Dimensions in Child Abuse

This volume has tried to provide the reader with the concepts, principles, and methods with which to diagnose, treat, and perhaps alleviate the condition we have come to know as child abuse. Child abuse knows no limits to socioeconomic level, race, creed, color, or national origin. Of all the developmental and psychosocial problems faced by children in our world, child abuse, sexual abuse, and maltreatment are the most destructive to the child who experiences it, to the caregiver who commits it, and to the society that allows it to take place (Veltkamp and Miller, 1991).

In addressing a multiplicity of issues related to child abuse and maltreatment, this volume has attempted to explore the critical elements at issue. It is clear that most clinical researchers agree that education is an essential component in addressing the recognition and prevention of child abuse and neglect. From the perspective of education, the following recommendations are suggested:

1. It is essential that public education programs be funded to acquaint all levels of society with the means to understand and recognize

this problem, and the steps by which one can do something about it.

2. Greater knowledge about family stress, its origin, and impact can be extremely important in preventing child abuse and child sexual abuse, and reducing its impact when it does occur.

3. A multidisciplinary undergraduate and graduate curriculum in universities must be established to address the needs of educating professional health care providers and clinical researchers in the issues relating to child abuse and neglect.

4. In-service education and training for medical- and health-related specialists would be a tremendous enhancement toward achieving early recognition and appropriate response patterns in dealing with child abuse and neglect.

5. Clinical research has the potential for yielding enormously useful information on the prevention and treatment of child abuse and neglect.

References

Adams-Tucker, C. (1984), Early treatment of child incest victims. *Amer. J. Psychother.*, 38:505–516.

American Academy of Child and Adolescent Psychiatry (1988), *Guidelines for the Clinical Evaluation of Child and Adolescent Sexual Abuse*. Policy Statement, Washington, DC.

American Humane Association (1988), *Highlights of Official Child Neglect and Abuse Reporting*. Denver, CO: American Humane Association.

American Psychiatric Association (1987), *Diagnostic and Statistical Manual of Mental Disorders*, 3rd ed., rev. (DSM-III-R). Washington, DC: American Psychiatric Press.

Boat, B. W., & Everson, M. D. (1986), Using Anatomical Dolls: Guidelines for Interviewing Young Children in Sexual Abuse Investigations, Hylands Anatomical Dolls, Inc., California.

Briere, J. (1984), The effects of childhood sexual abuse on later psychological functioning: Defining a post-sexual abuse syndrome. Paper presented at the Third National Conference on Sexual Victimization of Children. Children's Hospital National Medical Center, Washington, DC.

Brodsky, S. L. (1980), *Expert Witness Testimony and Tactics*, Audio Tape Series. Proseminar, Inc.

Burgess, A., Holmstrom, L., & McCausland, M. (1978), Counseling young victims and their families. In: *Sexual Assault of Children and Adolescents*, ed. A. W. Burgess, A. N. Groth, & L. L. Holmstrom. Lexington, MA: D. C. Heath.

——— ——— ——— (1979), Child sexual assault by a family member: Divided loyalty. *Victimol.*, 2:236–250.

——— Laszlo, A. (1976), When the prosecutrix is a child: The victim consultant in cases of sexual assault. In: *Victims and Society*. Washington, DC: Visage Press.

Carkhuff, R., & Berenson, R. (1968), *Helping and Human Relations*. New York: Macmillan Publishers.

Caulfield, B. A. (1978), *The Legal Aspects of Protective Services for Abused and Neglected Children*. Washington, DC: U.S. Department of Health, Education, & Welfare.

Cicchetti, D., & Olsen, K. (1987), The developmental psychopathology of child maltreatment. In: *Handbooks of Developmental Psychopathology*, ed. M. Lewis & S. Miller. New York: Plenum.

Conte, J. R., Berliner, L., & Schuerman, J. R. (1987), *The Impact of Sexual Abuse on Children*. Final Technical Report. Washington, DC: National Institute of Mental Health, Project Number MH 37133.

DeJong, A. R. (1985), The medical evaluation of sexual abuse in children. *Hosp. Commun. Psychiatry*, 36:503–509.

Despert, J. J. (1943), A therapeutic approach to the problem of stuttering in children. *Nerv. Child.*, 2/2:134–147.

Dinkmeyer, D., & McKay, G. D. (1982), *Systematic Training for Effective Parenting*. Circle Pines, MN: American Guidance Service.

Dohrenwend, B. S., Krasnoff, L., Askenasy, A. R., & Dohrenwend, B. P. (1978), Exemplification of a method for scaling life events: The PERI life events scale. *J. Health & Soc. Behav.*, 18:134–139.

Drucker, J., & Shapiro, C. (1979), First scribbles: The emergence of an ego function. *J. Amer. Acad. Child Psychiatry*, 18/4:620–646.

Faust, D. (1985), Declarations versus investigations: The case for the special reasoning abilities and capabilities of the expert witness in psychology and psychiatry. *J. Psychiatry & Law*, 13:237–241.

Finch, S. (1962), Criteria for Assessing Psychological Harm in Children. Typescript.

Finkelhor, D. (1979), *Sexually Victimized Children*. New York: Free Press.

Giaretto, H. (1981), A comprehensive child abuse treatment program. In: *Sexually Abused Children and Their Families*, ed. P. B. Mrazek & C. H. Kempe. New York: Pergamon Press.

Gold, E. (1986), Long-term effects of sexual victimization in childhood: An attributional approach. *J. Consult. Clin. Psychol.*, 54/4:471–475.

Gomez-Schwartz, B., Horowitz, J., & Sauzier, M. (1986), Severity of emotional stress among sexually abused preschool, school-age and adolescent children. *Hosp. & Commun. Psychiat.*, 36:509–512.

Goodenough, F. (1926), *Measurement of Intelligence by Drawings*. New York: Harcourt, Brace & World.

Goodwin, J., McCarty, T., DiVasto, P. (1982), Physical and sexual abuse of the children or adult incest victims. In: *Sexual Abuse: Incest Victims and Their Families*, ed. J. Goodwin. Boston: MA: John Wright-PSG.

——— Sahd, D., & Rada, R. T. (1982), False accusations and false denials of incest. In: *Sexual Abuse: Incest Victims and Their Families*, ed. J. Goodwin. Boston, MA: John Wright-PSG.

——— Willett, A., & Jackson, R. (1982), Medical care for male and female incest victims and their parents. In: *Sexual Abuse: Incest Victims and Their Families*, ed. J. Goodwin. Boston, MA: John Wright-PSG.

Green, B. L., Lindy, J. D., & Wilson, J. P. (1985), Conceptualizing post-traumatic stress disorder: A psychosocial framework. In: *Trauma and Its Wake: The Study and Treatment of Post-Traumatic Stress Disorder*, ed. C. R. Figley. New York: Brunner/Mazel, pp. 53–69.

Groth, A. N. (1979), *Men Who Rape: The Psychology of the Offender*. New York: Plenum.

——— (1982), The incest offender. In: *Handbook of Clinical Intervention in Child Sexual Abuse*, ed. S. Sgroi. Lexington, MA: Lexington Books.

Hjorth, C. W., & Harway, M. (1981), The body image of physically abused and normal adolescents. *J. Clin. Psychiatry*, 37:863–866.

Holmes, T. H., & Rahe, R. H. (1967), Social readjustment rating scale. *J. Psychosom. Res.*, 11:213–218.

Hultsch, D. R., & Plemons, J. K. (1979), Life events and life-span development. In: *Life-Span Development and Behavior*, ed. P. B. Baltes & O. G. Brim, Jr. New York: Academic Press.

Janoff-Bulman, R. (1985), The aftermath of victimization: Rebuilding shattered assumptions. In: *Trauma and Its Wake: The Study and Treatment of Post-Traumatic Stress Disorder*, ed. C. R. Figley. New York: Brunner/Mazel, pp. 15–35.

Kempe, C. H., Silverman, F. N., Steele, B. F., Droegemuller, W., & Silver, H. K. (1962), The battered child syndrome. *J.A.M.A.*, 181:17–24.

Klepsh, M., & Logie, L. (1982), *Children Draw and Tell: An Introduction to the Projective Uses of Children's Human Figure Drawings*. New York: Brunner/Mazel.

Koppitz, E. (1968), *Psychological Evaluation of Children's Human Figure Drawings*. New York: Grune & Stratton.

Kreiger, M. J., Rosenfeld, A. A., & Gordon, A. (1980), Problems in psychotherapy of children with histories of incest. *Amer. J. Psychother.*, 34:81–88.

Landis, J. (1985), Experiences of 500 children with adult sexual deviations. *Psychiat. Quart. Suppl.*, 30:95.

Lazoritz, S. (1990), Whatever happened to Mary Ellen? *Child Abuse & Neglect*, 14/2:143–149.

Loftus, E., & Davis-Graham, M. (1984), Distortions in the memory of children. *J. Soc. Issues*, 40/2:51–67.

MacCulloch, M. J., Snowden, P. R., Wood, P., & Mills, H. E. (1983), Sadistic fantasy, sadistic behavior, and offending. *Brit. J. Psychiatry*, 143:20–29.

Maultsby, M. (1984), *You and Your Emotions*. Lexington, MA: Rational Self-Help Books.

McCann, I. L., Pearlman, L. A., Sakheim, D. K., & Abrahamson, D. J. (1988), Assessment and treatment of the adult survivor of childhood sexual abuse within a schema framework. In: *Vulnerable Populations: Evaluation and Treatment of Sexually Abused Children and Adult Survivors*, Vol. 1, ed. S. M. Sgroi. Lexington, MA: Lexington Books, pp. 77–101.

McCann, L., Sakheim, D., & Abrahamson, D. (1988), Trauma and victimization: A model of psychologial adaptation. *Counseling Psychologist*, 16/4:531–594.

Miller, T. W., ed. (1989), *Stressful Life Events*. Madison, CT: International Universities Press.

——— Feibelman, N. D. (1987), Traumatic stress disorder: Diagnostic and clinical issues in psychiatry. In: *Stressful Life Events*, ed. T. W. Miller. Madison, CT: International Universities Press, 1989.

——— Veltkamp, L. J. (1986), Use of fables in clinical assessment. *Child Psychiatry & Hum. Develop.*, 16:590–596.

——— ——— (1989a), Use of fables in clinical assessment of contested child sexual abuse. *Child Psychiatry & Hum. Develop.*, 16/4:126–132.

―――― ―――― (1989b), Effects of child sexual abuse: The adult nonsurvivor. *J. Ky. Med. Assn.*, 87:120–123.

―――― ―――― (1989c), Effects of multigenerational sexual abuse in rural America. *Internat. J. Fam. Psychiatry*, 9:259–275.

Mischel, W. (1968), *Personality and Assessment*. New York: John Wiley.

Mrazek, P. B. (1981), Special problems in the treatment of child sexual abuse. In: *Sexually Abused Children and Their Families*, ed. P. B. Mrazek & C. H. Kempe. New York: Pergamon Press.

Murstein, B. I. (1961), Assumptions, adaptation level and projective techniques. *Percept. & Motor Skills*, 12:106–125.

National Center for Child Abuse and Neglect (1981), *Study Findings: National Study of the Incidence and Severity of Child Abuse and Neglect*. Office of Human Development Services, Administration for Children, Youth, and Families, Children's Bureau, National Center for Child Abuse and Neglect, Washington, DC.

―――― (1982), *Executive Summary: National Study of the Incidence and Severity of Child Abuse and Neglect*. Washington, DC: U.S. Government Printing Office.

―――― (1984), *Executive Summary: National Study of the Incidence and Severity of Child Abuse and Neglect*. Washington, DC: U.S. Government Printing Office.

―――― (1986), *Study Findings: National Study of the Incidence and Severity of Child Abuse and Neglect*. Washington, DC: U.S. Government Printing Office.

Nunnally, J. (1978), *Psychometric Theory,* 2nd ed. New York: McGraw-Hill.

O'Brien, S. (1980), *Child Abuse: A Crying Shame*. Provo, Utah: Brigham Young University Press.

Ressler, R. K., Burgess, A. W., Hartman, C. R., Douglas, J. E., & McCormack, A. (1986), Murderers who rape and mutilate. *J. Interpers. Viol.*, 1:273–287.

Russell, D. (1983), The prevalence of intrafamilial and extrafamilial sexual abuse of female children. *Child Abuse & Neglect*, 7:56–63.

Sgroi, S. M. (1978), Child sexual assault: Some guidelines for intervention and assessment. In: *Sexual Assault of Children and Adolescents*, ed. A. W. Burgess, A. N. Groth, & L. L. Holmstrom. Lexington, MA: D. C. Heath.

―――― ed. (1982), *Handbook of Clinical Intervention in Child Sexual Abuse*. Lexington, MA: Lexington Books.

―――― Porter, F. S., & Blick, L. C. (1982), Validation of child sexual abuse. In: *Handbook of Clinical Intervention in Child Sexual Abuse*, ed. S. M. Sgroi. Lexington, MA: Lexington Books.

Solnit, A., Freud, A., & Goldstein, J. (1973), *Beyond the Best Interests of the Child*. New York: Macmillan.

Sorkin, D., & Durphy, M. (1982), *Learning to Live without Violence*. San Francisco: Volcano Press.

Stemper, C. J. (1980a), Art therapy: A new use in the diagnosis and treatment of sexually abused children. In: *Sexual Abuse of Children: Selected Readings*. Washington, DC: NCCAN, pp. 54–63.

Stoller, R., & Geerstma, D. (1975), *Perversion: The Erotic Form of Hatred*. New York: Pantheon.

Sturner, R., & Rothbaum, F. (1980), The effects of stress on children's human figure drawings. *J. Clin. Psychol.*, 36:324–331.

Summit, R. (1983), The child sexual abuse accommodation syndrome. *Child Abuse & Neglect*, 7:177–193.

Thomas, J. (1980), Yes, you can help a sexually abused child. *RN*, 43:23–29.

Veltkamp, L. J., & Miller, T. W. (1984), Psychodiagnostic use of fables. Department of Psychiatry, University of Kentucky. Typescript.

――― ――― (1988), Effects of family mediation on disputed child custody in divorce. *Internat. J. Fam. Psychiatry*, 9/4:377–430.

――― ――― (1989), Fable assessments in evaluating child sexual abuse. *Child Psychiat. & Hum. Develop.*, 20/20:123–133.

――― ――― (1991), Workshop on child abuse and family violence. *Family Medicine Review*. Lexington, KY.

――― ――― Kearl, G., Barlow-Elliott, L., & Bright, K. (1992), Interdisciplinary treatment of child abuse. *J. Ky. Med. Assn.*

Ziskin, J. (1981), *Coping with Psychiatric and Psychological Testing*. Venice, CA: Law and Psychology Press.

Name Index

Subject Index

Abandonment, 18, 127
  shown in drawings, 56
Abandonment/left-alone fable, 46
Abuse. *See also* Child abuse; Neglect; Physical abuse; Sexual abuse
  adult adjustment to, 132–134
  future dimensions in, 149–150
  impact of, 4–5
  multigenerational pattern of, 13
  physical, 7–16
  sexual, 25–39
  types of, 4
Abuse victims, clinical assessment of, 41–60
Abusing parent, 103–105
Acceptance, 31–32
Adjustment, adult, 132–134
Adolescent
  physically abused, 14, 15–16
  sexually abused, 35
Adult adjustment, 132–134
Adult nonsurvivors, 126–132
Aggressive feelings, discharge of, 31
Alcohol abuse

in adult nonsurvivor, 127–128
assessment of, 46
eliminating, 105
American Humane Association, sexual abuse
  reports of, 25–26
Anal examination, 76–77
Anal wink reflex, 77
Anatomical dolls, 30, 48–49, 102
Anesthesia, 69–70
Anger, 127–129
  methods of handling, 104–105
  repressed, in sexually abused child, 111
Anger fable, 45
Anogenital findings, 82
Assertiveness training, 106
Assessment techniques, 42–60

"The Battered Child Syndrome," 3–4
Behavioral extremes, 22
Behavioral indicators
  of emotional maltreatment, 22–23
  of neglect, 18–19
  of physical abuse, 13–14

Flying Hoofs

Stories of Horses

Flying Hoofs

Stories of Horses

Selected by

Wilhelmina   Harper

Illustrated by Paul Brown

HOUGHTON   MIFFLIN   COMPANY   -   BOSTON

The Riverside Press Cambridge

1939

The Riverside Press
CAMBRIDGE · MASSACHUSETTS
PRINTED IN THE U.S.A.

To   My   Friends

Helen,   Sidney,   and   Henry   Wolff

FOREWORD

EVERY normal boy and girl has an instinctive love of animals. A more sympathetic understanding of these creatures naturally develops a kinder attitude towards all humans, and a finer character in consequence.

Those of us who have daily contact with young people are well aware that their reading interests lie definitely in the direction of the animal story. That is most natural, for what interesting companions and friends animals may become through the medium of books!

It seems to me that there has long been need for an anthology of horse stories. They are such intelligent and noble animals and their heroic deeds are legion. So, my object here has been to give young people some of the best horse stories available through the writings of representative authors.

It has been a most enjoyable work, not only because of my own genuine interest in animals but because it has presented opportunity to provide boys and girls with a book that I sincerely hope will give them pleasure.

WILHELMINA HARPER

ACKNOWLEDGMENTS

THE compiler makes grateful acknowledgment to the following publishers and authors for the courtesies extended in the use of copyrighted selections and others:

D. Appleton-Century Company for 'The Swede,' from *Men and Horses*, by Ross Santee; 'The Last Run,' from *Uncle Sam's Animals*, by Frances Fox; and for 'Belinda in the Fore-Room,' from *Stories about Horses: Retold from St. Nicholas*.

Thomas Y. Crowell Company for 'A Thoroughbred,' from *Tiger Roan*, by Glenn Balch.

Doubleday, Doran and Company, Inc., for 'The Indian Horse Race,' from *The Preacher of Cedar Mountain*, by Ernest Thompson Seton. Copyright, 1917. Courtesy of Doubleday, Doran and Company, Inc.

Harper and Brothers for 'A Herdboy of Hungary,' from *Herdboy of Hungary*, by Alexander Finta.

Henry Holt and Company, and Russell Gordon Carter, for 'Shaggy at the Front,' from *Shaggy, the Horse from Wyoming*, by Russell Gordon Carter.

Little, Brown and Company for 'The Black Horse,' from *Animal Pioneers*, by Catherine C. Coblentz. An Atlantic Monthly Press publication. Reprinted by permission of Little, Brown and Company.

Longmans, Green and Company for 'An Indian Boy and His Pony,' from *Waterless Mountain*, by Laura Adams Armer.

Acknowledgments

Julian Messner, Inc., for 'The Cream-Colored Pony,' from *Gypsy Luck*, by Chesley Kahmann.

William Morrow and Company, Inc., for 'Black Storm,' from *Black Storm*, by Thomas C. Hinkle.

Oxford University Press for 'Jock, the Pony of an English King,' from *Each in His Way*, by Alice Gall and Fleming Crew.

The Penn Publishing Company for 'Trustworthy,' from *Frog, The Horse That Knew No Master*, by Major S. P. Meek, used by permission of and arrangement with the publishers, The Penn Publishing Company, Philadelphia.

Charles Scribner's Sons for 'Pasha, the Son of Selim,' from *Horses Nine*, by Sewell Ford; and for 'Smoky and the Wolves,' from *Smoky*, by Will James.

Frederick A. Stokes Company for 'The Pony Express.' Reprinted by permission from *The Pony Express Goes Through*, by Howard R. Driggs. Copyright, 1935, by Frederick A. Stokes Company.

Montgomery M. Atwater for 'A Pure-Bred Pulls Through.'

Belle Coates, and *Child Life Magazine*, for 'Old Dude, the Mystery Horse,' reprinted from *Child Life Magazine*. Copyright, Rand McNally and Company.

Frances L. Cooper for 'Judy and Hammerhead.'

Lavinia R. Davis, and *St. Nicholas Magazine*, for 'Betsy's Horse-Show Ribbon.'

Constance Holme, and James B. Pinker and Son, for 'The Last Inch.'

A. F. Tschiffely, and Nannie Joseph, for 'Tale of Two Horses,' from *Tale of Two Horses*, published by Simon and Schuster.

Cornelia L. Meigs for 'Stable Call.'

Leonard H. Nason for 'Rodney.'

CONTENTS

LIST OF COLORED PICTURES

A PURE–BRED PULLS THROUGH

Montgomery M. Atwater

It was January. Far away in Kentucky, his birthplace, Kentucky Roamer's brothers and sisters and cousins were all blanketed and kept in heated stalls. Tuckee might have laughed if he had seen them. He wore no blanket, and the stable of his master, the forest ranger, did not have a furnace.

Burning heat or bitter cold are all one to an Arab horse, and Tuckee was an Arab. His desert ancestors had needed no coddling and neither did he, though their stout-hearted heritage came to him through generations of delicate race horses.

His red coat was as long and thick as a bear rug. January, the month of blizzards, bothered him no more than it did the two mountain horses who were his companions. But he did wish for summer, for now there were no long rides through the hills with the gray-green man on his back. The trails he knew so well were choked with three feet of snow, and when the forest ranger went out it was with queer, clumsy things — skis or snowshoes — tied to his feet.

Once a month, at the most, the gray-green man rode Tuckee

the few miles to town, leading one of the other horses to bring back a load of supplies. Most horses would have thought that hard work enough, in winter, but to Tuckee it was nothing at all.

Only yesterday they had made such a trip, and for Tony, in the next stall, it had certainly been hard enough. He had fallen down on a hidden patch of ice, wise veteran though he was, and strained one shoulder. He was feeling very sorry for himself and very disgusted, for he was known as the best snow horse in that part of the Rockies. He munched his hay deject-edly, and only flattened his ears when Tuckee put his head over the side of the stall and made a playful nip at him.

Kentucky Roamer turned back to his own well-filled manger. Nothing to do for another month. Really it was discouraging, when a horse's legs were fairly aching for some real exercise. Tuckee did not dream that before the close of the short winter day he was to have all the exercise he wanted, and possibly a good deal more.

In his office not far from the stable, Kentucky Roamer's master was looking at the barometer. Down three points since the evening before! With one finger he tapped it lightly and the needle dropped another half point. That meant a storm coming. Yes, the sky told him the same thing. At first glance it seemed clear, but a second look discovered a faint haziness. No doubt a blizzard straight from the Arctic Circle was getting close. It was about time for one.

The forest ranger went outside to look at the thermometer: the red column stood at fifteen degrees below. With his hand on the office door he paused at the sound of a faint droning overhead, and his keen eyes soon located the source: an airplane flying past several miles to the west. It was a little early for the mail plane to be going over, he thought, but perhaps the pilot was worried about the storm.

The plane disappeared behind a near-by mountain and its buzzing was heard no more. But still the forest ranger lingered, in spite of the cold. At the very last moment before it passed from sight the plane had seemed to drop into a dive. Now why should he have thought that? He shrugged finally, and went inside. His eyes must have played him a trick.

A few minutes later the telephone rang. He took up the receiver and recognized the voice of his chief: 'Did you see a plane go over your way a little while ago?'

'Why, yes,' he answered, 'just a few minutes ago. Why?'

'Reported by radio that they were making a forced landing. A Captain Craig, of our Air Service, and Wolfe-Arnold, the English Air Minister, making a tour of inspection in this country, are in that plane. It must be the one you saw. They're probably done for, but if there's any chance at all it depends on you to make it good.'

'You bet,' answered the ranger. 'I'll do all I can.'

'Just a second,' came the voice. 'What's the weather like out there?'

'Barometer says a storm's coming up.'

'I just wanted to be sure you knew. The Weather Bureau predicts a blizzard in less than twelve hours, so you haven't much time. Good luck!'

The gray-green man dropped the receiver on its hook and went to work. 'Poor devils,' he thought as he laced up his moccasins, 'they're certainly up against it, but there's still time.'

With the speed of long practice he assembled the things a man must take when he goes out against the wilderness in winter. A belt around his waist supported pistol, knife, and hatchet. Binoculars hung from a strap about his neck. For the aviators, in case they had managed to make a safe landing, he took two pairs of snowshoes. To the snowshoes he tied a bundle containing a first-aid kit, food, and a thermos bottle full of hot coffee.

As an afterthought he added to the bundle two pairs of heavy socks and mittens. If they were using a cabin plane the men would not be wearing the right kind of clothes for a snowshoe trip in fifteen-below weather. One hand, plunged into his pocket, made sure of his waterproof match-safe and the stub of candle which the woodsman always carries when a quick fire may mean the difference between life and death.

Outside the office he adjusted the fastenings of his skis, strapped the pack to his shoulders, and started off. The snow lay deep and soft, but the polished wooden runners carried him easily and swiftly over the surface. His course was up the side of the mountain which towered over his cabin. From its bald summit he hoped with the aid of his binoculars to locate the wrecked airplane. From there, in fact, he *must* locate it, if the flyers were to be saved. Without shelter, without proper clothes, injured perhaps, they could live only a few hours in the bitter cold; and there was the blizzard to reckon with.

An hour of unceasing labor brought him to the mountain-top, where he slipped his pack and took the binoculars out of their case. Above him in the sky the storm haze was now unmistakable. Below him was spread the endless confusion of the wilderness, cañon after cañon, mountain beyond mountain. On Tuckee he had ridden the length of every one of those cañons. He knew the name of the farthest mountain — and he knew, also, how inhospitable that wilderness could be to anyone caught helpless and unprepared in the midst of its vast expanse.

The ranger lifted his glasses and began patiently to search each meadow, clearing, and mountain park. A razor-keen wind bit through his heavy jacket, but he ignored it. If the aviators had managed to land in some open space he could search them out with his ten-mile eyes. If they had crashed among the trees or into a cañon, it would make little difference to them when they were discovered.

Little by little the binoculars swept the horizon; halfway around and still no sign of the plane. Suddenly the ranger's nerves tingled. There was no chance of a mistake. In a clearing only a short distance away was the airplane. The powerful glasses showed every detail. The machine lay on its side, with one wing crumpled, but it did not seem badly smashed. The ranger fired into the air three times and then watched for some indication that his signal had been heard; but there was none.

Finally he put the glasses back in their case, picked out several landmarks to guide him, and began the descent from the mountain. Downhill on skis is swift traveling. In a few minutes, with a hiss of dry snow under his runners, the gray-green man emerged from the timber and skidded to a halt beside the plane.

Anxiously he looked into the cabin. The men were there. One lay on the floor as though dead, wrapped in an overcoat; the other huddled in his seat, apparently only half conscious. He had heard neither the shots nor the sounds of the ranger's arrival.

The gray-green man jerked open the door of the cabin and cried: 'How about it? Anyone on deck?'

It was a wonderful thing to see the light of hope in the eyes turned toward him. The huddled figure in the seat stirred and then said, in the unmistakable voice of an Englishman, 'I say, how in the world did you get here?'

The ranger had unslung his pack and was working at the

knots. 'Never mind that,' he said cheerfully. 'Let this drive the cold out of your bones,' and he extended the thermos bottle.

The Englishman stretched out one cold-stiffened hand, then dropped it. 'Give the other chap some first. He's unconscious.'

In a moment the ranger had lifted the flyer's head and was pouring the hot fluid down his throat, a little at a time. The man choked, gasped, and took a deep breath. Only then did the Englishman take his turn. 'That makes a chap feel different!' he exclaimed after a few swallows. 'Y'know, you got here just in time. It's so beastly cold ——'

The ranger kindled a fire, using the fabric and framework of the broken wing. To its warmth he dragged the unconscious pilot and laid him on the snowshoes, to keep him from sinking into the snow. 'How about you?' he asked the Englishman. 'Need some help to get over here?'

England's Minister of the Air smiled ruefully. 'I'm afraid I do,' he replied. 'My leg is broken.'

The ranger's heart sank. The extra snowshoes were of no use. Less than six miles away was his cabin, and safety, but it might as well have been six hundred. He thought swiftly. The day was still young; could he go back and telephone for help? A glance at the sky warned him — the thickening haze showed plainly that the blizzard was not far off.

He explained rapidly to the Englishman: 'I'm going for horses. My cabin is only six miles or so from here, but there's a blizzard coming. We must hurry.'

'Righto,' answered the Englishman. 'But just a moment. A blizzard's pretty bad business. You really mustn't take any risks for our sakes, old chap.'

'Don't worry about that,' said the ranger. 'Just keep that

fire going. We've got plenty of time before the blizzard gets here.' But he turned away so that the Englishman might not read the truth in his face.

The gray-green man drove himself to the limit over the homeward miles, but once inside the stable, he paused with a feeling of dismay. In his excitement he had been counting all along on Tony. There was a horse, born and brought up in a deep-snow country, who would get through if any horse could. And until this moment he had forgotten Tony's wrenched shoulder. It was out of the question to use him. There were left only gallant, inexperienced Kentucky Roamer, and Brownie, too old for work like this.

Tuckee saw his master standing as though he did not know what to do next, and nickered inquiringly. At this the gray-green man seemed to make up his mind, and hurriedly saddled Tuckee and Brownie.

The red horse was surprised when his master turned him toward the mountains. He had expected nothing more than another gallop to town. Not for months had they gone in this direction. He snorted as his legs sank into the snow. The chilly white stuff came up to his broad chest. This wasn't going to be much fun, but it was up to his master. Before there had always been Tony to break the trail on trips like this. Only long training, added to unusual courage, can overcome a horse's instinctive fear of deep snow, and Tuckee had only the courage. Brownie held back on the lead rope. Did something warn him?

The forest ranger chose the path with care, going through the thickest timber, where the snow would not be quite so deep. But presently they came to a drift, where the snow was deep and crusted. The ranger dismounted, and Tuckee saw him sink to his waist, and farther, as he broke a way through.

No skis or snowshoes for him now. He must use his strength to save that of the horses.

Twice he went back and forth, then with a tug at the reins he urged Tuckee to try it. Obediently the red horse stepped forward. Now his feet no longer touched the ground. He trembled and stopped. There are not many things a horse fears more than to lose the feel of solid ground. But his master urged, 'Come on, boy, let's go.'

Kentucky Roamer gathered himself together and made a bound. Once, and again, and again. The sweat broke out all over him, but at last he was through. It was easier for Brownie now, though he balked and the ranger had to lash him.

So they pressed forward, stopping to rest only when forced to do so by sheer exhaustion. The ranger put one horse and then the other in the lead. As much as he could, he broke the trail himself. It is heart-breaking toil to walk in deep snow. It is like having a stone tied to each leg. The white flakes that seem so soft and light are like a million hands holding back.

More and more the ranger began to doubt the success of his desperate venture. Tuckee was bearing up splendidly, but Brownie was already nearly tired out. Only the thought of the helpless flyers drove the man on.

The distance the ranger had covered in an hour on skis took three times as long now, but finally they reached the goal. The fire was blazing cheerfully, and the American aviator had regained consciousness. He was even able to smile when the Englishman greeted the gray-green man with: 'Forgive our bad manners, old chap, if we don't rise,' adding as his eyes fell on Tuckee: 'I say, that's a magnificent horse you have there — a true Arab, or I never saw one.'

Tuckee was wringing wet with perspiration, and panting, but he could still prick his ears and arch his neck at the two strangers. Perhaps he wondered what in the world they were doing out here in the snow. For the airplane he had a snort of surprise. But there was no time to waste.

The haze had become a curtain that made half twilight of early afternoon. Already his master was helping one of the strangers into the saddle. What a queer way to ride, he thought, as the American slumped forward weakly. The other stranger was boosted into Brownie's saddle.

The trail was broken now, and the going was better, but Tuckee slipped and floundered. Why did the gray-green man keep urging him on, faster and faster? He would have liked to balk and shake the stranger off. It was hard enough to push his weary legs through that clinging, freezing blanket without a dead weight on his back to make it worse. But no, his master had put the stranger there and he must carry him, although his legs ached and his breath came in gasps.

He could see, too, that the gray-green man was very tired, stumbling on ahead, tramping down the snow to make it a little easier. He no longer turned his head to speak to Tuckee or the two airmen. Just behind him, Tuckee could hear Brownie laboring more and more painfully.

It was just after they had struggled through the deepest drift that the first catastrophe overtook them. Brownie was staggering now. Suddenly, without warning, he collapsed. The ranger had just time to pull the Englishman free. Tuckee looked around curiously at his friend lying half buried, with the air rattling in his lungs. Brownie could not get up. The snow had beaten him.

There was only one thing to do, and the ranger did it with his mouth set in a grim line. The pistol shot was short and harsh in the cold air. Just once he stroked Brownie's head. 'Tough luck, old sport,' he murmured. 'All over now.'

'I'll stay here,' said the Englishman. 'You've done all you can.'

The ranger only shook his head, and with a shrug the English flyer allowed himself to be boosted up behind the American. Tuckee braced himself against the double load. What was the matter here, anyhow? These people should have their own horses. His master spoke quietly to him and rubbed his nose for a moment. Then they started forward again.

Tuckee was dazed with fatigue. His legs wanted to crumple under him, as Brownie's had. The red horse kept his eyes on his master, plodding, stumbling, sometimes crawling, doggedly ahead. They were nearing safety, however. 'Careful here, old man,' croaked Tuckee's master.

They were going along the edge of a deep, narrow gully. The horse trod cautiously. A little farther and he would be past the dangerous place. But all at once he set his foot on a smooth log buried under the snow. He slipped sideways toward the ravine, and his weary muscles could not save him. At the last moment the gray-green man seized the riders and pulled them back. Then, with a crash, Tuckee went over and tumbled down.

He came to rest on his back at the very bottom, all four feet in the air. Desperately he struggled to turn, but the steep banks held him as in a vise. 'Easy, boy,' came the voice of his master, and Tuckee lay still. The gray-green man would fix it; the Arab horse was sure of that, and he fought down his fear.

Who could measure or describe the bitter hopelessness of the ranger? He himself could drag the two aviators to the cabin, now less than half a mile away. But what of Kentucky

Roamer? Must he lie there helpless, so close to home, until the blizzard finished him? No, there was a quicker way than that. Once more his fingers closed on the butt of his pistol.

He felt a hand touch him, and turned to look into the eyes of England's Air Minister. 'Too bad,' said the aviator. 'I wouldn't care so much — if it weren't for the plucky horses.'

'I can get you two in now,' groaned the ranger. 'It's only a little way. But I can't leave Tuckee like that.' He drew the pistol.

The Englishman raised his head. 'Only a little way? Why, then we must save him! All of us or none, I say.'

'It's no use. I can't turn him over alone.'

'Drag me over to that tree,' ordered the Air Minister. 'I can't walk, but I can pull.'

In their frantic haste they left the pilot as he had fallen, face down, in the snow. The ranger dragged the Englishman to a tree above the horse. Then he brought the lead rope and the two braced themselves.

Tuckee felt them tighten the rope. It pulled his head up and over his chest. Next his shoulders came away from the earth and rocks and snow of the ravine. He wanted to struggle; every fiber revolted against lying still in that helpless strained position. But the voice of his master held him quiet. He heard the sobbing breath of the two men as inch by inch they drew him up.

It must have been a grotesque and terrible scene there in the forest: the horse with legs pointing stiffly up and neck stretched out over his chest, the weary men braced against the tree, pulling with gritted teeth. A sharp gust of wind, first herald of the blizzard, powdered them all with tiny ice crystals.

At last they could do no more. Numbed fingers could no longer hold the rope; exhausted muscles could not pull another ounce. As the ranger tied the rope to the tree the Englishman suddenly fell back, his face as white as the snow.

The horse now lay partly on his back and partly on his haunches, a sort of half-sitting position, with his head pulled down between his forelegs. 'He'll have to do the rest,' said the ranger. 'If the rope holds, and he doesn't crack his neck, he can make it.'

He spoke to the horse: 'Try it, Tuckee! Try it, boy!'

Kentucky Roamer was not so tired now. While the men had been working, he had been resting, if only for a few minutes. For an Arab, a few minutes are enough. The muscles along his back tightened and the rope rasped against the tree. That rope gave the red horse a purchase, something to work against. With a surge he straightened the curve of his back and neck. Now his forefeet could touch the sides of the gully. In another moment he had clawed his way over, and stood up.

It was easy work to scramble out of the ravine, but then there was the long struggle to get the two flyers upon his back again. Both were unconscious now, and as the ranger pressed against Tuckee's shoulder, lifting them into position, the horse could feel that his master was trembling like one who makes his final effort. When they were safely up, he slapped Tuckee's haunches and said, 'All right, boy, go on home.'

Tuckee went forward ten feet. Then he stopped, for his master was not coming. He looked around and saw the ranger on his knees in the snow. What in the world was the matter now? He snorted impatiently. Again his master ordered him forward; but he would not go.

With the wail of a demon, a wind, sharp, cutting, and laden with ice particles, drove through the trees. The blizzard! Kentucky Roamer hung his head and stood. Then, through the uproar of the storm, he heard a faint dragging and scrap-

ing. The frightful cold that accompanied the wind must have
roused the ranger, for he was coming at last.

The gray-green man dragged himself along until he reached
the horse, pulled himself upright by means of the stirrup
leathers, and his hands joined those of the Englishman on the
saddle horn. Tuckee needed no order now. He started forward slowly, sidling a little to avoid stepping on his master's
dragging feet.

And so he brought all three of them home.

SMOKY AND THE WOLVES

Will James

A BIG moon came up and the light of it reflected a path that shined on the crusted snow. The air was mighty still, still with the cold that'd gripped the range and made everything that lived and carried hoofs come to a stand, so that no air would be stirred; a breeze at that temperature would of froze stiff every standing animal in that territory.

Smoky, the buckskin, and the bunch stood on a knoll where they could see well around 'em. They looked like petrified or froze there, so still they all stood; there was no sign of life from 'em excepting for an ear that moved once in a while and which was on the job to catch any sound that might come from near or far.

The 'yip, yip' and howl of a coyote was heard, another answered, and pretty soon them two filled the air with their serenading. The echo of that hadn't quite died down when the long, drawed-out, and mournful howl of a wolf made that of the coyotes seem like a joke. The little bunch of horses on the knoll hadn't blinked an eye while the coyotes was serenading, but at the sound of what followed, every head in the bunch went up, every ear pointed towards the sound, and the buckskin with a few others snorted.

Restlessness had got in the bunch. Smoky started out a ways and came back; then pretty soon, and keeping as close together as they could, they all begin moving. They moved on like shadows, and like more shadows three gray shapes had took up their trail.

The big buckskin had stayed in the rear of the bunch and he was first to notice the wolves. A loud whistling snort was heard from him as he landed in the middle of the bunch and kettled 'em into a stampede and the run for their lives. The cold air was split forty ways and crusted hunks of snow was sent a-flying as the ponies all wild-eyed broke their way through the drifts at the edge of a ridge and run on towards the big flat.

Smoky had stampeded with the rest and kept pretty well up in the lead through the run, but now that his blood was warming up in plowing through the deep snow, and being that that blood was circulating more free up his neck and into his brain, it all put somewhat of a different light on the subject. That brain of his was all het up, on hair trigger with the waking up the run was giving it, and pretty soon something hatched up in there that made Smoky slow down till the bunch went past and ahead of him. He was wanting to see what was all fired dangerous about them wolves so as to make the bunch run that way.

The big buckskin was the last to pass Smoky. He was busy keeping two little colts just a few months old from lagging behind too far; bucking the deep snow at the speed the bunch was making was beginning to show on 'em, and it was taking a lot of persuading from the big horse to keep them little fellers on the move.

The wolves was steady catching up with the bunch, and the attack would of took place some sooner if it hadn't been for Smoky. His lagging behind had fooled the wolves into thinking that the mouse-colored gelding had quit and was ready to make his last stand. It had been Smoky's intention to wait for the killers and paw the daylight out of 'em, but as the three rushed in on him he figgered it a good idea to postpone the pawing for a while and do a little running till he was some acquainted with their ways and tricks.

Head and tail up and fire in his eyes, he lined out and *led the wolves away from the bunch*. They'd figgered on making him their victim on account he was the handiest, but as the chase kept up they found the gelding had a powerful lot of speed left in him. In the meantime Smoky had somehow lost all hankering of stopping and fight it out with 'em. There was something about the three hungry-looking crethures that kept him a-moving, and his instinct was warning him strong that he should keep some safe distance between him and them.

He was doing that the best he could and as the running kept up and the wolves couldn't get any closer they finally figgered they was wasting their time. May be he got to looking too old and tough for 'em and calculated they'd rather have younger and more tender meat; besides, he was leading 'em straight away from the bunch, which might make 'em lose their chances of getting anything at all.

Smoky's play of leading the wolves off that way had been a great relief to the bunch and mostly the young colts; they'd had a chance to slow down some and get their second wind, and when the killers showed up on their trail once again they was all more able to sashay on and keep from reach of their tearing fangs.

When Smoky found that the wolves had left him and turned

back towards the bunch, it was his natural instinct to turn too
and follow up in their tracks. He had a hunch somehow that
he'd be needed there and he hadn't altogether lost the hope of
a chance of taking apart at least one of the outlaws.

It was a long and mighty hard run back till he caught up
with the bunch again, but Smoky wasn't the horse he was for
nothing. He made it in near as good a time as the wolves
themselves, and he got there just as the wolves circled around
past the buckskin and headed for one of the colts he'd been
hazing.

The buckskin hadn't hardly been noticed; the wolves had
passed him up as too old, specially when there was such as the
young colts which could be got easy. The old horse had
watched 'em catch up with the bunch and go past him for a
younger victim. He had no way to know that they didn't
want him, and he could of kept well in the lead of the bunch
if he'd wanted to, but he'd made hisself guardian over the
little colts and he couldn't for the life of him have left 'em
behind.

Of course the little fellers' mammies would of fought for
'em too but they was at the stage where they felt every horse
was for himself; they'd scared into a stampede and was all a-
running for their own lives.

The old buckskin knowed wolves; he knowed they had
their eye on him and it was best to keep neutral till they'd got
over being watched of every move he'd make; and as the three
grays passed him and was gaining on the scared little colts he
kept to one side and watched. It was just as the leader made a
leap for one of the little fellers' hamstrings that the big buckskin came to life, made a leap too, and went to fighting at the
risk of his own life.

The wolves hadn't looked for no such move from him.

They'd got over watching and figgered he was far behind and had put all their attention on dragging down the victim they'd picked. It was a mighty big surprise for them when from behind the big buckskin landed on the second wolf and buried him in the snow while on his way to the first.

A good-sized hoof came down just as that first wolf turned his head to meet the fighting buckskin. That hoof connected with his lower jaw as he made the turn and left that jaw hanging limp and plum useless. When the old pony looked back for the other wolves there was long gray hairs sticking between his teeth.

It was about then when Smoky arrived on the scene. He'd come up right behind the buckskin, and when the second wolf picked himself up out of the snow and made a grab which would of been the death of the old horse, Smoky done a side swipe that was quicker than chained lightning. A hind hoof came up and caught that wolf right under a front leg close to

the body and took that leg off of him like it'd been a tooth-pick; another horse that'd come up from behind and hadn't been reckoned with.

It was during this commotion of biting and kicking mixture of buckskin and mouse-colored horseflesh and flying gray wolves that the third and only able wolf disappeared into thin air. Them two fighting ponies had took away all his appetite for colt meat and left a hankering only to be gone from the reach of their destroying hoofs.

Three of his kind could of competed with the mad ponies if their attention had been on them from the start, but that's where the slip had been made, and as it was that lone wolf didn't feel at all equal of resuming what the leader of the pack had started. He left.

The moon faded away into the sky; break of day had come. Out on the flat the little bunch of ponies was knee-deep in the snow and a-pawing away for the grass that was underneath, there wasn't a scratch on nary a hide to show that any had ever seen a wolf; but if Smoky and his pardner the buckskin hadn't been in that little bunch there would of been another story to tell.

THE INDIAN HORSE RACE

Ernest Thompson Seton

EVEN far Montana heard the news of the coming horse race; and, winding through the hills, there came one day a band of Crows from their reservation on the Big Horn. They came with only their light traveling tepees; and the intense dislike in which they are held by the Sioux and Cheyennes was shown in the fact that they camped far away in a group by themselves.

The Crows are noted for their beautiful lodges and their inveterate habit of horse-stealing. They also have this unique fact on their record — that they have never been at war with the whites. They will steal a white man's horses fast enough, but they have never tried to take a white scalp. Their party consisted chiefly of men and a few surplus horses. But for the lodges and a few women, it might have passed for a war party.

The Crows are among the numerous claimants of the title 'best horsemen in the world.' If reckless riding in dangerous places without being thrown is good ground for the claim, then is the claim good; and it becomes yet stronger in view of the fact that most of their riding is barebacked.

When they came to the Fort that day, it was as though they were riding for their lives. They were but a score, and were admitted without question. They paid their respects to Colonel Waller; and then, after smoking, announced that they had money and goods to bet on the race. They were disappointed to find how much too late they were; everything was already up. So they rode away to their camp.

They did not go near the Sioux and Cheyenne camp; not that there was much danger of their suffering bodily harm, but they had been unmistakably informed that they were not welcome, though the action went no further than ignoring them.

Next morning, when Blazing Star and Red Rover were doing their turn, there were no keener onlookers than the Crows. By look and grunted word, they showed their appreciation of the noble horses.

The Chief came to the Fort to find out if the Colonel would sell Blazing Star after the race.

'We give twenty horses,' and he held up both hands twice.

'No.'

'Three hands ponies,' and they held up both hands spread three times.

'No, he is not for sale.'

Late that day, Red Cloud and Howling Bull came to Colonel Waller; and, after preliminaries, conveyed the information and warning: 'All Crows big heap thief. You watch him; he steal horse every time, heap no good.'

The third of July came, and the plain looked like a city of tents. Many traders were there to open temporary stores; and it is doubtful if any single race in the Western world has attracted more people or created intenser interest.

Among the spectators were the two Indian chiefs in their war-paint — Red Cloud of the Sioux, and Howling Bull of the Cheyennes. They spoke little to each other, for neither knew the other's tongue; but they made little gestures of the sign language, and any keen observer knowing it could catch the ideosigns: 'Good, good; by and by; we see good race; brave, swift,' and so on. Later: 'Yes, after one sleep. Rain heap, yes.'

The two chiefs, with their followers, conversed earnestly, and with much gesture. They looked and pointed at the Crow camp; and the rain sign came in many times, and emphatically.

It was four o'clock in the morning of the Fourth of July when the thunderbolt struck Fort Ryan. It was not very loud; it damaged no building; but it struck the very souls of men. A thousand thunder-claps, a year's tornadoes in an hour, could not have been more staggering; and yet it was only four words of one poor, wheezing Irish hostler at the Colonel's window:

'Colonel! Colonel! For the love of God — come — come — come at once — *Blazing Star is gone!* '

'*What?*' and the Colonel sprang up.

The reveille had sounded, the men were just rising; but one group there was already about the stable talking with an air of intense excitement. The Colonel went without waiting to dress — the officer of the day with him. In terrible silence they hurried to the stable; there was Rover in his box, whinnying softly for his morning oats; but the next — the box of Blazing Star — was empty; and the far end, the outer wall, showed a great new doorway cut.

Beyond, out in the growing light, troopers rode to every near-by lookout; but never a sign of horse did they see, or, indeed, expect to see. The case was very clear; the horse was stolen, gone clean away — their hope for the race was gone.

These were terrible moments for the hapless grooms and guards. Human nature, in dire defeat, always demands a victim; and the grooms were glad to be locked up in the guard-house, where at least they were out of the storm of the Colonel's wrath.

As the light grew brighter, a careful study laid bare the plan of robbery. The stables formed, in part, the outer wall of the quadrangle. They were roofed with pine boards, covered with tar-paper on cedar corner posts; the walls, however, were of sods piled squarely on each other in a well-known Western style, making a good warm stable.

It was a simple matter to take down quickly and silently this outer wall from the outside, beginning at the top, and so make another exit. This had been done in the dead of night. And the track of the racer told the tale like a printed page.

A general alarm had gone forth; all the Fort was astir; and the army scouts were by the case forced into unusual prominence. It was Al Rennie who spoke first:

'Colonel, it's a-going to rain, sure; it's liable to rain heavy. I suggest we take that trail right away and follow before it's all washed out.'

'The quicker the better,' said the Colonel.

Riding ahead on the trail like a hound went the old trapper-hunter-scout with a band of troopers following. They had not gone a quarter of a mile before the rain began to spit. But the line of the trail was clear, and it was easy for the practiced eye to follow. It headed east for half a mile; then, on a hard open stretch of gravel, it turned and went direct for the Crow camp. Rennie could follow at a gallop; they rounded the butte, cleared the cottonwoods, crossed the little willow-edged stream, and reached the Crow camp to find it *absolutely deserted!*

The rain was now falling faster; in a few minutes, it set in — a true Dakota flood. The trail of Blazing Star — clear till then — was now wholly wiped out. There was nothing but the unmarked prairie around them; and the guide, with the troopers, soaked to the skin, rode back with the forlorn tidings.

Under such a cloud of disaster, men cared little what the weather was; the deluge of rain seemed rather appropriate. There was even a hope that it might rain hard enough to postpone the race. But at ten it stopped, and by eleven it had cleared off wholly. The race was to be at noon.

Word had been sent to Red Cloud, asking for two days' postponement, which was curtly refused. 'White man heap scared maybe,' was his scornful reply.

The Colonel held a hasty council of war with his officers. Their course was clear. In Red Rover they still had a winner, and the race would come off as announced; such a horse as Blazing Star could not long be concealed; they would follow up the Crows and recover him in a few days. So, after all, the outlook was not so very dark.

Already the plain was surging with life. Gayly clad Indians were riding at speed for the pleasure of speeding. Thousands of gaudy blankets — put out to air in the sun — seemed to double the density, color, and importance of the camp. New wagons came with their loads, new life developed; now came a procession of Indians singing their racing songs, for the Indian has a song for every event in life; bodies of United States troops were paraded here and there as a precautionary and impressive measure; the number of Indians assembled, and their excitability, began to cause the authorities some apprehension.

The Indian Agent had many close conferences with the Colonel. He strongly disapproved the whole racing excitement, and plainly indicated that he held the Colonel responsible. What would happen when these excited fifteen hundred Sioux and Cheyenne warriors — not to speak of some five thousand women and children — met defeat, was a serious problem. Had the situation been sooner realized, the whites could have organized into some sort of home defence.

Red Cloud and Howling Bull, as far as could be discerned, contemplated the scene and the coming event with absolute composure.

At one o'clock, all the world seemed there. There were mounted Indians — men and women — by thousands, and at least a thousand mounted whites beside the soldiers. The plain was dotted with life and color from far beyond the Indian camp to Fort Ryan; but the centre of all was the race-track; and camped alongside, or riding or sitting near, was the thickest group of folk of both races, bound to lose no glimpse of the stirring contest.

The delay made for new excitement; the nerve strain became greater as each hour passed. The white soldiers did what they could to hold the crowd, and the Indians called on their own 'dog soldiers' or camp police to do the same. Fortunately, it was a good-natured crowd; and the absconding of the Crows had removed the largest element of risk, so far as violence was concerned.

At a quarter to two, the bugle of the Fort was blown, and there issued forth the proud procession with Red Rover in the middle, led beside his jockey, who rode a sober pony. It was Little Breeches.

Red Rover was magnificent, trained to a hair, full of life and fire. Of all the beautiful things on earth, there is nothing of nobler beauty than a noble horse; and Rover, in his clean-limbed gloss and tensity, was a sight to thrill the crowds that were privileged to see him spurn the earth, and arch his graceful neck.

Every white man's eye grew proudly bright as he gazed and gloried in his champion, and fear left all their hearts. At the starting post, they swung about, Little Breeches mounted, and a mighty cheer went up. 'Ho, Red Cloud! Where's your horse? Bring on your famous buckskin now'; and the rumbling of the crowd was rising, falling, like the sound of water in a changing wind.

Far down the valley, near the Ogallala camp, a new commotion arose, and a wilder noise was sounding. There was the shrill chant of the 'Racing Ponies' with the tom-toms beating, and then Red Cloud's men came trotting in a mass.

As they neared the starting point, the rabble of the painted warriors parted, and out of the opening came their horse, and from the whites went up a loud and growing burst of laughter. Such a horse as this they had never seen before; not the famous buckskin, but *the mysterious Pinto pony*, wonderful, if weird trappings could make him so.

On his head he wore an eagle-feather war-bonnet; his mane was plaited with red-flannel strips and fluttering plumes; his tail was even gaudier; around each eye was a great circle of white and another of black; his nose was cross-barred with black and red; his legs were painted in zebra stripes of yellow and black; the patches of white that were native to his coat were outlined with black and profusely decorated with red hands and horseshoes painted in vermilion; on his neck was a band of beadwork, carrying a little bundle of sacred medicine; and, last, he had on each ankle a string of sleigh-bells that jingled at each prancing step.

A very goblin of a horse! His jockey was Chaska, the Indian boy, stripped to the breech-clout, with an eagle feather in his hair and a quirt hung on his wrist.

Never, perhaps, was a more grotesque race entry in all the West; and the difference between the burnished form of Red Rover in his perfect trim and this demon-painted Pinto gave rise to an ever-growing chorus of shouting, laughter, rough jibes, and hoots of joy.

The Pinto seemed as tall as Red Rover, and, so far as trappings allowed one to see, he was nearly as fine in build. Diverse feelings now surged in the crowd. Many of the whites said, 'Well, it was true after all; Red Cloud, the old fox, he sent to Omaha, or maybe Illinois, and bought a racer.'

Old Red Cloud slowly rode by with his square jaw set, his eyes a little tight, observing all; but he gave no sign of special interest.

With two such keen and nervous racers, it was no easy matter to get a fair start; but at length they were manœuvred into line, side by side. The pistol cracked and away they went, while all the crowd held still, so very still for a moment that you could have heard for a hundred yards the medicine song of the Indian boy:

'*Huya! Huya! Shungdeshka, Shungdeshka!* (Fly! Fly! my Eagle! Fly, my Pinto Eagle!)' And that wild-eyed Indian pony sprang away as fast as the blooded horse beside him. So far as anyone could tell, it was an even match.

The white man had won the inside track again; and remembering how the Indian boy had got that advantage in the last race, he was on the watch. But nothing happened; the horses led off side by side, shoulder to shoulder. At the turning post was a mounted waiting throng that received them with a cheer, to follow again in their wake, like madmen let loose on hoofs. The horses seemed to thrill to the sound and bent to it faster.

Around the post they had swung, perforce in a large circle, and the Pinto lost a good half length. Now Little Breeches saw his chance; and, leaning forward well, he smote those bronzy flanks, while Rover bounded — bounded to his limit.

But the Indian boy's magic song rang out again: '*Huya, Huya, Huya deshka!* (Oh, Eagle, fly, fly, Eagle, my Pinto, fly!)' And the Pinto seemed to unchain himself, as a hawk when he sails no more, but flaps for higher speed. With thunderous hoofs, the wild horse splashed through a pool, came crawling, crawling up, till once again he was neck and neck with the wonderful flying steed in the coat of gold.

Little Breeches shouted, 'Hi! Hi! Hi!' Chaska glanced at him and smiled, such a soft little smile. The eagle feather in his hair was fluttering, and the smile was still on his lips as they reached the last half mile. Then, in weird and mouthing tone, Chaska sang of wind and wings:

> '*Ho, Huya, Huya deshka,*
> *Huya, Huya, Huya deshka,*
> *Woo hiya, Woo hiya, Woo hiya,*
> *Unkitawa, Unkitawa, Ho! Ho! Ho!*'

Strong medicine it must have been, for the Pinto thrilled, and bounded double strong. The white man yelled, Red Rover flinched, then sprang as he had never sprung before. But the demon pony in the motley coat swung faster, faster, faster yet; his nostrils flared; his breath was rushing — snoring — his mighty heart was pounding, the song of the wind and the flying wings seemed to enter into his soul. He double-timed his hoofbeats and, slowly forging on, was half a length ahead.

The white man screamed Red Rover was at topmost notch.

The demon pony forged — yes, now a length ahead, and in the rising, rumbling roar, passed on, a double length, and *in*. *The race was won, lost, won, lost* — the Pinto pony crowed; and the awful blow had struck!

The crack of doom will never hit Fort Ryan harder. When the thousand painted Sioux came riding, yelling, wild with joy, shooting their rifles in the air, racing in a vast, appalling hoof-tornado down the long track, and then to the lodge of all the stakes, they went as men who are rushing to save their own from some swift flood that threatens.

The whites were like men under a gallows doom; every man in the Fort, and most of those in the near-by town, were practically ruined.

'Stung, stung!' was all the Colonel had to say.

The Adjutant, an erratic officer, had lost half a year's pay. The magnitude of the disaster was almost national, he felt; and sadly, shyly, he said: 'Will you have the flag at half-mast, Colonel?'

'No!' thundered the Colonel. 'I'll be darned if the flag shall hang at half-mast for anything less than the death of an American.'

Colonel Waller had been telegraphing from Cedar Mountain to all reachable parts of the North where the Crows were likely to be, without getting one word of comfort. Then up to the door of his house the morning after the devastating race, came Red Cloud of the calm, square face, and behind him, riding, a dozen braves.

At precisely the right moment prescribed by etiquette, he opened: 'Me savvy now why you no run heap good horse.'

'Humph!' said Waller.

'Didn't I tole you watch them Crow come?'

'Humph!' was the answer.

'You no got him back yet — no?'

'No,' said the Colonel, with some asperity.

'Why? White scout no follow trail?'

'The rain wiped out all trail,' was the answer.

'Your scout heap no good,' said Red Cloud. Then, after a dozen slow puffs at his pipe, during which he gazed blankly and far away, the Indian said: 'Ogallala very good scouts. Maybe so they find trail. What you give for follow Crow? Maybe find, bring back your pony.'

Without a doubt, this was the easiest way. The Ogallala scouts would gladly pursue their ancient enemies, and force them to give up the stolen horse. These men knew which line the Crows would most likely take, and could probably pick up the trail in a day. Prompt action was necessary. The Indian bands were breaking up and going home laden with plunder; their fresh trails would render it impossible to follow the trail of the horse thieves. The Colonel's mind was quickly made up.

'Red Cloud,' he said emphatically, 'I'll give you two hundred and fifty dollars cash if you find Blazing Star and bring him back here in good condition within one week.'

The Indian Chief smoked for a few puffs and said: 'Seven suns, no good. Crow country far away; one moon maybe.'

Reckless riders like the Crows might easily ruin a horse in one month; so, at length, a compromise was reached, whereby Red Cloud was to receive two hundred and fifty dollars if within two weeks; and one hundred if a month passed before the return. Then the Sioux chief rose 'to find his young men,' and his party rode away.

It was nine the next morning when the sentry discovered a considerable body of mounted Indians in the northeast, riding rapidly toward the Fort. Had it been from the south, he would scarcely have made a report. Before ten o'clock they had arrived. They numbered about fifty warriors in full war paint.

At their head was Red Cloud. A hundred troopers were under arms, so they did not hesitate to admit the Indians. The warriors passed through the gate; then, spreading out before the Colonel's house, their opening ranks *revealed the noble form of Blazing Star.* Bestriding him was the boy Chaska, his bright eyes and clear white teeth gleaming in a smile.

A mighty shout went up among the white men as the blooded racer was led to the Colonel's office. One or two formalities, and the two hundred and fifty dollars was paid over to Red Cloud. Blazing Star was hastily examined, found in perfect trim, then handed over to the Irish hostler.

'You take him to the stable,' was all the Colonel said, but he said it in large capital letters, and it was full of grim threats and reminders. Hostler Mike led the lost darling back to the stable where a crowd of men were waiting.

Red Cloud crammed the new wealth into his tobacco pouch, and rode away at the head of his men.

Al Rennie felt sick with disgust that he should fail when the trail was fresh; while the Sioux, on a washed-out trail, made such a showing in so short a time. He was puzzled, too.

All that day the Indian bands had been going off. Their camps were breaking up; they were dispersing to their homes. The plain was nearly deserted that afternoon when hostler Mike took Blazing Star out into the heat of the sun to give him the thorough washing and cleaning that he surely needed. A minute later, Mike came rushing across the square to the Colonel's office.

'Colonel, Colonel!' he gasped. 'Come here, sir.'

'What's the matter with you?' said the Colonel, in a voice of wrath which boded ill for a new blunder.

'Colonel, come at once. Come, it's Blazing Star.'

There was a total lack of soldier decorum in the hostler's address. He was so intensely excited that the Colonel over-looked the informality and went quickly to where Blazing Star was standing tied to the washing post.

'There, sir; look there — and there!' ejaculated Mike with growing excitement, as he pointed to Blazing Star's legs. 'And look at that!' and he swept his bony finger round the big liquid eye of the racer. The Colonel looked, looked closer, parted the hair, looked down to the roots and saw *paint —
red paint, white paint, black paint* — traces of horseshoes, red hands, white patches, and stripes — not much, but enough to tell the tale.

Without a question, *Blazing Star was the Pinto that had won the race!*

The simple redmen knew that the buckskin was over-matched, so they secured the only horse on the plains that *could* win. They drove the Crows away at the right moment to leave a red-herring trail. Then, having captured the stakes, they calmly collected two hundred and fifty dollars for restoring the race-horse to his owner. The simple Redmen! The simple Redmen!

SHAGGY AT THE FRONT

Russell Gordon Carter

LIEUTENANT GORDON could see shells bursting along a crest far in front, where clouds of black smoke rose lazily. At the left smoke rose from a ruined village. As he guided his horse across a slashed and pockmarked field he could hear the pounding of American batteries behind him and the whirr and rattle of big shells passing overhead. Shaggy also heard them and was uneasy.

The lieutenant had ridden almost a kilometer when scattering shells began to land uncomfortably close. He waited beneath a clump of young trees, patting Shaggy's neck and talking to him quietly, reassuringly. He felt the horse trembling under him; nevertheless those sensitive, expressive ears were alert to catch the slightest word. Gordon lowered his voice to a faint whisper, and still the ears responded.

There beneath the trees he came to an abrupt decision. It was wrong to take the horse farther forward! He would slide to the ground, tether him to one of those slender trunks, and then go the rest of the distance on foot. 'Shaggy, boy, I'll have to leave you here for a while. It won't be for long ——'

Gordon had slipped one foot from the stirrup and was in the act of dismounting, when a shrill crescendo whistle sounded overhead. With shoulders hunched and eyes screwed shut, he waited an instant... a long horrible, agonizing instant. But he heard no sound. He was aware only of a bright flash, a strange swift rush of air... then blackness.

Out upon the brown rainswept field Shaggy raced, wild-eyed, his mane and tail flying, the empty stirrups leaping grotesquely. A spreading patch on the left side of his neck showed dark and red and ugly.

A mass of rusted barbed wire loomed in front of him, and he swerved sharply to the right, thundering past it. He leaped a yawning shell hole. His pounding hoofs clattered among loose stones along a brook. Sparks flew upward. The big stirrups striking against his flanks seemed to urge him to greater speed. With ears flat, he went skimming up a hill and shot across the crest. The opposite slope was steep, and he slackened his pace.

At the base of the hill he halted, trembling, his ears still flat, his head thrust forward. Steam rose in white clouds from his blowing nostrils. He shifted his feet, churning the soggy turf. Bewildered, still under the spell of terror, he remained there at the base of the hill while minutes passed and the rain beat down upon his shaggy coat.

At last he turned and, with head lifted, sent a shrill neigh ringing upon the heavy air. It echoed against the opposite hillside. The sound startled him. He leaped forward, and raced up the slope that he had descended; but he went down the far side at a walk, moving in zigzag fashion.

Now he was crossing the brown rainswept field over which he had first fled in pain and terror. Again he voiced a shrill neigh. This time there was no answering echo to startle him, but a crazily leaning stake at his left had a strange look to it. He halted, stiff-legged, staring with ears turned fearfully forward. There were strands of wire fastened to the stake; and from one of them hung a patch of soiled gray cloth. Suddenly it moved in the wind. With a snort of terror he bolted! His wild flight carried him into a mass of barbed wire. It ripped at his legs. He stumbled, plunged, thrashed frantically about.

At last he was free. He went forward at a nervous walk. Red slashes marked his white stockings, and he limped slightly. The rain increased. The hissing drone of it seemed to soften the pounding of the guns. From somewhere at the right came the sound of voices, muffled, far-distant. He arched his neck sidewise, halted, sniffed the air, then went on again.

The clump of young trees was just in front of him now. He quickened his stride. There on the wet earth lay a man creature, face downward, an arm wide-flung. His trench coat glistened; little pools of water gleamed in the folds of the skirt.

Shaggy halted beside the lieutenant and lowering his head, touched the outstretched legs with gently nibbling lips. He ran his nose inquiringly upward until it was against the man's shoulder. The hanging reins trailed across the motionless body. Shaggy continued to nuzzle and sniff at the prostrate figure as on the occasion when the lieutenant had gone out of the saddle during their first ride. But now the man lay silent, motionless — something was wrong.

Suddenly pawing the wet earth, Shaggy blew noisily, violently through his nostrils. Then he neighed once more — a prolonged, quivering, trumpet-like blast that went ringing forth across the field. As he repeated the sound, one of those outstretched legs moved slightly, but the horse failed to ob-

serve it. He stood there in the driving rain, turning his head now this way, now that, churning the mud with his nervously lifting feet.

Something was wrong — his nose against that strangely motionless body told him so. At varying intervals his troubled, ringing neighs rose above the sound of storm and guns.

He stood there in the driving rain while the gray of late twilight deepened into night, while the white flashes danced along the horizon and gilded the ragged edges of low racing clouds.

It was thus that a little group of advancing infantrymen found them — a wounded shaggy sorrel horse standing above a young infantry lieutenant, wounded and unconscious.

Under the care of the men Gordon came to his senses for a few brief moments. During that fleeting period he had a glimpse of his horse against a flickering background of gun

flashes, saw his pointed ears, his glistening head turned sidewise.

Then the lieutenant's eyes closed and as if from a vast distance, he was listening to men talking... something about
hearing a horse neighing in the darkness... something about
the horse being wounded... wounded also...

Gordon forced his eyes open, but they closed again almost
instantly. Once more there was blackness... only blackness...

On the morning of the fourteenth of November, three days
after the Armistice, Lieutenant Gordon was discharged from
the hospital and ordered to rejoin his outfit. He was eager to
go, for on the same morning a letter had come from his brother
officer, Lieutenant O'Ryan, and in it there was a paragraph
that relieved his mind of a great worry.

'Your Shaggy horse is still with us.' Gordon re-read the
paragraph while seated in the second-class compartment of
the train that was carrying him speedily eastward. 'He was
in bad shape that night when they brought him in — his legs
all scratched and torn and a terrible gash on his neck! Never
knew a man to curse the way Sergeant Boyd did at sight of
him! But the horse is in pretty good condition now, thanks to
the sergeant, and if you're sent back to the outfit, you'll find
him waiting for you. I thought maybe you'd like to know.'

Gordon stared out the window, his eyes open but unseeing.
Shaggy had come safely through the horror of that rainswept
night! Frequently during his period of convalescence the
lieutenant had pictured his favorite, wounded and terrified,
standing above him in the rain.

He had no doubt that it was Shaggy's repeated neighing
that had brought help. He had no doubt that, save for the

horse, he would have bled to death out there beneath the trees. And now Shaggy was safe and well; and in a few days the division of which the brigade was a unit would start on the long march into Germany.

It was then, while he sat alone that Lieutenant Gordon formed a solemn promise. He would befriend the horse always! He would keep him always! He would see to it, after Shaggy's army service was ended, that the horse had a pleasant and comfortable home for the rest of his days!

OLD DUDE, THE MYSTERY HORSE

Belle Coates

WHAT *will* you do now, Ronnie?' gasped Beth Posey as they stood beside old Dude, watching the roan pony from Pringle's ranch disappear toward the badlands in a cloud of dust.

'I'll have to borrow another horse,' answered Ronnie Garner grimly, shaking the dust out of his new tan angora chaps. Before running away the roan pony had spilled him into the sagebrush.

Ronnie began to pace back and forth across the Posey corral. Beth went on grooming old Dude before hitching him to the single buggy that would take her to the Rancher's Picnic. Thoughtfully she drew the currycomb across Dude's bony old ribs that ran like a picket fence across his stately white body.

'Of course you've got to get another horse, Ronnie.'

But where?

'I must have three horses or I can't enter the boy's relay race at the Rancher's Picnic this afternoon,' Ronnie went on, brushing off the gay cerise sateen shirt that he wore in honor of the day. 'With Pringle's borrowed roan gone I have only two — Comet and Sprint. So I'll have to find another horse.'

Determinedly Ronnie set his freckled jaw. 'I'm going to ride in the relay race, Beth. I'm going to win the prize twin calves so I can help my dad start up a new herd of cattle in place of those he lost last winter in the blizzard. I promised Dad I'd help ——' Ronnie's voice broke.

'I know, Ronnie,' Beth agreed gently. They had talked of nothing else all summer — this rancher boy from the tall white ranch house across the coulee and the homesteader girl who lived in the near-by tar-papered shack. Ronnie was going to ride in the boys' relay, win the twin calves and go into partnership with his dad, who was starting in the cattle business all over again.

No other boy in all northern Montana had any faster ponies or was any swifter at changing mounts and saddles; no other boy had practiced the movements of the relay any harder than Ronnie.

Then, less than ten minutes ago, just before leaving for the Rancher's Picnic, Ronnie had been practicing the last change from Comet to the roan behind his father's empty cattle-shed. And the roan pony had shied at a gopher, tumbled Ronnie into the sagebrush and run away. Ronnie had come stumbling across the coulee to Beth, because she never failed to think up a way out of his troubles.

Shakily Beth reached out and pushed Old Dude's funny loose-hanging lower lip up over his yellow teeth where it belonged. What horse could they get in place of the roan? Ronnie was depending on her to help. The race was at two o'clock. It was now nearly noon.

But she knew and Ronnie knew that every pinto, pony and horse in the country had been borrowed or bargained for by some boy to ride in the relay. There was no possible chance of finding another suitable horse to take the place of the runaway roan pony.

In despair Beth pressed her forehead against old Dude's white shoulder and heard his restless old heart beating strong inside. The old horse arched his long proud lumpy neck and nudged her with his nose. She tried to put her arms around him, but he was too big around and too tall.

Dude was all hers, all she had. Ronnie had three dogs, a yellow kitten, a fire truck, a cowboy outfit — chaps, shirt, kerchief, sombrero — but she had only old Dude. Old Dude was enough. No one could possibly understand how she felt about having Dude, unless it was Ronnie, who felt the same way about having the prize twin calves — and now he wouldn't have them.

Dude nudged her again, as if to tell her something — something that was very important to him.

Suddenly she knew.

'Here's Dude, Ronnie!' she cried triumphantly. 'Why didn't we think of him before? You can ride Dude in the relay race in place of the roan pony!'

Paul Brown '39

'*Him!*' Ronnie gave the old horse a scornful glance and almost laughed. 'Why, Dude wouldn't do at all.' Couldn't Beth see that for all his high-headed ways Dude was old and stiff and good-for-nothing?

No. To Beth, who loved him, Dude was as spirited and strong as any charger out of a book of knights.

'Dude can run,' she insisted loyally. 'He has long legs.'

'But he's too old, Beth. Like as not he'd get tired and lie down in the middle of the race, just as he lay down for the vanilla-and-spices man last spring outside your gate. That's why the vanilla-and-spices man gave him to you and bought a better horse from my dad. When a horse gets to be twenty years old he's no good for anything. Except,' Ronnie added quickly, with a good-natured smile lighting up his freckled face, 'to curry and feed and pet and maybe hitch to a single buggy. So he wouldn't do for a relay horse, now would he?'

'He might do,' the girl insisted stubbornly. 'No one knows what Dude is good for. He's a mystery horse. We don't know anything about him or his past life except that he is twenty years old by his teeth.'

'And that he tries to run away whenever anyone on horseback comes near him. That's a bad habit in a horse,' said Ronnie, who was a rancher and knew all about horses — more than homesteaders knew.

'Maybe,' said Beth, currying Dude's front leg that was as slim and trim as any colt's. One bad habit didn't spoil a good horse.

'And there'll be lots of boys on horseback at the race,' Ronnie went on, 'so the race is no place for scary old Dude. I'm sorry, Beth; I don't mean to be ungrateful.'

'That's all right, Ronnie,' she assured him quietly.

Ronnie began pacing again. 'I'll have to get another horse,' he muttered.

Suddenly Beth said: 'Charlie Bailey over in the Missouri breaks has a black pony, Ronnie. If he rides her to the picnic maybe you could borrow her.'

Ronnie brightened. 'So I could! I'll offer Charlie one of my dogs for the use of her.'

Ronnie rushed out of the barbed-wire corral and ran across the coulee toward home, shouting back jubilantly: 'I'll be seeing you at the picnic. Thanks for helping me, Beth. Thanks.'

Beth had expected to drive to the Rancher's Picnic with her father and mother, but at the last minute Mr. Posey discovered that the fence was down on the west line of his homestead. He must mend it at once before range cattle got into his wheat crop. Mrs. Posey would help him.

'But there's no reason why you should miss the ice cream and the relay race,' Mr. Posey told Beth. 'I'll hitch old Dude and Mother will put the picnic basket under the buggy seat and you can drive to the picnic yourself. It's only two miles away. Stay on the old trail past our fence, Beth. That way you won't meet anyone on horseback to make Dude nervous.'

Half an hour later Beth, in her starched pink gingham smock, sat very soberly on the buggy seat driving Dude down the old trail to the Rancher's Picnic. She had told Ronnie it was all right, but she *was* a little hurt because Ronnie had said Dude wasn't good for anything.

Dude didn't seem to care. His high head was higher than usual. His funny loose-hanging lower lip went pup-pup up and down like the lid on an upside-down coffee-pot as he trotted briskly along, picking his long-legged way carefully over little washouts and gopher holes in the unused trail.

In spite of herself she laughed softly at him. 'Funny old Dude. You're as gentle as Ronnie's yellow kitten and as dignified as a gentleman in a top hat and as mysterious as the sky at night. What were you raised to be? Cab horse, army horse, fire horse, circus horse, as some have said? *My* horse. That is enough. You lay down at my gate. Dear old Dude.'

Beth was late in arriving at the Rancher's Picnic. The foot-races and ball game and greased pig contest were over. It was about time for the boys' relay race to start. Already the boys were leading their ponies up to the circular track that had been laid out on the prairie like a great wheel in front of the grove of giant cottonwoods. Ranchers and homesteader families were leaving the picnic tables in the grove and gathering near the starting line to watch the boys and their ponies.

Sorrel ponies, bay ponies, piebald, spotted and rat-tailed ponies, shaggy ponies, sleek ponies, small ponies, tall ponies — they were nudging, snorting, whinnying, whisking about. How bright and merry and exciting it all was!

Beth tried to find Ronnie with Comet and Sprint and Charlie Bailey's black pony among them, but Dude was beginning to act nervous and needed all her attention. He looked eagerly toward the ponies across the way, his ears pricked, his long white body quivering with excitement. He shook his head stubbornly when Beth guided him quickly away from the ponies into the far edge of the cottonwood grove.

'Funny old Dude,' she chided him. 'Twenty years old and acting like a spring colt.'

She decided to unhitch Dude from the buggy and tie him behind a cottonwood tree out of sight of the racers. She was eleven; she could handle the light harness. As she loosened the tugs she wondered why old Dude always behaved so queerly at the sight of horseback riders. Ronnie always said someone on a horse must have frightened him once when he was young. But she wondered.

Then she heard the starter blow his whistle, calling the boy riders up to the line. She hurried with straps and buckles. She wanted to be at the race to cheer for Ronnie.

In the relay race, as Ronnie had told her, each boy must enter three ponies. On one of these he started the race. The other two ponies were held by their keeper in the group near the inner edge of the track. Then, when the boys raced their first ponies once around the track, they were to dismount swiftly, change their saddles to their second ponies and ride them around. In the third lap, they were to ride the third and last ponies.

It was the dismounting, resaddling and remounting from pony to pony that called for skill in the rider. Not a movement dare be wasted, not a second lost. The ponies themselves must be swift and sure. The boy who came in first on his third horse would win the prize twin calves. At this very moment they were being led out in the center of the wheel — two little red-bodied heifers with their round white faces sparkling in the sun. Everybody clapped at them.

'Oh, I do hope Ronnie wins them,' breathed Beth from the edge of the grove. Where was Ronnie?

Then suddenly Ronnie came running through the trees toward her. Something was wrong.

'Ronnie, why aren't you in the race?'

Ronnie turned away and began to pace back and forth, biting his lip to hide its trembling. 'I have only two horses; Charlie Bailey hasn't arrived yet with his black pony.'

'Oh, Ronnie!' she cried in disappointment.

What would they do? Ronnie *must* ride, he must win the twin calves. Her anxious eyes swept the picnic grove, the crowd of people, the prize calves, the ponies, the prairie beyond.

All at once she exclaimed, 'There's Charlie Bailey at the creek now, watering his black pony!' She gave Ronnie a little push. 'Go back and tell the starter you've found a third horse; start in the race with Comet and Sprint, Ronnie. I'll have your other horse there in three minutes,' she promised, and tying the last knot in Dude's halter rope she sped out of the grove toward the creek.

She heard Ronnie's joyful shout as he ran back to enter the race. 'Thanks, Beth.'

Beth found that Charlie Bailey wasn't watering his black pony after all. He had her left forefoot lifted and was looking anxiously at it.

'Got a stone in her foot,' he explained as Beth ran up. 'She limped so much the last mile I thought I'd never get here. It must be up high in the frog. I'll ask one of the men to help me get it out as soon as the race is over.'

Beth turned away. No use to ask Charlie Bailey for the loan of his black pony. The limping black pony could never win a race for Ronnie with a stone lodged in the frog of her foot. There wasn't time to get it out before the race. Beth had promised to bring Ronnie another horse in three minutes; and across the way the race had begun.

The youthful riders were starting their ponies around the first lap. In the lead Beth saw Ronnie's cerise sateen shirt flash below Comet's lowered head. Ronnie would certainly win the twin calves. If he had another horse!

She began to run blindly this way and that. Another horse!

Now the riders were coming in at the finish of the first lap. There was a flash of tossing manes, of quick young arms as the boys leaped to the ground, a gleam of brown saddles being changed swiftly from the first ponies to the second. Some boy in his haste made a blundering mistake. The crowd laughed.

Beth held her breath. It wasn't Ronnie. Ronnie was already started on the second lap with Sprint far ahead of the others. The crowd cheered him. He was the best rider.

In less than two minutes Ronnie would be around that track again. There must be another horse waiting for him to ride. What horse?

But why ask? There was only one other horse.

Dude.

A moment later the spectators began to laugh at the sight of a high-headed, long-legged old white horse that a frantic girl was leading out of the cottonwood grove toward the place where the keepers were holding the last relay of ponies.

Ronnie had known everybody would laugh. Ronnie had said that old Dude would lie down in the middle of the race. No time to think of that now. Ronnie, riding Sprint, was leading the other ponies swiftly down the second lap.

Again Ronnie came in first. He was off, the saddle with him. He turned without looking to throw it over the back of Charlie Bailey's black pony. He knew that the black pony would be there because Beth had promised. She had never failed him. His saddle fell expertly over a tall white back instead of a low black one.

Ronnie blinked. What was this? A white horse. Old Dude!

Beth, holding the quivering, prancing old horse in the hub-bub and scramble of boys and ponies at the edge of the track, saw Ronnie's dismayed face.

'Hurry, Ronnie!' she gasped. 'Ride him.'

Ronnie could only stare at old Dude. He was ashamed. He was beaten. One rider started out on the last lap. Another. The crowd cheered. Ronnie didn't seem to care. Dude began to toss his head, his funny, loose-hanging lower lip worked up and down — pup-pup pup! Beth could hardly hold him.

'Hurry, Ronnie!' she pleaded. 'Dude is all there is. Charlie Bailey's black pony has a stone in her foot.'

'Oh, well,' muttered Ronnie bitterly. He cinched the saddle, swung into it. They were laughing at him, but he would carry through. He was no quitter. But he knew the twin calves were lost to him.

There were four ponies ahead of them as Dude and Ronnie started out on the last lap. The ranchers and homesteaders all laughed and shouted good-naturedly at the bony high-headed old horse who trailed behind the fleet ponies.

Presently there were only three ponies ahead of him. Then only two. One. Old Dude was overtaking the ponies as surely and easily as a stately old stork might overtake a flock of fluttering chickadees. All the bottled-up restlessness in his long bony body seemed to have broken loose in his flying feet. The crowd stopped laughing, gasped, began to cheer for him.

Very quickly and breathlessly the boys' relay race was over. Ronnie Garner had won it. He came in far ahead of the others on old Dude. Someone was leading the twin calves up to him. Everybody was cheering.

Ronnie raised his sombrero and said thank you. Then he slid off old Dude's back to take the prize calves.

Beth was there, reaching for Dude's reins, pushing his funny loose-hanging lower lip over his yellow teeth, whispering lovingly, proudly to him.

'It wasn't a bad habit after all, was it — your wanting to run when you saw horseback riders? You only wanted to show us what you were born to be, not a mystery horse to be laughed at and guessed about — but a *race horse*.'

Ponies reared and galloped and wheeled all about him, but old Dude didn't notice. He was no longer nervous and restless. He lowered his proud head and nudged Beth with his nose as if to tell her that all that was past, that he was content and very tired and twenty years old, that all he wanted in life now was her arms about his neck.

And she understood and put them there.

Then Ronnie stood before her with his two white-faced calves. He was wild with joy, but Beth saw that he was humble, too. He wanted to tell her that he was sorry because he had said Dude was too old and had a bad habit and wasn't good for anything. He didn't know how to say it; boys were that way.

Suddenly he pushed one of the twin calves toward her. 'You take her, Beth.'

'What for?'

'For letting me use old Dude.'

She stared at him. Ronnie was giving her half of his precious partnership with his dad, half of his grateful heart. Ronnie, who had so many pets and playthings, could never understand that one was all she ever wanted.

She answered him gently with shining eyes: 'No, thank you, Ronnie. Old Dude is enough.'

The swede

Ross Santee

CARL was his name. He told the old man he'd been to sea. That was all any of us knowed of him. He wasn't a cow-puncher. The Swede's job was tendin' the pump down at the lower ranch and sort of lookin' after things around the place. He couldn't have been more than twenty.

Them pump men is usually a sorry lot, an' he bein' a for-eigner the punchers all let him pretty much alone. Of course it was funny to hear him talk. No one but the old man could understand him. But all the laughin' that I've did was done behind his back. An' no one ever called him Swede. At least not to his face.

He had an awful pleasant smile. But he wasn't the sort a man would ever get familiar with unless you knowed him mighty well. Except for the long knife in his belt and some funny kind of sailor shirt, he dressed just like the rest of us. But somehow with them straight legs an' that blond hair he never did belong.

The Swede never rode with the outfit. When he first came

he didn't know how to saddle a horse. The old man give him
an old pot-bellied gray to ride, when he was out workin' on
the fence. And it was a sight to watch the Swede come trottin'
up on that old gray. For he was plumb helpless on a horse.

Most of the time the Swede an' the old man was alone at
the ranch. For the punchers seldom came to headquarters unless we wanted a fresh mount of horses or maybe a pack-load
of grub. The Swede had been there 'most a month when the
outfit came into the ranch to gather horses for the fall
work.

I wouldn't have knowed the place. The ranch-house always
looked like a boar's nest. But the Swede had mucked things
out. An' anyone would have thought a woman was waitin'
on the place, it was that neat an' clean. He'd built a sink in
the kitchen an' had running water on the porch. An' he'd
even planted bluegrass in the yard around the house.

He was always busy at something. When he wasn't nursin'
that fool pump he was out somewhere a-fixin' fence. About
the only time I ever saw him still was at night around the fire.
Then he'd just sit an' puff his pipe an' hold that little fuzzy
dog. But he never said a word.

It was while we were down at headquarters that they give
Swede this new horse. I figured it was a lousy trick. But
Swede asked for him himself. 'All right,' the old man says,
'if that's the thing you're lookin' for, it's just as well you
get yours now as later on. You'll probably find him faster
than that old pot-bellied gray.'

He was a little bronc we called Shimmy. An' he was full of
TNT. He'd stand an' shake all over when anyone came near.
Then he'd strike out with both forefeet an' try to use them
teeth of his. Oh, he was a playful thing, all right. Slim Higgins rode him once an' turned him in. Slim was a rider, too.

Paul Brown '39

But Slim said he hired out as a cowpuncher an' not to work with dynamite.

Just why the Swede would pick out a horse like that was something we couldn't figure out. It wasn't as if Swede didn't know the horse. For he'd seen him fight too many times when anyone came near. Of course we wanted to see the fun. For we thought the Swede would try an' ride him that afternoon.

An' me and Slim offered to help Swede saddle him. But instead the Swede turned him into that little pasture down back of the house an' give him a big feed of grain.

The outfit pulled out for Black River next morning, an' we never came in again until the fall round-up was over. Once in a while a puncher would go in with the pack-mules after chuck. An' we heard there then that the Swede was still alive. Once when Bill Gilson went, Bill said the Swede was ridin' fence on Shimmy. But it was so seldom that Bill ever told the truth that none of us believed him. For none of us thought the Swede would ever get a saddle on him.

It was months before we saw the Swede again. An' it was awful good to see that smile of his the night that we rode in. For somehow a man gets awful tired of lookin' at them waddies that he's workin' with. The Swede came out and helped unpack. He'd ditched that funny sailor shirt. But he was still wearin' that long knife. An' I was surprised to hear him talk. For I could understand 'most all he said.

That night we all had quite a game around the fire. But it was the punchers that did most of the talkin'. For the Swede just sat an' puffed his pipe an' held that fuzzy dog. It was just before we all turned in that Shorty asked the Swede if he wouldn't like to ride with us tomorrow.

'We're pretty short-handed,' Shorty says, 'an' it'll be a good chance to try out that new horse of yours.' Most of us ducked our heads to keep from laughin'. But the Swede he flashed that smile of his and said he'd like to come.

Me and Slim Higgins was on wrangle next morning, an' we got into the ranch about daylight with the horses. Me and Slim hadn't had no breakfast yet, but we waited to see the fun. For the Swede was standin' in the corral with a bridle on his arm when we rode in.

I wouldn't have believed it if anyone had told me. But the Swede walked up to that fool horse an' slipped the bridle on. He didn't even use a rope to catch him. An' Shimmy never even tried to buck when Swede got on him. The old man give us both the laugh when we came in to breakfast.

An' then the old man said he couldn't understand the thing himself. He said the Swede had fooled with that blamed horse for days before Shimmy let him touch him. Then one day he looked out an' saw the Swede up on his back. An' all the Swede ever had to do was whistle an' the horse would come trottin' up to him. But Shimmy would never let nobody but the Swede come near him.

The outfit all went to town to let off steam after the round-up was over. An' the day me and Slim got back to the ranch we tried to steal a ride on Shimmy. Our horses was out in the pasture a mile or so from the house. An' we wanted to go into camp that night. We'd came as far as the ranch in the car. There wasn't no horses up to wrangle in. But Shimmy was standin' in the corral, an' so we picked on him.

Slim walked up with the bridle, but he never got to put it on him. For Shimmy struck with them forefeet the minute Slim came near. Slim wasn't hurt to speak of, but it made Slim fightin' mad. I never saw a horse fight so. I went an' got a rope, an' we finally choked him down.

Slim was puttin' the bridle on him when the old man came an' made us turn him loose. It was just as well we did, I guess, for just then the Swede came polin' in. An' the old man give us both the laugh again. For the Swede he saddled Shimmy up an' went an' brought our horses in.

As the months went by I came to likin' this Swede awful well. An' I often wondered why he came to drift away out here. One night when we was alone at the ranch he told me why he came.

'I was youst fourteen,' he said, 'when I leave home. Six
year I bane on sea. But once when I was little boy I saw some
pictures of the West. An' always I think sometime I like to go
out there. So once when we landed in New York I youst quit
ship an' come.'

There was always something about this Swede that none of
us could understand. He was hard as flint around the men.
But when it came to animals he had the softest streak I've
ever seen. The rest of us despised that fuzzy dog, for he was
always snappin' at your heels. But Swede would take this
fool pup every place he went. An' if the dog got tired Swede
would carry him.

During the drouth the Swede brought in some eighty dogie
calves, an' he carried most all of them in on that fool horse of
his. For whenever Swede found a calf whose mammy had
died, Swede would pick up the calf an' bring him in.

It made a lot of extra work for him just feedin' them blame
things. An' lots of nights he was 'way after dark just gettin'
through his chores. One day the old man spoke to him about
how much he'd saved the outfit by bringin' them calves in.
It made Swede fightin' mad.

'That wasn't the reason I brought them in,' says Swede.
'I youst feel sorry for them calves.'

It was the day the Swede was up on Slash cuttin' cedar
posts that he came near losin' Shimmy. There's lots of wild
horses up in there. But it never occurred to Swede that
Shimmy might pull out and leave him. The feed was pretty
good, so Swede pulled the saddle off and turned Shimmy loose
to graze.

Swede was busy with his posts, an' he never paid Shimmy
any mind. For the horse always hung around him just like a
dog. Swede had been workin' for an hour or so before he

missed the horse. He hunted everywhere. He finally saw Shimmy on a ridge about three hundred yards away. A bunch of wild horses had come in while Swede was busy, an' Shimmy had pulled out an' gone to them.

Anybody but the Swede would have kissed his horse good-bye right then. For once a saddle-horse gets in with them wild horses it takes the whole outfit an' the dog to ever catch him. But the Swede slipped back to his saddle an' got his rifle. Then he started crawlin' on his belly toward the ridge.

Shimmy an' three of the wild ones was a-playin' together a little way from the main bunch. An' Swede figured he might be able to cut them off when they started down the ridge. Swede had the wind on the bunch, an' he crawled within a hundred yards before they ever seen him. Then a sorrel stud threw up his head an' snorted, an' the wild bunch headed down the ridge a-runnin' like the wind.

Shimmy an' the three that he'd been playin' with was a-runnin' just behind. Swede made a run an' tried to cut them off. But it wasn't any use. It was then Swede opened up with that old 30–40.

Afterwards when Swede was tellin' me about it he said he thought he'd seen the last of Shimmy when they passed him on the ridge. It was then Swede started shootin'. Swede says there wasn't nothin' to it after Shimmy stopped an' saw him.

'For Shimmy he was pretty scared for all that shootin'. An' he youst stand an' shake all over till he hear me whistle. Then Shimmy he youst come to me.'

TRUSTWORTHY

S. P. Meek

FIRST call for evening parade sounded melodiously over Empire, the headquarters of the Nineteenth United States Cavalry in the Canal Zone. Lieutenant Scott emerged from the bachelor quarters, his riding gloves in one hand and a slice of fresh pineapple in the other. On his left wrist was a six-inch-wide binding of tape, but aside from that he showed no effects of the fall he had taken during the championship polo game, almost a month earlier.

Frog gave a whicker of satisfaction at the sight of his master. Although saddled for parade and standing at the hitching rack, the horse was not tied. With his reins dropped to the ground, he stood as motionless as though hewn from granite.

Scott handed him the pineapple and stroked his satiny neck while he ate it. When he had finished with the tidbit, Scott gathered the reins, tossed them over Frog's neck, then vaulted lightly into the saddle.

'Steady, Frog,' he said as the horse made a playful curvette.

At the sound of his voice, Frog ceased his prancing and started down the road past Officers' Line at a sedate walk. The lieutenant paid no attention to his mount, but carefully drew on his gloves, the neglected reins dropping loosely on Frog's neck.

In front of Captain Rembrandt's quarters, his friend, Elsie, was waiting for him.

'Oh, Scotty,' she called, 'I want to ask a favor of you.'

Frog stopped dead at a touch of Scott's knees. The lieutenant smiled at the eager-eyed child who faced him with flushed cheeks.

'Name your poison, Lady,' he said laughingly. 'I mean, what are you going to work me for now?'

'Are you going to ride Frog tomorrow morning?'

'I hadn't given the matter any thought, Elsie. Why?'

'Because, if you aren't, I'd — I'd like to — to borrow him.'

'What are you planning to do, start a bologna factory?'

'Of course not!' She looked up indignantly, caught the smile which lurked in Scott's eyes and laughed. Few grown-ups, and no children, could resist Scott's infectious smile. 'I'll tell you,' she went on quickly, the words tumbling from her lips in rapid eagerness. 'Sergeant Winsoton is going into the jungle tomorrow to get oranges and I want Frog ——'

Scott held up an arresting hand.

'Let Sergeant Winsoton ride Frog?' he exclaimed in mock horror. 'Never. Frog isn't a truck horse.'

'Of course not, Scotty,' cried the girl. 'He always rides Blaze, the spare fire-horse.'

'Oh, he does, does he?' said Scott, the twinkle still persisting in his eye. 'I'd been wondering what was the matter with Blaze. He's been looking awfully worn out lately. But go on with your story. What do you want with Frog, if you aren't going to let Winsoton ride him?'

'Why, it's this way,' said the child eagerly. 'I asked Daddy if I could go with Sergeant Winsoton and he said I could, if I could get a safe horse. I asked him if Frog would do, and he laughed and said yes. Will you lend him to me?'

Scott's merry laugh rang out.

'I smell a rat,' he declared. 'Does your father know that you've been riding Frog on the quiet?'

'No, I haven't told anyone. You said not to.'

'Just as I suspected. Your father thinks he has found a nice, diplomatic "out" on letting you go. You tell him that you've been riding Frog on the quiet for the last week. If he's still willing for you to go on him, you may have him.'

'Oh, thanks, Scotty; thanks ever so much.'

'You're welcome, Elsie. Have a good time.'

Scott touched Frog with his spur. The beautifully trained horse turned toward the parade ground, while Elsie Rembrandt, her blue eyes shining, turned and ran into her house. While Scott was at supper, Captain Rembrandt called him on the telephone.

'Do you think it's safe for Elsie to ride Frog tomorrow, Scott?' he asked. 'He's a pretty spirited horse, you know.'

'Spirited, yes, sir, but thoroughly trustworthy. He's a perfect gentleman, and would never misbehave with a child up. Elsie has ridden him every afternoon for a week and she handles him perfectly.'

'Well, you know your horse, Scott. I don't want to baby Elsie, and if you think it's safe, I'll let her go.'

'I'm sure it's safe, sir. Besides, Sergeant Winsoton will be along. He's a very dependable man, you know.'

'Yes, I know that, Scott. Well, all right, she can go.'

Scott chuckled as he hung up the receiver. 'She'll be as safe on Frog as on any horse I ever rode,' he said to himself.

He telephoned Sergeant Baker to put Elsie's saddle on Frog in the morning, and to send up Pedro for Scott's own riding.

There was dismay in Elsie Rembrandt's face as she faced Sergeant Baker at the corral the next morning.

'Sergeant Winsoton isn't here?' she cried.

'No, Miss Elsie. He was taken sick in the night and he's in the hospital. He said to tell you that he'd be out in three or four days and that he'd go after oranges with you then.'

'But I can't go in three or four days. Daddy won't let me go except on Frog, and I borrowed him for today. Can't you go with me?'

'I'm afraid not, Miss Elsie. I'm pretty busy today.'

The girl turned away with a disappointed face. 'It's maddening,' she declared. 'I had it all fixed up to go and get some early oranges for Christmas, and then something had to go and spoil it. Now I don't know what to do.'

Sergeant Baker thought rapidly.

'Why don't you take Frog, and go up the Paja Road a couple of miles and get some lemons?' he asked.

'I suppose I might as well,' she said, 'but I did want to go into the jungle. I've never been in during the wet season. Well, anyway, I'll get to ride Frog. Lend me a barracks bag, will you, Sergeant?'

'Surely, Miss Elsie.' He tied a heavy white bag which would hold about a bushel and a half to the cantle of her saddle, then helped her to mount. 'Have a good time, Miss Elsie,' he called after her.

'Thanks, Sergeant, I will. I'll return your bag tomorrow.'

She rode slowly through the post toward the end of the Paja Road. She carried herself proudly, wished that her father could see her as she rode the best polo pony on the post, holding him under perfect control. Frog stepped along with a dainty, mincing gait, holding his head high, as though proud of his burden.

Once clear of the post, Elsie touched him with her spur. He broke into a distance-eating trot, a gait that would carry him tirelessly at eight miles an hour for half a day at a time, even through tropic heat.

As she rode along, an idea formed in Elsie's brain. She could go after lemons any day. Now that she had Frog, why not go into the jungle alone and get some oranges? The trail was an open one, and she knew that the Tavares Grove was only two miles from the main road. She had specially planned on some oranges of her own picking for Christmas. Once the idea took root, it was not easily dislodged, and she ignored the groves of lemon trees which grew alongside the Paja Road. At the sight of the trail leading off toward the grove, her hesitation vanished.

'Come on, Frog, we'll do it!' she cried, and turned him off the road.

The trail was open and well marked. Her spirits rose at the thought of the adventure. She rounded a rocky knoll and a stretch of open savanna lay before her. A mile away she could see a grove of trees with dark green shiny leaves.

'I don't see why I should keep to this trail,' she said to herself. 'The last time I came out here with Daddy, I'm sure we went straight across this place to the grove.'

She turned Frog's head out of the trail. He went forward a few feet, then stopped and snorted. She urged him forward. He made a few gingerly steps, then whirled and bolted back to the trail. It was well that he did so, for this was the middle of the wet season and places which were readily passable a few months earlier were treacherous bog now. Before Frog reached the hard ground, he sank halfway to his hock-joints in thick, sucking mud. Elsie's cheek paled as he struggled back to the hard trail.

'Good horse,' she said, stroking his neck. 'You know what you're doing, don't you, Frog? We'll stick to the trail.'

Fifteen minutes of riding brought them to the edge of the grove. Elsie gave a cry of disappointment as she looked at the trees. They were loaded with fruit, but the oranges were no larger than lemons, and were a bright green in color.

'It's a shame,' she cried. 'I know it's early, but Sergeant Winsoton told me there would be some ripe ones. I won't find a single one here fit to take home.'

A sudden thought pierced her disappointment. Sergeant Winsoton had told her that they might not find any at the Tavares Grove, but that he knew another one, deep in the jungle, where the fruit ripened earlier. His description of the route was crystal clear in her mind.

'The trail starts at the far side of this grove,' she said. 'It branches in half a mile and you take the left fork. I'll see if I can find it.'

She gathered Frog's reins and rode through the grove. On the far side a trail led straight away into the deep jungle. Elsie hesitated.

'I don't know the road,' she confessed to herself, 'but Sergeant Winsoton said there was only one fork. I wouldn't get lost. Anyway, if I did, I could give Frog his head. He'd find his way back to the post.'

With this comforting thought in her mind, she rode off into the jungle. At the fork she turned left into a trail which was almost overgrown.

'I wish I had someone here with a machete to clear the trail,' she said, 'but I expect we can break through. We'll try, anyway, won't we, Frog?'

In half a mile she regretted that she had gone on. The tough lianas which grew across the trail threatened to sweep her from the saddle. She debated turning back, but a stubborn streak of pride in her nature forbade such a course. Crouching low in the saddle, she urged Frog on.

For three miles she forced her way until the trail opened up into a glade, grown high with underbrush, and lush, rank vegetation. She gave a cry of delight. Before her were dozens of orange trees, loaded with large oranges. Most of them were green, but quite a few had a golden blush, and some were evidently quite ripe. She would have no trouble filling her bag here.

She rode under the lofty trees and tried to reach the fruit. These trees were different from the low, squatty trees of the Tavares Grove. Most of the oranges, including all the ripe ones, were out of her reach. She dropped Frog's reins over his head and took her feet from the stirrups. Gingerly she raised herself until she stood on the saddle, but still only a few of the oranges were within reach, even with this added elevation. She would have to climb to get them.

She fastened the barracks bag to her belt, then stood once more on the saddle to reach a low-growing branch. She caught it, but withdrew her hand with an exclamation of disgust. Termites had attacked the living trees, and her hands had broken into one of their runways. She wiped the yellow slugs from her fingers with a grimace of distaste. Setting her teeth, she caught the limb again and swung herself up into the tree.

In a few minutes she had a dozen fine oranges in her bag. An usually luscious bunch a few feet out along a limb attracted her. Balancing herself carefully, she worked her way out along it. They were almost within reach. She moved a few feet farther, then gave a cry of alarm. The limb sagged beneath her with an ominous, cracking sound.

She strove to retreat, but it was too late. The termites had bored deeper into the limb than she had realized. With a tearing, rending sound it snapped off. Elsie gave a scream as she was hurtled off into the air. She strove desperately to grasp a limb, but in vain. She struck the ground with a dull thud, the broken limb beside her. She lay quiet, in a curiously crumpled heap.

As her scream rang out, followed by the crash of her fall, Frog gave a sudden leap forward. His trailing reins halted him. He paused, trembling like a leaf, his eyes rolling wildly. His fear soon passed. He made a cautious step toward his fallen mistress. He recoiled with a backward leap as a sudden hiss smote his ear. Coiled in the herbage was the reddish, yellow-brown of a six-foot fer-de-lance. The snake uncoiled and came forward, ready for battle. Frog backed away, snorting. The snake glided menacingly toward him.

Frog whirled about to run. His hindquarters struck a fallen branch. With a squeal of terror, he lashed out with both heels. The branch flew through the air and landed beside Elsie.

At the crash behind him, the snake paused and whipped into a coil, ready to deal his almost universally fatal blow. The limb which Frog had kicked settled with a sharp crackling. The snake instantly glided in that direction, straight toward the unconscious girl. Two feet from her hip it paused, whipped itself into a coil. Its head drew far back, then shot forward almost quicker than the eye could follow.

The head shot forward, but before it could land, a steel-shod hoof flashed between the death-laden fangs and the unconscious girl. Frog had whirled about when he had kicked,

just in time to see the snake, as he supposed, retreat. With a squeal of rage, he had charged after it with flashing hoofs.

The deadly blow struck harmless against the hard hoof. The snake drew back its head for another blow, but Frog, when aroused, could move as swiftly as the snake itself. His hoofs crashed down on the coils, breaking the snake's back in a dozen places. It writhed in pain and lashed out with its fangs, but Frog avoided the blows of the crippled viper with ease. Again and again the vicious hoofs fell with deadly effect until the snake was a mere battered mass of dead flesh. Still the horse did not pause until he had pounded it into a pulp. Then, and only then, did he turn his attention to the still motionless girl.

He nuzzled her softly and whinnied in her ear. He pawed at her gently, strove to roll her over with his nose, but she was wedged in a bush so that he could not move her. He whinnied his distress to the jungle, but there was no answer.

Slowly memory came to the horse. Once before he had seen his rider, Scott that time, unconscious before him. When he could not rouse him, he had galloped to the post and brought back aid. Scott had praised him and fed him pineapples to repletion the next day. Evidently that was the thing to do. Frog turned and started for the post.

He had gone but a few steps when another thought halted him in his stride. That snake! He came back at a gallop. The snake lay motionless, but the heavy reptilian odor which told of death hung heavy over him. With flashing hoofs, Frog drove again and again at the battered flesh. Satisfied at last that it represented no present menace, he once more strove to rouse Elsie. His efforts were fruitless.

Again he started for the post, but returned after a few steps to still further maul the dead snake. The problem was too much for Frog to solve. At the post he could get help, but to leave his mistress would be to expose her to that death which Frog could not be sure would not rouse itself at any moment and strike. He planted himself between the girl and the viper and stood guard, ready for instant attack should the snake stir.

Pedro had been brought to Scott's quarters that morning as he had ordered. The lieutenant mounted him and rode off to drill. Various duties kept him occupied most of the morning, and it was after eleven when he rode to the corral for his morning inspection. A glance at the picket line told him that Frog had not returned.

'Sergeant Winsoton isn't back yet?' he asked the stable sergeant.

'Winsoton is in the hospital, sir,' Baker answered.

'He is? What's the matter?' asked Scott quickly.

'Well, sir,' replied Baker, with a grin, 'it's a mixture of too much luck and bad judgment as to his capacity. You see, he won a good many chicken dinners on the big game last month, and Tubby doesn't exactly hate chicken. Well, he was in town last night and he ran up against two artillerymen who each owed him a dinner. They both had the money and offered to pay up then and there, or else never. So Tubby had to either eat two dinners — or lose one. He thought he could manage to get away with both of them so he tried. He succeeded. He ate those two dinners right through from soup to dessert, a double order of fried chicken in each one. He was a little purple when he got through, but he didn't say much. He just came home and laid down. During the night it got him, and we had to take him up to the hospital with acute indigestion. He'll be all right after they starve him for a week or so, but right now, if you say "chicken," he's liable to heave a rock at you.'

Scott laughed. 'Where's Frog this morning?' he asked, with a glance at the picket line.

'Miss Elsie got him this morning, sir. I put her saddle on him like the lieutenant told me to. She meant to go into the jungle with Winsoton, but after she found out what happened to him, she borrowed a barracks bag from me and went out along the Paja Road after lemons. That was at eight o'clock. She ought to be back any minute now.'

Scott's face was grave as he glanced at his watch.

'Three hours and a quarter,' he muttered. 'She ought to be back, even if she went clear to Paja. Of course, she's safe on Frog, but I wish she had someone along with her.'

He sat his horse a moment in thought, then turned to Sergeant Baker. 'I'm going out along the Paja Road to meet her,' he said. 'She may be having trouble tying her bag to her saddle — or something may have happened. If one of us isn't back here in two hours, start search parties out. Meanwhile, don't give out any alarm, and if Mrs. Rembrandt calls you, tell her I'm with Elsie. Understand?'

'Yes, sir.'

Scott turned his mount toward Paja. Once clear of the post, he clapped his spurs into Pedro and tore off toward the Zone line at a gallop, in utter defiance of the midday sun. He passed two lemon groves near the road, but a hasty examination told him that neither Frog nor Elsie had been there.

'I'll bet a month's pay to a Panamanian dime that she went into the jungle alone,' he muttered.

Three miles from the post a trail led off to the right toward Tavares Grove. Scott dismounted and examined the ground carefully. He gave an exclamation of satisfaction as his eye fell on a track made by a horse shod with a long inside trail on his hind feet. He had shod Frog that way himself a week before to overcome a slight tendency to interfere. It was proof that Elsie had come that way. He vaulted into the saddle and rode on.

As he came in sight of the grove, the torn-up ground attracted his attention. He vaulted off Pedro and studied the tracks. With no difficulty he read the story of the ill-advised attempt to send Frog off the trail straight to the grove, and of the horse's gallant fight back to hard ground.

'She was all right when she left here — thanks to Frog,' he said as he rode on.

Frog's footmarks were thick around the trees of the Tavares Grove. Scott studied the unripe fruit speculatively.

'She couldn't have got any oranges here,' he said. 'And no track leads back toward the road. She must have gone on to the Comegys Grove, or else the Alconte.'

He rode on through the grove and studied the trail leading into the dense jungle. Again he found Frog's tracks, still leading away from the post. He touched Pedro with his spur.

For a mile the trail led through unbroken walls of jungle, then forked and went in two directions. A glance at the torn lianas on the left-hand fork told Scott which way Elsie had gone. Even without this evidence, the way was clear, for Frog's tracks were plain in the oozy mud.

The trail mounted rapidly, became dry and rocky underfoot. The jungle pressed in until there was barely room for Pedro to squeeze through the thick underbrush. Frog had left no tracks on the hard ground underfoot, but dozens of broken branches and severed creepers bore testimony to his passage. Scott pressed his mount mercilessly. Sweat poured from him in streams in the dank, steaming heat of the jungle, while flecks of lather fell from Pedro's heaving flanks.

One last steep climb brought him to the edge of the grove. Unlike the comparatively open Tavares Grove, the Alconte Grove was grown up with dense brush which hid the lower part of the lofty trees composing it. Scott halted Pedro and stared around. There was no sign of either Frog or Elsie. He raised his voice in a loud halloo. From the brush a hundred yards away, a shrill whinny answered him.

'Frog!' he cried in relief.

He forced Pedro through the brush until he reached the more open space where Frog stood. At the sight of Elsie's prostrate figure he vaulted from his saddle with a cry of alarm.

'Policed!' he cried in dismay as he bent over her. He glanced up at the tree, and his face cleared. 'No, she wasn't,' he said. 'She was climbing and she fell.'

He laid his hand against her cheek, started as he found it cold despite the humid heat of the grove. Her left foot was twisted sideways in an unnatural manner. With deft fingers he examined it.

'Ankle badly sprained... or broken,' he decided. 'Suffering from shock, too.'

He straightened up, almost under Frog's nose. Frog moved sideways, then returned and struck viciously at the ground. Scott's cheek paled under his tan as he saw what the horse was pawing.

'A fer-de-lance!' he cried. 'If it hit her, she's done for.'

He kicked the mangled snake to one side and bent over the girl. The scream of a horse in terror smote his ears. He had kicked the remains of the reptile almost under Pedro's nose. The sight of the snake completed the rout of Pedro, already trembling at the reptilian odor of the glade. His hoofs thundered down the trail toward home and safety.

Scott followed him for a few steps, then turned and came back to Elsie. He bent over and laid his ear against her chest, straightened up with an exclamation of relief.

'Heart slow, but strong and steady,' he said. 'No snakebite, just shock. I know how to take care of that.'

With expert fingers he stripped the saddle from Frog and unwrapped the saddle blanket. He laid Elsie on it, and threw the loose folds over her. His knife soon procured him two straight sticks for splints. He padded them with the barracks bag, then gently straightened her twisted foot. A little moan of pain came from her unconscious lips. With Frog's reins he bound the splints to her leg, then led the horse alongside her.

'You may have a sore back, old fellow,' he said as he cinched the saddle into place with no blanket under it, 'but it can't be helped. Steady, now.'

Frog stood like a rock while Scott laid the unconscious girl across his withers. Once firm in the saddle, the lieutenant picked her up in his arms and held her close, arranging her crippled leg so that it would ride easily. He gave a grimace of pain as her weight came on his injured wrist, then set his teeth and ignored it. He touched Frog with his spur. The horse started down the trail at a sedate walk, Scott easing his burden from the unavoidable jolts as well as he could.

He held her close, hoping that the warmth of his body would help to overcome the coldness which frightened him. Her breath came slowly and in uneven gasps when they started, but as the effects of the heat began to make themselves felt, it came faster and more evenly. As they passed the Tavares Grove a little moan came from her lips. Her eyelids flickered, then rose.

'My leg,' she murmured faintly.

'It's twisted a little, but nothing serious,' said Scott with an attempt at cheerfulness. 'Are you comfortable?'

There was no reply. Scott shifted her in his rapidly tiring arms, groaned at the agony of his crippled wrist. He began to wonder whether he would be able to support her all the way to the post, but luckily, help was near. Along the trail from the Paja Road came three men at a gallop.

'Hello, Baker,' said Scott as they approached. 'You're just in time. Send a man to the post at full gallop for an ambulance. Ride alongside me in case my arms give out.'

At the Paja Road, Baker and the stable orderly took Elsie from Scott's numb arms and laid her on the ground. They covered her closely with the blanket and began, under Scott's direction, to chafe her hands and arms. It was a matter of only a few minutes before the ambulance clanged up. The post surgeon and Captain Rembrandt jumped out and bent over the girl.

'Nothing to be alarmed about,' said the surgeon when he had finished his examination. 'Left ankle bunged up some and a bad shock, but she's young and healthy. She'll be all right in a couple of months at the outside. It's a good thing she wasn't left for a couple of hours longer, though.'

Captain Rembrandt gulped for a moment before he could trust himself to speak. 'Thanks, Scott,' he said gruffly. 'I suppose she was policed,' he added with a venomous glance at Frog.

'No, sir,' Scott replied vigorously. 'Frog never policed a child in his life. She was climbing after oranges and a limb broke under her. Furthermore,' he went on as he noticed the direction of Captain Rembrandt's gaze, 'you've got Frog to thank for saving her life, not me. If it hadn't been for him, I would have found a corpse.'

In a few graphic words he told of his discovery of the trampled fer-de-lance under the tree.

'From all appearances, Frog nailed him just in time,' he said. 'Then he stood guard over her in case another showed up. Not one horse in ten thousand would have done that. Horses, as a rule, are deathly afraid of snakes, you know. Pedro bolted as soon as he saw the dead body. His arrival was what started Baker after me.'

Captain Rembrandt's eyes clouded as he looked at Frog. He moved over and stroked the satiny nose.

'I don't suppose you can understand me, Frog,' he said in a husky voice, 'but I appreciate what you did, even if I can't tell you. Scotty, is there anything that this horse especially likes?'

'Well,' said Scott with a grin, 'I've seen him eat pine-apples with every evidence of enjoyment. Not too many, though,' he hastened to add, 'or he'll get tummy-ache. Too much of anything will give it to a horse — or to a man,' he added with a chuckle to Baker.

'Then you'd better have the veterinarian stand by, Scotty,' said the captain with a tremulous laugh, 'because when I tell Mrs. Rembrandt that, she's going to feed him pineapple until he busts.'

BLACK STORM

Thomas C. Hinkle

NEAR a frontier cattle town of old Kansas on that memorable morning, John McDonald, the cattle-owner of the Chisholm Range, stood in the center of a corral holding the reins of a beautiful horse — a coal-black gelding.

Fully forty cowboys sat on the corral fence looking. The great black horse stood with his head high, a wild light of fear in his eyes, and he quivered in every muscle as he looked back at the stockily built man standing by the saddle.

'Well, here he is,' said McDonald to his men. 'They call him Black Storm. I got him cheap because nobody can ride him. He's been tried all the way from Texas to Kansas. No trouble to saddle him. He'll stand perfect as you see,' and the boss moved away, leaving the horse standing. 'There he is; he belongs to the man who can ride him!'

Instant excitement prevailed.

Certainly here was a good horse! Jet-black, long-limbed, graceful flowing mane and tail. But the men hesitated. Here was no broncho. A broncho may pitch violently but he is

small — small and therefore has not the strength of a big horse, and the broncho could not do to a rider what a big horse could — especially a horse like this!

Muscles of power were there. These men knew it. They had reason to know. They were not tenderfeet. They were among the best riders in the old American West, which meant they were the best riders in the world.

Black Storm was not hard to approach. He was easy to approach. That was his way.

The first man vaulted into the saddle.

A wild, black streak shot through the air; once, twice, thrice — the man fell hard.

Another mounted. The same thing. Then another and another and another. Twenty men Black Storm threw, and threw them like lightning.

Laughing and spitting dust from their mouths and some of them a little blood, they set up a wild shout: 'Where's Joe Bain, Mac? Here's one he can't stick. Get him in!'

A half mile away they found him.

Joe Bain, the silent, came riding in — Joe Bain, but a twenty-one-year-old youth — yet the able, trusted foreman over all the McDonald men and the tens of thousands of Texas longhorns.

The men sat as thick as crows on the top poles of the corral while shouting to Joe Bain: 'You can have him, Joe, if you want him! He's a purty hoss! But pick a nice soft place to light in! We all wanted a haystack but couldn't find any!'

The tall black horse stood in the center of the corral, his eyes shining, his ears not standing stiff, but moving back and forth. Joe Bain noted this as he walked slowly forward. On came the man; the horse shied a little, then stood trembling while Joe slowly came up.

He looked at the horse's head. He was wide between the ears. He looked into his eyes. They were not devil eyes, they were eyes of a mighty good horse but a terribly frightened one. Joe looked at the horse's sides. They were bleeding from the spurs of the men. Joe stood looking in silence, then bent down, removed his spurs, and tossed them aside; and he threw his quirt after them.

'Open the gate, Jim,' Joe ordered the nearest man. 'I'll mount him outside.'

Outside on the wild, level prairie, Joe carefully examined the cinch of the saddle, while the horse stood in a tremble, his eyes set back on his man.

Quietly, slowly, Bain gathered the reins, and then like a cat he was in the saddle.

Wild yells from many cowboys rent the air. The great black flashed up and down, whirled and leaped, reared high and leaped and whirled again, then up — and then that terrible drop to the earth on four stiff legs; and again he leaped with a greyhound leap, stopped short, leaped again.

More wild tricks he knew than any pitching horse ever seen on a range of the West. Up and down with terrific plunges, and up and down again, and still the long, lithe form of a sun-tanned youth held.

It seemed impossible that any man could stand all this and stay, but he did, and stayed on far beyond the limit of most pitching horses. A full half hour he stayed! And then, with a hush among the men, the tall, slim youth, blood running from his nose, dismounted from a groaning, foam-covered, quivering horse.

The youth held his red bandanna handkerchief a minute to his bleeding nose, while patting the horse gently on the neck.

He moved around in front of him, took the horse's nose

gently in his hands, and, the horse held down to him, closed his eyes and breathed peacefully.

Then the miracle. With low, soothing words Joe Bain put his foot in the stirrup, mounted slowly, and as slowly rode the horse a quarter of a mile on the prairie, rode back, dismounted and again held the horse's head in his hands, petted him and talked to him gently.

'Thank you, Mac,' said Bain simply to McDonald. 'He's a good horse. Somebody gave him a bad start, that's all.'

Bain fingered in his pocket for a trinket he had long carried. It was a bright silver star with a pin at the back. While the horse stood with his head down, Joe fixed the star permanently in the head-band of the bridle.

For a long time all the cowmen stood about talking of the horse, looking at him, admiring him. Then Joe Bain mounted again and with Black Storm fully at ease Joe said, 'Well, boys, it's time we were going on with the cattle.' All hands were soon ready, and in a brief time the long herd of Longhorns, temporarily halted here for rest, were started toward the east.

For two weeks it had not rained and as the vast herds, with Joe Bain on the black horse at their head, moved slowly forward into the deeper-cut cattle trails, a great cloud of dust floated up to settle down over cattle and men. At times through the dusty veil something in the morning sunlight flashed and gleamed and glistened. It was the silver star that Joe had fixed on the head-band of Black Storm's bridle.

Two of the cowboys were riding on either side of Joe and admiring Black Storm. They were nearing the river and at this moment John McDonald came galloping up. It was always necessary to swim the Longhorns across the river here as there was no bridge except a pontoon and this was too frail to support these vast herds of cattle.

It had always been Joe Bain who had ridden at the head of the herd on a trusted horse — one that would walk quietly into the deepest stream and swim, thus leading the cattle who would follow the familiar figure of Joe.

But now Joe was on the erstwhile intractable Black Storm. McDonald did not believe that the black horse could be trusted to enter the river and swim across in front of the herd. He was afraid also that if the horse did enter the stream he might, when below his depth, become frightened and so endanger the fearless rider.

McDonald rode up and said, 'Joe, you have a wonderful horse — but maybe you had better not try to lead the cattle across this time — I don't like to let one of the other boys try it either — but if you will take another horse ——'

'You wait and see us, Mac!' said Joe. 'Black Storm may hesitate a little at the edge of the water but when he knows what I want he'll go right in. I'll go ahead a little and talk to him.'

And still without spur or quirt Joe cantered on to the margin of the deep stream not far forward. He rode down the sloping bank to the water's edge where Black Storm stopped of his own accord.

Joe dismounted and took the horse's nose in his hands and petted him saying, 'We'll swim on across the river, Stormy, we'll go right across.' Bain knew the horse did not understand the words but he knew he understood the spirit behind them.

Joe mounted. Black Storm turned a little away from the stream but Joe pressed the rein on his neck, at the same time gently urging him to go in. Black Storm stood for an instant, his trim forehoofs at the edge of the water, his ears moving nervously back and forth as he looked across the river.

'Come, Stormy!' said Joe, leaning over and patting him on the neck — 'straight in and right across!'

Black Storm stepped nervously with his front feet a little, but he did not back away an inch, then he held his head down and looked at the water. He put one foot out and pawed the water a little, then looked down, then up and across.

'Come, Stormy!' Joe repeated, still patting him, and with that Black Storm surged in, his great black body sinking until only his head and upper neck were out of the water, and he was swimming like a veteran.

'Did you ever see anything like it?' exclaimed McDonald to three of his men who sat their horses beside him watching Joe and his horse.

'Joe's got that horse won for certain,' said the little under-foreman, Charlie Bliss.

'It's Joe's way,' said McDonald, 'and that horse has won Joe as completely as Joe has won him — look at him swim! Acts like it was all perfectly natural for him — a smart horse that — you wait and see! In a month Joe will have him per-forming all kinds of tricks.'

The Longhorn cattle had promptly entered the stream and were swimming behind Black Storm. They filled the river with a great mass of tremendous horns — some of them six and seven feet from tip to tip. As they swam their long horns frequently struck one another with a dull, clacking sound. But Black Storm did not seem at all concerned by the mass of swimming cattle behind him. He swam rapidly, his ears cocked forward, his large eyes looking eagerly across the river.

For the first time a man sat on his back talking gently to him and now and then lovingly patting that part of his neck above the water — a man who seemed so quiet and kind and who did not hurt.

Black Storm reached the opposite side, plunged up the sloping bank, alert and ready for Joe's slightest command. Arriving upon the level valley above the river, Joe waved to McDonald and Charlie Bliss, and then started on ahead of the cattle, now moving up the valley toward the bluffs on the east. McDonald, Charlie Bliss and the other cowboys were now swimming the stream behind the cattle and presently the whole herd was across.

From their position behind the cattle they could see at the head of the long herd the form of a beautiful black horse moving in the distance.

A HERDBOY OF HUNGARY

Alexander Finta

True Story of the Author's Boyhood Adventures on his Uncle's Ranch in Hungary, and of the Old Horse he Befriended

FRIENDSHIP between men and animals is not unusual. But the friendship between the old horse Mocskos and me was of a truly extraordinary intensity. It was so for a good reason. We were both in an equally forlorn situation.

Here was I, a very young boy, separated from my family and from all the cosiness, affection, and fun so dear to one of tender years. And here was Mocskos, redeemed from utter neglect only by treatment so cruel as to uproot every confidence she had ever had in mankind. Now, fated to live one astride the other day after day, the two came to depend upon each other with a completeness which drew a magic circle about them, and in it they were alone together.

On our ranch the herdboys were ranked according to age and length of service. The younger men were subordinate to the elder. You can imagine, therefore, with what relief and pleasure the youngest herdsman had seen me installed at the *puszta*. Now it was I and not he who would be the servant of all the herdboys and do all the disagreeable and lowly work both at the hut and around the herd. And, indeed, I had hardly got used to being on the ranch before I was assigned the dishcloth and the duties which went with it. It was my task to scrub all the greasy pots and spoons and, more, to obey all the orders flung at me by the others.

In the same fashion Mocskos was also at the very bottom of the heap. She was 'the good-for-nothing' whom nobody wanted or respected. No wonder, therefore, that our common destiny drew us together. We were always in the same mood and never wished to be separated.

It was soon apparent that if I left my horse for an instant she found it unbearable, and as I went about the hut to do my chores of cleansing the pots or preparing the simple soup for the herdsmen, Mocskos would drift back from her place at the edge of the herd and follow me about like a dog or wait near the door until I was ready to ride out on the prairie to join the ranchers.

Now it was no longer necessary for anyone to help me mount. For Mocskos herself had devised a way to assist me. What she did was to curve her foreleg and hold it stiff for me to stand upon while I reached the stirrup, and as I scrambled to the saddle she would lift her head and, keeping perfectly motionless, would watch to see that I did not fall down the other side. In return for such benevolence I would fill a pan with all the bread crusts left from the last meal and moisten them with water to make a mash for my toothless steed — an attention which pleased her very well.

Furthermore, I trained her to lie down so that I could wash her thoroughly and do my best to curry what hair she had. This earnest attention to improving her appearance seemed also to gratify her deeply. Naturally such mutual devotion caused infinite amusement among the herdsmen and we were the subject of eternal joking. But the fact only served to deepen our friendship more and more as time went on.

What troubled me most about Mocskos was the question of feeding her properly. She was half starved because with her few poor teeth she could not chew the rough, hard grass in which the herd was pastured. Such fodder was excellent for the strong young horses, but impossible for my ancient friend, and as hot summer weather came on the grass became so tough that she could not find one edible mouthful. My ambition had been to put some weight on her starving bones, and I had worked hard to succeed. But now, to my despair, the little fat she had gained dropped off and she began to lose strength.

The ranchman's job is to round up the horses and keep them from straying too far while grazing, and to prevent their getting lost. Mocskos and I had taken our share of this duty and galloped fast and far to head off wandering beasts and to drive them back to their fellows. But now, as the young horses grew stronger and more wilful, nourished as they were by a pasture which to them was crisp and rich, my nag was growing weaker and less able to cope with the situation.

'What ails your noble charger?' the cowboys would call out to me amid shouts of laughter. 'Why doesn't that handsome filly do her share of work? A mettlesome animal like that has no right to be lazy!'

Such hard-hearted derision filled my soul with bitterness toward my companions and toward the whole world. I grew sad and anxious. In vain I tried to seek out some part of the pasture land which would provide softer grass. Everywhere it proved only dry and hard, and Mocskos would leave it all for the young horses to nibble and crunch eagerly between their strong teeth. I was becoming almost brokenhearted over the failing strength of my horse, when one day the situation miraculously changed.

To keep together a herd of over five hundred wild young horses was as difficult a task as to hold five hundred flies in one hand. What made the matter more serious was the fact that half the pasture land was a perilous swamp. It was tufted with the very best grass for the herd, but offered a constant menace to our animals.

Their nervous high spirits kept us always on the watch. For young horses are like rascally boys in their eagerness to have fun at any cost. They are forever looking for an excuse to run away, and just let one mischievous horse annoy the others or let a single fly bite a ringleader, and a herd of five hundred horses will bolt as one. We cowboys had to nip this impulse in the bud or else watch some unfortunate beast be driven into the deep black quagmire whence no horse ever returned.

Sitting our horses and turning wary eyes this way and that, we kept lookout day and night to prevent stampedes. The instant one of the herd started to run away a cowboy was after it, racing like mad and whirling the lasso in air. If it could be quickly caught, quieted down, and returned to the pasture, all was well. But sometimes the entire herd scattered in panic and got away, and when that happened it would take us the whole day to collect them again.

One morning such a stampede occurred. The cause was too trifling for us to foresee, but to our rage all the horses turned mad in a single second and bolted in a hundred different directions. The cowboys, like agitated furies, galloped in wild pursuit. Mocskos started bravely off with the others, but after some five miles of chase showed signs of exhaustion and fell behind.

At last she could go no farther and was obliged to rest. As she came to a stop she lifted her head and eagerly sniffed the air. I, too, was aware of a delicious perfume floating up from near-by. I looked and saw that we were on the edge of a great field of thick clover. Even as I realized it, however, I remembered that this territory was the property of a famous Hungarian magnate.

Mocskos turned her head and rolled her eyes in my direction. She whinnied eagerly. It was a plain statement of her wild desire to have a mouthful of that luscious and tender food which was spread in such abundance under her hungry nose. Who could resist such temptation? Fearfully I hesitated, but in the end I slipped out of the saddle to the ground and took the bit from her mouth. An instant afterward Mocskos was in the clover.

Never did starveling eat with greater voracity! She did not stop to chew, but cropped up great mouthfuls of the succulent plants, still humid from the dew. As she gulped down this marvelous nutriment she gazed upon me with her beautiful eyes, speaking her joy and gratitude. Now on one side, now on the other she cropped eagerly and, although it was plain that her mouth was getting absolutely weary, although she often choked with suffocation because she left no room in her throat for air, she kept right on eating for half an hour.

Such joy was touching to see. At last, stuffed with the food of which horses dream, she lifted her head and sighed in complete satisfaction. Slowly she put out her foreleg. I mounted, and with great deliberation we left the scene of this happy luncheon. Behind us was a perfect circle stripped to the very turf in the heart of the clover-field.

That day Mocskos was the happiest creature in the world. As she took her leisurely way homeward she would often stop for a short look at me, and in lieu of words tears of thankfulness stood in her great eyes. Then after a time, although I had kept her walking slowly to prevent her being sick, she broke of her own accord into a gallop of such grace and strength as I never would have imagined her attaining. It was thus we crossed the last half-mile to the hut, and all the herdboys gathered in stupefaction to watch this astonishing approach.

Of course they turned their surprise into jokes about the style and speed of my old pal. But we two paid no attention. I got Mocskos a good drink, and when she had finished it she uttered many sounds of satisfaction. Thus she assured me that for once she had had a perfect day and was almost at peace with the whole world.

The next day I tried, as usual, to feed her with some of the finer grasses from the swampy land. But she turned coldly away from the proffered gift. Then, fixing me with her intelligent eyes and touching my legs with her head, she made a movement of starting off in the direction of yesterday's feast. I gave no sign that I understood, and pulled her about to another point of the compass. At this she shook her head and shot me a look of dark indignation. Soon she repeated her tricks and tried her best to persuade me to ride toward the field of tender clover.

But I did not wish to leave my duties without permission or excuse, and I did not want any of the other cowboys to get a hint of where we had been the previous day while they were rounding up the scattered herd.

Most of all I feared that if Uncle Miklos discovered that I let my horse eat up a large clover plot on my neighbour's property, he would punish me severely. No trespassing was allowed in our neighbourhood. It was bad enough for the runaway horses to damage the fields of other property-holders. For those who were caught deliberately feeding their animals on a stranger's territory no excuse was accepted and the penalty was stern. I knew that harsh law, but I doubt if Mocskos did.

All day she kept up her nervous attempts to set out again to the feasting-place, and all day I resisted her. Consequently she hadn't a bite to eat, and toward evening she began to whinny with the piteousness of a crying baby. She watched to see the effect of her behaviour and she saw that I was hard and unyielding toward her wishes. Disappointed and sad, she stood perfectly still and refused to move from the spot. Her ears were down. Her hair stood on end and she snorted with indignation. Without hope or interest she stood in that pose for long hours, a perfect model of resignation, and it gave me great sorrow to see her again in that mournful state.

On the second day after our adventure she seemed more nervous than the day before, and the eyes she turned upon me were more deeply appealing. She perturbed me with that look which seemed to accuse me. Suppose my old horse should die of hunger, what a sinner I should feel!

Pierced to the depth of my affection for her, I resolved that somehow, some time, I would sneak off without letting the other cowboys know. I had no idea how I might manage it, but I noticed that the moment I secretly resolved to try the adventure once more, my old pal grew quieter and her gaze was filled with an understanding satisfaction. The day seemed the longest of my life. The more determined I grew to slip away, the less could I see my way clear to doing so.

Several of the cowboys had to be on guard over the herd the entire time. They took turns at watching and tending the horses while the others ate and slept. This time it was my turn to come on before midnight as watch-boy. Some hours after supper I called Mocskos, mounted her, and rode around the herd. Yet in the half-light of late evening I didn't watch the horses, but spent my time looking left and right to see how I could make a get-away without attracting attention from my comrades.

Mocskos walked cautiously. She well knew what my idea was and wanted to help me. Slowly she went about the herd in ever wider and wider circles. By the time complete darkness was upon us we were well out of sight and my steed was striking off at full gallop. Her direction was certain. Her goal was the clover-field where two days ago she had had her succulent meal.

When we reached the edge of the fragrant patch, Mocskos stopped and waited for a time. Then, when she was sure no one was about and no trouble brewing, she stepped carefully into the centre of the clover-field. I heard her give the soft sigh which was my signal to dismount from her back, and the instant the bit was out of her mouth she was guzzling the silky clover with an appetite simply formidable.

With the rope in my hand I sat upon the ground. Now I watched the dark horizon in every direction and now I watched my horse. Sometimes that frenzy of eating would be interrupted for a moment while she lifted her head high to share my wary look about. Then with swiftly moving ears she continued her meal until she had reduced another huge patch of clover to stubble and filled every nook and corner of her stomach. Stepping close to me, she softly whinnied in joyous thanks and swiftly bent her foreleg as if to urge me to mount and be off without delay.

As soon as she felt me firm in the saddle she began to gallop. In the pitch dark she found her sure way and running like a magic steed in a nursery tale, like a winged horse which did not touch the ground, she reached the herd again. I realized that she must have found a short cut back, for she returned sooner than she had come. Slowly then she made the rounds, and it was soon apparent, to our mutual relief, that our absence had not been noticed.

Therefore I felt free to do what I often did during the day — take a short nap in the saddle. As I fell asleep it was with the sweet feeling that my old friend had enjoyed a fine dinner, and with a child's carelessness I no longer worried for fear our excursion would bring unhappy consequences.

Night after night we repeated our visits. After ten days of such feeding the effect on Mocskos was nothing short of miraculous. She began to be a gay animal. Gradually her bones sank from sight under a padding of firm flesh and she moved with fresh vigour.

One day a colt bolted from the herd. As usual, several cowboys raced after it, and I with them. But this time, far from lagging behind, Mocskos outstripped the fastest of the other horses and it was I who lassoed the runaway colt. It was my first triumph of the sort, and a prouder boy did not breathe in all Hungary. For this was a great honour and glory among the herdsmen.

That evening when Uncle Miklos heard of my exploit, he looked at me in astonishment. 'Big boy,' said he, 'what elf is working for you? Your horse is getting along nicely. It looks as if you would beat all the other cowboys. It is a *taltos* you ride.'

Taltos is the Hungarian word for magic horse, and when they heard that term applied to my ancient steed, the herdsmen burst into roars of laughter. It was evident that they had been mightily surprised by my exploit, but they only teased me the harder.

So far the outcome of our stealthy trips to the clover-field was well and good. But at last these produced another kind of consequence; one not so delightful for me. In fact, it was terrifying in the extreme. It happened after the tenth midnight feast. We were discovered — and no wonder! For in geometric formation ten circles had been cropped bare in the midst of the rich pasture.

It was a pitch-dark night. I had just dismounted and Mocskos had just taken her first great bites, when a startling sound struck our ears. It was the loud and angry challenge of a man's voice. Out of the blackness near-by it came to strike my heart cold with fright.

Too paralyzed to move, I was saved only by the wonderful sagacity of my horse. Motionless she stood, with ears pricked in the direction whence came that alarm, and at the same instant helped me to remount. As I clambered up I made out, to my horror, the vague outline of a figure approaching through the night. But hardly had I gained the saddle when Mocskos moved softly and swiftly away from the menacing shape. Soon she was galloping at full speed, and left far behind the spy who had almost caught the marauders.

But was Mocskos thus cheated of her nourishment? Not she. At the very opposite end of the clover-field she stopped again. Again I dismounted and, crouching close to the ground, lasso in hand, I kept uneasy guard while my horse earnestly devoured another large patch of tender leaves. My anxiety was superfluous, however. My four-footed companion kept sharper watch than I.

Strong as were my eyes, hers saw farther. Intently as I listened, she could hear better. One ear, like the antenna of some monster insect, she kept pricked upward and the other she bent to the ground. If from air or earth she caught the slightest vibration, she ceased cropping and waited. When perfect stillness followed, she munched swiftly on. Now and then her great head, with a thick tuft of clover dripping from her jaws, would jerk aloft and, although I hadn't heard the faintest sound, she would cautiously consider the horizon, and only when completely reassured would she continue grazing.

Next evening we found the ranch buzzing with excitement. An astounding piece of news had been brought in. While I was getting a drink for Mocskos, one of the cowboys strode over to share it with me.

'A mysterious horseman has been seen around the neighbourhood,' said he in a tone of great interest. 'He has been letting his beast feed in the rich clover-field belonging to the owner of the next ranch. A very reckless man, that!'

Naturally this news came to me as a great surprise. I learned that word of the pillage was spreading from ranch to ranch and from village to village. We were told that all about the patch where the robberies had occurred more guards, some on foot and some on horseback, were to be placed. For the owner was determined to stop that daring rascal from the destruction of his clover crop.

Even so, we never failed to go to that pasture, Mocskos and I. We went there every single night. Of course, our precautions had to be redoubled, and sometimes it took us a long time to find that portion of the field which was not being watched. Nevertheless, we always discovered some corner where my crafty mare could get the good nourishment she craved, and upon it she continued to wax strong and to gain in both weight and speed. As late summer drew on, however, a new difficulty arose. It was the fog. The thick mist rising from the fields made it harder not only to see, but to distinguish the direction of sounds. Sometimes my cautious and intelligent animal circled so far and listened so constantly that she scarcely got a bite to eat.

Meanwhile the vast improvement in my horse became the subject of much comment at the ranch. The cowboys had long observed the change. But at last Uncle Miklos himself noticed the difference in the appearance of Mocskos, and to a fresh outburst of jokes concerning her among the cowboys he answered with some sharpness. I could see that their fashion of treating me and their eternal scoffing at my mount were beginning to annoy him.

'All the same,' said he in a loud tone, 'I should like to see a race among you cowboys, and I am not at all sure you would beat Mocskos. After all, she has a great record from the past and even a horse has its honour.'

That wish of his soon came true. The very next morning, while we were all sitting around the pot of soup which I had prepared for breakfast, there came the hoofbeats and excited shouts which meant that once more a colt had bolted from the herd. Everybody sprang up and out. Uncle Miklos, who had once been a regular cowboy himself, rushed out with the others and shouted that the colt must be caught without fail.

'Up with you, Sandor!' he yelled to me. 'Do your best! Now perhaps you can take revenge for all these big laughs at you and your horse!'

I was the first to mount. For Mocskos was as eager as I, and before I had reached her had curved her foreleg to assist me. Quick as were the others, I was off at a gallop before them and got a long head start. Mocskos had understood the situation at once. She seemed to know that both my honour and her reputation were at stake. Indeed, there was nothing to equal the marvelous way in which that old mare conducted the cross-country race.

The others were close behind, but they could not catch up.

I was the first to come neck and neck with the runaway colt. Out flashed my whirling lasso and round the victim's head it fell. I had him fast, and as I coiled the rope end to my saddle I saw that in their astonishment and chagrin the other riders were behaving as if stricken with apoplexy.

Back I rode in triumph, and back the others had to come behind me. 'Well done, big boy!' shouted Uncle Miklos, in great satisfaction. Then, turning to the rest, he cried, reprovingly: 'And how was it you were so slow? Why could not you win the race from this old horse at which you have laughed all summer?'

It was a glorious moment. My heart was thrilled with gladness and pride. And Mocskos felt no less elation. She whinnied with joy, pawed the ground, and made every attempt to claim from horse and man her share of praise for the victory. It was not forthcoming, however. In jealous anger the cowboys turned away from us. They could not recover from their surprise at being beaten by the youngest rider and the oldest horse on the ranch. In revenge they contrived more work for me to do, and kept me running at their bidding until I had no instant's peace.

Before many days of this overbearing meanness had passed, however, Uncle Miklos became aware of it. He grew furiously angry. 'How dare you men act like this?' he roared at them. 'Do you want to break down a small boy's strength? Overcharging him with work in such a fashion! I'll not have it, I tell you! You have the power to make him obey your orders, but I notice you cannot beat him at a riding contest!'

Such words were sweet in my ears. They made me more than ever determined to get my beloved beast to that cloverfield where she could get the food to make her strong. I meant to go right on beating the others racing after runaways. And whenever I managed to do so my uncle was immensely pleased. But the rest of the herdsmen grew more bitter against me.

As Mocskos grew fatter and healthier these late summer days, however, I was running down in the same proportion. That prowling at night between the wary guards, my fearful anxiety and loss of sleep, were making me very nervous. I lost weight and strength with each passing day.

One night, while I was sitting in the clover-field, waiting for my companion to finish her stolen meal, I felt completely exhausted. Deep sleep suddenly enfolded me and I lay inert upon the ground. How long I slept there I don't know, but afterward I realized that Mocskos must have been trying for some time to make me wake up before I did so.

Once my eyes were opened, however, I knew that peril was upon us. Those armed peasant guards, furious to think that for weeks, despite their every effort, the ruin of the clover-field had gone right on, were now closing in around us. Mocskos had heard them for some minutes.

Too late I awoke. The trap was set. There wasn't an instant even to mount my steed. But so fully had she sensed the danger that before I was broad awake I felt her mouth close down over the collar of my jacket, felt myself lifted in air and borne swiftly and silently through the misty darkness. Mocskos was carrying me off to safety. Only when we had reached a point far distant from the clover-field did she drop her burden and let me climb upon her back. When I did so I found her trembling from head to foot with exhaustion from her terrific effort, and only very slowly did we creep back to the ranch.

By the time we got there the sun was up and all the herdsmen had come in for breakfast. They had spread the news of my disappearance and watched me approach in great astonishment. Uncle Miklos, who had been greatly alarmed, received

my laboured explanations with silent skepticism. Evidently
he did not wish to scold me before the others. But as soon as
he could get me aside, he gave me a very searching look.

'Sandor, Sandor,' he said in a tone of severe warning, 'it is
strange how you have managed to get your old vagabond
horse into such good condition. But I fear the cost may be too
great. Remember this — I do not stand for any lawbreaking
or dishonourable tricks. If you are doing such things, they
are on your own head. Besides, you are getting run down.
Have a care! You may be taking a rest-cure in the county
jail!'

To hear him express such well-founded suspicion made the
shivers run down my spine. But before I could reply I caught
sight of something more terrifying than his accusing face.
Around the hut near which we were standing came three
gendarmes. I spun about to hide the fear in my eyes, but not
before I had seen Uncle Miklos start toward them with a gesture of friendly concern. Quietly he gave them his entire attention.

'We have come to ask whether the mysterious horseman

who robs the clover-field might perhaps belong here,' said one
of the officers. 'Is there a horse which secretly leaves your
herd at night?'

As my uncle expressed his amazement at such an idea, the
men went on to say that both peasants and landowners were
at their wits' end to know how to catch the bold adventurer.

'He has the nerve and courage to visit that pasture every
night!' cried one gendarme, 'and the damage he has done is
beyond words to tell!'

Behind his back, still giving his visitors his courteous attention, Uncle Miklos gave me a secret signal. It meant that I
should go away from that spot with all discretion and speed.
You can imagine whether or not I obeyed the silent hint.

He said nothing further to me, but now and then looked at
me fixedly as if to repeat the warning that my crimes were on
my own head. Meeting that look and weighing his words, I
felt oppressed by guilt. Nevertheless, despite that weight
upon my world, despite alarms and dangers, Mocskos and I
went regularly to the pasture.

Torn between love of my horse and regard for the code of
honour on which I had been brought up, I didn't hesitate a
moment to act for my beloved beast. If anyone had called me a
thief I should have been horror-stricken. It didn't seem
exactly that to let Mocskos have the food she really needed.
Rather, our raids appeared to me as a perilous game of out-
witting a lot of adults who would have been furious to learn
that their enemy was a boy of ten.

Dense fog and cold rain came on with early autumn, and it
became more and more difficult to penetrate the circle of
guards without discovery. Yet we managed it. As a result,
the fame of the mysterious marauder grew almost into a legend
and the watchers grew hopeless about catching the invader.

My uncle seemed to have dismissed the matter from his mind. But one day, perhaps because he had heard some talk about it in the village, he looked me gravely in the face and said, 'The fox will pay some day with his skin.'

Oh, Mocskos was worth a risk! So I thought gleefully to myself, and besides, with a child's faith in magic, I had absolute trust in the cleverness of my steed. Hadn't she proved her wits and mettle again and again? I believed we would never be caught, and our expeditions were my delight and my resource in the lonely monotony of the plain.

Meanwhile, with every day and every venturesome night the friendship between Mocskos and me grew apace. Like two good pals, we understood one another completely. Never a moment of disharmony, never a treacherous impulse, disturbed a relationship made closer by the bond of a deep secret silently shared.

JUDY AND HAMMERHEAD

Frances L. Cooper

JUDY ROSSLYN, fifteen, pretty, her tall young figure clad in a man's striped shirt, whipcord riding breeches, boots, sat on a rock enjoying a crisp fall afternoon and caressing the nose of the beautiful horse before her.

'It's a shame, Hammerhead,' she addressed him. 'Just because I'm a girl Dad wouldn't let me help take those beef steers to the railroad. It's not fair! And me with the best horse in the country — though Dad doesn't know it yet!' Hammerhead flopped his lips suggestively. He wanted more of the sugar that had been his undoing and that had returned him into the toils of slavery.

For Hammerhead bore the wicked reputation of 'outlaw' — the worst word in equinedom, signifying an animal that fights mankind to the last gasp.

Dick Rosslyn, Judy's father and owner of the great Rosslyn cattle ranch, had acquired him a year ago for a mere trifle, smitten by his beauty and strength, thinking he would be a fitting mount for his own authoritative hundred and eighty pounds.

Hammerhead was a tall, eleven-hundred-weight six-year-old, of good blood. Dappled iron gray, his high, proud head flung back a massive mane, matched by the equally black and flowing tail. In his forehead was the peculiar white square, joining on to a thin white stripe down his nose, that had won him his name.

He was a horse gone wrong. His first owner, loving him, had broken him with care, but, meeting with financial reverses, had sold him into what he thought were safe hands.

Sold again, the great horse became the property of a rider noted for cruelty, a man who brought out the worst in a beast for the sheer pleasure of exhibiting his mastery. One jerk of the dreadful Spanish bit, a slash of the roweled spurs, and Hammerhead was transformed from an intelligent, tractable servant into a demon that believed all two-legged beings were monsters bent on torment.

From that day on no man had been able to stay on his supple back. He bucked like a fiend, seeming to know by instinct all the equine death-dealing tricks.

Rosslyn, after his best bronco-buster had suffered a broken leg, abandoned Hammerhead temporarily. He allowed him to run with the work and saddle horses, occasionally permitting some buckaroo of fame to tackle him.

Judy, from the moment Hammerhead arrived on the big cattle ranch, had coveted him secretly, wistfully, almost hopelessly. For, said Rosslyn, 'If I can ever get him gentled, Judy, he'll be as much yours as mine.'

Judy had then despaired of fulfillment. She knew her father loved to see her superbly mounted, but he was far too busy to squander time on a beautiful outlaw.

Later a chance remark of her father's had planted the germ of hope in the girl's heart. 'Why don't you make a pet of him?' Rosslyn joked one morning as they watched the big gray trotting nervously round the horse corral. Judy, her very soul going out to the wonderful animal, was absent-minded. She took the remark literally. The idea persisted. Why not try? It would be tremendous fun! Surprise her father to pieces!

Not a thought of wrongdoing, not a glimmer of the terrible danger she might encounter, entered Judy's confident, pretty head. The fall round-up was her golden opportunity. Her father and his cow-punchers were absent weeks at a time, covering the vast territory that comprised the Rosslyn holdings.

Cattle-stealing was prevalent, and it required constant watchfulness to preserve intact the hordes of roaming stock. And how Judy's father detested horse exercise! He much preferred to ride in the big, expensive new roadster — his delight and pride.

Judy's love for the big gray horse grew into a passion. And the horse pasture was a mile square — its upper end a long way from the house, where Mrs. Compton, her aunt and teacher, Milly the cook, and Ed, the rheumatic old chore-boy, ruled in her father's absences.

Accustomed to her independent outdoor habits, they paid little attention to her in the afternoon. When she had finished with the morning lessons she would saddle her own good horse and hurry to the upper end of the pasture. Here was a small flat, high on the great hill above the ranch and overlooking it.

Here, before the coming of Hammerhead, she read and dreamed, stretched along some fallen log, or sat and gazed at the panorama beneath her. Sometimes she practiced target-shooting with the revolver her father insisted she always carry.

But with the coming of Hammerhead her days were changed.

He was a perpetual, flamboyant challenge. What triumph if some day she were to ride him nonchalantly into the ranch just as her father and his men returned from some long trip!

If Rosslyn noticed his daughter's lack of desire to ride with him, he made no comment. Thieves had been rustling, and worries annoyed him.

After Rosslyn made his jesting remark, never dreaming his daughter would take it seriously, Judy began to turn her air castle into actuality by the provocative expedient of favoring her various horse friends with morsels of sugar. This diplomacy bore fruit. Hammerhead, boss of the less fierce creatures, resented their rewards.

He saw no danger in this unspurred, slender person with the kind voice, and it was not long until he accepted titbits from her hands. A wild thrill of mastery tingled through the girl when first his soft lips touched her outstretched fingers.

But he was very shy, and progress was slow. However, within ten days he was watching for her visits and gave every sign of enjoyment at the feel of her gentle hands. When he realized she meant no injury, he permitted her to rub him from head to hocks, to lean against him, to pick up his feet. Rosslyn would have turned gray to see his daughter then!

Judy never forgot the moment when, standing above him on a small bank, she eased herself on to his back. Would he, she wondered, give a crazy leap into the air, turn suddenly into the familiar man-killing demon? She had seen him too often in the corrals as he strove to trample some thrown cowboy.

But he didn't. He peered round as if to say, 'What *you* do is all right, Judy. I know you won't hurt me!' She perched there on his shining, powerfully muscled back, then slid off to give him a lump of sugar.

There was another shaky minute when she took the saddle

from her own horse and put it on him. The pressure of the weight, the tightening of the cinch, she knew, might rouse in him all his former unrest, fear, and hate. He accepted the burden calmly enough, with only uneasy twitches and quivers, turning once to give her a bright-eyed glance. And she remembered that once he was the loved pet of an easy-handed man.

For two days she saddled him, rubbed him, and led him round. Then she mounted. As she put her foot into the stirrup and swung lightly, softly up, Judy knew that this was the supreme test. Either she had won or —— He gave one frightful bound, nearly unseating her, then stopped, trembling from head to foot.

'Oh!' she murmured, knowing she had won, but frightened out of her wits. 'You have brains, haven't you? You knew I wouldn't hurt you, so you decided not to hurt me!'

Grinning with pleasure, she dismounted. When her heart stopped pounding she remounted and rode Hammerhead slowly two or three times round the pasture.

As her confidence in the great horse increased she rode him farther afield. Once Bill, the foreman, gave her a scare.

'Didn't I see you,' he asked, 'a-ridin' a gray horse away over there by Ansell Point?'

'A gray?' she countered, not wishing to lie, yet terror-stricken. She so wanted to surprise her father, and Bill might spoil it all! 'How come I'd be riding a gray horse when mine's sorrel?' she said. 'Seeing things, Bill, seeing things!'

'Oh, well,' he grumbled. 'Must have been somebody else. Ain't but one gray horse here, an' it's a cinch you couldn't be ridin' him!'

Bill's shock came sooner than Judy had planned. As she sat there on her rock this beautiful afternoon, lamenting to the attentive Hammerhead because she couldn't help drive the collected beeves to the shipping point, some twenty-five miles to westward, Hammerhead jerked his muzzle up and stared in the direction of the ranch, ears pricked.

Judy followed his gaze. In that clear atmosphere she could see the buildings plainly — the house, the garage, the corrals, the minute figure of old Ed moving about his chores. She saw, too, a couple of mounted men lope into the house yard and begin to hold conversation with Ed.

Then she jumped to her feet, startled. Both men dismounted; then Ed was on the ground. She saw her aunt run from the house, meet one of the men, then scurry back as if in terror. Next Judy saw the strangers dash into the garage; her heart pounding, she saw them emerge seated in her father's beloved roadster. Faintly she heard the motor's roar, saw Ed scramble to his feet, heard the far-off crack of a rifle, saw the old man fall.

For a breath, she watched the speeding car as it fled down the road. A bound, and she was on Hammerhead's back.

'Get going, boy!' she shouted. The big gray went leaping down the pasture with the speed of wind. She tied him to the hitching rack and flew into the house. Her aunt and the cook were bending over Ed and crying.

'Pshaw! 'Tain't nothin'!' he expostulated angrily. 'Just nipped me. Should a-knowed better'n to draw my gun on 'em!'

'What's happened?' shrieked Judy.

'Them two guys your pa fired last week 've stole your pa's car an' shot Ed — that's what they've done — the murderin' brutes!' blubbered the cook.

'I tell you I ain't hurt much — just nipped me in the leg. If we had a telephone, we could head 'em off. But as 't is we've just give away a good car. Couldn't catch 'em now, and if they get to the border it's good-bye.'

Judy's aunt, a mild, ineffectual woman, and the cook shed tears. Judy thought. She remembered an important fact. The gasoline gauge on the tank didn't register. It was Judy's fault. Two days before, learning to drive, she had backed the car into a wagon and injured the device.

So now the dial hand stood permanently at three-fourths full. Actually there were a scant three gallons in the tank. And three short gallons would not take the bandits more than fifty miles, for the road to the border, which branched away from the main road to town, was rough, and no car could make good time.

According to Judy's estimation, the bandits would believe the gas register, fail to look, and find themselves from ten to three miles from the border without gas. And there were no towns, except the one at the line, and they would have to pass through.

If she could get to El Sol, the shipping town, find her father,

have him telephone the border guards, there might be a chance
— provided she got there within a couple of hours.

The bandits' trail led through deserted country; it was unlikely that they could obtain gasoline. She chuckled, pictur-
ing their rage. An empty tank — nothing to do but walk.
Excitedly she told Ed, picking him as the most collected one
of the group, what she planned to do. Her aunt and the cook
wailed. Ed took her seriously.

'Might be done, but there ain't a decent horse on the place.
If your pa hadn't took your sorrel, he might do it, but ——'

'I have a horse! I'm riding Hammerhead!' Judy cried, tast-
ing her moment of triumph. For what was the big horse made
if not for just such an emergency?

Ed's eyes fairly popped as he took in her jerky story. Admiration lighted his face.

'Well — then, if that's the case, Judy, go to it!'

She fled from the house, unheeding her aunt's timorous ex-
postulations. Ed raised himself from the floor to see the huge
gray thunder by.

'She's off! Y-y-ip-pee!' he whooped. But Judy never heard.
She was too busy calculating the familiar road, where to race,
where to save and coddle, the big engine beneath her.
'Twenty-five miles!' she whispered. 'Got to do it in at least
two hours, or they'll have time to find gas and steal that
lovely car. And Daddy worships that car, Hammerhead, as
much as I do you!'

And they did it under two hours, but it was a horse, once
gray, now black with sweat and foam that slid, quivering, to
a halt where Rosslyn was tallying beef steers.

'What ——' he shouted, staring with incredulous eyes at
the apparition and losing his count, as the gray tossed froth
into his face. Judy shrieked at him racing words.

A moment to grasp her story, a pounce for his horse, and he was gone. Presently he returned. 'Done all I can,' he announced briefly. 'Telephoned all the rangers and every sheriff I can get hold of. If we catch 'em they're your meat, Judy!'

Then he scowled, taking in Judy's mount for the first time. 'Where did you get that horse?'

Judy quaked. Her peak of triumph was vanishing. Was he going to be furious? Doubts of her conduct entered the girl's straightforward mind. Surely, though, there could be nothing wrong in making a pet of a horse he himself had not had time to train. And her father was always boasting about her horsemanship. Tears filled her eyes. Excitement was beginning to react upon her.

'It's — it's only H-Hammerhead — that — that you said I might make a pet of!' she explained quaveringly. Then a bit of her former exultation flared. 'And — and I did!' she finished.

Her father glowered at her, wrath and amusement striving within him. Crazy little fool! Abruptly he decided. He whacked his daughter between the shoulder blades as he would a son, nearly toppling her over.

'One on me, girl! But I'll never joke with you about an outlaw again! I'm going to write out a long list of things you can and can't do on that ranch of ours!' His booming laugh was echoed by his cow-punchers — all old friends of Judy's.

Judy laughed through gathering tears. A car came snorting up. 'They got 'em, Rosslyn!' shouted the driver. 'Caught 'em walking down the road for gas! They never dreamed they'd get pinched. They're two guys you fired a week ago. They were sore! Laid low and picked a time to steal your car when there weren't any good horses or riders left on the ranch!'

'Well, they sure fell down there!' said Rosslyn grimly. And he added, 'For here's the best rider and the best horse in the whole country!'

An Indian Boy and His Pony

Laura Adams Armer

SOMETHING was making Younger Brother restless. At night he dreamed of strange experiences and new places. He dreamed of floating down a river on a raft of logs. The river grew so wide he couldn't see its other side. The water was blue, the color of turquoise.

Younger Brother could feel himself gliding smoothly on the water until he hit something and awoke. Every night he had that dream of gliding in watery space until he hit something that woke him. He never knew what it was that he hit. In the daytime he tried to reason it out and he grew restless.

He wanted to glide in the daytime and find the thing that awoke him. He knew he glided toward the west. It must be the wide water of the west that he saw in his dream. He had always wanted to go to the wide water. Perhaps if he did he could find the Turquoise Woman of the western sea.

He was terribly restless. Mother's weaving was beautiful on his pony; so was Father's bridle, but he knew the Turquoise Woman was calling him to the west. Every morning he drove the sheep toward the west. Maybe if he went far enough he could find the wide water.

He grew to hate the sheep because he must take them back toward the east every afternoon.

One morning, after awaking from his gliding dream, he told Mother he would not take the sheep out that day as he must be about other business.

'Son, are you crazy? The sheep must be herded,' said Mother.

'Then you must herd them, for today I travel west on my pony.'

Mother looked at him and did not say a word. What she had been dreading had come to pass. Her younger son was leaving her.

She packed dried meat and corncakes in a flour sack and tied them on his pony's saddle. She rolled a sheepskin in a blanket and tied that on.

Younger Brother put his bow and arrows in front of the saddle and was ready to leave. He shook hands with his father, merely saying:

'I ride to the west.'

He put his arms around his mother, who clung to him for a moment, then said:

'When you are hungry, the mutton will be ready.'

He mounted his pony and was off without once looking back at the hogan. When out of sight and hearing he sang wildly as he rode,

> The Sun Bearer travels a trail to the west,
> The Moon Bearer travels a trail to the west,
> Westward the stars move. Westward move I.

The rocky cliffs answered back, 'Westward move I.'
The pony neighed as he scented a coyote howling on a hill.

A hawk screeched as it flew toward the west. Above the crooked rocks Yellow Beak the eagle circled in the blue. The boy stopped his pony and called to him:

'My trail goes to the west.'

He skirted the crooked rocks and rode far beyond. By the time the Sun Bearer had reached the zenith the boy had passed the Waterless Mountain. He never looked back. The west was calling.

When he stopped to rest on top of a cedar ridge, he tied the pony to a tree and lay flat on his back. Dim in the distance he could see the blue peak of the western mountain. In the valley ahead he could trace the wash by a rolling line of dust blowing along its course.

'That means a sandstorm,' he said to the pony. 'We had better move quickly to shelter.'

As he rode toward the valley, which must be crossed, the storm increased. The sand blew higher in the air until it obscured the sun. The pony struggled on against the wind. The boy knew that shelter must be found. He couldn't keep his eyes open. His ears and hair were full of the fine dust. He dismounted. It was impossible for the pony to struggle further against the fury of the storm.

Younger Brother unrolled his blanket, put it over his head, and stood close to the pony as if to shelter him. The sand was blowing so thick it was like a fog enveloping them. The boy knew there was nothing to do but wait.

He could not see ten feet ahead of him. Loose tumbleweeds flew past him. Sometimes they were hurled into the air, out of sight. Sand piled up against the sagebrush and in some cases covered the lower shrubs. Clouds of dust enveloped the boy and the pony, each standing with bowed head and closed eyes, helpless before elemental fury.

Darker and darker grew the atmosphere; colder and colder the wind. Younger Brother thought of his mother's warm hogan with the sheepskins around the fire, but he said to himself, 'I must travel to the west.'

While he stood there fighting the thought of the cosy family group, he was startled by a cry — a long shrill cry of despair. He could see nothing.

The cry was human. Out of the wilderness it came, adding terror to the storm. Younger Brother did not move. The pony trembled. The cry came nearer.

Younger Brother opened his eyes for a second. He could see nothing but whirling sand and tumbleweed. He shut his eyes again and leaned close against the trembling pony.

Another cry pierced the air. It sounded nearer, much nearer. When Younger Brother opened his eyes again he could distinguish a form moving toward him.

He, too, trembled and clutched the pony's bridle to hold him. The pony reared in an effort to escape the phantom-like form in the dust. The boy's impulse was to mount and ride away, but something kept him rooted to the spot.

Before he knew what was happening, the phantom figure fell at his feet. The cry was silenced. Younger Brother looked down on the limp figure of a white boy. He was dressed in khaki and wore high laced boots. His hat was missing and his blond hair curled in a tangled mass about his forehead.

Younger Brother leaned over him. The white boy looked up at the Navaho, with eyes as blue as Hasteen Tso's. He spoke the only Navaho word he knew, 'Toh.'

Younger Brother untied a canteen of water from the saddle and the white boy lifted it to his lips. The *toh* revived him. Together the two boys sat by the pony with Younger Brother's blanket about them. The wind was abating.

By sunset the dust no longer flew and the boys could see the western mountain dark against a vermilion sky. Younger Brother rolled his blanket, mounted his pony, and motioned the white boy to sit behind him.

Together they rode toward the western mountain.

Mile after mile of gray sagebrush stretched toward the purpling mountain, the only distinctive landmark in sight.

The white boy was straining his eyes in search of a lone cottonwood where he had left his roadster early in the afternoon.

Younger Brother kept a lookout for smoke from some hogan, as he had no desire to sleep out on the desert.

The pony was the first to find a camp, for he scented water and galloped gladly toward it. Younger Brother let him have the rein and soon, around a little rise of ground, they came upon a spring. The white boy shouted with joy as he recognized the lone cottonwood by the spring; and there was his roadster, the cause of all his trouble. It had run out of gasoline, five miles from a trading post. The boy had started to walk to the post for help, when he was overtaken by the sandstorm and lost.

He motioned to Younger Brother to dismount and the two boys proceeded to set up a tent that was stored in the back of the car. The white boy took out his pots and pans while Younger Brother made a campfire of sagebrush. Soon the smell of coffee brewing and bacon frying made the boys realize how hungry they were.

'Gee, this is the real thing,' said the white boy, as he opened a can of sardines and put two of them on a cracker.

'Have some?' he asked the Navaho. Younger Brother shook his head, 'No.'

When the big yellow canned peaches were passed, they were not refused. They are not taboo for Navahos, but fish is. My! They tasted good! Younger Brother watched every move of his new friend. He was a big boy about fifteen and though strong and muscular, seemed tired out after his fight with the wind. That was because he had become frightened and lost his head.

After supper Younger Brother watered the pony, removed the saddle, and took the blanket and sheepskin into the tent. Then he hobbled the pony so that he couldn't wander too far away.

The boys slept soundly all night, and in the morning the white boy tried to make Younger Brother understand what he wanted to do. He pointed to the auto and he pointed down the road, said 'Toh' and shook his head for 'No.'

The Navaho boy thought he wanted water and started toward the spring with a bucket. The white boy gesticulated, 'No.'

Then Younger Brother had an inspiration. He said excitedly:

'Jedi-be-toh. Jedi-be-toh.'

Suddenly the white boy recalled that the Navahos call gasoline 'jedi-be-toh.' He was delighted that they understood each other. He realized that *jedi* meant the sound of the engine. *Toh* meant water and *be* meant its, so there was the Navaho word for gasoline — 'automobile its water.'

He was so delighted he shook Younger Brother's hand and pointing down the road and to the pony said, 'Jedi-be-toh.' After a while he succeeded in making himself understood and the two started out again, riding the pony.

At the post the trader interpreted for the boys. He asked Younger Brother where he had come from.

'From the Waterless Mountain,' said the boy.

'Why are you with the Pelicano?'

'The Pelicano boy was lost in the black wind. I put him on my pony. Tell the Pelicano my pony needs hay.'

The trader told the white boy it was up to him to pay for hay as well as for gasoline.

'Sure thing. I expect to, but how am I to get back with this gas?'

'Where are you heading for?' asked the trader.

'Grand Canyon. I expect to meet my folks there.'

'I'll ask the kid what he will do for you.'

Younger Brother said he was riding west and if the Pelicano wanted him to he would go with him. Of course they could not pack much gasoline on the pony, but enough to get the car to the post, where the tank was filled and everything set for a western trail.

The white boy led the way in his roadster and Younger Brother followed his tracks.

As he rode alone again he noticed clouds piling in the sky. The land was strange and new to him but the sky he could always read. He said to his pony, 'The voice of the thunder will be heard in the land today.'

It wasn't long before drops of rain spattered in the dust and on the sagebrush. It smelled so good, so fresh, just as it smelled at home near the Waterless Mountain.

The little pony jogged along, glad of the clouds which made shade for his going. He still followed the track of the roadster.

The white boy was in the best of spirits. He thought what a lucky thing it was for him that he met the Navaho boy. He wished he could tell the Navaho that he liked him. Of course Younger Brother knew that he did, but white people always like to talk.

While the tent was being set up for the next night, Younger Brother called the pony with a low, sweet whistling sound. The white boy, busy driving tent stakes, thought he heard a mourning dove calling. He didn't know that Younger Brother had taught the pony to obey that call. It had taken months to teach him but now he always answered.

The pony came up to have the saddle removed. He was a pinto pony marked with big white spots on red. A small white crescent between the eyes was the only mark on his red face.

Younger Brother took the buckskin hobble from the saddle and put it on the pony's flanks. He went off to graze in the sagebrush.

A bucket of water was brought from the wash and left to stand overnight. It was so muddy that it would take all night to settle. Everything was as cosy as possible inside the little tent, and for the second night the two boys lay down to sleep.

The white boy was still wishing he could talk with the Navaho. There were so many questions to ask about cliff dwellings and arrows and old pottery and hunting. He knew that the boy had a bow and arrows but he hadn't seen him use them yet. They were lying close to him with the bridle and the saddle blanket.

Younger Brother didn't miss the talking. Being an Indian he found entertainment in just lying still and doing nothing. He was content because he was headed toward the west. He fell asleep listening to the water roaring down the wash. It too was headed west and would some day lose its red, muddy self in the wide water, where the kind mother of all lived in her turquoise house.

'Hurray for the desert!' shouted the white boy as he turned a somersault in front of the little tent next morning.

'Hurray for the coffee and bacon,' he called, and turned another somersault.

Younger Brother stopped poking the sagebrush fire to watch the antics of his friend. He supposed he was performing some morning ceremony of the whites. Maybe it was his way of greeting the sun. Probably it was, for the whole valley shimmered in the glory of early sunlight. Everything was fresh and clean, washed by the rain of yesterday.

The white boy knew he could not ford the stream for some time, so after breakfast he motioned to Younger Brother to go for the pony, indicating that he would clean camp, pack the car, and stay by the saddle.

So Younger Brother started out to follow the clear hoof-prints in the damp sand. They led into the brush where the pony had grazed.

Probably he wasn't far away. He never wandered too far

from camp. For about a mile the boy walked, when he noticed the traces of two more horses. Still there was no sight of his pony. He was alarmed for he could tell by his pony's tracks that the hobbles had been removed.

With great anxiety he followed the marks back to the road he had traveled the day before. At a lone cedar tree the tracks led to the left and entered the brushy ground again.

Younger Brother was discouraged. Following on foot was slow, but he kept on with only one thought: He must find his pony. On and on he trudged until he came to the edge of a deep gully made by the water from heavy rains.

Looking down the gully he saw a thin blue smoke rising above the far side of a bend. Carefully and quietly he walked in its direction, keeping on the crest of the bank. When he was ready to turn the bend, he hid in the bushes and listened.

He could hear two Navahos talking. One was saying, 'The pony will bring thirty pesos.'

'Who will buy it? No one has thirty pesos.'

'If no one buys him, I myself will ride him.'

'Yes, you say you will ride him, but what shall I ride then?'

'As you ride now.'

'Half of that pony is mine. We worked together.'

Younger Brother listened in wrath. That was his pony. Uncle had given it to him and he had trained it to do his will through the long days of sheep-herding. They were the closest of friends. No one should steal the pony from him. No one could. He would get him back.

He crawled stealthily among the bushes until he was directly above the campfire of the horse thieves. He could see his pony with the two horses of the Navahos. He looked so beautiful, with the white crescent shining on his forehead and the pattern of big white-and-red spots marking the rounded grace of his body. He was not tied and was nibbling a few stray blades of grass on the margin of the gully.

Younger Brother crawled noiselessly through the brush to reach the windward side of the pony. There was just a little stir in the pure air and he figured it would carry the scent of him to his pony.

After a little while of patient waiting, he saw the pony lift his nose and sniff. Then he whinnied a little and pricked up his ears. The horse thieves noticed the actions and one of them said, 'What does he hear?'

'Nothing,' said the other. 'I hear nothing.'

The pony decided to graze again, moving in the direction of Younger Brother. The two Navahos resumed their quarreling, and while they were talking Younger Brother breathed his own special note of the mourning dove.

Immediately the pony ran toward the sound, whinnying as he went. He started right up the wet, sandy bank of the gully. In his haste he dislodged big chunks of dirt, precipitating a small landslide.

The horse thieves jumped to their saddles to pursue. Younger Brother trembled with excitement as he saw them start toward the bank.

Again he whistled the mourning dove note and he could see his pony leap to the top of the bank. His head was held high and his nostrils distended.

Another big piece of dirt fell from behind him, uprooting a yucca plant which rolled down the bank, landing in the path of the horse thieves.

Younger Brother remained hidden, expecting to be discovered at any minute. He was alert, waiting for the right moment to emerge from the bushes. He could not see the thieves.

Suddenly he heard them yell in terror. They were calling 'Chindi, chindi, ghost,' and as the boy peeked out from behind the bush he could see the two rascals riding up the opposite bank as fast as their horses could carry them.

Younger Brother was amazed. He wondered what had frightened them. Maybe they had seen his eyes peering through the bushes. He didn't know what the dislodged yucca plant had uncovered. From the top of the bank he couldn't see the prehistoric grave with its beautiful big pottery jar standing beside an ancient skeleton.

The thieves had seen it and they were horrified. They had no desire to own a pony who must be chindi himself. Why had he whinnied and looked in the direction of the grave? He must have known it was there.

So the thieves rode away frightened out of their wits.

Younger Brother walked boldly to the edge of the bank and looked over. He could see the beautiful jar, so big it would take both of his arms to reach around it.

He would like to take it to the white boy but, when he ran down the bank and saw the bones, he wouldn't touch the jar. He knew it belonged to the ancient people. Uncle had always told him to leave such things alone.

So he went up the bank and mounted his pony, happy to have him again. He rode bareback to camp, where he found the white boy rather anxious.

Younger Brother was excited and tried to tell his story with gestures. He could not make himself understood.

Once more the boys were westward bound. They stopped at the next trading post for gasoline. The trader was good-natured and allowed them to camp near the store and put the pony in the corral with a good supper of hay.

The boys spent the evening with the trader in his living-room. It was a splendid big stone-walled room with Navaho blankets hanging on the walls and piled halfway to the ceiling in one end of the room. The floor was carpeted with the blankets. A big stone fireplace suggested cosy evenings in the winter-time.

The white boy asked the trader to find out what had happened to his Navaho friend that morning, and Younger Brother told about the horse thieves.

'They tried to steal my pony,' he said.

'What did they look like, my boy?'

'Like the spittle of snakes, like dried coyotes, like *chindi*.'

'Hard to identify,' said the trader. 'Try again.'

'One was squint-eyed, with a mouth that could kill.'

'Sounds like Cut Finger. He's a bad egg,' said the trader, turning to the white boy. 'The government's looking for him. How did you get the pony back, boy?'

'He came when I called him.'

'Well, well, as easy as that!' laughed the trader. 'What became of the thieves?'

'They rode to the north when my pony found the pot and the bones.'

'Found what pot, what bones?'

'The big red pot with the black snake on the outside.'

The trader was excited by this time. 'How big was the pot?'

'So big my arms could not reach around it.'

'Will you show me the place tomorrow?'

'No, I must travel to the west. It is not good to disturb the ancient people.'

Nothing could induce Younger Brother to guide the trader to the place of the pot.

The white boy was excited about the pot because his father

was an archaeologist looking for old things. He decided to investigate for himself. He wanted to find the pot.

So the next morning he and Younger Brother parted company. He gave the Navaho boy a dollar for a present and watched him ride his pinto pony into the west.

Younger Brother was again free to dream of the wide water. He couldn't help feeling a bit homesick as he rode past hogans or watched a flock of sheep herded by some child; but coupled with the feeling of homesickness was the urge to be free.

THE LAST INCH

Constance Holme

THE woods were wet, that morning. Horses and men scrambled and slithered on the steep riverbank, and when finally the butt of the big beech was drawn out into the open park, it left a deep trench to mark its course. Buck Drummond set his men to 'tidy' the big log with the cross-saw, while he himself snigged the tops across to the timber-carriage, which had been left standing on the drive, in order to disfigure the turf as little as possible.

It had taken six horses to fetch the butt out; six horses straining and scrambling, with chains clanking and brasses swinging. Buck Drummond had only a man and a boy to help him, but then Buck was a host in himself. He was not only a waggoner born, his father having been one before him, but he was also a born organizer; he was, moreover, an artist.

Ted Hutchinson, the timber-merchant, counted him his best man — Ted Hutchinson, who could turn out thousands of pounds' worth of Shire horses from his various stables, but was content for his own part to race about the country in a ramshackle Ford.

Buck was young for a foreman, being only about thirty, but his capacity could be gauged by that quaint air of wisdom beyond his age which is also to be seen in a good young dog. He was slightly above middle height, with curly sandy hair and a pleasant Scotch face on a beautiful body. He was slim but not thin, hard but not stiff, supple but not sinuous. His small feet lifted themselves lightly in their heavy boots.

Good timber-hauling is not only a matter of body but of brains, demanding a knowledge of angles and stresses, together with an eye for delicate adjustments and distribution of weight. The born waggoner in Buck came out in the way he sized up his loads before he touched them; the artist in the ease and grace with which he assembled them; the efficient organizer in the fact that he wasted neither time, strength nor speech.

He could fetch, lift and place a log within five minutes, and without even the slightest appearance of effort or hurry. He was unusually quiet, both with his horses and his men, giving few orders, and those almost in an undertone. And he never gave an order twice.

He used only three of his team for taking the tops up the slight incline that led to the timber-waggon — Lauder, Elspie and Haig, with Lauder leading as usual. The leader of a timber-team corresponds to the foreman of the gang in that he must have brains, and in this case it was Lauder who had them. He was a brown about nine years old and as clever as paint, but nothing to look at, either from a timber point of view or any other. He was rather undersized for a timber horse, to begin with, and he was thin and rat-tailed and looked like a bad feeder.

Probably because of his extra intelligence, he was inclined to be temperamental, apt to excite himself if he had a man

at his head, and to pull too fiercely; so, because of this, Buck
worked him by voice alone. Backing up the slope, he called
to him by name, and the three horses, taking a circular 'cast'
like that of a sheep-dog, followed him with a rush, the log
dragging inertly at their heels.

If they narrowed the cast by attacking the slope too directly,
the log would roll over and refuse to follow, and they would
have to be sent back to straighten it up again. Then once
more they would make their rush at the little hill, their
coats and brasses gleaming in the fresh sunlight which had
followed the wet night.

Arrived at the timber-waggon already stationed under the
triangular 'legs,' the young waggoner loosed Elspie and Haig,
afterwards harnessing Lauder alone to the lifting-tackle.
Here again he worked him only by voice, often without even
glancing in his direction. 'Come to me, Lauder!' he would
call, and Lauder would turn to him like a child; or — 'Another inch!' and the brown horse would move backwards or
forwards, lowering or lifting the load as the foreman fitted it
into position.

The first two 'tops' settled themselves comfortably enough,
but the third, a heavy, curved bough, with a tiresome twist
in it both to right and left, promised to give trouble. Buck
lowered it once or twice, only to swing it up again, climbing
about the load with that peaceful sureness of his that neither
loitered nor hurried. He moved carefully as he prized the logs
apart to make a safe resting-place for the awkward customer,
for both his boots and the smooth skin of the beech were slippery with the wet.

Lauder, harnessed at right angles to the load, moved forward or yielded a step according to orders. The big, curved
limb, swung on block and pulley and clipped by great hooks,

hung suspended between the 'legs' like an unusually clumsy sword of Damocles. Buck studied it first from one point and then another; once, when he was on the ground, catching the end of it as it was hauled upwards, and allowing it to lift him completely over the waggon.

Presently, however, he got things as he wanted them, and, climbing back on to the load, steadied the bough as Lauder lowered it for the last time. He lowered it gingerly, as if conscious, even with his back to it, of the delicacy of the operation, and stopping for further orders at discreet intervals. 'Another inch!' Buck called, as the bough still hung, and, slipping at that moment on the logs beneath, fell forward across them. Lauder backed obediently without hesitation, lowering the great limb lightly on to the prostrate waggoner.

It was so neat and efficient an accident that the neat and efficient mind of Buck Drummond must surely have appreciated it if he had been in a position to do so. That little slip had dropped him face downwards across the load, with the bough not yet wholly in place, pinning him across back and elbows. It was pressing on him, but not heavily enough to hurt him; it merely held him there a complete captive.

He could neither raise himself by his hands in order to lever the weight off him, nor turn himself ever so slightly in order to swing it aside. He felt about cautiously with his feet, but could find no foothold. He was as helpless and as neatly pinned as a trussed chicken. And if Lauder moved again, feeling the weight of the log still more or less on the pulley — well, Buck did not need telling what several tons of 'wood' were capable of doing to you if you happened to be beneath them.

He found presently that he could lift his head just a very little, and by turning his eyes up he could watch the move-

ments of the horse in front of him. He would have called to
him to move forward and free him, but he felt too uncertain of
his voice in his constricted position.

Lauder knew as well as he did that the log ought to be in its
place by now, and if he did not recognize his voice, might
possibly misinterpret the order. Buck finally decided to wait
until the men came up after finishing the cross-sawing; trusting
to Lauder's training to keep him motionless in the meantime.

It was wiser to wait — he had settled on that; but, however
wise it might be, it was certainly not pleasant. Each time
his glance climbed from the brown hocks to the brown
quarters, he expected to see them giving under the strain.

A great stillness seemed to have fallen upon the world which
had lately been so full of cheerful and musical movement — a
stillness in which the only sound was the faint buzzing of the
cross-saw. The men were still at work, then, he said to himself, and there was no knowing how long they would be.
Certainly, they might wonder, after a while, why he did
not return, and climb the little slope to see what kept
him.

But they were as well aware as he that the last load would
probably be difficult to tackle, and so would not expect him to
be through with it very soon. And by the time they did begin
to think he ought to be finished, it would probably be too
late. By that time Lauder would probably have yielded the
last inch, letting down the full weight of the big bough upon
Ted Hutchinson's best waggoner.

The tiny sound of the cross-saw seemed to go on intermin-
ably. It seemed to Buck, listening, that they must have cut
the whole of the butt to pieces by now, instead of just trim-
ming off the limb-sockets that would have made it awkward
to handle. 'I'll hae to tell 'em off aboot that,' he said to him-

self mechanically, forgetting for the moment that he was not in a position to 'tell off' anybody.

He remembered it as once, however, because he tried to move a leg, and found that he was beginning to get cramp. But by this time, indeed, he hardly dared to move at all, in case Lauder, wondering at the silence and wearying of the whole business, should take the least motion of the log as an excuse for that last inch.

And still the sound of the cross-sawing went on.... Other sounds came to him presently, equally disturbing, though after a different fashion. Elspie and Haig, he could hear, were beginning to fidget, evidently becoming puzzled by the continued lull. Like all well-trained timber-horses, they would stand for hours while work was in progress, but no doubt they found something sinister in this particular pause.

He could hear them stamping and fussing behind him, and knew that they were moving about by the sound of the chains. He began to be afraid that they might wander round the waggon in search of amusement, and so irritate or startle Lauder into yielding that last inch.

But still Lauder stood quietly, awaiting the final order....

His head was slightly bent, as he braced himself against the continued strain. Once he bent it lower still, and the log quivered in response, lifted a useless fraction and settled itself again. Once he switched his rat-tail as if getting impatient, and Buck caught his breath, or would have caught it if the log had not caught it for him already.

Once, too, he turned his brown head, though carefully, without moving his body, sending a questioning glance in the direction of the waggon. Buck saw him do it, and was stirred by the humanness of the action into trying to call to him, only to find that his voice remained in his throat. And still over the little hill the buzz of the cross-saw went on.. . .

Buck did not hear it stop. By that time he was engaged in trying to twist his neck to watch Elspie and Haig, as they came, blundering and inquisitive, round the timber-carriage. The first that he knew of the men was when they were right upon him with frightened shouts, sending his heart into his mouth for fear they should startle Lauder. But Lauder still stood, unstartled, unstirred.

He stood while the load was swung aside and the foreman helped into an upright position; while the men, getting no answers to their questions, stood back, panting; and when Elspie and Haig had come up and were nosing him fondly but interferingly, Lauder was still standing.

Buck slipped off the waggon without vouchsafing any information to his puzzled underlings. He was a trifle stiff, a trifle red in the face, but otherwise he seemed exactly as usual. Once on the ground he signalled his men to swing the log back to its former angle. Then — 'Another inch!' he called to Lauder, and the horse stepped back instantly.

The big bough dropped delicately into place.

PASHA, THE SON OF SELIM

Sewell Ford

LONG, far too long, has the story of Pasha, son of Selim, remained untold.

The great Selim, you know, was brought from far across the
seas, where he had been sold for a heavy purse by a venerable
sheik, who tore his beard during the bargain and swore by
Allah that without Selim there would be for him no joy in
life. Also he had wept quite convincingly on Selim's neck —
but he finished by taking the heavy purse.

That was how Selim, the great Selim, came to end his days
in Fayette County, Kentucky. Of his many sons, Pasha was
one.

In almost idyllic manner were spent the years of Pasha's
coltdom. They were years of pasture roaming and bluegrass
cropping. When the time was ripe, began the hunting lessons. Pasha came to know the feel of the saddle and the voice
of the hounds. He was taught the long, easy lope. He learned
how to gather himself for a sail through the air over a hurdle
or a water-jump.

Then, when he could clear an eight-foot ditch, when his wind was so sound that he could lead the chase from dawn until high noon, he was sent to the stables of a Virginia tobacco-planter who had need of a new hunter and who could afford Arab blood.

In the stalls at Gray Oaks stables were many good hunters, but none better than Pasha. Cream-white he was, from the tip of his splendid, yard-long tail to his pink-lipped muzzle. His coat was as smooth as silk plush, his neck as supple as a swan's, and out of his big, bright eyes there looked such intelligence that one half expected him to speak. His lines were all long, graceful curves, and when he danced daintily on his slender legs one could see the muscles flex under the delicate skin.

Miss Lou claimed Pasha for her very own at first sight. As no one at Gray Oaks denied Miss Lou anything at all, to her he belonged from that instant. Of Miss Lou, Pasha approved thoroughly. She knew that bridle-reins were for gentle guidance, not for sawing or jerking, and that a riding-crop was of no use whatever. She knew how to rise on the stirrup when Pasha lifted himself in his stride, and how to settle close to the pigskin when his hoofs hit the ground. In other words, she had a good seat, which means as much to the horse as it does to the rider.

Besides all this, it was Miss Lou who insisted that Pasha should have the best of grooming, and she never forgot to bring the dainties which Pasha loved, an apple or a carrot or a sugar-plum. It is something, too, to have your nose patted by a soft gloved hand and to have such a person as Miss Lou put her arm around your neck and whisper in your ear. From no other than Miss Lou would Pasha permit such intimacy.

No paragon, however, was Pasha. He had a temper, and

his whims were as many as those of a school-girl. He was particular as to who put on his bridle. He had notions concerning the manner in which a currycomb should be used. A red ribbon or a bandanna handkerchief put him in a rage, while green, the holy color of the Mohammedan, soothed his nerves. A lively pair of heels he had, and he knew how to use his teeth. The black stable-boys found that out, and so did the stern-faced man who was known as 'Mars' Clayton.

This 'Mars' Clayton had ridden Pasha once, had ridden him as he rode his big, ugly, hard-bitted roan hunter, and Pasha had not enjoyed the ride. Still, Miss Lou and Pasha often rode out with 'Mars' Clayton and the parrot-nosed roan. That is, they did until the coming of Mr. Dave.

In Mr. Dave, Pasha found a new friend. From a far Northern state was Mr. Dave. He had come in a ship to buy tobacco, but after he had bought his cargo he still stayed at Gray Oaks, 'to complete Pasha's education,' so he said.

Many ways had Mr. Dave which Pasha liked. He had a gentle manner of talking to you, of smoothing your flanks and rubbing your ears, which gained your confidence and made you sure that he understood. He was firm and sure in giving commands, yet so patient in teaching one tricks that it was a pleasure to learn.

So, almost before Pasha knew it, he could stand on his hind legs, could step around in a circle in time to a tune which Mr. Dave whistled, and could do other things which few horses ever learn to do. His chief accomplishment, however, was to kneel on his fore legs in the attitude of prayer. A long time it took Pasha to learn this, but Mr. Dave told him over and over again, by word and sign, until at last the son of the great Selim could strike a pose such as would have done credit to a Mecca pilgrim.

'It's simply wonderful!' declared Miss Lou.

But it was nothing of the sort. Mr. Dave had been teaching tricks to horses ever since he was a small boy, and never had he found such an apt pupil as Pasha.

Many a glorious gallop did Pasha and Miss Lou have while Mr. Dave stayed at Gray Oaks, Dave riding the big bay gelding that Miss Lou, with all her daring, had never ventured to mount. It was not all galloping, though, for Pasha and the big bay often walked for miles through the wood lanes, side by side and very close together, while Miss Lou and Mr. Dave talked, talked, talked. How they could ever find so much to say to each other Pasha wondered.

But at last Mr. Dave went away, and with his going ended good times for Pasha, at least for many months. There followed strange doings. There was much excitement among the stable-boys, much riding about, day and night, by the men of Gray Oaks, and no hunting at all. One day the stables were cleared of all horses save Pasha.

'Some time, if he is needed badly, you may have Pasha, but not now,' Miss Lou had said. And then she had hidden her face in his cream-white mane and sobbed. Just what the trouble was Pasha did not understand, but he was certain 'Mars' Clayton was at the bottom of it.

No longer did Miss Lou ride about the country. Occasionally she galloped up and down the highway, to the Poindexters' and back, just to let Pasha stretch his legs. Queer sights Pasha saw on these trips. Sometimes he would pass many men on horses riding close together in a pack, as the hounds run when they have the scent. They wore strange clothing, did these men, and they carried, instead of riding-crops, big shiny knives that swung at their sides. The sight of them set Pasha's nerves tingling. He would sniff curiously after them and then prick forward his ears and dance nerv-ously.

Of course Pasha knew that something unusual was going on, but what it was he could not guess. There came a time, how-ever, when he found out all about it.

Months had passed when, late one night, a hard-breathing, foam-splotched, mud-covered horse was ridden into the yard and taken into the almost deserted stable. Pasha heard the harsh voice of 'Mars' Clayton swearing at the stable-boys. Pasha heard his own name spoken, and guessed that it was he who was wanted. Next came Miss Lou to the stable.

'I'm very sorry,' he heard 'Mars' Clayton say, 'but I've got to get out of this. The Yanks are not more than five miles behind.'

'But you'll take good care of him, won't you?' he heard Miss Lou ask eagerly.

'Oh, yes; of course,' replied 'Mars' Clayton carelessly.

A heavy saddle was thrown on Pasha's back, the girths pulled cruelly tight, and in a moment 'Mars' Clayton was on his back. They were barely clear of Gray Oaks driveway be-fore Pasha felt something he had never known before. It was as if someone had jabbed a lot of little knives into his ribs. Roused by pain and fright, Pasha reared in a wild attempt to unseat this hateful rider. But 'Mars' Clayton's knees seemed glued to Pasha's shoulder.

Next Pasha tried to shake him off by sudden leaps, side-bolts, and stiff-legged jumps. These manoeuvres brought vi-cious jerks on the wicked chain-bit that was cutting Pasha's tender mouth sorrily and more jabs from the little knives. In this way did Pasha fight until his sides ran with blood and his breast was plastered thick with reddened foam.

In the meantime he had covered miles of road, and at last,

along in the cold gray of the morning, he was ridden into a field where were many tents and horses. Pasha was unsaddled and picketed to a stake. This latter indignity he was too much exhausted to resent. All he could do was to stand, shivering with cold, trembling from nervous excitement, and wait for what was to happen next.

It seemed ages before anything did happen. The beginning was a tripping bugle-blast. This was answered by the voice of other bugles blown here and there about the field. In a moment men began to tumble out of the white tents. They came by twos and threes and dozens, until the field was full of them. Fires were built on the ground, and soon Pasha could scent coffee boiling and bacon frying.

Black boys began moving about among the horses with hay and oats and water. One of them rubbed Pasha hurriedly with a wisp of straw. It was little like the currying and rubbing with brush and comb and flannel to which he was accustomed and which he needed just then, oh, how sadly. His strained muscles had stiffened so much that every movement gave him pain. So matted was his coat with sweat and foam and mud that it seemed as if half the pores of his skin were choked.

He had cooled his parched throat with a long draught of somewhat muddy water, but he had eaten only half of the armful of hay when again the bugles sounded and 'Mars' Clayton appeared. Tightening the girths until they almost cut into Pasha's tender skin, he jumped into the saddle and rode off to where a lot of big black horses were being reined into line.

In front of this line Pasha was wheeled. He heard the bugles sound once more, heard his rider shout something to the men behind, felt the wicked little knives in his sides, and then, in spite of aching legs, was forced into a sharp gallop.

Although he knew it not, Pasha had joined the Black Horse
Cavalry.

The months that followed were to Pasha one long, ugly
dream. Not that he minded the hard riding by day and night.
In time he became used to all that. He could even endure the
irregular feeding, the sleeping in the open during all kinds of
weather, and the lack of proper grooming.

But the vicious jerks on the torture-provoking cavalry bit,
the flat sabre blows on the flank which he not infrequently
got from his ill-tempered master, and, above all, the cruel
digs of the spur-wheels — these things he could not understand.

Such treatment he was sure he did not merit. 'Mars'
Clayton he came to hate more and more. Some day, Pasha
told himself, he would take vengeance with teeth and heels,
even if he died for it.

In the meantime he had learned the cavalry drill. He came
to know the meaning of each varying bugle-call, from reveille,
when one began to paw and stamp for breakfast, to mournful
taps, when lights went out, and the tents became dark and
silent. Also, one learned to slow from a gallop into a walk;
when to wheel to the right or to the left, and when to start
on the jump as the first notes of a charge were sounded. It
was better to learn the bugle-calls, he found, than to wait for
a jerk on the bits or a prod from the spurs.

No more was he terror-stricken, as he had been on his first
day in the cavalry, at hearing behind him the thunder of
many hoofs. Having once become used to the noise, he was
even thrilled by the swinging metre of it. A kind of wild
harmony was in it, something which made one forget everything else.

At such times Pasha longed to break into his long, wind-splitting lope, but he learned that he must leave the others no more than a pace or two behind, although he could have easily outdistanced them all.

Also, Pasha learned to stand under fire. No more did he dance at the crack of carbines or the zipp-zipp of bullets. He could even hold his ground when shells went screaming over him, although this was hardest of all to bear. One could not see them, but their sound, like that of great birds in flight, was something to try one's nerves.

Pasha strained his ears to catch the note of each shell that came whizzing overhead, and, as it passed, looked inquiringly over his shoulder as if to ask, 'Now what on earth was that?'

But all this experience could not prepare him for the happenings of that never-to-be-forgotten day in June. There had been a period full of hard riding and ending with a long halt. For several days hay and oats were brought with some regularity. Pasha was even provided with an apology for a stall. It was made by leaning two rails against a fence. Some hay was thrown between the rails. This was a sorry substitute for the roomy box-stall, filled with clean straw, which Pasha always had at Gray Oaks, but it was as good as any provided for the Black Horse Cavalry.

And how many, many horses there were! As far as Pasha could see in either direction the line extended. Never before had he seen so many horses at one time. And men! The fields and woods were full of them; some in brown butternut, some in homespun gray, and many in clothes having no uniformity of color at all.

'Mars' Clayton was dressed better than most, for on his butternut coat were shiny shoulder-straps, and it was closed with shiny buttons. Pasha took little pride in this. He knew his master for a cruel and heartless rider, and for nothing more.

One day there was a great parade, when Pasha was carefully groomed for the first time in months. There were bands playing and flags flying. Pasha, forgetful of his ill-treatment and prancing proudly at the head of a squadron of coal-black horses, passed in review before a big, bearded man wearing a slouch hat fantastically decorated with long plumes and sitting a great black horse in the midst of a little knot of officers.

Early the next morning Pasha was awakened by the distant growl of heavy guns. By daylight he was on the move, thousands of other horses with him. Nearer and nearer they rode to the place where the guns were growling. Sometimes they were on roads, sometimes they crossed fields, and again they plunged into the woods where the low branches struck one's eyes and scratched one's flanks. At last they broke clear of the trees to come suddenly upon such a scene as Pasha had never before witnessed.

Far across the open field he could see troop on troop of horses coming toward him. They seemed to be pouring over the crest of a low hill, as if driven onward by some unseen force behind. Instantly Pasha heard, rising from the throats of thousands of riders, on either side and behind him, that fierce, wild yell which he had come to know meant the approach of trouble. High and shrill and menacing it rang as it was taken up and repeated by those in the rear.

Next the bugles began to sound, and in quick obedience the horses formed in line just on the edge of the woods, a line which stretched and stretched on either flank until one could hardly see where it ended.

From the distant line came no answering cry, but Pasha could hear the bugles blowing and he could see the fronts massing. Then came the order to charge at a gallop. This set

Pasha to tugging eagerly at the bit, but for what reason he did not know. He knew only that he was part of a great and solid line of men and horses sweeping furiously across a field toward that other line which he had seen pouring over the hill-crest.

He could scarcely see at all now. The thousands of hoofs had raised a cloud of dust that not only enveloped the onrushing line, but rolled before it. Nor could Pasha hear anything save the thunderous thud of many feet. Even the shrieking of the shells was drowned. But for the restraining bit Pasha would have leaped forward and cleared the line.

Never had he been so stirred. The inherited memory of countless desert raids, made by his Arab ancestors, was doing its work. For what seemed a long time this continued, and then, in the midst of the blind and frenzied race, there loomed out of the thick air, as if it had appeared by magic, the opposing line.

Pasha caught a glimpse of something which seemed like a heaving wall of tossing heads and of foam-whitened necks and shoulders. Here and there gleamed red, distended nostrils and straining eyes. Bending above was another wall, a wall of dusty blue coats, of grim faces, and of dust-powdered hats. Bristling above all was a threatening crest of waving blades.

What would happen when the lines met? Almost before the query was thought there came the answer. With an earth-jarring crash they came together. The lines wavered back from the shock of impact, and then the whole struggle appeared to Pasha to centre about him. Of course this was not so. But it was a fact that the most conspicuous figure in either line had been that of the cream-white charger in the very centre of the Black Horse regiment.

For one confused moment Pasha heard about his ears the whistle and clash of sabres, the spiteful crackle of small arms,

the snorting of horses, and the cries of men. For an instant he was wedged tightly in the frenzied mass, and then, by one desperate leap, such as he had learned on the hunting field, he shook himself clear.

Not until some minutes later did Pasha notice that the stirrups were dangling empty and that the bridle-rein hung loose on his neck. Then he knew that at last he was free from 'Mars' Clayton. At the same time he felt himself seized by an overpowering dread. While conscious of a guiding hand on the reins Pasha had abandoned himself to the fierce joy of the charge. But now, finding himself riderless in the midst of a horrid din, he knew not what to do, nor which way to turn.

His only impulse was to escape. But where? Lifting high his fine head and snorting with terror he rushed about, first this way and then that, frantically seeking a way out of this fog-filled field of dreadful pandemonium. Now he swerved in his course to avoid a charging squad, now he was turned aside by prone objects at sight of which he snorted fearfully.

Although the blades still rang and the carbines still spoke, there were no more to be seen either lines or order. Here and there in the dust-clouds scurried horses, some with riders and some without, by twos, by fours, or in squads of twenty or more. The sound of shooting and slashing and shouting filled the air.

To Pasha it seemed an eternity that he had been tearing about the field when he shied at the figure of a man sitting on the ground. Pasha was about to wheel and dash away when the man called to him. Surely the tones were familiar. With wide-open, sniffing nostrils and trembling knees, Pasha stopped and looked hard at the man on the ground.

'Pasha! Pasha!' the man called weakly. The voice sounded like that of Mr. Dave.

'Come, boy! Come, boy!' said the man in a coaxing tone, which recalled to Pasha the lessons he had learned at Gray Oaks years before. Still Pasha sniffed and hesitated.

'Come here, Pasha, old fellow. For God's sake, come here!'

There was no resisting this appeal. Step by step Pasha went nearer. He continued to tremble, for this man on the ground, although his voice was that of Mr. Dave, looked much different from the one who had taught him tricks. Besides, there was about him the scent of fresh blood. Pasha could see the stain of it on his blue trousers.

'Come, boy. Come, Pasha,' insisted the man on the ground, holding out an encouraging hand.

Slowly Pasha obeyed until he could sniff the man's fingers. Another step and the man was smoothing his nose, still speaking gently and coaxingly in a faint voice. In the end Pasha was assured that the man was really the Mr. Dave of old, and glad enough Pasha was to know it.

'Now, Pasha,' said Mr. Dave, 'we'll see if you've forgotten

your tricks, and may the good Lord grant you haven't. Down, sir! Kneel, Pasha, kneel!'

It had been a long time since Pasha had been asked to do this, a very long time; but here was Mr. Dave asking him, in just the same tone as of old, and in just the same way. So Pasha, forgetting his terror under the soothing spell of Mr. Dave's voice, forgetting the fearful sights and sounds about him, remembering only that here was the Mr. Dave whom he loved, asking him to do his old trick — well, Pasha knelt.

'Easy now, boy; steady!' Pasha heard him say. Mr. Dave was dragging himself along the ground to Pasha's side. 'Steady now, Pasha; steady, boy!' He felt Mr. Dave's hand on the pommel. 'So-o-o, boy; so-o-o-o!' Slowly, oh, so slowly, he felt Mr. Dave crawling into the saddle, and although Pasha's knees ached from the unfamiliar strain, he stirred not a muscle until he got the command, 'Up, Pasha, up!'

Then, with a trusted hand on the bridle-rein, Pasha joyfully bounded away through the fog, until the battle-field was left behind.

Of the long ride that ensued only Pasha knows, for Mr. Dave kept his seat in the saddle more by force of muscular habit than anything else. A man who has learned to sleep on horseback does not easily fall off, even though he has not the full command of his senses.

Only for the first hour or so did Pasha's rider do much toward guiding their course. In hunting-horses, however, the sense of direction is strong. Pasha had it — especially for one point of the compass. This point was south. So, unknowing of the possible peril into which he might be taking his rider, south he went. How Pasha ever did it, as I have said, only Pasha knows; but in the end he struck the Richmond Pike.

It was a pleading whinny which aroused Miss Lou at early daybreak. Under her window she saw Pasha, and on his back a limp figure in a blue, dust-covered, dark-stained uniform. And that was how Pasha's cavalry career came to an end. That one fierce charge was his last.

In the Washington home of a certain Maine Congressman you may see, hung in a place of honor and lavishly framed, the picture of a horse. It is very creditably done in oils, is this picture. It is of a cream-white horse, with an arched neck, clean, slim legs, and a splendid flowing tail.

Should you have any favors of state to ask of this Maine Congressman, it would be the wise thing, before stating your request, to say something nice about the horse in the picture.

Then the Congressman will probably say, looking fondly at the picture: 'I must tell Lou — er — my wife, you know, what you have said. Yes, that was Pasha. He saved my neck at Brandy Station. He was one-half Arab, Pasha was, and the other half, sir, was human.'

THE PONY EXPRESS

Howard R. Driggs

THE first time that I met 'Uncle Nick,' as he was familiarly called, was up in Jackson's Hole, Wyoming. This old pony rider always kept on the edges of the frontier. He didn't take kindly to barbed-wire fences; and his dislike for paved streets and telephones was such as made him shy clear of them as much as he could. A child of nature always, he had kept close to her heart till when, as an old man, he was pioneering that beautiful valley under the shadow of the Tetons, up near the Yellowstone Park.

It was at his cabin on the edge of the ranch village of Wilson — named in his honor — that I found him one day when I was out on a fishing-trip. I had heard of his thrilling story of the days when he had lived as an adopted papoose of old Chief Washakie's mother, for two years among the Shoshones. I was eager to get the whole of that story, but he did not warm up to giving me much of the tale until I got him around the home fire one night. Then I began to get it in its charming naturalness and vivid reality.

This was the beginning of our friendship, which grew until his death the day after Christmas, 1915, up there in the frontier valley he loved. Out of that friendship came the saving of Uncle Nick's stories — or some of them — in *The White Indian Boy*. But those were not the only tales of the West in the storehouse of the man's memory.

It is another tale of the Pony Express, which I drew out of him one night while my two boys were listening with eager ears, that you are to get in this sketch — the story of a horse that tricked the Indians.

The horses that carried both mail and riders in that famous relay race, by the way, are entitled to unstinted praise. If it hadn't been for them, there wouldn't have been any Pony Express; and if all the stories of those four-footed heroes could be told, there would be a thrilling series of them.

There was Black Billy, for instance, who always made a home run. He never failed to bring his rider through. One day he came in carrying two arrows, one in his shoulder, another in his flank; but he reached the station with his rider. He wasn't black at that time; blood and foam and desert dust had changed his color. Black Billy got tender treatment and a 'lay-off' till his wounds healed.

And there was another horse, a gray one — 'American Boy,' I believe they called him — a high-spirited steed. One day when they were changing mail, he broke away and went dashing along the trail, leaving the hostlers and rider at the station. But he did not fail in his duty, even though he was riderless. He carried the mail clear through to the next station, beating the pony rider, who had hurried after him on another horse.

And there was Nigger, the trick horse that Nick Wilson was given to ride when he had to run the gauntlet past the Gosiutes and Pahvants, who had vowed they would burn every station and kill the riders and keepers of the Pony Express.

I can hear Uncle Nick's quiet voice again as he told his story. I can see him sitting there in our big rocker. He filled it rather comfortably, for, though short of stature, he was a bit plump in his last years. And I can see the eyes of my two listening boys, alight with the moving pictures Uncle Nick's words are bringing to their minds.

'Nigger,' he is saying, 'was raised out on Antelope Island in the Great Salt Lake. The Utah Pioneers had bought a herd of California horses shortly after they first came to Utah; and they had swum the herd over on to this Antelope Island for safekeeping. They established a ranch there. A family by the name of Garr was put in charge of the ranch.

'One of the boys was named John. The Indians called him "Shantanamp," which means "much foot." John had six toes on each foot. I don't know whether that was what made it easy for to stick onto a horse; but "Shantanamp" was a great broncho-buster.

'They used to drive in the band of horses every so often and catch a few for breakin'. One day there was with the herd a yearlin' colt — black as the ace of spades, not a white spot on him. When they had roped and tied all the horses they wanted, they turned the rest out of the corral. The yearlin' stayed with the horses they had caught.

'John Garr made a pet out of "Nigger," as he called the colt. He taught him some tricks. One of these was to lie down whenever his front legs were stroked.

'Well, the colt grew up in a few years to be a fine horse, and John broke him to ride. He proved to be the best saddle animal on the ranch. John thought a great deal of him; but he got hard up at one time and sold him to "Sol" Hale.

Sol used Nigger on all of his Indian campaigns. Later he sold him to "Cap" Hooper; and Hooper turned the horse over to the Pony Express for a good sum of money.

'I never knew anything about Nigger till I got to ridin' on the Pony Express. He was put out where I was — on the deserts of Utah and the country that's now Nevada — the worst part of the trail. And then when the Indians had cleaned up all of the way stations between Fish Springs and Simpson's Springs, Nigger was given that hard stretch of fifty miles to run.

'If the mail was to be carried at all, one horse had to make that distance; all the stations had been burned between, or the keepers killed. Only the best animals could be used there. They took Nigger and others of their finest horses for that long run. I was chosen to be one of the riders, and Billy Fisher, I think, was the other.

'One day I had to take the mail from Fish Springs east. There was a certain point on the trail that was pretty dangerous — just a little way from Fish Springs. The water from the springs there spreads out and makes a swamp which reaches up pretty close to a rocky point of the mountain which then was covered with cedars. This point made a good hidin' place for the Indians, and they used it to get up close to the trail and shoot at the riders.

'But we had to run the gauntlet if the mail was put through. There was no way around it. So I got up all the courage I had and struck out. I was scared, I tell you, for I felt sure that the redskins would be layin' for me.

'When I came up towards the point, I kept my eyes peeled, but I couldn't see a sign of Indians. They wouldn't show up, I knew, anyway until I had got right into the trap where I couldn't turn back. I rode on cautiously; then, just as I reached the danger point, I touched Nigger lightly with my spurs. He leaped into a dead run, and the first thing I heard was a yell up in the rocks and cedars. A few bullets and some arrows came whizzing past me. By good luck none of them hit either my horse or me.

'I looked back over my shoulder and saw them comin' — about thirteen of the devils, as hard as they could right in after me, yellin' and shootin'. But Nigger's grain-fed muscles soon got me out of the danger of their arrows and the few old guns they had. Their grass-fed ponies couldn't keep long within gunshot.

'Pretty soon I noticed that the Indians were giving up the chase, so I reined in my horse to give him a chance to get his breath. Then I got off to look over my cinch. As I stood there I began to pet Nigger, and in doing so I happened to stroke his front leg. The first thing I knew down he went flat onto the desert. I couldn't imagine what had happened to him. The first thing that came to my mind was that he was either sick or wounded.

'The Indians evidently thought so too, for they let out another yell and came after me again on the jump. I was getting a little excited, when suddenly my horse jumped to his feet. Sol Hale told me afterwards that that horse was better than a watchdog when it came to smellin' Injuns. He had either heard or smelled them, for he was up like a shot, and I was just as quick jumpin' on his back. We soon put distance between us and the yellin' devils.

'That night when I reached Simpson Springs I was telling the boys about the experience. Then they told me about the trick the horse had been taught as a colt. There were some of the Johnson Army soldiers at the station. They listened to us, and then one of them suggested a plan to get even with the Indians.

'The soldiers would make a night march over to some hills not far from Fish Springs, and be ready for the Indians if I would agree to try to bring them into the trap. I was willing to do my part.

'About three days later it was my turn to ride past the ambush point again. I came up with my eyes open and Nigger was watchin' this time, too. He seemed to sense the danger. When we got into the mouth of the trap he didn't need any warning. He was off like a shot.

'The Indians were ready too. This time they shot before they let out any yell. They come close to getting me. An arrow hit my saddle, and another clipped off a lock of Nigger's mane just in front of me.

'I kept him going his best until I felt safe enough; then I slowed up a little to tease them on. The Indians followed me about two miles this time before they began to lag and give it up. Then I got off my horse and stroked his leg on purpose. Down he went again, while I began to act excited over him.

'The next thing I knew the band was comin' on full tilt. Their smell or their yell brought Nigger back to his feet and I leaped onto him. This time I had trouble to hold him back, but I managed to keep from getting too far in the lead until finally I had most of them among the hills where I wanted them. Finally I gave a yell and the soldiers rose out of their hidin' places and began to fire.

'Two or three of the Indians were killed. The others scooted back to tell the tribe what had happened. We did not have any more trouble with them after that. The way stations were rebuilt, and Nigger was given a good rest; but the fine horse was kept in service till the last run of the Pony Express.'

JOCK

Alice Gall and Fleming Crew

The Pony of an English King

KING GEORGE V of England always looked forward to the times he spent at Sandringham, one of his favourite residences. He liked the peace and quiet of this particular countryside in Norfolk. When he and Queen Mary went there, as they did frequently, to rest from the affairs of state, they both enjoyed the simplicity of Sandringham, and the beauty of the country round about.

In his stables on this great estate King George kept many fine horses: big Shire horses standing sixteen hands high and weighing a ton or more; sturdy farm horses for use in the fields and meadows; and horses that were graceful and fleet of foot for riding.

But of all the horses there was none that King George really loved as he did a grey pony named Jock. Whether he went for a canter about the royal estate, or set off for a day of hunting, it was always Jock that he rode, and the two of them spent many hours together at Sandringham.

Sometimes they would go leisurely along the pleasant woodland trails or through the broad, quiet meadows. Sometimes, when the King took along his dogs and his gun, the course lay along the hedgerows and through the bracken, where partridges and pheasants were to be found. But it made no difference to Jock where they went, for he loved the woods, the meadows, and the thickets equally well. As long as he was with his master the pony was happy.

On an afternoon when King George was riding Jock he overtook a small boy walking along one of the hedge-bordered roadways near Sandringham. The King loved children even better than he loved horses, and bringing his pony to a stop he smiled down at the boy.

'Good afternoon, my little friend,' he said. 'I hope you are enjoying this fine winter weather.'

'Oh, yes, sir, thank you, sir,' the boy answered, taking off his cap respectfully. 'I like to be out of doors on a day like this. I have been to the village to buy some poultices for my grandfather's rheumatism,' he added.

'I see,' said the King. 'Then you have had a long walk. My pony and I just came out to enjoy a bit of sunshine for a while.'

'I often see the little pony when his groom leads him about for exercise,' the boy told him. 'My grandfather says that nobody but Your Majesty ever rides him. That is my grandfather's cottage you can see over there through the grove of trees.'

'Indeed,' replied the King, glancing toward the grove. 'It is a pleasant spot. I know your grandfather. He has been a tenant here at Sandringham for a great many years. He is a stout-hearted Englishman.'

The boy's eyes brightened. 'That will please him, Your Majesty, when I tell him,' he said. 'My grandfather is very

The first thing I kne

Paul Brown

t flat onto the desert
(*See page 148*)

proud of being an Englishman, and he often tells me what a wonderful country our England is, and how brave and true our people are. My grandfather knows a great deal about such matters, Your Majesty.'

The King looked into the boy's earnest eyes. 'It is such men who have made England the great country she is,' he said quietly. 'And such a man as your grandfather, you, too, will grow to be, my little friend, and will help to keep England great.'

The King took up the reins, which he had allowed to fall free on the pony's neck. Jock lifted his head and stood ready to start forward at a word of command from his master.

But before going on King George looked down at the boy again with a kindly smile. 'We are Englishmen, all three of us,' he said, 'your grandfather and you and I. And we are friends and neighbours here at Sandringham.'

The pony moved off at a slow jog, and when the turn in the lane was reached King George looked back and waved good-bye.

The boy, a strange new pride surging inside him, stood for a while at the spot where he had last seen the little pony and its rider. And scarcely knowing that he did it, he spoke the words his grandfather had taught him: 'God save our country and our King.'

And so the King returned to Sandringham House and the boy trudged on toward the cottage of his grandfather.

It was late afternoon when he reached home, and his mother was busy in the kitchen preparing the evening meal. She stopped her work to take from the boy the bundle of poultices he carried. 'Thank you, my son,' she said. 'I do not know what your grandfather and I would do without you. Your father would have been proud if he had lived to see what a fine big boy you are growing to be.'

When supper was over and the grandfather was seated in an easy chair before the fire, the rheumatic leg resting on a footstool, the boy came quietly into the room and glanced anxiously at the old man. 'Does it feel easier now, Grandfather?' he asked.

'Yes, a good bit easier,' his grandfather told him. 'Once I get a poultice exactly where it is needed the pain is pretty sure to disappear. Rheumatism is a queer thing. But come and tell me about your trip to the village.'

The boy sat on the floor near the hearth, and crossed his legs under him. 'I saw our King, Grandfather,' he said with a note of pride in his voice. 'He stopped in the lane, and we talked together.'

The grandfather raised his shaggy eyebrows as he always did when he heard an interesting piece of news. 'And what did you talk about?' he asked.

'Well,' replied the boy, 'we talked mostly about England and Sandringham, and about the King's little pony. And, Grandfather, our King called you a stout-hearted Englishman, and he said it was men like you who have made England great.'

The old man's face flushed with pride. 'His Majesty is very kind,' he said.

'He called me an Englishman, too,' the boy went on eagerly, 'and he said that when I grow up I will help to keep our country great.'

'And so you will,' replied the grandfather, 'so you will. I, who am old, cannot hope to serve my King and my country much longer, but you will carry on in my place, Grandson.' The old man smiled proudly as he noted the sturdy little body and the frank, fearless eyes that looked at him so earnestly.

'Grandfather,' the boy said presently, 'if I were a king I

would have a little pony just like Jock. He is ever so much nicer, I think, than those big clumsy Shires.'

'Jock is a fine pony,' answered the grandfather. 'I remember well the day he was brought to Sandringham. He came from the Highlands, you know, from Inverness Shire in the north of Scotland. So you see, you and the little pony are countrymen in a way, for your ancestors came from the Highlands long ago.'

The boy thought about this for a while. 'Tell me about the Highlands, won't you, Grandfather?' he said at last. 'And about the day that Jock came down to Sandringham.'

'Very well,' the grandfather answered. 'But first I think I had better tell you something of Jock's ancestors, for the little pony comes from an old, old race, older even than England herself. There was a time, thousands of years ago, when the land that we now know as England was nothing but a lonely island covered with a wilderness of forests and swamps.

'The people who lived here in those days called themselves "Britons," and they called our Island "Britain." They were a half-civilized people who lived in little settlements of rude huts, and who wore clothes made from skins of animals that roamed wild over the land.'

'What kind of animals?'

'That I do not know for certain,' answered the grandfather. 'But there must have been deer, and I think perhaps wolves and foxes.' He moved his poulticed leg a little and continued:

'These savage men kept little horses that were almost as wild as themselves — ponies, we would call them. And these ponies wandered wherever they chose, finding such forage as they could in that wild land, and serving their masters when needed to carry heavy burdens over difficult forest trails. It was a rough and trying life, but it gave the little horses sturdy bodies and muscles that were as hard as iron.

'All this was such a long time ago that the memory of things which happened then has almost faded from men's minds. The wilderness is gone, the swamps are gone, and the lonely island of Britain has become the greatest kingdom in all the world.

'But that sturdy race of little horses lived on, and today their descendants are scattered here and there in the British Isles. Such were the ancestors of Jock, the grey pony. Every inch British! So you see, Grandson, it is very fitting that he should carry Britain's King.'

'He is a fine little pony,' the boy said, looking into the fire. 'His mane and tail are as white as snow, and his eyes have a friendly look.'

'In the Highlands where he came from there are many like him,' the grandfather went on. 'I have seen them in the streets of Aberdeen and along the mountain roads of Inverness Shire. That is a rugged country, my boy, a brave country, a land of great deeds and mighty men; and a beautiful country, too, with its rolling moors where the purple heather grows, its clear mountain lochs, its dashing streams, and towering over all the giant of Scottish mountains, old Ben Nevis: "The Ben," as all Scotsmen call it. Ay, it is a good land.

'But I am forgetting about the grey pony. He was six years old when he came down to Sandringham. His groom told me that for a day or two, just at first, he was a bit restless and would look about him in the strangest way. It would have been queer if he had not done so, for a Highlander, be he horse or man, must grieve a little for his mountains and his moors when first he leaves them.'

'Tell me again, please, about how Jock follows the King

around Sandringham Park just as a dog would,' coaxed the boy, 'and how the King feeds him carrots.'

'I have told you that story so many times that you know it as well as I do,' smiled the old man. 'Surely you do not want to hear it again. Besides, I am afraid my rheumatism will start up again if I do not stop talking so much. Talking is bad for rheumatism, they say.'

'Oh, Grandfather!' laughed the boy; 'you are just making that up. I know you are.'

'Maybe so,' admitted the grandfather, his eyes twinkling, 'maybe so. But nobody can tell what rheumatism is going to do from one minute to the next, and I am not making *that* up!'

When the boy had gone to bed he lay for a time repeating the words the King had spoken. 'We are Englishmen, all three of us: your grandfather and you and I.' Just a few words — and they meant so much. They made him feel very proud. 'And Jock, the little pony, is British, too,' he murmured as he fell asleep. 'Maybe the King will ride him again tomorrow.'

But King George V of England did not ride out again. Instead, word came from Sandringham that he was gravely ill. For weeks people everywhere waited anxiously, hoping for his recovery. But on a day in January the sad news was flashed round the world that the King of England was dead.

And now the day came when the people at Sandringham must say a last farewell to their beloved sovereign, for he was to be taken to London to lie in state in the great church of Westminster Abbey.

The morning of this day dawned fair and the sun shone with a tempering warmth. It was one of those gracious winter days that come to the south of England now and then. After a brief service at the little church of Saint Mary Magdalene in Sandringham Park the royal family began their journey to the railway station, accompanied by a procession of guards and officers, and by friends and neighbours.

Along the road that morning young and old had assembled as a last mark of respect to their friend, their neighbour, and their King. Among those gathered there were an old man and a little boy. They had been standing a long time by the side of the road, these two, and the old man leaned heavily on his cane. From time to time the boy looked up at him anxiously, and finally he pulled the old man's sleeve to attract his attention. 'Grandfather,' he said, 'is your rheumatism hurting you again?'

'Never mind my rheumatism, my boy,' the old man told him. 'It is a little thing and it does not matter now.'

'But it does matter a great deal,' the boy said quickly. 'You must take care of yourself now more than ever. Don't you remember that the King said you and I must help to keep England great? Don't you remember that, Grandfather? And besides,' he added, 'I don't want your leg to hurt. If it aches badly we must go back home right away and put a poultice on it. I am sure the King would want you to, Grandfather.'

'Yes, perhaps he would, perhaps he would. But my leg is all right now, so do not bother about it.'

Just then the notes of a bagpipe came to them and the grandfather put his hand to his ear and listened. 'The King's piper,' he said softly. 'The King's own piper.'

Moving at a quick march, the procession came into view, and the old man brushed away a tear with the back of his hand. 'That is the Chief Constable in front,' he whispered. 'Just behind him are the Grenadiers. See how tall and straight they are.'

The boy took the old man's hand and held it and so they stood, two loyal Englishmen, while a gun carriage, drawn by six handsome horses, went by bearing a black coffin over which was draped the royal standard. King George V of England was passing, and every head was bowed.

Next came the royal family. Edward and his brothers walked ahead followed by Queen Mary and the royal ladies in their carriages.

And now the grandfather felt the boy's hand tremble and he pressed it gently with his own. For the next marcher in that sad procession stirred them both deeply.

It was a grey pony, led by its groom; a riderless pony, saddled and bridled as though ready to bear its master on this strange new journey upon which he was setting out. 'The little shooting pony of the King,' someone whispered.

The boy's lips moved, but the words they framed were spoken in a voice so low that not even the old man at his side heard them. 'God save our country and our King,' he said.

The rest of the procession, high officers of the royal household, tenants, and servants, moved like a blurred shadow before the boy's tear-dimmed eyes. And then there was only the empty road. The procession had passed. King George V was gone from Sandringham.

After a little while the grandfather looked at the boy and smiled. 'Come, young man,' he said. 'We must be getting home, you and I. Our new King will need us now. We must help carry on for England.'

Slowly they went back along the road, neither of them speaking until the little cottage appeared through the grove of trees. Then the boy slackened his pace. 'It was right here that I saw him, Grandfather,' he said, 'the day he was riding Jock.'

'Yes, I know,' the grandfather answered quietly.

They were almost at the cottage door when the boy spoke again. 'What will become of Jock now the King is gone, Grandfather?' he asked.

'He will remain at Sandringham, I think,' the grandfather told him. 'Sandringham is Jock's home, and I believe the King would want him to stay there as long as he lives.'

'Oh, I hope he will,' the boy exclaimed as he opened the door for his grandfather to enter.

It had been a longer walk than the old man was accustomed to take, and he was growing tired. 'Grandson,' he said, 'I think you will have to let me lean on you a little; this door-step seems high today.'

The boy squared his shoulders sturdily under the old man's hand and together they went into the cottage.

The people of England had lost a great and good friend when King George V died, and they sorrowed for him. But they returned to their daily tasks.

And what of the grey pony, Jock?

As winter passed and spring came again, he could be seen

grazing in the peaceful meadows of Sandringham. Sometimes he lifted his head, put his ears forward, and looked off across the fields, as though listening for a footstep that he knew, for a familiar voice that he loved, as though wondering why his kind master did not come to ride him along the pleasant countryside.

But the grass was fresh and green in the meadow, the air was sweet with spring smells and warm with sunshine. Jock's nostrils quivered, he tossed his head and whinnied, then went on with his grazing.

He did not know it, this small grey pony, but he had found a place in the heart of every British subject. He had become the best-loved pony in all England.

BELINDA IN THE FORE-ROOM

Ethel Parton

THERE had come a sea-turn in the early afternoon of a hot August day. Tilly and Achsah Binns, their dishwashing done, escaped joyfully from the kitchen, and sat down side by side on the broad door-stone at the back of the farmhouse, drawing deep breaths of the moist, salty air as they watched the silver sea-fog swirl and billow higher and higher along the slope of Two-Top Hill.

Already Tilly's buff sprigged calico was limp and clinging with dampness, and Axy's brown hair, neatly laid in bands behind her ears, was rippling and roughening its decorous satin surface, and threatening presently to break downright into curls.

Tilly had rolled her hands, yet red and puckery from the dishpan, loosely in her apron, and leaned her back against the door-jamb with a long sigh of comfort. Axy sat upright, her chin in her hand, her sharp bare elbow resting on her knee, her eyes following absently the strong, soft pouring of the mist through the hollow cleft in the hilltop that held and sheltered the farm.

The mounting tide had risen beyond where the girls were sitting, but it thinned visibly as near as the eaves and chimneys of the house, and often in its swirling and shifting allowed the twin round summits of Two-Top to break into view, with a gleam of watery blue above them.

The High Farm, in its lofty nest, was plainly almost at the upper height of the fog-drift, but below it all the world was lost in streaming gray.

There was heard not far away a sudden sound of clattering and scrambling, followed by a thud and a rattle as of falling stones.

Tilly, who was easily startled, clutched Axy's arm.

'Oh!' she cried, 'what was that?'

'I don't know,' said Axy, staring vainly down the hill, where only the nearest boulder and a clump of barberry bushes loomed dimly through the fog. 'It's down there, somewhere in the pasture. Listen! — it sounds as if a horse were coming over the stone wall that crosses the ridge. Maybe somebody's got lost in the mist, and left the road. He'll break the horse's legs, if not his own neck, I'm afraid. There — there it is again!'

There was indeed a nearer thud and scramble, followed by a startled snort; and then a dark bay horse with a white foot and star, ridden by a hatless, wide-eyed boy, burst swiftly out of the smother only a few yards away, leaped the last flat-lying juniper bush, and halted, sweating and panting, at the door.

'It's Zeb!' cried Tilly, with relief. 'Well, Zebedee Thyng! What are you thinking of, riding such a crazy rig; and, good land! — that's Belinda! Whatever will your father say?'

The boy slipped to the ground and leaned against the horse, breathing hard, and bending his head sidewise, with a motion of his hand to the girls to keep still.

He was evidently listening; and Tilly took fright again, and caught her breath in a whimper. But Axy sharply bade her keep quiet, and she tried to control herself, only striving nervously to untie her apron-strings, and sniffing softly as they pulled into tighter and tighter knots and refused to come undone. Zeb glanced at her impatiently, and spoke to Axy.

'They've sent out more parties to bring in horses,' he said. Axy nodded. She knew he meant the British, who had been quartered for a week past in and about the nearest town, and had already carried off many horses from the neighboring farms.

'Do they want Belinda?' she asked.

'Yes,' said Zeb; 'they do. She's the finest horse anywhere round, and they've heard of her — seen her, too, when Father was at the camp looking after some of their sick soldiers. One of his patients there thought it rather poor pay for doctoring to steal the doctor's horse, I suppose, for he sent him a warning to hide her. We got it just in time. You ought to have seen Father!

'You know how proud he is of Belinda. He vowed and declared he'd shoot the first outrageous red-coat that dared put his finger on her hide; and the more he talked the angrier he made himself. He threw his wig across the room, and pounded his fist on the table, and pretty nearly danced, he was so angry! Then he saw I had to laugh, and he tried to be calm and dignified and take a pinch of snuff; but his hand shook, and he took so much he nearly sneezed his head off; and before he could stop *kerchooing*, we saw them coming up the street.'

Tilly, who had giggled faintly, grew serious again, and asked breathlessly:

'What did he do?'

'He stopped just a second to think,' answered Zeb, 'and

then he told me to take her and get away with her. He said
he wouldn't even tell me where to go, so he could say honestly
he didn't know where she was; but guessed if I used my wits
I'd think of the best place.

'I meant to take her over to Uncle Joseph's by way of the
woods, and that's the place I started for; but there are parties
out on both roads, and I couldn't get there. I was chased, and
I only got away by coming over the stone wall and right up
the hill here; and I couldn't have done that but for the fog.
They didn't dare follow over such rough ground when they
couldn't see and didn't know the way. I don't know how I
did it safely, myself.'

'It's a queer place to hide,' said Axy, anxiously — 'the top
of the tallest hill in the county!'

'It's worse than queer,' agreed Zeb, ruefully. 'Belinda can't
go any farther: she's shaking all over, poor thing; look at her!
And she cast a shoe coming over the wall. If the fog holds,
and they come, maybe I can hide her down the side a little
way, in a clump of bushes. They couldn't tell what was horse
and what was barberry bush ten yards off.

'But if it clears there's no chance at all. They'll just come
up and take her. They can see her half a mile away, if we try
to escape by the pastures; and there's nowhere to hide her if
we stay.'

'But do they know where you went to?' asked Axy. 'Are
you sure they'll look for you up here at all?'

'Oh, yes; they know,' Zeb answered, forlornly. 'There —
there's the sun!'

Sure enough, the mist parted, and both summits of the hill
shone bright and clear, with the cresting boulders and low
bushes standing plain against the glistening blue.

'Whatever shall we do?' wailed Tilly. 'Oh, dear! oh, dear!

Oh, Axy, do you suppose they've started yet? It's so thick in the hollows, I can't see. Oh, isn't that something red?'

'No, it isn't,' snapped Axy, who was apt to be cross when she was excited; 'and do be quiet, Tilly, and let us think. If there was only any *sort* of hiding-place big enough to hold Belinda! But there isn't; there's not ——'

'Put her in the barn,' interrupted Tilly, distractedly.

'The barn! Where do people look for horses first of all, simpleton?' cried Axy, with scorn.

'Well, the *house*, then,' suggested Tilly, timidly.

Zeb laughed rather shakily, and answered that Belinda wasn't parlor company, and he guessed Mrs. Binns would have a word to say; besides, it couldn't be done; and if it could, it would get them into trouble; and it wouldn't be any use, anyway.

But Axy broke in abruptly on his objections.

'We'll try it!' she cried. 'It's the only thing, and it's a chance. Mother's away, and so's Father; and Aunt Nancy is so deaf she won't hear a thing; and there's nobody else at home but just us two. She's out in the storeroom, and doesn't even know you've come; and we'll get you in without telling her, and then she can tell 'em there's nobody here; don't you see? And we'll muffle her feet, and you must stay and pat her nose and keep her from whinnying.'

Axy did not stop for such a trifle as to untangle Aunt Nancy and the mare from the maze of pronouns: her hearers would understand.

'And the parlor shutters are always shut, so there'll be nothing odd about that; and I don't believe, honestly, they'll ever think of looking there. And I couldn't *bear* to lose Belinda — the beauty! — and let some hulking, rough trooper ill-use her. And besides that, Zeb, what would they do with *you?* They might carry you off to prison; and if they didn't——

'Oh, Zeb, don't you remember how the soldier thrashed Reuben Jenks, and told him that was a lesson for rebel lads who ran away with the horses that were wanted for His Majesty's army? And it was only their old cart horse he had tried to get away with, that's twenty years old, and as slow as a snail. Surely they'd be angrier to near lose Belinda.'

'Axy, will you truly do it?' Zeb interrupted, his pleasant, freckled face, so downcast the moment before, flushing with hope as he comprehended the possibility of her scheme. 'I do believe it is a chance — and Father has trusted me to save her.'

Axy nodded a firm little nod by way of answer. Then she bade Tilly run round to the storeroom window and peep in to see if Aunt Nancy was still there and busy enough to be likely to remain. Next she pulled off her big apron, and, tearing it into strips, handed them to Zeb to tie up Belinda's hoofs.

'Woolen would be better, but I can't stop to find any,' she explained, 'at least, not till we get inside; and she mustn't make dents in the hall floor if we can help it. Mother'll say it's right to help you, but she won't like things spoiled, all the same. Besides, if they're already coming up the hill they could hear her ever so far, tramping on wood.'

'They can't be near yet. Besides, it's as thick as porridge down at the bottom,' returned Zeb, as he stooped low, handling the puzzled mare's fore foot. 'And the road's so rough, they may wait till the sun's out clearer. They know if I'm here I can't get away, with the river looping round the hill, and their men blocking the road. They can take their time. But all the same we haven't a minute to lose.'

'No,' agreed Axy. 'We must get Belinda in as quick as we can. Open the door, Tilly.'

So Tilly, who had returned, reporting Aunt Nancy safely occupied for another half-hour, flung open the back door of the wide hall that ran straight through the roomy old farmhouse, and darting indoors, presently came back with a big red apple in her hand, and stood on the threshold, extending it coaxingly toward Belinda.

Belinda, poor bewildered creature, saw it, but even such a delicacy could not entirely distract her mind. She would prick one ear forward and sniff; but then, just at the critical moment, she would remember her bundled hoofs, and lift them uneasily up and down, shying and sidling, craning her pretty head forward and trying the lower of the three stone steps with her fore foot, only to draw it back, a moment later, and begin again her fuming and fidgeting.

It was not until Zeb relinquished the bridle to Axy, and, taking the apple himself, backed slowly before her, that he was able, with much coaxing and many reassuring whispers, to beguile her up the steps, and reward her as she crossed the door-sill. She would have instantly retreated, but he took the bridle again and urged her forward, while just beyond him Tilly held out more apples, a gleaming and fragrant apronful.

And at last, with one twitching ear turned forward and one back, and mingled appetite and anxiety expressed in her great, brown, rolling eyes, Belinda danced gingerly sidewise down the long hall after the excited pair. She started violently and swung around with a snort and a toss as the sunlight was cut off by the closing of the hall door behind her, and a subdued clash and the sound of a bolt shot home signaled that she was a prisoner.

'We have her now!' cried Axy, triumphantly, as she ran ahead to open the parlor door, and invited her guests to enter, Tilly, of course, coming first with the enticing apples, and Zeb following. He had released Belinda, guessing that if she were left to herself she would presently choose society and more apples of her own free will, in spite of her manifest dislike to doorways, rather than remain in the loneliness of the hall without.

She looked after him dubiously; but she followed, and stood gracefully allowing herself to be fed and petted, in the very middle of the beautifully sanded 'best' floor. Her sleek bay sides and dainty head were reflected in the narrow looking-glass, in the dim green window-panes, in the glittering fire-dogs on the hearth, and in the polished brass knobs of the tall highboy, until there seemed more horses in the cherished precincts of the Binns fore-room than the big Binns barn without had ever held.

Axy presently flitted away, to return bearing a load of braided rugs, bags of 'pieces,' and worn-out comforters. These she heaped on the floor, and Belinda was led upon the pile, that her feet, if she should prance or paw, might be more effectually silenced.

'Put the rest of the apples on the mantel, Tilly,' she ordered, looking about her with the eye of a little general; 'they'll do if Belinda gets uneasy; but she does crunch so loud it makes me scary! I wouldn't give her any more unless you have to, Zeb. Tilly, now run round outside and see if there's anybody in sight. We can't open these windows to look.'

Tilly slipped out. 'Do you think of anything else we can do?' asked Axy, who felt she must be pale herself, and noticed how big and dark Zeb's freckles looked on the unfamiliar whiteness of his cheeks. His face wore a listening look once more, and he was breathing fast.

'Only just to wait,' he said. 'I hope they'll come soon, and get it over. I hate waiting, worse than anything.'

'So do I,' agreed Axy. 'We've thought of all the things we ought to think of already, and it just gives us time to think of all those we *oughtn't* and to get frightened. I haven't had time to be frightened before; but this is — it's — I don't like it a bit!'

Belinda munched a bite of apple, and shifted nervously on her feet, and the boy and girl stood silent for a while beside her. Then Zebedee asked:

'If they get her, and take me, too, you'll let Father know?'

Axy nodded her little jerky nod; but she added:

'They won't; and there's no need. You can leave her here and go and hide yourself. There are plenty of cupboards and closets.'

'She wouldn't keep quiet without me.'

'I'll stay with her.'

'She doesn't know you as well; and if anybody stays, I'm the one. She's in my charge.'

'But they wouldn't hurt me: I'm a girl.'

'I don't suppose they would; but I wonder what sort of boy I'd be if I left you alone to find out whether they would or not!'

'I'm willing, truly.'

'I'm *not*, and I'm going to stay.'

Belinda suddenly lifted her head and pricked her ears; she raised a muffled foot and tried to paw with it, but Zeb dropped quickly to his knee and caught it in his hand. She thought he was taking off the bunch of rags that cumbered her, and stood patiently letting him hold it lifted, though still listening. After a little he set the foot gently down, and rose, ready to smother against his shoulder the whinny which he feared would be the next thing.

The mare's loud breathing, as she puffed her nostrils and

drew them in again, and the hurried beating of their own hearts seemed to fill the room as the two young rebels waited, and waited, and waited. But the thundering knock which they expected to hear did not come. Instead, there were only a few faint sounds from without, they could not tell exactly what or whence, though they seemed to come from the direction of the barn. They were not even quite sure they heard anything.

And then, suddenly, a horse neighed almost under the window, and Zeb had caught up an old shawl from the floor and buried poor Belinda's nose in it, and was hugging and soothing her with his arms round her neck and his face to hers, clinging only the tighter in silent desperation as she started away.

Axy, prompt and pale, snatched up an armful of the soft woolens as Belinda's fore feet quitted them, and tossed them behind her heels to deaden the sound of her movements as she backed.

It was over in a moment — the answering whinny smothered in time, the startled creature freed again from hasty blindfolding, and her more startled guardians panting beside her, close in front of the wide hearth.

'Do you suppose they heard?' Zeb breathed rather than whispered.

'No,' Axy whispered back; then, very anxiously: 'Where can Tilly be? Why didn't she warn us?'

She paused and added: 'I'm going out. Aunt Nancy may miss me and ask questions. And I'm going to lock you in and hide the key. That would give you a minute to get out by the windows if they try the door. But I'll keep them away if I can, and don't you think of anything but just keeping Belinda quiet. Tilly and I'll do the rest.'

She was gone, and he heard the key click cautiously in the

lock; and then he was left alone with Belinda in the dim, shuttered room.

As Axy came round the corner of the house, the first thing she saw was Tilly, pale and tearful, standing between two soldiers, one of them held her by the arm, while Aunt Nancy, her black eyes snapping with wrath, confronted the group. She must have just demanded their errand, and received a reply which, it was plain, had not been understood; for now one of the men was roaring at her, while his comrade and a third soldier near-by, mounted, and holding the horses of the others, were laughing heartily at his efforts to make himself heard.

'A horse!' he fairly shouted. 'Horse! *Horse! Bay* horse — *boy* — came this *way!* (Oh, confound it all! — she's as deaf as an adder!) *Boy — horse!*'

'There's no horse here,' Aunt Nancy replied with spirit. 'You have been in the barn and seen for yourselves there is not. And pray let go of my little niece there. You are frightening her to death. Sure, do you think the child keeps a bay horse hidden in her apron pocket?'

'We won't *hurt* her!' shouted the soldier, 'but she *refuses —* to *answer — questions*, and we *think* — she knows *more* — than she'll *tell!* You had best *speak out* if you want us to let her *go!* Have you *seen — a bay horse —* a fine bay horse with a white *star* — red-headed BOY?'

His voice broke with the strain of yelling so long an address, and he mopped his brow with his red sleeve, while his comrades grinned appreciation of his difficulties.

'I have seen neither horse nor boy. You may see for yourselves if there be either about the place,' responded Aunt Nancy, angrily. 'A likely thing, indeed, to hide away a horse and rider on the top of a stony, bare hill with not so

much as a tree on it for cover! Let my niece go, you blundering boobies! She is too frightened to answer your questions.
But I will answer as many as you please, and you may make
the most of what I say. Nancy Binns is afraid of no man; no,
nor soldier, either!'

'One deaf and t'other dumb!' groaned the exhausted soldier. 'I've had enough of the pair. Here, little maid' — he
turned to Axy — 'can *you* talk — and hear?'

'Both, sir,' said Axy, curtsying.

'That's better,' said he, good-naturedly enough, and plainly
relieved. 'Now, then, you have heard what we want to know.
Have you anything to tell us? Be careful; 'twill be a dangerous thing for you if we catch you fibbing.'

'I'll tell you no fibs, sir,' answered Axy quickly; 'but I can
only say what my aunt has said already: There's no such
horse in our barn, and you can see for yourself there's none in
our pasture; and the only other place is our house — if you
please to search that.

'There's the attic, and the cellar, and the woodshed, and all
the closets; and if the bay horse with the white star is as clever
at curling his legs up under him as he must be at stretching
them to run away, or maybe to scramble up and down stairs,
he might even be stowed away in the pumpkin-bin! I have
often hid there myself, and indeed it's a good place to lie
snug. Will you look?'

Now, the sergeant was already thinking he had made a
mistake in searching a hilltop, and that the boy must have
slipped past them somehow in the fog; and, moreover, he was
a kind man, who did not enjoy frightening a little girl as desperately as he seemed to have frightened Tilly; and besides, if
the horse was not there, it must be somewhere else, and
time was being wasted.

So the puzzled sergeant looked hard for an anxious minute from Axy to her aunt; and then, growling only 'Saucy tongues aren't safe for little girls!' he flung upon his horse, tossed a quick order to his comrades, and away went the three scarlet figures together, clattering swiftly down the hill.

Nobody spoke till they were well beyond the first 'thank-you-ma'am' of the rough road. Then Tilly, lifting her streaming face from Aunt Nancy's scrumpled kerchief, where she had buried it, sobbed hysterically:

'Oh, Axy — oh, Axy! they asked me if I'd seen 'em — and I had! And so I wouldn't say anything at all. And they said they'd take me away with 'em if I didn't; and I was so frightened I didn't know what to do; but I didn't tell — I didn't tell!'

She dropped her face again against the soaked kerchief; and Aunt Nancy patted her shoulders and murmured:

'There, my dear; there, there!' She added more sharply, 'What is the poor child talking about, Axy?'

'Come into the house and I'll show you,' said Axy; and taking Tilly's hand, she led the way to the parlor, whisked the key from behind the hall cupboard, and threw open the door. For a moment they could not see into the dim room, and before their eyes had grown used to the darkness Belinda neighed a greeting — neighed unchecked, so loud and long that even Aunt Nancy heard, and jumped as if she were shot!

A minute later Axy was pouring out explanations, and Zeb thanks, while Tilly still sobbed softly; and Belinda, forgotten in the excitement, walked slyly over to the mantelpiece, and laying her nose down sideways, and curling back her lips, chased the last remaining apple up and down the smooth ledge, with her white teeth snapping, and little snorts and puffings of enjoyment.

At nightfall she was led to the barn, where she remained safe during the few remaining days before the British marched out of the vicinity. Then Zeb took her home.

And a little later Doctor Thyng — who, scarcely less than the parson and the squire, was a great man of the neighborhood — rode out in his Sunday coat and best ruffles to make a formal call on 'Miss Achsah and Miss Matilda Binns,' and to thank them for all they had done; and which had done the more he declared he could not tell; and he praised them both till Tilly blushed like a peony, and Axy held her chin so high with pride it tipped up skyward almost as sharply as her little turn-up nose!

And if the two sisters did not really enjoy this visit as much as the many less imposing which Zeb — their warm friend from that day — made in less stately fashion, yet it was a great honor and a great event, none the less.

Standing on the doorstep, curtsying their good-byes, they felt, as the doctor in his saddle lifted his fine cocked hat, shook the reins on Belinda's glossy neck, and cantered away, as if something had lifted them quite out of little girlhood and added a good ten years to their dignity.

THE BLACK HORSE

Catherine C. Coblentz

THE Black Horse hoped something important was going to happen to him. There was expectation in each high-stepping foot, in the way he arched his neck, in the tilt of his nose.

Proudly and happily he led all the other Spanish horses. Forgotten was the ocean journey of several weeks from the Island of Cuba to Mexico. Forgotten, too, were the battles with the Indians when he had carried first one master and then another on his back.

Now his rider was Cortez himself, that Spanish Conquistador who had conquered the Aztecs and all Mexico for Spain. The Black Horse had heard him say that he was going southward next to Honduras.

It didn't matter much to the Black where they went. He liked to glimpse from the corners of his slanting eyes that black silken banner with a scarlet cross in its centre waving over the Spanish soldiers. He liked to hear the bugle playing, and didn't mind at all the high shrill shrieks from the herd of pigs taken along to provide food for the soldiers in case game should be scarce.

But gradually the pace of the Black slowed a little. Cortez was not a light person to carry, and besides he was dressed in heavy armor. The Black remembered that he had no idea how long the way might be to Honduras.

He was glad later that he had saved his strength. He had never dreamed there would be such high chains of mountains to be crossed, such rivers that must be conquered. Sometimes he swam across them. Sometimes he was carried across by Indians in canoes.

Good grass was often scarce. Flies settled on the Black's coat by day and mosquitoes by night, even though he switched his tail or twitched his skin constantly to shake them off.

Sometimes in the dusk horrible bats would descend upon him and plague him almost as much as did the insects and flies, and the bats were not so easily dislodged.

Day after day went by, and the Black still led the way southward. After all, he once thought, this was probably the most important thing that could happen to him.

One morning he came to a wide river. It flowed fast in places, but along the shores it seemed hardly to move at all, and it was filled with alligators. The Black had heard it said that alligators were fond of eating horses. So he waited eagerly for the bridle rein to tighten. If Cortez urged him into the water, he knew he would obey.

But after he had cantered up and down the river-bank for a little, Cortez patted his neck and said, 'No, my Black, that river is not for *you* to swim.' And the man slipped from the horse's back and led him over to the shadow of some ceiba trees.

There for four days the horse of Cortez rested with the other horses, watching while the Spaniards cut down trees and built a narrow bridge. When it was done Cortez led the Black across the bridge, while the other Spaniards followed, leading their steeds. The Black switched his tail triumphantly at the hungry alligators. Surely now the worst of his troubles were over.

Even as that idea passed through his mind his left fore foot sank under him. Quickly he placed the other front foot on what appeared to be solid ground. It, too, sank out of sight.

Then the third and fourth foot plunged into black mud and ooze. All the horses that had followed after him were sinking also. He could hear their frightened breathing; somewhere one of them screamed. What had looked like solid earth was a terrible marsh.

He glimpsed Cortez jumping from grassy hummock to grassy hummock. Then he heard the voice of his master calling his horse to follow him.

Vainly the Black tried to obey. But the more he struggled the deeper he sank into the muck. His two front legs were in the mire to his knees, his hind quarters to his body.

Desperately he lunged, and succeeded in raising his front feet for a moment on what seemed to be firm ground. But as he attempted to free his hind quarters even this ground failed him, and the front feet sank down once more, until he felt the mire along his whole body. The morass was filled with struggling, snorting, and neighing horses.

Taking another quick glimpse, the Black saw that all the *men* had crossed, and he was glad of that. He heard Cortez shout an order and caught the answering voices of the men, who were coming back again toward their horses. They had picked up anything on which they could lay their hands, and brought armfuls of long reed-like grasses and fallen tree branches, and threw them down in front of the animals, urging them to attempt to use even this frail support. Some of

the horses succeeded in partially raising themselves in this way.

But the Black, after getting one foot upon the armful of stuff Cortez thrust before him, saw both foot and the green grass disappear again in the dark slipperiness.

Deeper and deeper he sank. The mud was cool against his sides, but he did not appreciate the coolness. He was afraid, desperately afraid.

Then the mud closed over his spine with a sucking sound. He flung his head up and back as far as he could. But it seemed useless. The black stuff drew him down, down. Now it was at his mouth, his nostrils. Taking one last, long breath of air, he sank out of sight. Only his ears were to be seen, little points above the black mud.

And then, 'Swim, my Black One, swim,' came the voice of his master. 'Swim, swim! I tell you, *you can swim*. Black One, come, *come! Swim!*'

Was the master out of his mind? What horse could swim in *mud*? But the horse of Cortez obeyed the voice. He thrust his feet out in the swimming motion. And he moved. Slowly but surely he moved forward.

The sucking mire seemed to leave his nose. He felt men's hands pushing down through the mud to his hind quarters, propelling him forward. He heard the voice of Cortez calling, coaxing. Valiantly he struggled.

Suddenly he was freed. He was swimming quite easily. He shook the mud from his eyes and opened them. A few feet ahead of him some Spaniards were standing and calling. Others were jumping frantically from grass spot to grass spot at one side of the horses. Horses were swimming to the right and to the left of the Black. Ahead of him he saw one scrambling out of the mire and standing erect with four feet securely on firm ground. The Black made for that spot.

Afterward as he lay panting on the ground he listened to the men explaining how the struggling of the many horses in the mud had caused a middle lane of water to gather, and by this narrow waterway the steeds had finally been able to swim to safety.

The Black looked around him happily. He was a ridiculous sight, covered from his eyes to the end of his tail with drying mud. But he did not mind. The sky had never seemed so blue, or the trees so green.

He struggled to his knees. Suddenly Cortez was beside him and all the Spaniards likewise fell on their knees. There in the sunlight, under the gray moss that swayed from dead tree branches, the men gave thanks for the saving of their horses.

The Black, too, felt very thankful.

The Cream-Colored Pony

Chesley Kahmann

THE new gypsy camp was a world of its own. All the men had disappeared for the day, but women in long, bright skirts dragged feather mattresses into the newly erected tents and stirred the food in the kettles over the smudgy, blazing fires. Already the smell of onions and sage and burning wood had come into the air. And everywhere there was shouting and laughter as children fed the horses and gathered twigs for the fires.

Linji, however, stood a little apart from everyone, staring at old Eldorai, who was hobbling away from her.

'I just can't believe it!' she gasped.

But there it was on her arm, the bracelet that old Eldorai had given her. And Eldorai's words still were in her ears: 'It's your own, dearie, for all the good turns you've done an old woman!'

'Even Nareli has nothing so precious!' Linji thought. It sparkled in the sun and the white stones seemed to flash a hundred colors. It made all the other beads and bracelets Linji wore look shabby.

The next moment Linji started toward her sister, Nareli, her wide, ankle-length orange skirts swishing grandly and her jewelry jangling. Nareli was going to tell fortunes at the next fair, but even Nareli had nothing as valuable as this new bracelet.

'Oh!' cried Nareli, who had been stirring a stew in one of the kettles. 'Let me see it! Whose is it? Let me have it in my own hands for a small, wee moment!'

'It's mine!' said Linji. 'Eldorai gave it to me!'

'Why'd she give it to *you*?' asked Nareli, her face darkening. 'You aren't going to tell fortunes at the fair! Here, give it to me!' She grabbed at the bracelet, but Linji jumped back.

The next moment Nareli said, 'I'll give you my purple scarf for just one moment's wearing of it.'

'No,' said Linji, fearful that her sister would not return it.

'I'll give you my red skirt,' offered Nareli, impatiently. 'And my green earrings.' Quickly she took off her earrings and held them out. 'See, they're yours!'

But still Linji shook her head.

At that, Nareli reached forward and gave Linji's arm a deep pinch. Linji screamed.

'Hush! hush!' said Nareli. Then, in a low voice: 'I won't forget, and that's God's truth! May the dazzling stones in the ugly bracelet bring you the worst of luck!'

'You've no right!' shouted Linji, angrily. 'You — you ——'

But the next moment she was stalking out of camp, past the three green wagons with yellow wheels, past the tethered horses. Then she was alone in the wood, but still thinking, 'She's no right!'

It was a new neighborhood to explore, and Linji began to take deep breaths. To rest her legs she ran forward, stopping only when she had splashed into a hidden spring. She took off her sandals and waded in the water. From that moment, Nareli was forgotten.

Soon she caught sight of a squirrel above her in a tree. At once she began to make strange little sounds in her throat. The squirrel sat listening, his small gray head cocked to one side. Then he, too, made sounds, as if he understood all that Linji said.

For an hour or more he followed Linji, chattering and scolding. Occasionally there was a trill from a bird or the sound of a woodpecker drilling. Linji made bird calls, too, waiting after each one to see if there would be an answer.

But suddenly, above the chattering of the squirrel, came other sounds. Linji stood still and listened. Voices and laughter — but not gypsy laughter — and hoofs upon the ground. She stole toward them. Finally she stood very, very still, peering through a clump of bushes. Beyond were two Gorgios, a girl and a boy. The boy was riding the most beautiful pony she had ever seen — cream-colored with a black mane and tail. He was slightly larger than an Indian pony, and he raised his feet nicely, proudly, and held his head high. The girl rode a brown pony.

Linji, behind bushes where she could see and not be seen, moved closer, hearing talk of school which would open soon, and a dance. She could tell that the boy liked the girl and wanted her to think him superior to other boys. At least he seemed to, with all that talk about football and what he was going to do. He called her Helen and she called him Bob.

Linji followed, thinking: 'If I could just ride the cream-colored pony! If I just could!' Cautiously she crawled from bush to bush. 'Oh, I've just *got* to ride him!' Perhaps the boy would let her!

She circled away from the Gorgios and, when far enough so they could not hear her, ran ahead as fast as she could, then back to the path they were following. She climbed a small tree. And there, sitting on a limb which jutted out over the path, she waited for Helen and Bob.

Before long she heard their voices and the feet of the ponies. She sat very still until they were under the tree. Then she moved her legs.

As she had expected, the ponies swerved to one side. With a laugh, Linji sprang out of the tree and grabbed both bridles. The girl, frightened, screamed. The boy pulled on the reins and tried to turn his pony around.

'Oh, don't be scared!' said Linji, repentant of the trick. 'I did it only for fun.' She wondered what would have happened had the girl fallen and got that clean gray riding costume dirty. Her hair was tucked in under a clean black hat, too, with light curls sticking out.

'Go away!' said the boy.

But Helen stared at Linji's uncombed hair that had never known a hat, at the dirty blouse and wrinkled sash, and the orange skirt that fell to Linji's ankles.

'Who — who are you?' she finally asked. 'And where do you live?'

'I live everywhere,' Linji said. Then, to Bob: 'Come, give me a ride! Give a poor gypsy a ride on the cream-colored pony, and bring yourself a little luck for the kindness!'

At the word 'gypsy,' Helen seemed to shrink back and at the same time to be interested.

'You — you've just come here?' Helen asked.

'Don't talk to her,' advised Bob. To Linji, 'Move aside, and hurry up about you!' Again he tried to turn his pony.

'You wouldn't go without giving me a ride, would you?'

Linji asked quickly. She still kept her hands on the bridles.

'I'd be smart, now, doing that!' said Bob. 'It'd be good-bye, pony!'

At that, Linji's black eyes flashed angrily.

'Do you think I'd steal him and be caught for it, and get my people into trouble?' she cried. 'I'd be smart, doing that, I would!'

'Move!' commanded the boy.

'I can ride the fastest ponies in the world and not fall off,' said Linji in a softer voice. Then, seeing that that kind of talk did not help either, she said, 'Here, let me tell your fortunes.'

'Do you really know how?' Helen asked.

'Of course,' said Linji. She wished with all her heart that she did know how, that she had paid more attention to the older gypsics when they had talked of fortunes. 'Here, give me your hand.' She looked into Helen's eyes, trying to find a sign which would tell her what to say.

Helen reached her hand toward Linji, but Bob said, 'Come on, we haven't time to waste on that!'

Linji ignored the remark, taking Helen's hand into her own, saying quickly, 'Your name is Helen.'

'Did you hear that?' Helen gasped.

'All the boys like to dance with you,' continued Linji, remembering Helen's conversation.

Bob cleared his throat. Oh, surely this fortune would win a ride on the pony!

'Can you tell me what his name is?' asked Helen, pointing to Bob.

'I'll have to look at his hand,' Linji said, pretending that she could not know the answer otherwise.

'Give her your hand,' said Helen.

'Aw, she couldn't tell!' said Bob. But, obviously because Helen had asked the favor, he condescendingly stretched out his hand. 'She hit yours accidentally. Helen's a common name.'

Linji turned Bob's hand this way and that. She puckered up her face as if puzzled, finally saying, 'Your name begins with a B. It might be Bob.'

'Listen to that, now, would you!' said Helen disdainfully.

'Oh, I've got to have a ride, I've got to!' Linji kept thinking. Aloud, she said, 'You're going to school sometime.' Sooner or later all rich boys went to school. And Bob looked rich.

'That's right,' said Helen. 'Maybe next year.'

'Sure, she can tell a fortune!' said Bob. 'You tell her everything, yourself!'

'If you don't believe in fortunes,' said Linji, 'then you shouldn't listen to them! But from those lines in your hand — several little lines right there' — grabbing his hand and brushing over a number of lines — 'it says you are interested!'

'Show me the lines!' said Helen.

'You couldn't see them,' said Linji. 'You're only Gorgios!'

'Go on, tell him some more!' said Helen.

'You've met a dark-haired friend,' said Linji, quickly. 'All you have to do is give her a ride on the pony.'

At that, Bob jerked his hand back, saying: 'Oh, so that's it! All this, so you'd get a ride! Nothing doing!' He said triumphantly to Helen, 'What'd I tell you!'

'Oh, I'm foolish, trying to go so fast!' thought Linji, miserable at the thought of failure. Eldorai often spent a whole week getting something she wanted. But aloud, she said desperately: 'You're a good dancer, too. No wonder your friend likes to dance with you.'

'Who said she did?' shouted Bob.

Then Linji realized that she had said too much. She must be more careful or the Gorgios would discover that her information came from their own conversation. But she covered her mistake by adding, 'Well, her dancing line is the same shape as yours, that's all.' She should not have mentioned dancing at all. Why hadn't she said something about football? That would have appealed to Bob more. But it was too late now.

'Come, give me a wee ride!' Linji begged. When Bob refused, she continued, 'You'd let me go to all this trouble, and then not give me a tiny, short ride?'

'Go on, let her!' said Helen. 'She won't be long.'

'Oh, and that's the truth!' agreed Linji. She stripped herself of all her jewelry except the new bracelet and thrust it into Helen's hands. 'Keep it, to prove I'll come back.' She patted the cream-colored pony's neck, and the pony rubbed his nose against her hand.

In the end Bob dismounted, but it was plain that he would not have done so had it not been for Helen.

'What's his name?' Linji asked.

'Gregory,' said Bob. 'Now don't go far away from us.'

Linji unfastened the girths of the saddle. 'I could never get along on such a thing!' she said. 'You keep it.' She put the saddle upon the ground, then took hold of Gregory's mane, and in a moment was on his back, her legs squeezed close to his warm sides.

Off she rode, patting Gregory's neck, telling him that she was his friend. If Nareli could just see her riding this cream-colored pony with the black mane and tail! How grand she must look! And how the bracelet sparkled! It was not far to the gypsy encampment. She would show them.

She rode to the tents. Children shouted as she drew near
and begged for a ride. Women crowded about.

'What a grai!'

'Let me on his back!'

'Keep away!' warned Linji. 'Where's Nareli?'

Learning that Nareli had gone to a farmhouse for food,
Linji brushed the children aside and rode to the main road.
Sure enough, there was Nareli, trudging along in the dust,
dragging a sack behind her. Linji rode to her and stopped.

'*This* is the bad luck the bracelet brought me!' boasted Linji.

But Nareli only said, 'The potatoes are heavy, fine sister.'
She rested the sack on the ground, looking at the pony. 'And
the day is hot, so let's just put the sack behind you on the grai.
I'll walk along and steady it.' She looked, too, at the sparkling bracelet.

'What!' said Linji. 'Use him for carrying potatoes! He'd be
black instead of cream-colored, after that!'

Then, as Nareli's face darkened, she touched Gregory's sides
with her heels. The pony started down the road at a gallop,
leaving Nareli in a cloud of dust.

With Bob and Helen again, Linji said, 'Oh, he's a good one,
and he can go like the wind, just the way I like to ride!'

Helen returned the jewelry. Linji dismounted and gave
Gregory back to his master, who promptly swung the saddle
over his back. Bob seemed less suspicious of her now.

'A circus wanted to buy him, once,' he said.

'But Bob wouldn't sell him,' said Helen. Then, 'My pony's
named Morovan and I call him Moro.'

Linji, feeling guilty that she had not paid Moro any attention before, patted his nose. But she stole glances at Gregory.
In all the world there was not another pony like him.

A squirrel darted across the path.

'Let's catch him,' said Linji. If she could interest Bob enough, she might get another ride.

'Could you?' asked Helen.

'We'll see,' said Linji. 'Here, tie your ponies to a tree.' She imitated the squirrel's chuckles and chatter and saw the squirrel, who had moved on a short distance, turn to look back at her.

'I'll bet she does have a way!' whispered Helen. She dismounted from Moro. 'Come on, Bob, let's see if we can catch him! Wouldn't it be slick if we could learn a trick like that?'

Bob and Helen tied their ponies to a tree. Then they followed Linji as Linji crept almost up to the squirrel. The squirrel darted farther away. Linji coaxed him back a little. The squirrel scolded, chattered, darted away again.

After perhaps half an hour, Bob said: 'You're no nearer catching him than you were in the first place! I don't believe you *can* catch him!'

'I guess he's not used to you,' said Linji. 'I guess maybe he's afraid of you.'

'We got pretty close, anyhow,' said Helen.

'1 guess maybe we could have had him in a little while,' said Linji. But perhaps it was just as well that they gave up the chase. Bob did seem impatient.

They walked back toward the ponies — over twigs and matted leaves and brushing against prickly bushes. At last they came to the tree where they had tied the ponies. But only Moro was there.

The cream-colored pony was gone!

Seated cross-legged on the ground around kettles of stew, the gypsies ate with special gaiety. For Linji's father, Taimi, had announced that the county fair would open the day after tomorrow and the gypsies had been given permission to tell fortunes there. With the tribe so sadly in need of money, that had been joyous news.

But Linji paid little attention. Instead, she watched the flames rise into the blackness of night, watched burned wood turn white and curl into thin, paper-like pieces.

'Oh, he was such a fine grai!' she kept thinking. 'And he had such straight legs, and his mane was so black against his body!' She had searched the wood with Bob and Helen until dark, finally confident that Gregory had gotten loose and gone home by himself, the way a horse would do if he had the chance. Bob had been very angry about everything, but he would see! He would find his pony in his own stable!

Her own people had scolded her for ever having spoken to the Gorgios — and then everyone had forgotten the pony at Taimi's news of the fair.

The meal finished, someone tuned a violin. Two girls moved into the center of the ring and began to dance. Nareli clapped her hands and jumped to her feet, too, swaying this way, that way, to the rhythm.

But suddenly the music stopped and the dancers moved back.

'That's the girl, right there!' someone cried.

Bob, accompanied by four men, rushed toward Linji.

'Maybe you know where the pony is!' one of the men said. 'I'm the sheriff.'

Linji tried hard not to show the anger she felt. So Bob had come with a bodyguard, had he?

Taimi stood before the sheriff, saying: 'We wouldn't steal a pony. Not us. But we'd be glad if you'd look around.'

Bob kept shouting out the whole story of Linji's riding his pony as the men searched the camp. The more Bob talked, the more silent Linji became. She calmly denied knowing any more about Gregory than Bob did.

'Well, he's not here, that's true,' admitted the sheriff, finally. 'But tomorrow morning, early, you're to move on — the whole bunch of you. And don't come back, unless you want to camp in jail! Understand?'

It made no difference to the sheriff that the gypsies needed to earn money at the fair. Nothing made any difference. The Gorgios departed, repeating the warning to move on.

'If there's trouble, it's us that're blamed!' wailed old Eldorai.

'There's the one we have to thank for it!' shouted someone else, pointing to Linji.

'Yes, why'd you so much as look at the Gorgios? Don't you know what they are by this time?'

'Yes, it's your fault if we starve!'

Voices rose in indignation and anger, and Linji heard her name on almost every tongue. Miserably she sat before the fire, feeling very much alone. Suddenly Nareli slid over toward her and sat down at her side.

'How fine a ride you could be having in the moonlight while the Gorgios sleep!' Nareli whispered. 'It was a fine grai, and he did travel like the wind.'

'I wouldn't touch him again!' said Linji, disturbed that Nareli had come so close to her thoughts. 'I've forgotten him.'

'Oh, no, you don't forget,' said Nareli, softly. 'Such a pony was made for us who'd understand his ways, not for Gorgios.

'I said to myself,' Nareli continued, '"Linji should have him to ride." Ha, I saw clear into your very heart.'

Linji turned over a log. The wood crackled and gave off a smudgy, sweet odor. The voices of the old women grew louder, grumbling against Linji.

'Come, let's take a walk,' said Nareli.

Linji, glad to escape, was soon walking into the black wood with her sister.

'It wasn't my fault the pony ran away,' Linji said.

Nareli turned her flashlight from the path to Linji's face, saying, 'I thought you understood!'

'Understood what?' asked Linji.

'I said to myself: "I, and I, alone, can do my dear sister a favor. She won't do it for herself. Only I can borrow the pony and let her have a ride, when the night's quieted down and the Gorgios have given up the search until morning,"' said Nareli.

'You took him?' cried Linji. 'And ran the risk of jail, and ——'

'It was only borrowing,' whispered Nareli. 'There's no crime in doing that. After you have had a little ride on him, you can turn him loose and he'll find his own stable fast enough by himself.'

'Where is he?' demanded Linji.

But Nareli was in no hurry to tell. She simply said, 'He's safe enough.' And added that she herself had fed him.

'Oh, I will turn him loose!' Linji thought, 'after one little ride!' Already she could feel her legs against Gregory's sides, the breeze in her hair.

'And what'll you do for me — for the favor?' Nareli asked.

'Oh!' said Linji, angrily. 'You did it for yourself, then, not me!' But the next moment, she was saying: 'Show me the pony! And what do you want?'

'Ah, pretty, loving sister, what about the bracelet, for instance?' asked Nareli.

'Show me where he is first!' insisted Linji. 'Then I'll give it to you.'

The two hurried through brush and over sticks, Nareli saying, 'Oh, and I was afraid, after the sheriff came!'

'But not afraid to let them think I stole the pony!' said Linji, angrily.

'I didn't mean any harm!' said Nareli.

But when they came upon Gregory in a place sheltered by three huge rocks, Linji began to forgive the trick. She untied the pony, felt his nose upon her shoulder.

'Here's the old bracelet!' said Linji.

With Nareli lighting the way, Linji rode through the darkness to a road, not the main road but one she knew would surely lead to the town.

'If you'd like to have me watch for you, I will,' said Nareli.

'No,' said Linji. 'Go away.'

She galloped down the road, the breeze blowing her hair, night air upon her face. The stars were above, and a long road lay ahead with fields and woods at the side.

'You're as good as my own for the hour!' she whispered.

Three times she let him reach the edge of town, then turned him back into the country, saying: 'Oh, not quite yet! One more ride, Gregory!'

The moon slipped under a cloud and the wind blew a little more strongly. It looked as if it might rain. Before long, Linji found herself not only at the edge of town, but on paved streets. The streets were dark except at the corners where there were street lights. Gregory's hoofs clattered in the stillness.

'I ought to turn him loose right now,' Linji thought. But as she saw no one upon the streets, she thought she would wait until the next corner. Before she had gone that far, however, a group of boys appeared. Linji never could be sure where they had come from, but one called out, 'Hey, that's Bob Baxter's pony!' and the boys rushed forward.

Linji found herself surrounded by them. Her first thought was to jump and run, but she realized that would be foolish, for the sheriff would know who she was.

'Give him to us!' one of the boys demanded.

'How smart you are!' said Linji. 'Why'd I give him to you after all the trouble I've had to get him this far? Didn't I find him in the woods, caught so he couldn't get away? You should have seen him! Twenty men couldn't have found him!' Then, seeing their wide eyes, she continued, 'So you've come just in time to show me the way to the Baxter house.'

'Gee!' said one of the boys. 'Where was he?'

'Caught, I said!' Linji repeated. 'And he could have stayed there for weeks, with no food and no water, and all you would have stumbled on had you ever come upon him would have been his bones!'

The boys were glad enough to lead the way to Bob's house. Linji, towering above them, rode through the streets proudly, feeling more like a hero than she had imagined one could feel. More boys joined the procession and to them, also, Linji told the story.

At the Baxter house, Bob and his father and mother rushed out.

'She knew all the time!' Bob said. 'She got afraid when the sheriff went out, so she brought Greg back!'

'Bob!' said Mr. Baxter, sternly.

'That's the way it looks!' insisted Bob.

Linji dismounted and handed Gregory over to his master, explaining once more how she had found him when she least expected to; how she had taken the trouble to return him.

Not for worlds would she tell about Nareli's part in the

finding. She and Nareli might quarrel within the tribe, but neither would be false to the other outside.

'Come into the house,' said Mr. Baxter. 'I'd like to talk to you, but it's too noisy out here.'

As Bob took Gregory around the house to the barn, Linji followed Mr. and Mrs. Baxter up to the porch. Mr. Baxter opened the front screen door and Linji, head high, walked through proudly. She had never been inside a house like this before. Several times she had gone into the kitchen of a farm-house, but never into a brick house like this one, through the front door!

Inside, Linji found another world. The living-room was large, with polished furniture everywhere — furniture without a speck of dust. And the rug was so thick it made her want to take off her sandals and wade in it.

'Sit down,' said Mrs. Baxter.

Linji sat down carefully on the edge of the red silk sofa. She looked about her at the several lamps, the pictures on the wall, the magazines and books on a table. She wished she could touch the keys of the piano across the room. And the long curtains were silk. And the chairs were so soft-looking and clean! How could people keep them so clean? She must remember it all so she could tell her people.

'What is your name?' asked Mr. Baxter.

Linji told him. Then, she told once more of that black wood where she had found the pony caught by his reins. She told about the dense thicket in such detail that it seemed more and more true.

'And my own sister fed him his supper,' she added.

'Ugh!' Mrs. Baxter shuddered. 'I'm glad Bob didn't prowl around in that awful place tonight!'

Linji wondered if all Gorgio mothers were like that. What was there to be afraid of? She wanted to laugh.

'Well,' said Mr. Baxter, digging a hand into a pocket, 'I should like to thank you for bringing Gregory back.'

'Oh, that's all right,' said Linji, rising to go.

'Any money in the house?' Mr. Baxter asked his wife. 'I haven't — what I want.' Mrs. Baxter shook her head.

'Oh, I don't want any money,' said Linji, 'if that's what you're talking about.'

She heard rain outside. It pattered against the window-glass. She was glad it had begun, for she liked to walk along the road in it. But as she started for the door, Mrs. Baxter said: 'I can't let you go all that way alone. Your mother wouldn't want you to!'

Linji stared at her. Her mother not want her to! How strange!

'You'd better stay all night,' Mrs. Baxter said.

'All night in a house?' thought Linji. 'Never. I shouldn't sleep a wink!' But aloud, she said, 'The rain doesn't bother me any.'

Just then Bob came into the house. His hair was quite wet.

'Yes, stay all night!' said Mr. Baxter.

Bob frowned. He shook his head at his father, as if warning him not to let a gypsy stay all night.

Linji's eyes flashed. There was no reason for Bob to continue this hostility. Not once had he even thanked her for returning his pony. And now he didn't want her in the house!

'I'll stay!' she said, so suddenly that even Mrs. Baxter looked surprised. To herself, she was thinking: 'I'll show him! I'll stay in his old house! Oh, I will, even if it kills me!'

'Here's a nightgown for you,' said Mrs. Baxter when she had taken Linji to her room. Then she showed Linji the bath-room, giving her two towels and a washcloth.

It was very, very funny, Linji thought. As soon as Mrs.
Baxter had gone downstairs, she very carefully hung the
towels and cloth on the glass rods with the other towels.
They were far too clean ever to use. Then she examined the
tub and looked into the mirror over the washbowl where she
saw her own dark gypsy face.

She turned on the water. Some was hot; some was cold.
The hot water burned her hands. So the Gorgios didn't have
to heat it! The tub had both kinds of water, too, she found.
Also, she found that the water stayed in the tub when she
turned a certain knob. Off came her sandals in a great hurry
and in splashed her feet.

'If Nareli could only see this!' she thought.

Before long, she dried her feet on the rug and went to her
bedroom. She had seen Mrs. Baxter turn on the lights by
pressing a certain button. She pressed it now, herself. The
room became dark. Another push, and it became light. For a
while she played with the mysterious button, laughing to
think how easy it all was.

Then she looked at the bed. Mrs. Baxter had turned down
the spread, and the white, unwrinkled sheets showed. The
nightgown lay at the foot.

'Ha, did she really think I'd wear it!' thought Linji.

As she walked across the room, she caught sight of herself
in a full-length mirror. For a moment she stood looking at her
wide orange skirt. She had not known it was so dirty. She
retied the sash to make herself look a little better.

On the dresser lay a piece of silver which, overturned, became a hand mirror.

'The Gorgios certainly like to look at themselves!' she
thought. 'Wouldn't Nareli like to have this, though!' Already she had forgiven her sister for taking the pony.

She could hear the rain now, but not well enough, so she opened a window, letting the rain come into the room and spatter her face. She felt better. How stuffy a Gorgio house could be! As she stood there, she discovered a roof outside. She stepped out onto it. There she could smell and feel the rain better. But the roof was slanting and slippery. She finally returned to the room.

She felt the bed. It was soft and springy.

'But it's just too clean for sleeping!' she thought. It was for a Gorgio, not for her

She lay down on the floor, but she did not stay there long, for she kept wondering what was behind the door by the dresser. She got up and cautiously opened the door, finding, to her surprise, a room full of dresses.

Her eyes fell upon one dress in particular — a bright red one. She took it out of the closet and stood before the mirror, holding it up in front of herself.

'Gorgeous!' she thought.

She slipped it over her own dress. It was too big, but it looked well. It was by far the reddest red and most beautiful dress she had ever seen. For several minutes she paraded back and forth.

'I'd look better if my hair was combed, maybe,' she thought.

But there were so many snarls that the comb she found in the top drawer would not go through. She tried to brush it next. The brush wouldn't work well, either, and she finally gave up and pulled her hair back as far as she could and stuffed it down the back of her dress.

Then she took a yellow dress from the closet. It had a blue flower on the shoulder and lace around the neck. She put it on over the red one. She tried several others, too, one on top of the other. But she liked the red one best of all.

'I'll take it to Nareli,' she thought.

One by one she took off the dresses and returned all except the red one to the closet. The red one she folded carefully and stuffed under her blouse. But in the mirror she could see that it bulged too much around the waist. Anyone would be suspicious. So she pulled it out and took off her own dress. Then she folded Mrs. Baxter's lengthwise and wound it around her waist. Over that she put on her gypsy dress and tied her sash as tightly as she could.

'You'd never know it was there!' she thought, proudly. How surprised Nareli would be!

But the next moment, she was shaking her head sadly, thinking, 'No, it won't do!' Nareli might wear it and the gypsies find themselves in jail. To protect her people she must not take it.

Slowly she untied her sash, took off her dress, and unwound her new possession. It was badly wrinkled.

'Mrs. Baxter'll know I tried it on!' she thought. She smoothed it out on the bed the best she could and sat on it to press it, but that did not help much. She finally hung it back of all the other dresses, next to the wall where Mrs. Baxter would not see it when she opened the closet door.

'But what a shame to leave it here when it looks so well on me!' she thought.

Her own clothes on again, she dropped to the floor, tired. The rain had stopped. She lay looking up at the ceiling. The ceiling began to worry her, and the four walls seemed to move in on her every time she closed her eyes.

'If only I could let the outdoors into this room!' she thought.

She rose from the floor and sat in the rocking-chair. As she rocked back and forth, she wondered what her people would say if they knew she was in a Gorgio's house, under a ceiling! Why was she here, anyhow? Because Bob had not wanted her to stay!

'Making myself uncomfortable, just to spite a Gorgio!' she thought. 'Oh, it's not worth it! I won't do it!'

She jumped up from her chair and crawled out through the window to the slanting roof. It was still wet, but she moved slowly toward the edge on her hands and knees, feeling sure that she could find a way to the ground. Rid of the stuffy Gorgio's room, and under her own sky again, she took a deep breath, filling herself with that damp, fresh smell of things after a rain. But there was something else in the air, too. She sniffed again. Was it smoke?

She looked back toward the window through which she had come. Was the house afire? For it was smoke, all right! Then she looked over toward the barn. It was dark there, but as she looked, she saw a burst of flame in an upper window.

'Gregory!' was her first thought.

Linji scrambled back into the house and ran into the hall, screaming: 'Get up! Get up! Your barn's on fire!' She kicked loudly at every door she saw. Then, the family aroused, she dashed downstairs, unbolted the front door, and ran out to the barn. By now the smoke came faster and faster from the upper window.

'Oh, the poor grai!' she cried, pulling at the barn door. But the door would not budge. She kicked it, pulled again.

Then she ran around to the back, hoping that there might be another door. But there was not. There were, however, two open windows. She crawled through one. From somewhere she heard Gregory stomping and whinnying, but grope as she would in the blackness, she could not find his stall.

Then she heard a fumbling of keys at the door. A moment later the door slid open and someone switched on lights.

'Get Gregory!' said Mr. Baxter to his son. 'I'll get the car out or the place'll blow up! Hurry, Bob!'

'Listen,' said Bob, turning to Linji, 'you don't need to feel so important around here! It's funny how the barn caught fire *tonight* ——'

'Get the saddle!' cried Linji. 'Something he's used to! So he'll leave the barn!' Smoke was coming into the stable from the hay chute. 'Or get a gunnysack! Or something to cover his eyes!'

'Go on out!' said Bob, shoving her. 'I can get him myself. Whose pony is he, anyhow? Come on, Greg!'

But Gregory showed no signs of moving. Rather, his legs seemed glued to the floor. He stiffened them, and no matter how hard Bob pulled on the halter rope, they would not budge.

'Get the saddle!' Linji cried. 'Don't you know *anything*?'

'Are you crazy?' shouted Bob. 'The important thing's to get him out!'

'But he — won't move' — coughed Linji — 'without — a saddle — or a gunnysack ——' No horse would leave a burning stable unless his eyes were covered or unless one could make him think he was going to be ridden. Oh, the stupid Gorgio! Did he know nothing about his own pony?

A spark from the haymow above fell into the manger. Linji struck the flame with her hands and threw what water was in Gregory's pail onto it.

'Oh, the poor, poor grai!' she wailed. She ran out into the main part of the barn, but she could not find the saddle, or a sack, or anything. Back in the stable again, she found Bob still jerking the halter rope.

Linji's eyes smarted from the smoke that still was coming out of the chute. Suddenly she clutched Bob's arm with her strong fingers. With a quick twist she sent him flying away from the pony.

'That's only a little of what I can do!' she cried. 'Now, be quick! Get the saddle! Or you'll have a dead pony and maybe be dead yourself!'

Bob, obviously surprised at Linji's strength, dashed out of the stable, returning a moment later with the saddle. Suddenly the lights went out.

'Oh, and maybe the ceiling will cave in!' Linji kept thinking. She jerked the saddle from Bob, threw it over Gregory's back, and tightened the girths. Then, quickly, she ripped off her long, wide skirt. That she threw over the pony's head and eyes. Then she took hold of a certain place low down on his nose with her other hand, ignoring the halter rope, and led Gregory out of his stable into the blackness of the main part of the barn. Gregory kept shaking his head up and down, trying to free himself of the skirt.

'It's all right,' Linji kept saying. 'Don't be afraid.'

Outdoors, she pulled her skirt from Gregory's head and eyes and led the pony to a tree a safe distance from the barn, telling Bob he need not bother any more if he didn't want to.

But Bob had already dashed off.

A screeching siren seemed to have awakened the whole town, for neighbors, half-dressed, were rushing into the yard, and a fire engine clanged up the driveway. Soon men in rubber coats and hats were erecting ladders and splashing water over the unburned part of the barn as well as into the haymow.

'But it was me that saved you!' boasted Linji to Gregory. 'Me, and not your own master!' She started to pull on her skirt when suddenly she cried: 'Oh! Just look, would you! Look what's happened!'

Her skirt was torn from hem to waistband.

Gregory rubbed his nose against her shoulder.

'Oh, I'm not blaming you,' Linji said. 'No, you're worth a lot more than a torn skirt. But look at him, now!' — she pointed to Bob — 'Running around like a wild man, trying to get someone to find his bicycle! Not thanking me, even!'

Firemen spread big rubber sheets over the roof of the garage so the garage would not catch fire. Everywhere there was noise. A hundred helpers, it seemed. Shouting, running about, yet only a few actually doing anything. Linji watched, contemptuously. She put on the skirt with a jerk. It tore in still another place.

Someone was now throwing sacks of grain out of the haymow door. Linji watched. Did the stupid Gorgios think Gregory would eat grain that had been smoked?

Flames were red against the dark sky. Columns of smoke

puffed upward. But Linji stood by Gregory, stroking his smooth back, rubbing his nose.

Everybody was giving directions. Bob dashed about as if his excitement would help put out the fire. Everywhere was the smell of burned wood, and pieces of charred wood flew through the air when the hose was turned upon the roof.

Under the chemicals and water the flames gradually turned into smoldering smoke and Linji could see that the fire was under control. And then she caught sight of a tall man she had not noticed before.

'The sheriff!' she gasped, uneasiness instinctively overtaking her. To Gregory she said: 'Oh, I've got to go now! The next thing the sheriff'll say is that I started the fire! Well, good-bye ——'

She gave Gregory's neck a squeeze and hastily rubbed his nose once more. Then she started to steal away.

She had gone only a few steps, however, when someone behind her cried: 'There she is! Here, Dad!'

Turning, Linji caught sight of Bob.

'Oh, they've thought of it!' Linji said to herself. 'Thought of blaming me for the fire!' The picture of jail loomed up before her. 'Oh, and what'll my people say?' Already her people were angry at her for having associated at all with the Gorgios. They would be angrier than ever, now, when they found she had been blamed for the fire, too.

In defense, she turned to Bob, saying: 'You needn't speak a word! Look at me! Torn from head to foot, I am, for helping you get your pony out!' She showed him the long rip in the skirt, showed him that anybody could now see the whole length of her green petticoat.

'Gee!' said Bob. 'Gee, I'm sorry. That's too bad! Look, Dad, look how she's torn ——'

Linji could only stare at Bob. Had she heard right? Or *had* there been a tone of pleasantness in his voice?

But Mr. Baxter was there, too, saying: 'Linji, we want to thank you. You ought to give my son a few lessons on horses in general. You saved Greg, all right. Bob never could have. And we'd like you to know we appreciate it. What can we do for you?'

'I ——' Linji began. 'Oh, I ——' For the life of her, she couldn't think of anything. If only she had been a little more prepared for this sudden change in the Gorgios!

Then she realized that Mrs. Baxter was there, too, adding a thank-you.

'We ought to get her a new skirt,' Bob was saying. 'Look how hers is torn.'

Suddenly Linji began to seem a little more herself. In a flash she remembered the bright red dress in Mrs. Baxter's closet.

'Oh!' she said. 'If you're — going to all the bother of getting me a new skirt, maybe — maybe you'd get it the color of the dress upstairs — the red one ——'

Then she stopped abruptly, realizing that she never should have examined those dresses. But Mrs. Baxter was saying kindly, 'Which one, Linji?' quite as if everything was all right.

'It's — well, it's a red one,' said Linji. 'And it's a little wrinkled and ——' As well as she could she described it, adding, 'It's the one clear in the back of the closet — behind the other dresses.'

Mrs. Baxter was nodding her head, saying, 'I know the one you mean.' Then suddenly, 'Linji, how would you like to have *that* dress?'

'Oh!' said Linji. A strange feeling came into her throat.

'Oh, it was gorgeous!' She remembered exactly how she had looked in it. 'Oh, it was!'

The next minute Mrs. Baxter had gone into the house, asking Linji to wait.

'Sam! Come over here a minute!' called Mr. Baxter.

And then the sheriff was standing beside Linji, clearing his throat loudly.

'He's got something to say to you,' said Mr. Baxter.

'I guess,' said the sheriff, looking straight at Linji, 'you can stay awhile in the neighborhood if you want to. I guess it'd be a good idea to stay for the fair! I guess maybe we need a few good fortune tellers at our fair!'

At the same time Bob was saying: 'Listen! Could you come over this afternoon and show the gang how you can ride without a saddle?'

'Oh, I don't hear right!' Linji thought. Inside, she felt very fluttery. But aloud, she found herself answering: 'Yes, I could. Oh, I could, without any trouble at all!'

Then Mrs. Baxter was back with the red dress. In a second, the dress was over Linji's arm — her own. And finally Linji was starting out for her camp, calling back a promise to meet Bob that afternoon to show his friends how well she could ride.

Then, out of sight of everyone, she sighed deeply.

'I'd never have believed it if I hadn't heard him with my own ears!' she thought. 'A Gorgio sheriff inviting us to stay for the fair! Saying it as if he really meant it. Oh, what's come over the Gorgios!'

Her feet kept going faster and faster. For above everything that had happened, something else awaited her at camp — her own people's praise. Nobody would be angry now.

As for Nareli . . .

She sighed again. She had done something that even her older sister, Nareli, could not have done.

Stable Call

Cornelia Meigs

Was it the rustle of the tent flap, moving in the soft prairie
wind, which had roused Rodman Phelps to raise his head
from the pile of army blankets and listen?

All about him the camp was sleeping. Even the horses had
stopped jerking at their ropes and were still, in those small
hours when everyone is wrapped in deep slumber after a long
day's march. The guards were awake, of course; now and
then Rod could hear their slow tramp going back and forth
beyond the last line of tents.

But in all that company his were the youngest ears, and
they had certainly caught some sound, faint and far off, but
unusual enough to signal even to his dreaming senses that
there was danger. And most certainly there was only one real
danger for which they all were on the lookout. The moment
anything out of the ordinary happened, there was but one idea
which instantly leaped into every mind.

Although there were soldiers all about him; although the
camp was set up in rows of army tents, with arms stacked be-

fore the doors, and horses for the soldiers tied in long lines beyond, it was no real errand of war upon which they were all bound. If it had been war, there would have been no place in that company for Rodman Phelps, aged fourteen, and in no way enrolled in the United States army.

No, this was a bold adventure of a different sort. The soldiers were those sent out to be a guard for a great project — the laying out of a railroad across unsettled country full of broad plains, difficult rivers, broken hills, and unfriendly Indians.

In the early 1870's the Northern Pacific Railroad was only in its first beginnings; so that this was no matter of building roadbeds and laying rails, but merely of seeking out the best line across that great unknown territory, of surveying the chosen way slowly and exactly all the way from the Great Lakes to the Missouri River and from the Missouri to the Yellowstone. There were but six engineers who were doing the work, but the body of troops sent to keep them safe amounted to a small army.

It was only a month ago that the news of this march had come to the fort where Rod's father, Colonel Phelps, was in command. Every young officer, every enlisted man of any spirit, was anxious to be one of those chosen to go.

And it seemed almost too wonderful to believe that Colonel Custer of the Seventh Cavalry, who was to be in charge of the soldiers on the journey, should have said, with his easy good nature: 'How about my taking the boy along, Phelps? He can go if he wants to; he seems to me the kind who wouldn't make a nuisance of himself. There will be some good hunting — buffalo and elk and antelope. And, after all, as I see it, with such a big force there's not too much danger. We may never even be attacked by the Sioux.'

Rod had held his breath while his father thought it over. There was not time to think long. 'Why, yes, he may go,' was the glorious permission finally given. 'Only, as you say, he must be sure not to be a bother to anyone in any way.'

The boy could see that Custer's second in command, Lieutenant Tracy, was none too well pleased with the plan. 'Trust a boy to get himself in the way, somehow,' Rod heard him mumble. But it was not his place to speak aloud. A horse was found for Rod, his things were got together, and they were off.

Through all the march, which had been long and hard, he had been careful above all else never to make a nuisance of himself, never to be in the way or to cause any delay. He was never the last in saddling up in the morning; he always got his horse tied and fed and watered as soon as any of the more experienced soldiers; he always leaped at the sound of the bugle call, no matter what its message.

But he burned to do even better than that; to be of some real and active use, if only to show his bravery to that watching, doubtful eye which Lieutenant Tracy never failed to fix upon him whenever they met. 'This sort of journey is no place for a boy,' he said aloud, more than once in Rod's presence.

Rod swore to himself that before the march was over he would show Tracy something, he would prove that he had as good a right in that company as any other. Perhaps, he thought, as he now sat up in the dark and strained his ears, perhaps it might be this very night. Suppose he were to be the one to give warning of a Sioux attack.

He listened, holding his breath, but he heard nothing. The great prairie was still, except for the far-off cry of a wolf; a horse whinnied and shifted its feet; the guard tramped past. That was all. Rod was very sleepy.

From where he was lying among the blankets he could look past the open tent flap to the broad Dakota prairie, dim in the faint starlight; the tall grass bending a little in the wind; the low, round hills rising against the sky. No, it was just as it had been on every other night. The breeze of late summer was chilly; he snuggled down between the blankets again; his eyes were closing.

Then suddenly there arose outside the most terrible of uproars, a nightmare of noise, shouting, stamping, yelling, and the crash of guns. A dark form went running past the tent door; a half-dressed soldier came after it, and another, and another.

Horses snorted, reared, broke loose, and went galloping through the camp. Shots were fired in every direction; officers roared orders, and men shouted in reply; but above everything there rose, high and terrifying, the Indian war cry. A bullet sang past Rod's ear and nicked the tent pole. A moment later a loose horse stumbled against the canvas wall and brought the whole thing down about his ears.

When he crawled out of the tangle of blankets, ropes, and smothering canvas, the uproar was over. The soldiers were gathering in ranks, the horses were being caught, flying reports were beginning to shrink down to sober truth. The actual facts were at last made clear. A half-dozen Indians — certainly no more — had ridden, shouting and shooting, straight through the camp, charging down the narrow lanes between the tent rows, and emptying their guns into the tents.

Their object had plainly been to stampede the horses; to make them break loose from their posts and gallop away into the dark, where they could be gathered by the red men and driven away.

The enemy had not succeeded in their plan, however; for

only a few of the horses had managed to break away, and of these nearly all were caught. The shooting in the dark had done little harm; for this was not meant to be a serious attack. It was mostly an act of daring on the part of the Sioux, the proof to the white man that they were close upon his heels.

But when morning came and men and horses were counted, it appeared that there had indeed been one great loss. Colonel Custer's best horse, Ajax, swift and big-shouldered, was gone. A few others which had got loose were seen galloping here and there, not far from the camp, and were caught again, so that it seemed that the Indians had not had a real chance to drive them away. But Ajax had completely disappeared.

Rod went back and forth through the camp. The men were either mourning or laughing over the events of the night.

'Six Indians threw us into a good deal of an uproar,' one gray-haired old soldier admitted. 'We won't get off by our usual time today. There's broken harness to mend and slit canvas to repair, where the horses put their hoofs through. It's sure bad luck that Custer's horse was the one to be lost. He was the best in the whole regiment. The colonel's sending out a group of men to see if they can find him. But they mustn't take long, for we've got a long march ahead of us today.'

For a boy of Rod's ability and energy an idea needed only to be a minute older than the performing of it. When the men, with an officer in command, went galloping out on the back trail to look for the lost horse, the boy was trailing behind them. His long-legged horse was not so sturdy or so experienced as theirs. Rod had to urge it again and again to keep up with the speed of the others.

The searchers swung over one hill and then another, and at last saw a galloping animal which the officer, with the colonel's field glass, made out to be the lost horse. They quickened their speed and bore down upon him as he grazed and ran and then stopped to graze again, once in a while pausing to stare at them as they came closer.

'He always was a wild thing,' the sergeant said. 'Even the Indians couldn't catch him in the little time they had for a chase. But I shouldn't be surprised if we couldn't get him back, either.'

It proved true enough. The big creature stood once for a minute on the height of the hill; then stretched his neck and sped away more swiftly than they could follow, swinging down the long slope, and disappearing into a group of cottonwoods around a water hole. The sergeant looked back over his shoulder.

'The line's getting under way,' he said, 'and we're too far away from them now. We'll have to give the horse up and go back. Remember that we've been ordered never to forget that the Indians are always watching.' He gave his command, and the men swung their horses obediently.

But Rod, so he argued with himself, was not strictly bound to follow military orders. Riding last in the line, he looked back again and again. The horse had grazed out beyond the clump of trees, a single, lonely figure in that great empty waste. Rod had patted him often; the animal would know his voice if he came near and called. The others were mounting the hill and disappearing on the other side. The boy turned his horse.

Down he rode; down the long slope out into the broad basin with its scattered clumps of thicket and faint line of green where the water trickled away and lost itself in the dry ground. He was nearing the horse, who raised his head and stood looking. His own horse whinnied, and Ajax answered, the shrill greeting of one horse friend to another.

Rod was not many yards away. He rose in his stirrups and called, ʿAjax! Ajax!ʾ For an instant the animal stood motionless; then he swung about and was off in a thunder of hoofs — a long, regular beat which stood for such wild, fleet escape that there was no hope of overtaking him.

Rod pulled up and let his own horse breathe for a minute. He had been so sure; but he had been wrong. He was beaten. And had it been, perhaps, the wisest thing in the world to lag so far behind? He took one more glance backward at the fleeing Ajax. The ground the horse was mounting went up, up to a long roll of hill; and just below the top something moved, and something else — now three moving dots and now four — riders, seemingly heading downward toward the level. There could be no doubt that they were Indians.

They would stop, he was sure, to catch the loose horse; for such an animal as Ajax was a rare prize. He rode on, urging his mount to the top of its clumsy speed, but not wanting to seem to flee too hurriedly. After a stretch of yards he looked back again. They had not stopped to go after the colonel's horse; they were after more valuable game. They were following him.

He turned about and galloped on. He would not look back again, he told himself — not until the shots began to sing about his ears; not until he would have to turn finally, draw the army revolver from its holster, and sell his life for what it was worth — not much, he thought painfully, for he realized now the foolishness of what he had done.

This was just what the men had always been warned against. This was the very thing for which the Indians had waited so long. Sometime or other a person in that marching column would grow careless, bold, and forgetful; would stray away from the safety that numbers brought and let himself fall into danger. Rod thought himself so wise and responsible, and now he was the one to bring about the special thing they had all sought to avoid.

'We don't want to have to stop to waste time and blood fighting the Indians,' he had heard the colonel say more than once. 'With the season so late, it's our business to get on.'

Would they have to try and save one thoughtless boy who had got himself into danger by making a stand and a battle? No! The one thing he desired now was that they should leave him behind and think no more about him. It might ruin the success of the whole journey if there was a halt, a fight, and the engineers were kept from their work. How could he have done this? Should he look back? He had told himself he would not, but he did.

The Indians were close; they were within shooting distance. They were still riding on the level, and Rod was mounting the hill, so that they gained on him rapidly. He could see them spread out like a fan, swinging their rifles into position. There was a report, and he ducked without thinking, although the ball flew high. One more effort and he would be over the hill. But the second shot was very close, and the yell that followed it and the drumming of hoofs sounded at his very heels. It was time to turn and make a stand now. His hand closed on the handle of his pistol.

But what was this? A shout ahead of him, and heads rising over the edge of the hill! How good the blue uniforms looked as they swept into sight! The soldiers had been sent back to his rescue! He had hoped that they would go on without him, but how glad, how gloriously glad he was that they had not.

The group opened, and he and his stumbling horse rode into the midst of it, followed by a last scattering of bullets. The Indians swung out, circling to right and left. They did not care for a fight; they had only been enjoying themselves, chasing a foolishly bold boy. The little company of soldiers galloped away toward the column, with its great cloud of dust hanging over it as it marched along.

The immediate joy of relief in Rod's heart gave place, little by little, to hot shame and regret. It was just his luck, he thought unhappily, that the officer who had been sent back to fetch him should be Lieutenant Tracy. He did not say a word to Rod as they rode back, but it was plain that he made sure that the boy heard what he said to the man beside him: 'This is just the kind of thing I expected from the very first. Anyone would know that the fellow would make trouble.'

It was just before they rode even with the marching ranks that Rod pushed his horse up beside Tracy and spoke. 'Couldn't — couldn't you tell the colonel that it was only because I wanted so to get back Ajax — that it was because Ajax was his horse ——'

'I'll tell him no such thing,' replied the other. 'That isn't my business. And it's yours to see that you obey orders and don't delay the column again.'

Rod knew that the report would be harsh and unpleasant, and he felt that he had deserved it. And then, in a sudden burst of anger, he knew that he had not earned all those harsh words. He had been foolish; but there had really been a good chance that he could get the horse, and every horse was valuable. 'And I'll make up for it yet,' he found himself promising suddenly. No matter what should happen, he was bound that he would clear himself from blame in the eyes of the colonel and the company. Somehow he would prove that he was not so foolish as he had seemed.

The march went on, day after day, following the basin of a winding river. Rod would take his turn with the rest at guard duty, looking abroad for the enemy or glancing down into the green hollow; he would watch the engineers, with their instruments, measuring and marking curves, mapping and surveying. He tried to think of the rails and the thundering trains that were to follow; how they would soon go roaring through that empty country and make it a place where men could win a rich living from those spreading plains. There was room for both white men and Indians if the proper plans could be made.

He would look across the hills, watching for the enemy and thinking there should not be a war. Some of the Indian tribes had sent word that they were willing to let the railroad cross their lands, but the Sioux would never give in. They would hate and hate and hate forever. Had they got Ajax? Rod often wondered. He never put aside the idea that somehow he himself would get him back.

Sometimes he went with the hunters to get game for food, since the company had come a long way from headquarters and supplies were getting low. Buffalo, elk, bear — how welcome the meat was as a change from the usual salt pork and beans! Rod learned to be a good shot and a wise hunter of game. He had learned also to be patient when the day's ride was a long one and many of the men around him were grumbling and complaining over their hard lot.

The Indians still hung at their heels, never risking an open fight, but always a cloud of danger that never was lifted, that never allowed a moment of freedom from peril.

They passed the deep cuts of rivers; and Rod saw, put down on the rolled paper sheets, the plan for bridges which would extend over those difficult streams, and the long raised banks which would give level roadbeds through the broken country. 'Will you ever really build them?' he asked curiously of one of the engineers.

'Next year,' was the cheery reply. 'There'll be an army of men with picks and shovels where you see this army camped with its guns. And the year after that the trains will be running, and this will never be wilderness again.' To Rod it seemed like a fairy tale, but these men saw it all as surely as though it were built already.

The survey had reached the Yellowstone River, and the procession turned back. That was as far as they could hope to go before the blizzards of the prairie winter would shut down upon them. They must make haste now back to the headquarters on the Missouri; for the autumn was nearly at an end, and winter must not catch them unprepared. The march was rapid, difficult, and discouraging. Food was scarce, the game had been frightened away, and they found little hunting on their homeward track.

Horses had given out and had to be turned loose, and a number of soldiers who usually rode had to march on foot from lack of horses. There was one day when the whole day's march was almost stopped because the colonel's horse had gone lame and he had no spare mount. 'If we only hadn't lost Ajax!' Rod heard him say again and again.

Rod offered his own horse, but the colonel only smiled. 'He's not up to my weight,' he said; and certainly he was not — a sorry beast who had never been very good, and now, tired and stubborn, he was very little to offer in the way of horseflesh. The colonel thanked the boy, however, and Rod felt that for the first time he was half forgiven for his foolishness so many weeks ago. Lieutenant Tracy had seen to it that the affair was not forgotten.

The boy felt himself to be an experienced soldier now — tough, brown, and dusty as were all the men. He had made friends with almost everyone. He could clean and feed the

Paul Brown '39

Rod put the bugle to his l

od up in his stirrups, and blew
(*See page 224*)

horses, bring them grain, set up a tent, and make up a bed roll
as well as any of the rest. One of his best comrades was the
bugler, Tom Davis, a young man not much older than Rod.
He taught Rod the camp calls, and there were several morn-
ings when Tom got a few minutes of extra sleep while the
camp was awakened by Rod's slightly uncertain notes calling
them to rise.

'I can't get 'em up! I can't get 'em up!' thus the soldiers
had long ago put words to the notes which he blew, clear and
loud, although a little unskilled. He could sound stable call
also, when all the horses were driven up to be fed; and taps,
when the camp settled down to its sleep.

The Indians heard it, too, he was certain, as they circled
the dark hills, always watching. They had got a number of
horses. More than once a buffalo or an antelope, wounded by
the white men on their hunt, fell into the hands of Indians
when the soldiers could follow it no farther. They would see
the fires on the hills. The Indians were feasting, while the
troopers went to bed hungry.

They had come back into the basin of the Heart River,
where the first daring ride through the camp had occurred.
'Watch for Ajax' was an unnecessary order; for all eyes were
searching the hills and levels, as the long column, always at-
tended by its wrapping of yellow dust, went crawling across
the plain. Moving dots in the distance were sometimes antelope, now and then an elk, more often Indians.

But one day Lieutenant Tracy, leveling his field glass, announced suddenly: 'There he is! And the Indians got him.
There's a Sioux riding him.'

Very grudgingly he let Rod look. It was true. There was
the tall horse, with an Indian on his back, standing at a great
distance, watching the column pass. A force of men was sent

to try to get him. The colonel was talking to Tracy, who was
to be in charge, giving orders.

'You can risk a good deal to fetch him back,' he was saying.
'I never thought losing a horse could make such a difference.
I'd give anything to get him again.'

Rod stepped up with a boldness he had not felt in many
weeks.

'May I go?' he asked. He saw it in Tracy's eye to refuse
immediately, but it was the colonel's part to decide.

'Yes, let him go,' he directed. 'It seems to me he wasn't so
wrong in trying to get him before.'

Rod was happier and more excited than he had been for a
long time, as they all galloped away, Tracy in the lead and
Rod and his friend Tom Davis riding together.

It was a useless search. The Indian saw them coming; and
as the company bore down upon him he rode away toward the
hill. Clouds of red warriors suddenly appeared from nowhere,
circling and shouting, plainly hoping for a fight. Tracy drew
rein; the Indians stood still also. 'The colonel ordered us not
to attack,' he said. 'We're not sent out to start a battle.'

He turned to go back; and immediately all but a few of the
Indian riders disappeared, while the rest followed the white
men at a distance, their laughter and insults coming faintly
down the wind. The soldiers stopped and turned, and the Indians fled away; then gathered and followed as once more the
soldiers rode toward camp.

The men growled and muttered; it is hard to be laughed at
by the enemy. But orders were orders. At the head of the
bold half-dozen Indians was the man who seemed to be their
leader and who was riding Ajax. Rod was near enough to see
the rise and fall of the cruel whip.

The soldiers came back toward the camp, then swung about

once more and charged; but it was of no use. The Indians were too quick and skillful, and their horses had not been worn down by the long, grinding march across the plain. And Ajax himself, after the months in the wilds, seemed to have developed fear of white men. He snorted and shied as he came closer to the camp and the guns and the tents came into plainer sight.

Once more the soldiers turned, reached their own ranks, and dismounted. It was a failure. They would have to give over the best horse in the regiment to the enemy. Rod heard Tracy reporting to the colonel, 'They are too many and too quick for us, sir,' and the colonel's regretful reply, 'Yes, we'll have to march on.'

Suddenly the boy was seized with an idea. He rushed through the camp, found the tent of Tom Davis, snatched the bugle from its peg, and flung himself on his horse. He rode some yards out from the camp, the six Indians circling near but safely out of reach of the soldiers' guns.

No one ordered the boy back; they all watched, spellbound, wondering what he meant to do. Now he was almost out of rifle shot of his companions — so far away that the fire of the soldiers could scarcely protect him from attack. The Indians, accepting his challenge, advanced nearer and nearer, circling carefully, within shot now, the leader, on Ajax, coming closer than all.

Rod put the bugle to his lips, stood up in his stirrups, and blew. Stable call — those were the notes that sounded, the order that rang through the camp at evening when the march was over and the horses were gathered and fed. It had never been so steady or so clear.

> Come all who are able,
> And go to the stable ——

Rod heard the rustle and tramp of the horses behind him; they were pulling at their bridles, answering naturally the signal they all knew so well. The men held them steady — watching, watching. Ajax heard; he pricked up his ears; he stood still; he snorted.

And give your horses some oats and some corn.

The big horse leaped forward; the Sioux's whip sung brutally, but it was of no use. Habit and training were too strong. Ajax lowered his head, snorted again, and bolted. Straight toward the ranks he shot like a flash of lightning, his rider yelling, jerking, lashing. The rude bridle was as nothing against the horse's charge.

Nearer and nearer they came, and the Indian at last threw himself from his horse's back, rolling in the dust, and jumping up to flee on foot, out of reach of gunfire. A great roar went up from the watching soldiers, joined even by the insulting laughter of the Indian's own comrades.

A Sioux on foot is no warrior at all, but a creature to be despised even by his own friends. He ran, a bullet or two following him, kicking up the dust at his heels. One of his companions rode close, took him up behind, and the whole band sped away.

Rod had dismounted and caught Ajax by the rude loop of the Indian bridle under his jaw. The animal was trembling and so was the boy. The colonel strode out alone and laid his hand on the mane of his horse.

'I offer you the thanks of the regiment,' he said quietly.

TALE OF TWO HORSES

A. F. Tschiffely

(*Two young Patagonia horses, Mancha and Gato, relate some of their adventures on a real journey they took to the United States with their master.*)

Mancha Speaks

THE first day of our journey was most unpleasant, to say the least. The pack-saddle tickled me, and every now and again I saw something that frightened me. To make things worse, it rained hard, and the road was so muddy that we sank in deep with every step.

We were made to go north; further and further away from home. After the first few days' travelling, one day was like another. We trotted over a vast prairie which looked like a limitless sea of grass. We followed a wide track which was fenced in on both sides, the posts and wires stretching in two dead straight lines until they were lost from view at the horizon.

Heavy rains continued to pour down every day, and in many places the track was so soft that it was hard work to plod through the mud and water. We were so bored that we didn't even look at the prairie-owls who sat on fence-posts screeching at us. When we occasionally saw horses in the distance we no longer called them, for by this time we knew that we were in a strange land where we had no friends.

By degrees we got to know Master so well that we began to like him, and as time went on our liking grew into love and affection.

Gato and I took it in turns to carry Master, the one with the pack following behind.

On and on we jogged. Sometimes we spent the night in a ranch, but when we camped out in uninhabited parts Master slept on the ground near us. If a stranger came near, we heard or scented him long before he saw us, and on such occasions we snorted to wake up Master, but if he slept so heavily that he didn't hear us, we pushed our noses against him.

One evening, after a long day's plodding through water and mud, we arrived at a humble little ranch-house. Torrential rains had beaten down on us all day, and to make things even more unpleasant, a strong wind began to blow as an early dusk fell on the dreary plains.

As we approached the ranch-house, a number of barking and snarling dogs came dashing towards us, but Master took no notice, and made us go on. When we were near the house he clapped his hands and called 'Ave Maria!' — the customary manner for travellers to announce their arrival in the Argentine pampas. No stranger ever gets off his horse until he is invited to do so. Even the dogs seem to know this, for they keep on barking and threatening until their master calls them away.

Presently, several men and women appeared at the door, and although Master was a stranger to them, they politely asked him to dismount, and invited him to enter into the hut. These kind people even helped him to unsaddle us, and when we had been turned loose, they and Master went into the house, where a big fire roared up the chimney.

We grazed for a while, but it continued to rain in torrents, and the wind was so cold that we preferred to take shelter behind the walls of the house. Occasionally, when we heard Master's voice, we peeped in through the door to see what he was doing.

The people inside had obviously just finished a meal, for a spear — on which they had roasted a side of sheep — was still stuck in the mud floor near the fire. The dogs were gnawing bones which had been thrown to them, while the men were sitting close to the fire in a semi-circle.

Several children cuddled up against their mothers, their black eyes gleaming as they looked at the fire, over which hung a large kettle which hummed and chirruped as the water was beginning to boil.

Presently one of the gauchos (Argentine cowboys) poured some of the hot water into a little gourd which was filled with mate tea, and when the bombilla, or metal tube, had been stuck into it the gourd was handed round, and everybody sucked a little of the green tea.

For a long time nobody spoke, and only the crackling of burning logs and the crunching noise of dogs gnawing bones broke the silence. When a particularly strong blast of wind roared down the big chimney, sending a mass of whirling sparks and smoke into the room, it sounded just like the snort of a wild horse.

On such occasions a grizzly old cowboy shook his mop of long white hair, and pointing a horny finger at the darkness beyond the open door said, 'The snorting of the Bragado.'

From where we were watching and listening, we heard Master ask the old man to tell the story of the Bragado. Finally, when the old man had seated himself in a more comfortable position, he started to speak very slowly, and in a deep bass voice.

'The Lagoon Bragado,' he began, 'is still infested with wild ducks, flamingoes, and many other varieties of wild birds, very much as it was over a hundred years ago, when my story opens.

'"Bragado" is the name of a beautiful stallion who was first seen by two trappers who were on their way to a distant store. In those days the pampas were quite uninhabited, and only a few settlements snuggled against the mountains to the far southeast. These settlements were fortified so as to make them safe from attacking Indians and fierce bands of outlaws, who were a great danger in those days.

'Here and there the prairie-land was covered with patches of thorny bush, and only an occasional *ombú* tree broke the monotony of the seemingly endless plain.

'The two trappers who first sighted the "Bragado" were earning money by the sale of hides and skins. Once day, whilst they were creeping along a brook, stalking some ostriches, they beheld a sight which made them stop as if spellbound. On a hill, like a sentry on guard, stood a stallion, a magnificent, blood-red beast with white-blotched flanks. He was nervously quirking his ears as if to locate by some sound the place in which his instinct told him were enemies. On the lower ground about him was his herd, over which the stallion towered like the statue of a horse on a pedestal — motionless save for his twitching ears and slightly quivering, wide-open nostrils.

'When the two trappers arrived at the next settlement they told everybody about the beautiful stallion they had seen, and soon the name of the "Bragado" became famous. So many were the extraordinary tales that were told about him that expeditions were being organized to go in search of him. However, in spite of all these efforts to capture the animal, the "Bragado" always escaped easily, only to appear again in some other part.

'On several occasions he even allowed his would-be captors to come quite close before whirling round and uttering the call that brought his herd to heel and sent it off like a cloud of mist before the wind. Sometimes, in a spirit of mockery, the "Bragado" had even galloped through the advancing line of cowboys, and in a cunning manner dodged the lassoes which were thrown at him.

'Soon the fame of the stallion reached the distant cities, and a wealthy trader decided to organize an expedition and send it into the pampas in search of the "Bragado."

'Two hundred men, some hired and others volunteers seeking adventure and glory, joined together. Covered wagons and provisions were bought, and for defence against Indians every man was armed with a rifle or some other weapon. Slowly the wagon train wound out of the city and was soon lost from sight on the horizon.

'The expedition had been on its way for several weeks when, one evening, as the men were sitting about the camp preparing food, some scouts came back with the report that they had sighted the famous stallion. All the gauchos rushed to saddle their mounts, and soon they were advancing on their gallant prize. Riding in fan formation, they had planned to entrap the horse between themselves and a high, precipitous river-bank.

'The attack was so sudden and cleverly carried out that the

Paul Brown '39

"Bragado" was separated from his troop. The dodging of men was no new thing to him, but this time every possible avenue of escape was cut off by the advancing riders, who were swinging their lassoes and *boleadoras*, a dangerous weapon the stallion had long ago learned to fear. As an attempt to break through the advancing line of enemies was impossible, he climbed up to the highest rock that projected above the river. Murmurs of admiration and calls of triumph escaped the cowboys as they realized the animal was at last securely trapped.

'He looked beautiful now, pawing and snorting, his body showing to full advantage with the setting sun behind him. The cool evening breeze played with his mane and flowing tail, and as if admitting defeat he tossed flecks of foam into the air.

'For a few seconds he stood at bay, and then, uttering a shrill neigh of defiance, he sprang into space and his beautiful body hurtled downward into the river, sinking immediately from sight; never to reappear.

'Silently the men returned to their camp near the lagoon, where later a village was founded. With the passing of years this village grew into a small town, its neat houses standing as a monument to the "Bragado," who, like many men, preferred death to bondage.'

After we had travelled over the prairies for many long days, the country began to change. The sun became hotter and hotter, and the ground was very sandy and dusty. Here there were no more fences, and in many places it was difficult to see the track. Vast stretches of the country were covered with a mass of white salty crystals, which made the place look as if it had snowed. Here and there grew huge cactus plants, some being as big as chestnut trees — forty to sixty feet in height.

In the daytime it was terribly hot, and when we had our midday rest there was nothing to eat, except a few tufts of coarse salty grass. Sometimes Master cut the long and sharp thorns off cactus plants with a big knife, and chopped the thick bulgy leaves into slices which he gave us to eat. At first we were not keen on this new fodder, but when we tasted it and found that it was quite sweet and good, we ate every scrap Master prepared for us.

In this region we saw only two or three human beings, and very few animals, excepting lizards and an occasional snake. Some of these lizards were very big and beautiful, and as we approached them they waved one fore paw as if beckoning to us to come nearer. Early in the morning and towards evening, flocks of little green parrots flew about, screeching loudly, but during the heat of the day they slept in shady spots among the cactus plants or in their big nests, in which several families live.

At night foxes prowled about, and owls flew silently above our heads. How I hated the mournful hooting of these birds, whose eyes sometimes stared at us like two bright yellow disks.

We were glad when we came out of this desolation of cactus plants and sand, for fodder had been scarce, and we had gone thirsty for hours till we found water, which was warm and tasted of salt.

Master was lucky to have us with him, for more than once when we were so thirsty that our tongues began to swell and prick as if pins were being stuck into them, we showed him the way to water-holes he would never have found without us. Men are intelligent, but in some ways we horses are cleverer than you are. We can smell water long before we see it, and, moreover, we never lose our way.

On one occasion it was just as well that Master didn't interfere with us when we showed him the way to a water-hole, or
else he might not be alive today. This is how it happened.

We had travelled for many hours, and the sun was so hot
that it burned through my hide. Master, too, must have felt
the heat, for he was unusually silent. As a rule, he chatted
with us, and although we couldn't understand all he said,
we liked to listen to his voice.

The region through which we were jogging was a desert
where nothing grew but here and there a few shrubs and soli-
tary cactus plants. Every time we came to a hollow, I noticed
that Master looked for something, and I soon guessed that it
was water he wanted. 'How stupid!' I thought to myself.
'Fancy looking for water with the eyes!'

For a long time we continued, and I was beginning to feel
quite bad with the terrible thirst that tormented me. Suddenly a lovely smell of water reached my nostrils, and I
sharply turned to the left where it came from.

Master seemed annoyed with me for having changed our
course, but in spite of his efforts to make me go his way, I refused. Trying to make him understand that I was leading to
water, I raised my head, pricked up my ears, and sniffed the
air.

It was lucky for the three of us that Master guessed what I
wanted to tell him, for as soon as he gave me my head I took
him straight to a hole where we found precious water.

After this, whenever we were in difficulties, Master always
left the finding of water-holes to us.

Gato Speaks

When I was young I never guessed that the world is so big, and I didn't know that so many strange people and animals live in it.

For thousands and thousands of miles we went north from Patagonia. We crossed the whole of South and Central America, and then jogged through Mexico, and from there trotted on to Washington in the United States of America. Sometimes we travelled through huge prairies, then we plodded through tropical swamps, or we climbed up giddy mountain-sides till we came to regions of eternal snows, high above the clouds.

Again, we fought our way through wide rivers and raging mountain streams, most of which had no bridges, and therefore had to be crossed by swimming. Some of the tropical waters were full of alligators and crocodiles; and we were lucky that no electric eels touched us, and that we were not stung by rays, whose poison can even kill a horse.

Electric eels live in some of the slow flowing streams and rivers in the hot parts of South America. They are about four feet long and black, and as thick as a man's arm. Their bodies are like electric batteries, for they are filled with enough electricity to stun a horse if they touch any part of his body.

Before entering some rivers and streams, Master had to look us over very carefully to make quite sure that we had no cuts or scratches anywhere, for if the cannibal fishes — who infest these waters — smell blood, they tear their victims to pieces in a few moments. These cannibal fishes are called *carribes* or *paraňs*. We encountered many other perils on the way.

What strange people we saw in some places! We lived

Paul Brown '39

among Indians who went about practically naked; and we even saw some who painted their bodies and faces.

Now I must tell you what happened when we left the cactus forests behind us and came to much nicer country where there was plenty of good grass and water.

Whilst we were trotting over an open stretch of grassland

in the forest region in the north of Argentine, we had a very exciting adventure.

I was carrying Master, who seemed to be half asleep, when the smell of an enemy I dreaded came to my keen nostrils. In a flash I turned and tried to flee in the opposite direction, but before I had gone ten yards Master stopped me and, much against my will, turned me round again. However, in spite of all his efforts to make me go ahead, I refused to make another step forward, and as he didn't seem to realize that a puma lay hidden somewhere ahead of us, I snorted and reared up, trying to make Master understand that I had scented danger. When he finally guessed that something was wrong, he dismounted and, having tied the two of us to a tree, went to investigate.

He hadn't gone far when I heard a warning snarl which made me tremble with fear.

Presently Master came running back to us, and having unstrapped his rifle — which was always on top of the pack — he slowly advanced towards the place where the puma lay hidden.

At the time we didn't know what a rifle is used for, and we had often wondered what this strange stick on the pack might be.

Step by step Master advanced through the dry grass, whilst the two of us watched with horror, expecting him to be killed at any moment. After a while — which seemed like a whole day — he stopped and slowly raised the rifle to his shoulder.

With heads held high, we both looked on, our nostrils wide open so as not to miss the faintest smell which might come our way.

Suddenly a flash of fire came out of the muzzle of the rifle, and at the same instant there was a noise like a thunderbolt. I really don't remember what happened after, for the fright I got was so great and sudden that I can't tell you what I did. In trying to run away I got such a violent tug on my neck that I fell, and when I managed to scramble to my feet I fought madly to tear myself loose.

After a while I heard Master's voice, and when I could see clearly again I saw him standing near me. Having calmed down a little, I looked around me and saw Mancha, who was still tied to a tree near-by, and I noticed that he was every bit as scared as I was.

Master spoke to us and stroked our necks, and, as soon as we were less nervous, he went over to the place where the puma had been hiding in the grass. Only when we realized that our enemy was dead could we be persuaded to proceed on our way, but for a long time after that we were on the look-out for a sudden attack.

Later on Master taught us not to fear his firearms. After a few weeks we got so used to the deafening noise they made that we took but very little notice when he shot birds and animals, which were often his only food.

Every day we travelled far, until, after many long journeys, we saw mountains ahead of us. We were in very wild country now. There were no roads, and the few villages we came to were small and dirty. The people we saw there were much darker than those in Buenos Aires; in fact, most of them looked like Indians.

The country was getting very mountainous, and as not even trails existed there we were obliged to travel along the dry river-beds. Slowly we penetrated further and further into the mountains. Sometimes we were shut in by high walls of rock, which rose straight up into the sky.

It was just as well that we had arrived during the dry season, for if we had been caught in one of these valleys when it rains in the high regions, and the wild waters come thundering and seething down the deep gorges, we should have been drowned like rats.

When we had crossed the whole of the Argentine we came to a country called Bolivia. Every now and again Indians with their troops of laden llamas passed us.

The first time I saw llamas I was terrified, but when Master made me understand that they are quite harmless, I plucked up courage and looked at them with curiosity. How strange they look with those long, upright necks and woolly coats!

Very soon we got so used to seeing llamas that we took practically no more notice of them. Before I go on with my story I must tell you something funny about them.

You know that to defend himself a horse kicks, a cat scratches, and a dog bites. In fact, most animals have some kind of defence; but, as far as I know, llamas have no way of defending themselves, for they neither bite nor kick, nor do they scratch. However, they have a very nasty and most unpleasant habit. They spit! Yes, when they are annoyed they — spit!

Sometimes when we passed a troop of these llamas on a narrow mountain trail where animals and men have to walk in single file, it was very unpleasant if they didn't like the looks of Master. If the first llama made up its mind to spit, all the others which followed behind did the same; and you can guess what sort of mess Master was in when a troop of llamas had passed him!

Travelling became more and more difficult as we advanced into the network of mountains. Sometimes we slowly picked our way through stony river-beds, where we struggled ahead for hours, stumbling over rocks and stones.

I have never seen anything more imposing and dreary than

these enormous and deep valleys. There wasn't a trace of animals, and for days we saw nothing green, excepting here and there a cactus plant. Icy winds swept down from the snow-capped mountains ahead of us, and where these winds struck some rocks they produced a mournful, booming sound, which, together with the clattering of our hoofs, were the only noises to break the mysterious silence.

Sometimes we came to rivers we couldn't cross, and so we were forced to follow Indian foot-trails which led us up steep mountain-sides and along giddy precipices. In such places we had to be very careful and watch every step we took, for a slip or a careless movement would have meant certain death.

Soon we had so much confidence in Master that we went wherever he guided us. When we came to a steep incline, he always went afoot to make it easier for us, and we didn't mind it a bit when he caught hold of our tails to be pulled along. He was always very careful with the pack and saddle, and every now and again he stopped to see if they had slipped out of place. We got to understand each other so well that we could guess what Master wanted us to do; and by this time he understood us as easily as if we had been able to speak.

If one of us suddenly stopped, he guessed at once that something had gone wrong, and immediately came to investigate. Sometimes a stone had stuck in a hoof, the pack or the saddle had slipped, or perhaps one of us wanted to rest a minute.

We were now so high above sea-level that the air was very thin. The lack of air-pressure causes *mountain sickness*, which is very unpleasant, and sometimes even dangerous. The slightest physical effort makes the heart beat violently, and the sufferer vainly gasps for breath. Very often he bleeds from the nose and feels giddy, and sometimes even faints.

Master always told us to climb up these mountain-sides slowly, and whenever we stopped he never drove us on, but waited until we had recovered our breath.

At first we used to tremble and shiver with fear when we looked down some of these giddy precipices, but we soon got so used to them that we didn't mind so much.

Once one of my feet got stuck between two rocks, and in the struggle to pull it out I tore off the shoe. Master had often taught us to lift our legs; and to show us that he would do us no harm, he tapped the underneath part of our hoofs with a stone. Thanks to these lessons I didn't mind standing on three legs whilst he nailed on another shoe. He always carried several spare irons in the saddle-bag, and he also had a hammer and other tools which are necessary for shoeing a horse.

When I remembered the fight I put up when men tried to shoe me for the first time, I couldn't help smiling to myself. But I wasn't tame at the time, and I thought the men wanted to do me some harm.

With all the lessons Master gave us, we quite enjoyed the fun when he said 'Left' or 'Right,' and soon we got to know by sound which leg he wanted us to lift. You see, even a wild horse becomes tame and affectionate when he is taught with kindness and patience.

A THOROUGHBRED

Glenn Balch

WHEN he came West, Redston, the gambler, brought with him a beautiful bay mare that had originally come from Kentucky. Redston had a natural horseman's eye, and he could see in that mare things that made him proud to own her.

His luck held until he reached the Du Chesne country, but there it started to break, and twice he found himself reduced to such an extent that he was forced to use the mare for capital. Presently he awoke one morning to find that on the turn of a card she had passed from his possession.

Redston, no welcher, went to the corrals with the new owner to transfer control of the animal. He stood and looked long and regretfully at her trim bright form.

'She's hot blood,' he told the man. 'Her ancestry reads like the social register. There ain't no better breeding. She's got all the aces in the deck, spirit, intelligence, speed. . . . Say,' he broke off to throw a shrewd glance at the new owner, 'did you ever handle hot blood?'

The man's thick bearded lip curled disdainfully. The eyes in his coarse face were little and liquor-reddened. He wore the rough, dusty garb of a rancher.

'Hot blood or cold, she's a hoss, ain't she?' he retorted. 'I've handled hosses all my life, an' I can handle her. She don't look so salty to me. When they git too tough for me to tame, then you might as well shoot 'em or turn 'em out. I don't reckon you can tell me anything about handlin' hosses, mister.'

Redston's shrewd, calculating eyes were still on the man's face. Presently, with a hopeless sigh, he said, 'No, I don't reckon I could.'

The new owner carried his lariat in his hand. Back of them his saddle-horse, a flea-bitten gray, stood to trailing reins. It was the abuse which the gray showed that was causing the misery in Redston's heart. Inwardly, he cursed himself and he cursed the cards by which he made his living. Men like this, he knew, were few in the West; yet fate had decreed that he should lose his beautiful mare to such a one. Redston felt sick inside.

'Well, I'll be ridin',' the man said, and he opened the corral gate and stepped inside, shaking out a noose in his rope.

'Wait a minute,' Redston told him quickly. 'Don't rope her.'

The gambler stepped past the man and advanced into the corral. 'Dolly,' he called in gentle tones. 'Come here, Dolly.'

The mare whinnied low, trotted up to him, setting her round, trim hoofs down in the dust with the springy lightness of a greyhound. He caressed her nose, slipped an arm about her neck. 'Bring your rope,' he instructed the man.

'So that's how you catch her,' the fellow sneered. He

advanced roughly and, when within a few feet of the mare, tossed a small loop at her beautiful head.

With a startled snort she ducked free of Redston's arm and wheeled away. The rope fell to the dust. The mare raced, head high and puzzled eyes wide, to the opposite fence, stood there eyeing them with nervous uncertainty.

'You fool, you'll ruin her,' Redston cried angrily.

'I'll show her who's boss,' the man retorted heatedly, jerking the noose up out of the dust and catching it with an experienced hand. Slinging out a loop, he advanced upon the mare. The gambler swung in front of him.

'Don't do that, man!' he cried.

The fellow paused, and his eyes narrowed to angry, bitter points of light. 'She's my hoss, ain't she?' he snapped.

During the long half minute of tense immobility that followed, Redston's fists clinched and unclinched convulsively. Then with a mighty effort of will he jerked himself to one side and left the corral without looking back.

The mare retreated nervously as the man with the rope approached. Presently he had her hemmed in a corner. Twice she whirled about, now thoroughly frightened. He continued to approach, bearing slightly to the left, his big hands that held the rope hanging low. Suddenly she broke out along the fence, to the right as he had planned, a beautiful bundle of swift-flowing muscles under her satiny coat.

The man's right arm darted forward, the loop swirled expertly before the mare's eyes, and the next instant the strands bit into the tender skin of her neck. Distracted by this strangling new terror, the mare plunged and bucked around the corral, dragging the man behind her. When presently he succeeded in getting her halted she was breathless and wild-eyed.

He attempted to approach her and she leaped away, snorting. He cursed her fluently, braced himself on his high heels. Getting her halted again, he tied the rope to one of the corral posts. Then he went outside, mounted his gray, and rode back. Taking the rope from about the post, he wound it around his saddle horn, then turned his gray horse and rode out the gate and down the road that led toward his dilapidated little ranch. Choked into submission, the mare followed reluctantly.

Early the following morning the man came to the corral to view his prize. Standing there in the little enclosure with her trim, intelligent head high and the bright sunlight striking gold glints from her red coat, she was a picture to bring joy to any horseman's heart. There was strength and grace in the long, supple lines of her body, and the vibrant elasticity of physical perfection in her movements. Alertness and intelligence showed in her eyes and her ears and her nostrils.

The man halted but a few seconds to watch her. He had never owned a horse like her before, and he was anxious to get on her back. He dropped into the corral with his coiled lariat, and the mare snorted alarm at the action. The man paused thoughtfully. For a few seconds he eyed her highstrung, trembling nervousness. Presently he spoke his first words to her.

'Dolly, come here,' he said.

A striking tableau they made there in that little dilapidated corral situated in a scraggly clearing in the juniper, the man, shoulders hunched and stern, on one side, and the nervous, high-headed mare poised for flight on the other. The bright sun gave a yellowish hue to the dust beneath their feet, and the mare's black tail and mane swayed slightly under the impulse of the gentle breeze. Dust recently stirred by her restless feet drifted in a little cloud through the low, sagging rails behind her. A thirsty old range bull was a red blotch coming down to the creek through the trees of the opposite slope.

The words struck a familiar chord in the mare's memory, but the voice was not the low, confidence-inspiring voice of the man, Redston, who had taught her their meaning. And this man held in his hands that feared coil of rope which she unerringly associated with the choking pain about her neck of the day before. She stirred restlessly but came no nearer to him.

'Come here,' he repeated sharply. 'Come here, Dolly.'

The mare shook her head and snorted loudly, a puzzled nervous snort.

'Come here!' He shouted the words, a note of irritation creeping into his voice. He took a step toward her; she sprang away, raising a flurry of dust.

Trying to restrain his temper, the man followed, hemmed her in a corner, sought with voice and hand to cajole her into approaching him. She held, but with obvious difficulty. The man continued talking to her, approached slowly, his hand outstretched. This way of catching was new to him; a hard-twisted merciless rope was what he always used. But Redston had done it, and he could do anything that tinhorn could.

'Come here, Dolly.... Come here.... Here, girl.... Here, Dolly....'

But his voice lacked assurance and his hand was shaky. The mare stood it as long as she could, then whirled, presenting to him a pair of powerful hindquarters with muscles bunched for action.

With a sharp curse the man leaped back, out of range of

those hard, round hoofs. She didn't kick, but that didn't
appease his anger and chagrin.

'I'll l'arn you how to turn yore tail on me,' he shouted,
and as his arm swung in a quick-tempered arc a long bight
slid out of the coil of rope. It made a dusty U across her
satiny hips.

The pain of the blow added to the mare's fright. With a
terrified snort she wheeled on her hind feet, broke out of the
corner along the fence. The man shouted his rage at her, and
the bight pulled the hair again, this time across the back.

She slowed, circled the next corner, and cast a look over
her shoulder. The man was coming across the corral, at stiff-
legged jumps. Curses tumbled from his loose-lipped mouth
and his bearded unkempt face was twisted in anger and determination. The long bight of the lasso whistled in circles
about his thick, powerful right hand.

'Come to me,' he shouted.

The mare was in another corner now, trembling and shrink-
ing, her heels toward him. Crack! The bight bit hard and
deep. She whirled to break away, but he was there before
her. The rope fell on her withers as she wheeled desperately
back, stood humped in the corner.

Crack! Crack! He rained a succession of savage blows on
her cringing hips. Hard-twisted rope whistled again and
again through the dust-laden air with all the weight his arm
could give it. 'I got you now,' he grunted in savage triumph,
and her satiny rump rapidly became a criss-crossed maze of
dusty welts.

His savage cruelty got the better of his judgment; he closed
in through the dust, and the end of the bight went over the
mare's hips and tore at her tender flanks on the opposite side.

'When I git through with you, you'll be danged glad to

come to me,' he grunted between blows. 'Never saw a hoss I couldn't...'

The pain had become unendurable and at last the mare retaliated. Through the dust her two hard, round hind hoofs shot up and back. One missed; but the other caught the man squarely in the middle, just a few inches above the big brass buckle of his belt. His talking was shut off as if some giant hand had been suddenly clapped over his loose mouth. He landed on his back in the corral dust, his cruel face frozen in an expression of surprise and helplessness.

The mare whirled frantically out of the corner, raced across the corral. The old range bull raised his dripping nostrils from the creek as her golden form came sailing over the rail fence. He snorted and retreated as she flashed past him, racing madly up the valley.

On she went at a swift run, streaking over the green grass and darting through the trees. Presently she topped out at the head of the little draw and there paused a moment to look back, sharp-etched against the sky in her wild frightened beauty, before she tossed her head and galloped on toward the high, rugged Uinta mesas, where some instinct told her perhaps that the wild bands roved.

BETSY'S HORSE-SHOW RIBBON

Lavinia R. Davis

'THERE he is, Betsy, going around the ring now!' Johnny Travers pointed out the little hackney pony across the ring. Betsy watched as the pony came near them. It was trotting hard, throwing up its knees to its chest. As it flashed past them Betsy caught the sheen of its sleek, black sides.

'That's Bad Boy,' Johnny said, turning toward his sister. 'You're in luck to be riding him.'

Betsy wasn't so sure. She watched the pony again as it came pounding past them. Flaherty, the Martins' groom, was riding it now. Flaherty was so big that he and the pony looked top-heavy, but Bad Boy didn't seem to mind. Bad Boy acted as though he had nothing on his back at all, or something so light that it could hardly be noticed. He trotted as though he were a trotting machine, knees and hoofs snapping.

As he left the ring after the class Bad Boy made a neat, compact kick at the horse behind him. 'Look!' Betsy said. 'Did you see that?'

Johnny grinned. 'Not scared, are you?'

Betsy shook her head. She wasn't really. Or if she was it didn't make any difference. She was going to ride Bad Boy anyway. Hadn't she wanted to ride in a horse show all her life, and now this summer for the first time she'd been given the chance? And it was on the Martins' pony at that, and Mr. Martin was the Master of Fox Hounds in Milldale Valley. Betsy hurried along to keep up with Johnny.

Johnny was going to ride in the jumping class for children under eighteen. Betsy watched him get Melissa ready. Melissa was Johnny's hunter. She'd been a farm horse when he'd seen her and been convinced that she could jump. He'd finally gotten the family to buy her and he'd been right about her jumping.

Melissa had a head that made you think of a camel, she had great bony knees, and her gray coat looked flea-bitten. Melissa was not beautiful but she could jump.

Betsy held her while Johnny bridled and saddled her and then swung himself into the saddle. When Johnny did anything with a horse it looked easy, and natural and right. Johnny was as good a horseman as his father, and that was saying a good deal.

Betsy watched him go over the jumps with her heart in her mouth. She wasn't afraid that he'd fall, but just that Melissa might be careless and clip the top of one of the fences with her big feet. But Melissa outdid herself and Johnny went twice around the course without touching a jump.

About a half hour later Johnny came out of the ring with his silver cup in his right hand. Johnny had won the children's jumping class without anyone even being close to him!

'You win a ribbon this afternoon,' Johnny said as he slid

off Melissa, 'and we will have something to tell Father when he gets home tomorrow.'

For the first time Betsy thought of her parents. Mother was in Europe with Grandma, but Father was off on a business trip that would be over tomorrow. He would want to know every detail of how she had ridden Bad Boy.

For the rest of the morning Betsy couldn't get Bad Boy out of her mind. She was to ride him in the class for children under twelve, riding only to count. The class was coming soon, and Betsy wasn't quite sure that she was ready for it.

Johnny and Betsy lunched at the show grounds on frankfurters. Soon after they had finished, the grandstand began to fill up. The boxes blossomed with bright dresses and gay hats as people came for the afternoon.

At quarter to three Flaherty came looking for Betsy. She saw him first but she didn't say anything. 'Time to get ready,' he said when he saw her. 'Major Chase is the judge, and he's always through his classes sharp-like.'

Betsy followed Johnny and Flaherty to the stable. Bad Boy was all ready, and Flaherty folded back his cooler and pulled it down his gleaming rump. Bad Boy's black sides were so shiny that they looked as though they had been oiled.

'I'll give you a leg up,' Johnny said, and the next minute Betsy swung into the saddle and her knees were seeking to grip on Bad Boy's unrelenting sides.

'Walk up and down slowly,' Flaherty said, 'and get him used to the other children. He's not used to such big classes.'

Bad Boy didn't like being in a class with nearly forty children. He threatened every horse or pony that came within six feet of his tail.

'Class 58 — Best Child Rider under Twelve — this way, please.' The 's' of the announcer's 'please' sent a little shiver down Betsy's neck. The bugle blew and Bad Boy trotted briskly into the ring. It would have been fine, but Betsy felt that he was trotting that way because he wanted to, and because the bugle made him feel frisky, and not because he was doing what she directed him to do.

The horse-show grounds were filled. There were people everywhere — in the boxes, in the reserved seats, and two deep around the fence that lined the ring. They held programs, purses, gloves, a hundred and one shining objects for Bad Boy to shy at.

Before she was halfway around the ring for the first time Betsy saw the band. Twelve men in red coats carrying brass instruments. She saw them going to a little platform behind the judges' stand. In another moment they would strike up, and what would Bad Boy do then?

It happened just as she and Bad Boy passed behind them! The bandmaster lifted up his baton. One, two, three — they crashed into 'Marching through Georgia.'

Bad Boy nearly turned inside out! He arched in a sharp curve to the right. Betsy could feel her legs loosen. He plunged away from the band in a series of businesslike bucks.

Betsy's seat was all gone now. She held onto the reins and grabbed shamelessly at the saddle pommel. Bad Boy curved away from the band once more and ended up with one big buck. Betsy sailed off over his head!

The ground came toward her with a rush. She held the end of her reins and fell. She hit the earth hard, very hard. She lay still for a second while the other horses circled some distance away from her. They were still trotting carefully, evenly around the ring. She was away behind them. None of the other children had even seen her.

Betsy sat up. The reins were still in her hands. She had

held to them consciously, desperately. 'You've got to learn
to keep your horse when you fall,' Johnny had said. 'If you
lose him when you take a spill in the hunting field you're
through.'

Betsy stood up and walked toward Bad Boy. He stood
looking at her, head down, sharp ears back. He looked a
little like an irritated goat.

They were well beyond the regular line of riders behind the bandstand. Johnny and the rest of the audience had not seen her fall. The judges even hadn't seen her.

Betsy knew she didn't have any choice. When you fell off you got on again right away as long as you could still walk. Johnny had told her that over and over again and so had Father, and there wasn't anything else to do.

Betsy shortened her reins in her left hand and reached for her stirrup with her right. 'Steady now, Bad Boy,' she said. 'Steady.'

She swung herself upward, and instantly Bad Boy bounced off. She saw the surprised face of one of the ring attendants who had run toward her when she had fallen. She was on again by the time he reached the spot! She was on again and riding toward the front part of the ring, posting carefully to Bad Boy's high trot.

For the rest of the class Bad Boy outdid himself. He trotted hard, as fast as he could, his legs hitting up toward his chin. Betsy caught her breath and tried to keep up with him. She knew her hat was on crooked and that there was dirt on her back. She wriggled her head a little and felt the cardboard disc that had her number on it. She'd kept that on by luck.

They passed the band from the front and from the back, but this time Bad Boy had nothing to say about it. He'd acted up and now he was quite content to go past them as quickly, as efficiently as possible.

'Walk, please.' The horses and children stopped trotting with varying degrees of speed. Bad Boy stopped instantly before Betsy's hand touched the reins. In another minute the announcer shouted, 'Canter, please,' and Bad Boy was off like a small sky rocket.

'Walk, please.' The class settled unevenly to a walk.

'Numbers 5, 14, 16, 37, and 7 in the middle of the ring, please.'

Betsy could hardly believe her ears. They were being called into the middle of the ring. And she was one of the ones called!

She heard the announcer say something and the rest of the class, thirty or more, trooped out of the ring. She started to look at the four other children lined up near the judges' stand. She saw Hughie Martin on one of his father's hunters — but just then Bad Boy started curvetting about and she didn't have time to look any further. She had all she could do to keep Bad Boy anywhere near where he was meant to stand.

'Numbers 5, 14, 16, and 37 out in the ring, please.' Betsy understood now. They'd kept her out but she wasn't going to get a ribbon. Anyone on Bad Boy would be sure to be noticed, but that didn't mean you were going to get a ribbon. They were trying out the other four, but not Bad Boy and herself.

They put the other children through their paces and then called them back to the centre of the ring. 'Number 37 first, please,' the announcer called. 'Number 14; number 16.'

Betsy began to turn Bad Boy toward the gate. 'Number 7.' Betsy could feel little prickers of excitement down her back. They were calling her number. She had won a fourth! A glistening white ribbon! They couldn't have seen her fall! What would Johnny say, what would Father say when, with forty-odd children in the class, she'd won a ribbon?

But Bad Boy didn't like ribbons. When the man leaned toward him with the ribbons he edged away, curvetting like a kitten. It ended with Major Chase himself tucking the ribbon into Betsy's riding-coat pocket. 'You gave a nice performance,' he said. 'Very.'

Paul Brown '39

At last the mare retaliated.   Through the

two hard, round hind hoofs shot up and back

(*See page 248*)

Betsy smiled at him and followed the other horses round the ring. She should have said something about the fall. Should have told him that she had fallen when she was just behind his stand. But she couldn't. Not possibly. There wasn't time, and then there was the ribbon. Betsy could feel the round silky rosette in her pocket. After all, if the judge hadn't seen her? And it was her first ribbon.

In another minute they were all out of the ring and Johnny was holding her bridle. 'Nice work,' he said, and there was a grin all over his face. 'Nice work.'

'Well done, miss, very well done. That was a stiff class to be in the ribbons.' Flaherty swung Betsy out of the saddle.

Betsy patted Bad Boy's nose and let Flaherty take him off. She looked after them unbelieving. Had nobody seen her fall?

'Let's see your ribbon,' Johnny said, and she took it out to show it to him. It was a creamy satin rosette with Milldale Valley Horse Show written on it in gold letters. 'That's wonderful,' Johnny said. 'When Father gets home tomorrow he'll be awfully pleased.'

Betsy put the ribbon carefully back in her pocket. She wanted it more than she'd ever wanted anything in her life. If Johnny hadn't seen her fall maybe nobody'd seen her? She glanced at the attendant who'd run to pick her up. He didn't know her number, and anyway it meant nothing to him. Betsy felt the ribbon with the tip of her finger. Major Chase would never know that she'd fallen off. He'd never have a chance to give Betsy's ribbon to number 5. The ribbon was Betsy's for keeps.

But the rest of the afternoon wasn't quite as much fun as Betsy had thought it would be. She and Johnny walked around the horse-show grounds and they kept meeting Major

Chase. He wasn't judging after the children's class, and he and the Martins, with whom he was visiting, strolled around the temporary stables. It seemed to Betsy that they ran into them regularly every ten minutes.

Johnny and Betsy went home after the very last class of the horse show. When they got there Johnny fastened his ribbon over Melissa's stall and put his cup on his own bureau where he could see it from his bed.

Betsy put her ribbon on the table beside her bed. But when she woke up once during the night she didn't want to look at it. It caught the light and Betsy quickly turned the light off. She'd taken it under false pretences. She'd taken it without telling Major Chase that she'd fallen off when he couldn't see her.

Betsy turned over in bed. All of a sudden she knew what she had to do. She had to take that ribbon back to Major Chase the very first thing in the morning. It was a good thing he was staying with the Martins, who lived only a half mile down the road. Betsy pulled up the covers and tried to go to sleep. But she couldn't; she thought first of Major Chase's face, then Johnny's, and finally Father's.

Early in the morning before anybody else in the household was up Betsy was out and walking along the dirt road that led to the Martins'. It was very quiet so early in the morning, and the shadows of the maple trees were long and dark.

Betsy hurried along, holding on tight to her ribbon. She hoped that Major Chase would be up and nobody else. To tell her story in front of Hughie Martin and all the others would be even more terrible.

When she got there Major Chase was walking around the rose garden all by himself.

He looked very surprised when he saw her. 'Why, hello,' he said. 'Who are you?'

Betsy's heart sank. It was going to be harder than ever to explain. He didn't remember her. He'd seen hundreds of ponies and children in his three days of judging. How should he remember?

'I'm Betsy Travers,' she said. 'I rode in the children's horsemanship class yesterday. I — I — that is, you gave me the fourth prize.' Betsy held out the ribbon. 'But you shouldn't have. You see, I — well — I fell off when you weren't looking.'

She pushed the ribbon into Major Chase's large hand and started off. She wanted to run, to fly, to get out of that garden and on her way home. But Major Chase caught up to her and held onto one shoulder.

'Look here,' he said. 'Not so fast. I don't understand. At least not all of it. Were you the child on the black hackney?'

Betsy told him the story all over again. For the first time she felt an uncomfortable lumpy feeling in her throat. The morning was very hot, and she hadn't slept much, and Major Chase wasn't helping her a bit.

When she was all through, Major Chase sat down on one of the stone benches and pulled Betsy down beside him. 'And you thought that disqualified you?' he said gently. 'And you came all the way up here to tell me about it?'

Betsy looked at him and nodded. 'But doesn't it disqualify me?'

The Major looked at her and shook his head. 'It's the reason why I gave you the ribbon,' he said. 'I watched you take your spill and I watched you get on again. Recovery after a fall's a big part of horsemanship.'

'Then it's mine,' Betsy said. 'For keeps?'

'It certainly is,' said Major Chase. 'And I never knew a rider who deserved it more.'

A few minutes later Major Chase took her home in his car. Just as they got there Father drove up to the front porch. He and Major Chase shook hands and then the Major told him the story of Betsy's early morning visit. 'You've got a daughter to be proud of,' the Major finished. 'She's a rider and a sportsman.'

'I knew it right along,' Father said. 'But it's nice to hear it from someone else.'

Betsy held onto Father with one hand and the ribbon with the other. She could say nothing, only beamed.

RODNEY

Leonard H. Nason

In an Army post, by ten o'clock in the morning, the morning's work is very nearly finished. Reveille at 5.45, breakfast
at 6.00, first call for drill at 6.45, assembly at 7.00, and then
off to the drill field. By 10.30 the troops begin to move slowly
back to quarters to groom, clean equipment and police up
generally before dinner.

Upon an October day, when the sun shines golden through
the turning leaves and the mists hang smokily above the
Virginia hills, two officers stood side by side and watched
the troops come slowly home from drill. One of the officers
was a colonel in a many-ribboned blouse, shiny boots, white
cuffs and riding-crop; the other a captain, in a campaign hat
and O.D. shirt.

A soldier would guess, because the colonel was wearing
the black stripe of the General Staff, that he was an inspector,
and that the captain, because he was in working clothes, had
been snatched from his organization to guide the colonel
inspecting about, and also to be pumped very genially on the

side as to what he thought of his commanding officer and the way the post and garrison were handled in general. A soldier would also know that the inspector had posted himself there to watch the troops come in; the hour of their going out being rather early for a field officer to be up in the morning.

Two batteries of artillery clattered by, the men dust-covered, horses sweating, brass hub caps on limbers and caissons glittering. The colonel replied absent-mindedly to the salute of the officer in charge.

'Some lounging in the saddle there!' he commented. 'Ought to correct that.'

'There are a lot of recruits in that battery,' observed the captain. 'They're probably suffering from saddle sores.'

A squadron of cavalry in full pack went by, machine rifles, field radio and medical detachment complete.

'What's the idea in that, Captain Black?' snapped the inspector.

'I believe they're off next week for a month's practice march. They've been turning out full pack for some time. Gets the men accustomed to making up packs, pitching camp, packing saddles and that sort of thing. Then, they've never made a march with air-cooled machine guns in pack, and they want to see how they ride. We aren't very familiar with the gun.'

'Hurump!' grunted the inspector. 'Well, where is your outfit?'

'The headquarters detachment does not go to drill,' said Captain Black quietly. He seemed to settle himself as a man might that expected a blow.

'Why don't they? Don't they think they need it?'

'Colonel,' said the captain, 'my detachment furnishes the telephone operators, the orderlies, the chauffeurs, the messengers, the mail carriers, the radio men and the office boys for this entire post and half the city of Washington. I couldn't get them together for drill if I wanted to. Anyway, in time of emergency, they'd do just as they're doing now. A trained telephone operator or radio man wouldn't take the field.'

'But who looks after your animals?'

'We only have two — my own mount and a horse that does odd jobs around the post.'

'Your own horse is a private mount, of course?' asked the inspector. 'The other one a public animal? Where is he? I want to look at him.'

Captain Black turned and led the way across the parade ground toward the stables. An escort wagon loaded with hay stood before the last one on the end, and from this wagon, by means of a block and tackle, the bales were being hoisted into the loft.

At the end of the rope that did the hoisting was a big chestnut horse, well built, sturdy about the back and loins, one that in his day must have been a beautiful wheeler, but that now was so old his muzzle was quite white. At his bridle was a man in stable clothes and a battered campaign hat, decorated with a cord that still held some faint suspicion of its original red.

'That's the horse,' said Captain Black, pointing. 'His name is Rodney.'

The inspector strode clankily toward the group about the wagon, and the men at once came to attention. But the inspector halted before the chestnut horse and his attendant.

'You!' barked the inspector, addressing the man at Rodney's bridle. 'Don't you ever shave?'

The soldier in the dilapidated hat was old. The two days' beard that sprouted from his leathery cheek was quite white, and his eyes were bloodshot and watery with the perpetual tears of age. But he stood at attention as straight as a ramrod.

'Yes, sir,' he replied, 'for Saddiday inspecshun.'

'What battery are you with?'

The old soldier's eyes wandered to Captain Black.

'Headquarters detachment, sir,' he replied.

'How's this, Black?' demanded the inspector, turning. 'Don't you ever visit quarters? Your first sergeant ought to do it if you don't!'

'The headquarters detachment have no quarters, sir,' said Captain Black. 'The men are mostly married, and they are scattered about Washington, so that it was not practical to have them all come back to the post to sleep.'

'But this man must sleep somewhere. He lives on the reservation, does he not? Isn't there someone to keep him up to snuff?'

'He lives in the stable shack here with the horseshoers. Such duty as he has he performs well, and since he has seen so much service, we allow him — I allow him — a little liberty from strict observance of regulations.'

'The commanding officer know about this?' asked the colonel coldly.

'I don't know,' replied Captain Black. 'I have never discussed it with him.'

'I see the colonel has the Cuban Pacification medal,' observed the soldier, nodding toward the ribbons on the colonel's chest and smiling politely. 'Was the colonel at Camp Columbia? I was there. I was outta G Troop of the 'Leventh Calvary. Terry McGovern won the boxin' championship o' the camp that year. He was our top. G Troop was always a great troop for boxers. I was in China too. In aught seven.'

'How much service have you got in?' asked the colonel, bending his brows sternly upon the old soldier.

'I got two more years to go to retire, sir. I'm on my last hitch.'

'And what's the highest grade you've held?'

'Well, sir, now, I never paid much attention to grades. They come an' go. I been a private first-class for a good many years. That's good enough for me. I seen too many o' my buddies made noncoms, and then, when they lost their stripes for no reason at all, it about broke their hearts.'

'Did you get overseas in the last war?'

'Yes, sir.' The old soldier looked with affection at the old horse. 'I drove Rodney. Him an' me an' Jefferson was the wheel team of the first piece in A Batt'ry.'

The colonel, his attention once more drawn to the horse, walked over and opened Rodney's mouth. He inspected the horse's teeth, lifted his feet, one by one, then finally turned to Captain Black.

'That's a damned old horse,' said the colonel. 'Well, come, Black. Let's be moving on!'

Captain Black immediately fell in on his superior's left, and they walked away.

'Come on, you, Benny!' called the driver of the escort wagon as soon as the two officers were out of hearing. 'Git Rodney into his collar and let's git to hoistin' in this hay! You know who that old buzzard was? Well, he's here to make economies. Come from the General Staff. His chauffeur's livin' in my squad room, told me about it. Look out he don't sell you an' Rodney for glue!'

'Don't worry about me!' jeered old Benny. 'I seen inspectors come an' inspectors go.... Come, Rodney, boy; up goes a bale o' hay! Tchk! Tchk!... Huh. You recruit, pull your hand down outta the air! Why, that colonel was just lookin' Rodney over for his fine points. I mind one time on the Border, Black Jack Pershin' judged a horse show we was in. "Fine horse that, Benny," sez he. He always called me "Benny." I was with him in Jolo, time I done one o' my hitches in the calvary. "Fine horse that, Benny." "Yes, general!" 'sye. "I'm goin' to give him the blue ribbon," sez he.

'Next time I see General Pershin' was in Andernach. Army of Occupation. We was havin' a horse show. When it come I win the blue ribbon with Rodney, an orderly comes over and says they want to see me over by the grandstand. General Pershin'. "Ain't I seen you an' that horse before?" sez he. 'Sye: "Yes, sir. El Paso, in 1915." "My, my!" sez he. "There's a lotta wind been blown through the trumpets since then. An' Rodney still collectin' ribbons!" "Well, general," 'sye, "we all collected a few since those days, but I'd just as soon not go through any more shows like this last one. Some o' them jumps is a little high for a feller my age."

'Well, we lifted a cup that afternoon in the battery competition, and when we went by Black Jack, he waved his hand to me, and Marshal Haig, he was there, he give me a grin, because they'd told him who me an' Rodney was.'

'Yeh,' observed the driver, 'but don't let's talk about liftin' cups right now. Let's see how good Rodney is at liftin' a little hay.'

Meanwhile the inspecting colonel and Captain Black were roaming about the outside of one of those long portable buildings that were put up everywhere during the war and that are still housing Army personnel. This particular one had a sign over the door that said Headquarters Detachment, but within all was dark and silent.

'What's this building serve for, Captain Black?' demanded the inspector.

'My orderly room is in one end, sir. That's all it serves for now. In the summer, when the reserve officers are here, we have a tailor shop, a store, barber shop, cafeteria and day room. We give out the concessions, you know, and collect ten per cent of the gross for the mess fund.'

'What do you do with a mess fund if your company doesn't eat in quarters?'

'They do in the summer, sir. Then, anything that's left over we use to buy the men tailor-made uniforms, or for athletic goods. Basketball, baseball, that sort of thing.'

'These old temporary buildings,' said the inspector, 'are a great source of expense. There is no reason so valid in the Army for anything becoming permanent as that it was only intended to be temporary. The paint and maintenance cost for these pasteboard affairs is terrific. I have orders to condemn them wherever possible.'

'Well, colonel,' smiled Captain Black, 'I don't know what we'd do for quarters for the headquarters detachment. In the summer, when the civilian components of the Army are out here — the reserve officers, the R.O.T.C., the C.M.T.C. and the National Guard — things are pretty congested.'

'Perhaps,' said the colonel, 'that can be arranged.'

They went into the orderly room at the back, where, having dismissed the clerk, the inspector sat down and began going through the company records.

'This forage return is a needless expense,' said the inspector suddenly, taking off his eyeglasses and thumping the table. 'I'm surprised that you should keep on that one useless animal, eating his head off in the stables. Why can't one of the wagon mules be unhitched to hoist hay into the loft, and if that's not practical — and I don't understand why it shouldn't be — why should the one horse that does it be carried on your returns?'

'Well,' said Captain Black, 'I suppose it simplifies paper work somewhere. That was the arrangement I found when I took over the company.'

'And that old file that looks after him there? What's his name? What's he done to rate a gravy train like that?'

'His name is Benny Walsh. He's been in the regiment twenty-two years. When he was younger, there wasn't a better soldier in the United States Army. If it hadn't been for one failing, he'd be a sergeant major now, at least.'

'Drink, of course?'

'But between pay days,' said Captain Black sadly, 'he certainly performs his duty well.'

'I see no reason for coddling him there!' snapped the inspector.

'No, sir, that's not the reason. He was Rodney's driver during the war. Together they pulled off some kind of a gallant deed up there on the lines. The regiment has felt grateful to them ever since.'

'And what was that?'

Well, it was quite a story. Captain Black had not seen it. He had not been with the regiment then. The battalion commander at the time had been lieutenant colonel when Black joined, and there had been some old sergeants that remembered it, but they were all gone now, and he had not heard the story for years. He had rather forgotten the details. Something up in the woods. On the Marne. H'm'm. Oh, yes. Rodney had been a wheel horse in A Battery then.

The battery had been sent up, early in July, direct from training camp, to a position along those hills through which the Marne trailed its slow way like a lazy snake. They were in thick woods. It was all woods up in that part of the country, with isolated stone farmhouses. Woods on this side of the river, woods on that side, where the Germans were, though there was never a sign of them.

Never a shot fired, nor a sound, nor the bark of a dog or the rattle of a wheel to show that there was anyone across the river, and only the wreckage of the shattered bridge below Jaulgonne to hint that war was going on. A Battery was on the crest of a hill, with a field of fire up and down the river, but they saw nothing to fire at. There were Americans in front of them somewhere, but they never saw them. They saw French soldiers once in a while, going about in their shirts, without helmets or gas masks, carrying water or bringing in wood.

The battery grew sick of the place rapidly. This was no way to fight a war. They grew more and more careless about walking on the paths; even the officers took short cuts through the wheat. It was cold at night, even though it was summer, and after the first week of vigilance the cooks used to leave their fires going in the kitchen after dark.

The men of A Battery played baseball one afternoon against a team of the second battalion and would — had it not been too far away — have gone down and had a swim in the Marne to cool off afterward. Then, upon a night of fine rain, when everyone was celebrating France's Independence Day, the scene was suddenly shifted with a roll of thunder.

The curtain went up to the accompaniment of full orchestration, peal after peal, and the men, throwing off their blankets and coming out from under the guns, half awake, saw that the wooded heights across the river were crowned with heat lightning that never ceased its flickering for an instant.

All those paths the careless men had trodden through the wheat, the kitchen where the fires had burned all night, the shallow dugouts where officers had sat and smoked through the soft summer evening, all went skyward in the first quarter of an hour. The battery, for some strange reason, was un-molested. What was happening to the rest of the regiment was conjecture, for all the telephone wires were out and runners sent into the shell-lit woods did not come back.

At daybreak, the battery commander crawled out with the executive to an open space along the ridge, and there could see what was going on. There was smoke everywhere like brush fires, and men running like startled bugs. On the upper side of the bend there was no smoke, but there was firing farther back in the trees. Black shrapnel, which meant German shells. The river was black with boats. The Germans had got across there, and that firing back up the slope was their rolling barrage.

'We've got to get out of here!' decided the captain. 'They'll go down to Conde-en-Brie and cut us off!'

He did not fire on the boats because he had run out of ammunition. He went back to his guns, where a pale French lieutenant told him that the Germans were at St. Eugene, on the west side of the hill, and that it would be only a matter of minutes before that whole sector would be pinched out. At this moment a tooth-chattering sergeant reported that there was not a surviving horse on the picket line. Yes, said somebody else, there was. There was Rodney, and Jefferson; his team-mate Benny Walsh had taken them in to the farm the night before.

'We can't move a battery that requires fifty horses with only two!' cried the executive.

'We can try!' said the captain. 'I'm not going to leave my guns to the krauts in my first engagement!'

There are supposed to be six horses to each gun, and six more to each caisson. They hitched Rodney and Jefferson in and Benny Walsh drove, while the weary gunners, death staring them in the face, shoved on the wheels. They got three guns out — away over the hill to the new support position. But the enemy had balloons up by then, and spotted what was going on.

An airplane, zooming like an angry hornet, descended upon them just as old Benny had started out with the last piece. A fistful of machine-gun bullets scattered the battery, and another struck down Rodney's team-mate. But those that fled saw Benny leap from the saddle, draw a knife and hack away at the traces.

The airman swung back in a low bank, and fired another yard or so of clip that knocked Benny into a heap beside his off-wheeler. After that, those present went their way, but in the afternoon, still harnessed to the gun, Rodney arrived at the support position. One horse, dragging gun and limber — a load for six — and with old Benny stretched out insensible on his back.

That was the story. Captain Black had heard it many a time from men who had been witnesses. They were mostly all gone now, and the thing was beginning to be forgotten.

'Humph!' commented the colonel. 'They should have tried that captain for letting his men give away the position like that. But in wartime, with an army full of civilians ——' He finished the sentence with a vague wave of his hand, and went back to his inspection of the records.

The colonel ruffled books, unfolded reports, inspected records and added figures. Finally he closed the correspondence book with a bang.

'Black,' said the colonel calmly, 'I see no way out of it.

We're going to have to disband this headquarters detachment. Too much waste here, unnecessary paper work. This
building costs too much in upkeep. We can tear it down.
We'll send the men to duty with troops, or transfer them to
the Signal Corps or Motor Transport Section of the Q.M.
That will take their pay and maintenance off the artillery
accounts.

'That old horse there, I'll have condemned and sold. The
man Walsh I'll recommend be discharged for the good of the
service.'

'Benny?' gasped Captain Black. 'Why do you want to
discharge Benny?'

'You told me he did nothing but look after the horse, and if
the horse is sold he'll have nothing to do.'

'But he's only got two years to go to retire.'

'That's the point,' said the colonel. 'We'll save Uncle
Sam the cost of his pension all those years. Why, some of
those old horned toads live to be a hundred!'

'I know, colonel,' protested Captain Black, 'but he won't have anywhere to go; he'll be destitute.'

'Bah!' said the colonel. 'He can go to the Old Soldiers' Home, can't he? It'll be good enough for him!'

The news of the disbanding of the headquarters detachment spread rapidly, but aside from its value as an interesting event, and something to talk about, it aroused little interest. The men in it lived in town, their duties kept them away from the post, and, after all, it meant little more to them than changing their collar ornaments.

The other recommendation — that Rodney was to be condemned and sold, and old Benny discharged — did not come out until later. The sergeant major whispered it to the first sergeant, who told the stable sergeant, who told the saddlers and the horseshoer that lived in the stable shack with Benny.

'What's the matter with you Johns?' demanded Benny angrily one night. 'You're too danged polite all of a sudden! You ain't been goin' through my foot locker, because there ain't ary thing in it worth stealin'. You're puttin' up some kind of a shine on me, though; I c'n tell by the sneakin', guilty look in your eye!.... Tom Parsons, you leather-spoiler, you put cement in my shavin' powder again?'

'No, Benny,' said a saddler contritely.

'That reminds me,' said Benny thoughtfully; 'speakin' o' shavin' powder, I gotta get some new. I'll go over to the exchange after supper. There's a pair o' breeches there I've a mind to buy. The tailor'll sell 'em to me jawbone. They was made for one o' them recruits in the headquarters detachment that's got sent to the Q.M. and he don't want 'em now. Cheap, they be.'

'Better wait until next week,' advised the horseshoer.

'Wait another week, Benny. Be sure you make up your mind first. Maybe next week you won't want 'em.'

There was a solemn hush, while Benny looked all around the circle, blinking his watery eyes.

'That's right,' said he slowly; 'so I won't.' Quickly he jerked up his head. 'Say, is that what's been botherin' you terrapins? About them dischargin' me? Huh? Don't let that bother you. Cap'n Black, he broke the news to me this afternoon. What's in that to look sad about? Ain't I gettin' outta this madhouse? All my friends is on the outside, anyway. Black Jack, he's been out for years. The army's full o' recruits. I'll be better off out of it.'

No one made any remark. Benny's face was calm, his voice steady, and the hand with which he calmly sorted over the things in his foot-locker tray never trembled.

'The only thing,' said Benny, 'is that you boys gotta take good care o' Rodney.'

'Why, didn't you know?' spoke up the blacksmith, without thinking. 'He's been condemned. They're goin' to sell him at auction.'

Old Benny recoiled as though he had been struck.

'No!' said he. 'Straight goods?'

'Yup,' nodded the saddler. 'They're gonna put the I.C. on him tomorrow morning.'

'Well, well,' marveled Benny, shaking his head from side to side. 'Goin' to condemn Rodney. Old Rodney, that never bucked, nor never refused to pull, nor never went in a horse show he didn't win! Overseas with the outfit and back with it! And now they condemn him! Man, I'll tell the horntanglin' universe that that's the best one I ever did hear! You Johns listen to me. Since I come in the outfit they've wore five different styles o' puttees, and they finished up by putting white collars and cuffs on enlisted men, but I'll tell you this is the biggest surprise I had since the time I thought coneyac was the French word for "soup"! So me an' Rodney is gettin' condemned! Well, whaddyuh think o' that for curb chains?'

The other men in the stable shack said nothing, and Benny went on about his sorting. But they noticed, now, that he kept taking out the same two pairs of socks, unrolling them, rolling them up, and then putting them back again, and that his hands shook ever so slightly while he did it.

At noontime, some three weeks later, Captain Black went into the officers' club for lunch. Nearly all the former members of his headquarters detachment had gone, and he had nothing to do now but wait for his own orders. He tossed cap, gloves and riding-crop into a corner and, going into the reading room, spoke to an officer there that he knew, the post quartermaster.

'They have the auction this morning?' asked the captain.

'Hello, Black!' greeted the quartermaster. 'Yes, all over. Sold 'em all off, horses and mules, as well as a flock of condemned shelter halves.'

'About Rodney — that old horse from my outfit — do you know — that is, have you any idea who got him?'

'No. Not the slightest.'

'I sent my striker over there to bid up to fifty dollars for him,' said Captain Black sadly. 'I had in mind having him destroyed. I hate to think of that horse pulling a junk cart.'

'Well, you didn't get him,' said the quartermaster, 'because the cheapest a horse went for was seventy dollars. Oh, by the way, I paid off one of your men yesterday. Old Walsh. He drew quite a lot of money on his final settlement. Clothing allowance, savings deposited with the quartermaster — can you imagine the old bum saving money? — a biggish amount. I thought I'd warn you so that you could get him off the reservation as soon as possible, before he gets into a crap game and they take it all away from him.'

One of the club servants came softly across the room and touched Captain Black's elbow.

'There's a Mr. Walsh would like to see you, sir,' said he.

'Mr. Walsh?' repeated Captain Black.

'It's old Benny!' laughed the quartermaster. '"Mister" is right. He's a civilian now.'

Captain Black went out to the hall, where his visitor awaited him. It was old Benny. He was still wearing his 'Saddiday inspecshun' breeches, puttees and army shoes, but over his olive-drab shirt was a threadbare, cast-off coat, two sizes too large for him, and his gnarled hands twirled a civilian hat. The old soldier. He had taken off his blouse, taken off his cap, someone had given him an old coat, and he was a civilian!

'Good day, captain,' greeted Benny. 'I'm through now, and I been paid off, and I just wanted to stop by and say goodbye to you, sir.'

'Well, Benny,' said Captain Black, finding words with some difficulty, 'you know I'm sorry to see you go. Er — these things happen, you know! These are evil times! Er — have you any plans for the future, Benny — that is ——'

'No, sir,' said Benny. 'I hadn't just give it much thought. But I'll find somethin' to do. There's no hurry. I'll want to take a little vacation fust, from gittin' up at revvely, an' the like o' that!'

'I understand,' went on Captain Black, 'that you drew quite a lot of savings of one kind or another. That's fine, Benny, to have saved up all that money! How much was it?'

'Hundred and forty dollars, sir. I always tried to save a little. But what with blinds, and equipment I had to pay fer now and again, you know it took a long time. I been over twenty-five years savin' that hundred and forty. When I come in first, a private only got twelve dollars a month.'

'Well, you want to hang onto it now. Don't go getting into any crap games with it. Keep it for emergencies.'

Old Benny grinned. 'It's all gone a'ready,' said he.

'What? Did somebody take it away from you? You give me his name and I'll have it back for you, don't fret! Who got it? What did you do with it, Benny?'

'I bought Rodney with it!'

'You bought Rodney?' gasped Captain Black. 'You bought Rodney? Rodney, the horse? What on earth did you do that for?'

'The cap'n's heard tell, ain't he, about the time that Rodney pulled the guns outta the woods up on the Marne so the battery wouldn't get captured by the Germans? Well, sir, I got hit that day. Bad. But I got up on old Rodney's back again, an' I sez in his ear, "Rodney, I'm passin' out, but you take care o' me."

'I woke up in the hospital. Why should he keep on goin' draggin' that great gun all alone if he hadn't heard me? He got me outta there. I'd been planted if it hadn't been for Rodney! Captain, I don't mean no offense, but a man that's been through one o' them shellin's ain't got no fear o' hell no more, no, sir-ree!

'Well, anyway, there was my old pal, and I went round to see him to say good-bye, and there was some iceman gittin' ready to buy him. An' it come over me that no buddy o' mine was gonna pull no ice cart. An' so I bid for him. An' when it come to a hundred an' forty dollars, the iceman quit, an' Rodney belongs to me.'

The post commander, being married, of course ate in his own quarters, but the adjutant, who, after all, was the commander's right hand, ate at the club, and he, wiping his mouth with his napkin, walked into the card room to meet someone who said he wanted to see him on a matter of the utmost urgency.

'Why, Captain Black,' began the adjutant with some surprise, for Black was known to be a sober and somewhat cold-blooded officer. 'What's the excitement? I thought we were getting a warning for M day at least!'

'No, no,' said Captain Black impatiently, 'but we've got to work fast here. You know, of course, that my old headquarters detachment had a big mess fund, and it's all been audited and found correct, and since the outfit has been broken up, each organization to which one of my men goes gets his share of the fund. I'm to turn it over to the Finance this afternoon. Now you know all the rules and regs! Old Benny Walsh has gone and bought Rodney with his last cent, and how can I get authority to reimburse him out of the mess fund? After all, the horse belonged to the detachment anyway! A hundred and forty dollars! A dollar less per man's share!'

'You can't do it!' said the adjutant. 'Even if the fund hadn't been audited. That mess fund isn't to buy animals with; it's for extra food and comforts for the men!'

'Pigweed!' snapped Captain Black. 'Somebody can give me authority to disburse those funds. Can the Old Man?'

The adjutant laughed. 'Not now. Nobody short of the Secretary of War can do it now.'

'I'll go see him.'

He swung on his heel, but the adjutant seized his arm.

'Captain!' he pleaded. 'Here; let's cool down on this

matter! You can't go over everybody's head that way. You know that! If you try to see the Secretary, it will mean your commission!'

'I doubt it,' said Black calmly. 'The Secretary was a cavalryman first. He was through most of that sausage-grinding in France too. I think he'll understand! We'll try it anyway. Who makes the biggest bet — old Benny with the last cent between him and starvation, or me with a problematical career? I'm off for Washington. Meanwhile, until this is straightened out, I'd like authority to keep Rodney and Benny on the reservation.'

'That's simple,' said the adjutant, 'but you stay out of the State, War and Navy Building.'

The rumor that old Benny Walsh had bought Rodney at the auction with his last cent, and that Captain Black had gone to appeal to the Secretary of War, brought Rodney into a prominence he had not enjoyed since the war. There was eager discussion of the affair that afternoon, and when Captain Black returned from Washington, the officers eagerly demanded if he had been able to see the Secretary, and if so, what the Secretary had said.

'I got it,' replied Black to all queries, 'and he let me talk. When I had finished, he said he'd look into it. He'd look into it, and that I'd hear from him.'

'Yeh,' murmured the listeners, 'you'll hear from him! And how!'

Among the enlisted personnel, there was a sergeant here, and a caisson Jack there, and one or two old privates who remembered Rodney when he was the best wheel horse in the Army, and they refreshed their souvenirs for the memory of the recruits. People suddenly realized that the old horse which so faithfully hauled hay into stable lofts every morning was in a class with Traveller, that bore General Lee all through the Civil War and years afterward, and with Comanche, the sole survivor of the Custer fight, that never had a man on his back after Miles Keogh.

Someone dug up the ribbons Rodney had won, and got permission to have them grouped and mounted separately, to be hung in headquarters. Someone else, in A Battery's storeroom, found the old name board with 'First Section. Piece. Wheel. Rodney' on it, and this was taken down to the Battery station and put up over his old stall.

Meanwhile the result of Captain Black's call on the Secretary of War was not known. The officers gloomily remarked that the least he would get would be immediate orders for Fort Forgotten or Camp Cactus, with an old-issue hump-crawling in the bargain, just for the good of the service. Otherwise, every time an organization commander was displeased with higher authority, he would be off to take his case to the Secretary of War, with resultant destruction of good order and military discipline.

But after a week of excitement there arrived a curt order that the sale of Rodney was declared null and void, and that his purchase money should be refunded. Ah! well, that took care of Benny Walsh. But the old soldiers shook their heads.

'It ain't over yet,' said they. 'Keep your heads down. Them War Department orders got delayed-action fuses on 'em.'

The following afternoon, just before evening parade, Captain Black burst into the stable shack where old Benny had been a guest until his affairs could be arranged.

'Where's Walsh?' demanded the captain.

'Why, sir, we ain't seen him since yesterday,' replied the saddler.

'Did he say where he was going, when he was coming back — anything?' demanded the captain. 'I've got to get hold of him. The War Department is retiring Rodney. A formal retirement order and everything! They're going to give him a review, just as if he were an old noncom going out after thirty years or so!'

'Hot dog!' cried the saddler. 'I didn't hear anything about it! That's what you get for not standin' formations! If they was to declare war, they'd never give us no hint of it! I gotta see this. I'm glad the captain told me.'

'I should have come down before,' said Captain Black hurriedly, 'but I've been so busy myself. I didn't hear about it until an hour ago. I've been ordered to the École Militaire in Paris for two years! Why, I've put in for that detail since I was a shavetail, with no more idea of getting it than that I'd be made Chief of Staff! And now I've got it, with a week to get ready in!'

'The captain must 'a' kinda acquired a drag with the War Department,' grinned the blacksmith.

'Ugh!' replied Captain Black. 'I don't know about that. But that's neither here nor there. I want old Benny to see this review! Now, how can I get hold of him?'

'Sir,' said the blacksmith, 'I don't think it can be done. As quick as he got his hundred and forty dollars back he high-tailed outta here with it, and it's too soon afterward for him to be in any shape to appear in public, assumin' you could find him, anyways.'

Captain Black went out and, leaping on his horse, hurried to the parade grounds. Everyone in the post was there, and a lot of people, sensing the unusual, had come in from the surrounding country and even across the river from Washington. The ceremony had begun by the time Captain Black got there, and

Rodney, his coat shining in the setting sun, had been led
'front and center' to hear his retirement order read.

'By direction of the President,' read the adjutant, 'the ex-
ceptional record of service of the horse Rodney is brought to
the attention of all organizations. Eighteen years in the same
battery of field artillery, from the thirst and drought of border
stations to the drenching rains and everlasting mud of France,
this animal continually performed more than his share of
work allotted to his organization.

'Without complaint, silently, obscurely, without thought
of favor or reward, for eighteen years Rodney has fulfilled
every mission assigned to him by his superiors, his only
thought one of steadfast service to the limit of his ability.
In consideration of which, the President directs that Rodney
be, and hereby is, placed upon the retired list of the United
States Army, with full ration of oats, for the period of his
natural life.'

When the order was finished, Rodney was led up to his post
beside the commanding officer, the band struck up 'When the
Caissons Go Rolling Along,' and the entire garrison — horse,
foot, guns and tanks — went by in review. There was more
than one throat that was dry and catchy when the review was
over.

As for Captain Black, he turned and rode slowly back toward the stables. Old Benny would have enjoyed that! But
he had not known, and a hundred and forty dollars in his jeans
at once was too much for him! Poor old sot, he labored, as did
Rodney, only to the limit of his intelligence!

Suddenly, turning the corner by the riding hall, Captain
Black came upon Rodney, preened and shining, being taken
back to the stables. But what was a civilian leading him for?

'Oh, there! You with the horse! Just a minute!' called

Captain Black. He rode up, then suddenly reined in his horse with astonishment. The civilian was Benny Walsh. Benny Walsh, garbed modestly in dark blue, clean-shaven, a derby hat on his head, gloves on his hands, a large cigar in his mouth.

'Benny!' choked the captain. 'In God's name, where did you get those clothes?'

'How do you do, cap'n? The cap'n see that review? Now, I thought that was just fine. Rodney enjoyed that. He understood, sir; don't the cap'n think he didn't. Yes, sir, that was a right nice thing to do for Rodney. . . . Oh, yes, these clothes! I bought 'em, sir, with some o' my retirement money. I got reimbursed, sir, for what I spent, so I bought some clothes with it.'

'Oh, Benny,' cried the captain, clapping his hand to his brow, 'why didn't you come and talk it over with me first? I'd have given you some clothes. Why didn't you save that money until you got yourself some kind of a job or something?'

'Oh,' chuckled Benny, 'don't let the cap'n worry about me. Hoh! I got me a job! I still got some friends. The minute they found I was outta this John outfit, they got me a job.'

'What kind of a job have you got?' demanded Captain Black.

'I'm a civilian employe, Quartermaster Corps, salary thutty dollars a week. Purty goo, I calls it.'

'Civilian employe, Quartermaster Corps, good Lord! And what do you do?'

Old Benny drew a long puff from his cigar and exhaled it before replying.

'Rodney,' said he, ' has been, by order, placed in the custody of the Quartermaster Corps. My duties is to look after him.'

THE LAST RUN

Frances Margaret Fox

A NEWSPAPER reporter once wrote a plea on behalf of the last regular team of fire horses in the District of Columbia, begging contributions for the purchase of the beloved old horses, that they might not be sold at auction to the highest bidder. Here is what that kind-hearted reporter said in his paper one June day in 1925.

'Three faithful servants of humanity, the last regular team of Washington's once petted battalion of sturdy fire horses, are stamping the cement floors of unfamiliar stalls today, eagerly listening for the gong that is never again to strike on this earth for them.'

Right there the reporter made a mistake. The gong did strike again for the fire horses, thanks to work done by this very reporter. Something better happened than even he had dreamed of.

The horses' names were Barney, Gene, and Tom. For ten years they had been faithful servants of the fire department on Uncle Sam's payroll in our capital city. Now the fire department would never again require the help of horses in putting out fires. Motor fire-engines had taken their place. Horses must go, and Barney, Gene, and Tom were the last old team to leave the service.

To save these horses from being sold to draymen, the newspaper begged the people of Washington to buy them.

That newspaper article saved the three horses, though not in the way the reporter suggested. The very next day came the good news that the horses were to be given to the Home for the Feeble and Infirm at Blue Plains, there to live the rest of their days in comfort and happiness. The District Commissioners had so decided. The managers of the farm at Blue Plains, who had seen the newspaper article, had said that they would gladly give the three old horses a good home for life. They could earn their board by taking the old folks out for 'straw rides.'

The chief of the fire department was glad when he heard these plans. He agreed that it would be a great pity if the faithful old horses should be made wretched by hard work in their old age. They were great pets, and so gentle he was sure the old folks at Blue Plains would enjoy driving out in the sunshine in a big wagon drawn by Barney, Gene, and Tom.

The poor old fellows would live only a short time, he said, if draymen bought them. They were chosen by the fire department in the beginning for their speed and intelligence, and not for their strength. Almost their entire lives had been passed in active fire-service, and they were not fitted for hauling great loads through hot city streets.

Then he declared that the last regular team was to be sent to its retirement with every honor the department can bestow and with the clang of the stirring fire-gong ringing in the horses' ears once more.

'As soon as he learns the day, Superintendent Fay of the farm at Blue Plains will call for the old fellows. He will order them removed to their original stalls,' said the chief. 'When they leave their former home for the last time, it will be in the shining livery they have worn so well for more than a decade, and in the presence of many of the men who have served along with them, and before the officials of the fire department.'

Then said he: 'I want to do this, not only for Barney, Gene, and Tom, but to give the people of Washington an opportunity of seeing what a noble crusade this has been. We will have a regular fire-run for those old fellows, the last they will ever enjoy, and it will be a sight worth seeing, too.'

Next day there was gay news in the paper. The preparations had been made for the retirement of the horses the following Monday morning.

Long before ten o'clock on Monday, thousands of children and grown people were in line to see the dear old horses make their last run.

Meantime Barney, Gene, and Tom had been taken back to their old home engine-house. There they found their stalls gaily decorated with flowers. The three horses were given a breakfast of oats. The men who had cared for them for seven years dressed them for their farewell party. Their manes were combed and their gray coats curried until they were like satin. The horses' big hoofs were polished until they shone.

At ten o'clock the fire-gong sounded. Barney, Gene, and Tom were ready for the dash the instant their shining harness was snapped on. Nine times the gong sounded, three strokes for Barney, three for Gene, and three for old Tom.

The horses must have believed they were headed for a bad fire.

When the last gong sounded the firemen throughout the city stood at attention for one minute.

In twenty-two seconds from the time the first gong sounded, the three horses were dashing from the engine-house, dragging their old fire-engine behind them.

Thousands of men, women, and children saw the race, and how that crowd cheered! The streets were lined with people. Motion-picture photographers took pictures of the ceremony, that millions of Americans might later see just how those fine horses ran that day.

Perhaps Barney, Gene, and Tom were disappointed when their run ended in front of a fire-hydrant at Lincoln Park, only a few blocks from their engine-house — and no fire in sight.

Anyway, after they had trotted slowly home again, wreaths of roses were hung round their necks and speeches were made. One of the District Commissioners said in the beginning of his speech, as he handed the reins of the glorious trio to Mr. Fay, superintendent of the farm at Blue Plains: 'When a fireman has served the department with loyalty, he is pensioned and returned to the rest he has earned in the twilight of his life. These old fellows are no less firemen than the men of our department, and it is only right and fitting that they too should be protected now that their service is over.'

Barney began to eat the roses in his wreath before the speech was ended, and Gene and Tom were trying to help him, when the fire chief noticed and placed the wreaths out of reach.

The horses then stood at attention while Mr. Fay made a speech, in which he said:

'We accept the trust reposed in us by you and the thousands of admirers and lovers of this wonderful trio of horses. We have afforded refuge to many an old fellow, both man and

horse, who have been buffeted by old age and adverse circumstances. You may rest assured that these faithful veterans,
like many of their predecessors, will find a haven in the green
fields and shady pastures beside the Potomac at Blue Plains.'

Then Barney, Gene, and Tom, garlanded with roses, at-
tended by their grooms, walked the five or six miles to Blue
Plains, cheered by their admirers all along the line of march
to their new home.

THE OLD CAVALRY HORSE

An old cavalry horse was much surprised one day, when he
was mustered out of service. It was a fate he could not understand. He had lived long years at a Western post and had
always served Uncle Sam faithfully. The old horse loved his
garrison friends, because they had always taken good care of
him. That is, he loved the old soldiers. Young recruits had
so much to learn that he felt superior to them. He believed it
beneath his dignity to take orders from newly enlisted men.

Perhaps one reason why the old horse carried himself so proudly was because he had long been the trumpeter's horse. Even so, the day came when he was sold to a milkman and home he went with that milkman to live.

The old cavalry horse must have believed that some officer at the fort had made a bad mistake and that one of his friends would soon come galloping over the hills to his rescue. However, he was kind and polite to the milkman. He didn't hurt his new master's feelings by asking why he didn't blow a trumpet at mealtime and have a little more ceremony in his stable. He didn't object when he was harnessed to the milk-cart, with never the sound of a bugle-call to make the peddling of milk more interesting.

The good old horse peddled milk like a gentleman. The work was easy and there were no young recruits to drive the milk-wagon and tell him when to stop and go. The old horse didn't blame the milkman for the change in his fortunes and he was grateful for kind treatment.

Then one day when the driver was jogging along delivering milk at one door and another, the most upsetting thing happened. As the old cavalry horse approached the drill-ground, where a troop of his garrison friends were drilling, he pricked up his ears and stepped a bit faster. Suddenly the trumpet sounded the order to 'Charge!'

Instantly Uncle Sam's old horse obeyed that call. He bounced the milkman off the seat of the cart, and then away he flew to the drill-ground with the milk-cans rattling behind him.

Another minute and the old horse, milk-cart dragging behind, was charging with the cavalry troop. Milk-cans were scattered over the field and the old horse's heels beat like drumsticks on the dashboard.

That was a merry occasion for everyone but the milkman. It gave the old horse something cheerful to think about, while day by day in his stable, far from headquarters, he waited for the trumpeter he loved to come riding over the hills to take him home.

THE END